Exclusion of Śūdras From Brahmajijñāsā

Adventure of Consciousness

- Analytical Ayurveda/ Dr. K.A. Latheef
- Upaniṣads and Edith Stein: *A Dialogue on Models of The Person*/ Thomas Marottipparyail
- Tirthaṅkarāsana: *A Work on Jaina Yoga*/ Shantilal D. Parakh
- Aparokṣānubhūti: *The Essence of Self Realization*/ Dr. Shrikrishn Deshmukh
- A Critical Study in the Schism in Early Buddhist Monastic Tradition: *Dasavatthu and Pañcavatthu*/ Lokananda C. Bhikkhu
- Mystical Poems of Jnaneshwar: *Original Translations from the Marathi*/ Anand Mundra
- Exclusion of Śūdras From Brahmajijñāsā: *Re-Reading Apaśūdrādhikaraṇam of Brahmasūtra Śāṅkara Bhāṣya*/ Jaison Vadakkan
- Kashi Satsang: Pt. Nar Choubey
- Bhagavad Gita Natyaroop: PK Agarwal

Exclusion of Śūdras From Brahmajijñāsā

Jaison Vadakkan

Re-Reading Apaśūdrādhikaraṇam of Brahmasūtra Śāṅkara Bhāṣya

MOTILAL BANARSIDASS PUBLICATIONS

EXCLUSION OF ŚŪDRAS FROM BRAHMAJIJÑĀSĀ

First Edition : Delhi, 2019

ISBN : 978-81-94-0111-4-9

Published by
Motilal Banarsidass Publications
93, Shyam Lal Marg, Darya Ganj,
New Delhi-110002 (India)
mlbdbooks@gmail.com

MLBD Cataloging-in-Publication Data
Exclusion of Śūdras From Brahmajijñāsā
Re-Reading Apaśūdrādhikaraṇam of Brahmasūtra Śāṅkara Bhāṣya by Jaison Vadakkan
ISBN : 978-81-94-0111-4-9
Includes Glossary, Bibliography and Index
I. Philosophy II. Brahmasūtra Bhāṣya of Śaṅkara III. Brahmajijñāsā
IV. Apaśūdrādhikaraṇam V. Vadakkan, Jaison

Printed in india by Replika Press Pvt. Ltd.

TABLE OF CONTENTS

PREFACE

Śāṅkaradarśana is an evergreen philosophy and theology which is discussed widely. It is a living tradition having great followers. This work titled, Exclusion of *Śūdra*s from *Brahmajijñāsā,* is primarily a critique on Śaṅkara and it looks into the problem of *śūdra*-exclusion by analysing *Apaśūdrādhikaraṇam* of *Brahmasūtra Śāṅkara Bhāṣya.* With the insights received, it tries to make an *advaitic* response to the problem of exclusion which has become a threat to the well-being and integrity of the society.

This work is my doctoral dissertation submitted to the Faculty of Philosophy, Jnana-Deepa Vidyapeeth (Pontifical Institute of Philosophy and Religion, Pune), defended on July 28, 2017 for the Degree of Doctor in Philosophy (Ph D).

With a joyful heart I thank God, the Almighty who has been my light in the task of this research. It was He who enabled and availed me with all the necessary help in various ways, especially by providing me with persons who were generous to support me.

I consider it to be providential and great blessing to have Dr. John Peter Vallabadoss OFM Cap. as my guide. I express my sincere gratitude and profound appreciation for his scholarly guidance, honest critique and insightful suggestions. It was his availability with a joyful spirit and encouragement with a brotherly concern that kept my enthusiasm untiring.

I am thankful to Dr. Selva Rethinam, SJ, the president of Jnana-Deepa Vidyapeeth (JDV) Pune, and Dr. Kuruvilla Pandikattu, SJ, the Dean of the Faculty of Philosophy, for their encouragement. I am grateful to Dr. Nishant A. Irudayadason, who always extended his wholehearted support at every stage of this work in his capacity as the Chair Person for the Doctoral Committee of the Faculty of Philosophy.

At this moment, I would like to express my sincere gratitude to Rev. Dr. Raphie Paliakkara OFM Cap., the former Provincial Minister of St. Thomas Capuchin Province, Kerala, to which I belong. It was he, in consultation with his councillors, who suggested me to have this research and made all the necessary arrangements. I am greatful to Rev. Fr. Pauly Madassery, the present Provincial Minister, who with all his blessings supported and encouraged me to get this work published.

I thankfully remember Dr. Stephan Chundanthadathil, SJ, Dr. Henry D' Almeida, SJ, Dr. Sebastian Pynadath, SJ, Dr. Kancha Ilaiah, Dr. Jose Thachil, Dr. Johnson Puthenpurackal OFM Cap., Dr. George Pattery, SJ, Dr. Anto Cheramthuruthy, Dr. P.T. Mathew, SJ, Dr. Yesudas Karunanidhi, Fr. Antony Thekkinieth OFM Cap. and Dr. Jijo Kurian OFM Cap. for spending their precious time for me with discussions at various stages of this project, and for their help in finding out the needed resources.

With heartfelt gratitude I remember Fr. Vincent Crasta, SJ, the registrar of JDV and the moderator of JDV PG Block, Fr. Alex, SJ, the administrator of JDV and Dr. Francis Ezhakunnel, the former moderator of PG Block, for their encouragement and support for my stay and study in JDV.

I take this opportunity to gratefully acknowledge the scholarship provided by *Missio*, which supported me financially.

I gratefully remember the generous service rendered to me by Dr. Thomas Reddy, SJ and Dr. Biju Joseph, SJ, the librarians of JDV, and other library-staff.

I acknowledge, with a grateful heart, the help that I received from Dr. George Menachery OFM Cap., Fr. Aloysius Vilayil CMI, Fr. Joseph Peedikathadathil CMI, Fr. Rarish Mukkam, Sr. Jamsey CTC, Sr. Johncy SMI, Fr. Lijoy Chiriyankandath OFM Cap., Dr. Ivan D'Souza and Fr. Stephen Kachapilly OFM Cap. It was they who patiently and carefully did the proof-reading, and also offered me methodological and technical assistance whenever I needed.

This work reached its completion because of prayerful and friendly support of many. I acknowledge the warmth of love and care from the Capuchin community of La-Verna Theologate, Pune, and also from the Capuchin fraternity at large. I too extend my thanks to my companions in JDV and in PG Block. I thankfully remember the encouragement that I received from my family members, relatives, friends, and well-wishers.

Once again, I joyfully admit that it was my loving God who gave me all these generous persons and the setting conducive for carrying out my research.

Jaison Vadakkan, Capuchin
Calvary Ashram, Poothole P.O.
Thrissur, Kerala - 680 004 (India)
Ph. #09496417862, Email # jaisonvadakkancap@gmail.com

ABBREVIATIONS

Ai Ār	*Aitareyāraṇyaka*
Ai Br	*Aitareyabrāhmaṇa*
Ai U Bh	*Aitareyopaniṣad Bhāṣya*
Āp Dh S	*Āpastamba Dharmasūtra*
Āp Śr S	*Āpastamba Śrautasūtra*
AV	*Atharvaveda*
Ba Dh S	*Baudhāyana Dharmasūtra*
BG Bh	*Bhagavadgītā Bhāṣya*
BG	*Bhagavadgītā*
Bh Pu	*Bhāgavatapurāṇa*
Bṛ U Bh	*Bṛhadāraṇyakopaniṣad Bhāṣya*
Bṛ U	*Bṛhadāraṇyakopaniṣad*
BS Bh	*Brahmasūtra Bhāṣya*
BS	*Brahmasūtra*
Ch U	*Chāndogyopaniṣad*
Ch U Bh	*Chāndogyopaniṣad Bhāṣya*
Dr Śr S	*Drāhyāyaṇa Śrautasūtra*
Ga Dh S	*Gautama Dharmasūtra*
Ja Br	*Jaiminīyabrāhmaṇa*
Ja Mī S	*Jaimini Mīmāṁsāsūtra*
Ka Br	*Kauṣītakibrāhmaṇa*
Kā Śr S	*Kātyayana Śrautasūtra*
Ka U	*Kaṭhopaniṣad*
Ka U Bh	*Kaṭhopaniṣad Bhāṣya*
Ke U Bh	*Kenopaniṣad Bhāṣya*
Ke U	*Kenopaniṣad*
M Bh	*Mahābhārata*
MS	*Manusmṛti*
Mu U	*Muṇḍakopaniṣad*
Mu U Bh	*Muṇḍakopaniṣad Bhāṣya*
Pr U	*Praśnopaniṣad*

RN	*Rāmāyaṇa*
ṚV	*Ṛgveda*
Śa Br	*Śatapathabrāhmaṇa*
Sa Śr S	*Satyāṣāḍa Śrautasūtra*
ŚYV	*Śukla Yajurveda*
Ta Br	*Taittirīyabrāhmaṇa*
Ta Sa	*Taittirīyasaṁhitā*
Ta U	*Taittirīyopaniṣad*
Ta U Bh	*Taittirīyopaniṣad Bhāṣya*
Upad	*Upadeśasāhasrī*[1]
Va Dh S	*Vasiṣṭha Dharmasūtra*
YS	*Yājñavalkyasmṛti*

[1]*Upadeśasāhasrī* of Śaṅkara consists of two parts: Metrical Part and Prose Part. Throughout this dissertation Upad 1 indicates the Metrical Part and Upad 2, the Prose Part.

INTRODUCTION

Brahmajijñāsā, the quest for *Brahman,* which is the desire and search for self-realisation, is very fundamental to *Advaitic* tradition. In satiating this quest Vedas are considered as the excellent recourse by the entire Vedic tradition. On the basis of *varṇa* and *āśrama*, Vedas and the religious tradition related to it disqualify and exclude some groups of people, such as *śūdra*s, women of all *varṇas*, non-*sannyāsa āśramis*, and those who do not belong to any *āśrama* such as widower, from this quest. This idea of exclusion is fostered by the subsequent texts of the tradition such as *Manusmṛti*. It is carried over to the succeeding age of the Vedic tradition reaching up to the time of *Vedānta*. Śaṅkara, the great *Vedāntic* philosopher and theologian, also seems not an exception to this. *Apaśūdrādhikaraṇam* of his *Brahmasūtra Bhāṣya* argues for the exclusion of *śūdra*s. This dissertation attempts for a critical account of the problem of exclusion in Śaṅkara.

Śaṅkara: The *Vedāntic* Thinker

There were various attempts to understand the Upaniṣadic truth with the help of *Bhagavadgītā* and *Brahmasūtra* in addition to Upaniṣads. These attempts were in the form of interpretations given to these texts. Various philosophical or theological developments based on such interpretations are generally known as *Vedāntic* systems.

Śaṅkara interpreted the Upaniṣadic wisdom from the standpoint of strict non-dualism (*a-dvaita*). Ontologically *Brahman* is the essence and reality-giving cause of everything. This does not deny the plurality and differences experienced in the phenomenal world but uphold the transcendence of ultimate reality, *Brahman*. The enlightenment consists in the intuitive experience of this non-dual reality which comprises the realisation of the identity between *Ātman* and *Brahman*. In order to have this realisation the aspirant has to take up *jñānamārga*, the *śravaṇa* (listening), *manana* (reflection) and *nididhyāsana* (contemplation) of scriptures. Using reason as a tool, the aspirant takes up the means for realising the ultimate reality, *Brahman* which is trans-rational and extra-textual.

Critiquing Śaṅkara

A sound critique on Śaṅkara invites our attention to some of the important points. Understanding the mind of Śaṅkara is comparatively difficult. One of the reasons is, his textual works—except *Upadeśasāhasrī*—are commentaries on the texts of Vedic tradition such as Upaniṣads, *Bhagavadgītā* and *Brahmasūtra*, and therefore, the reader may not find his own ideas systematically developed. Secondly, the vocabulary he uses are sometimes confusing, because he borrows terms from other known philosophical systems of his time, such as *Sāṁkhya* and *Mīmāṁsā*. Thirdly, many literary works are attributed to him. Some of them present Śaṅkara inadequately and improperly. Due to all these, it is possible that the *Advaita* tradition after Śaṅkara misrepresent him. A critique has to take this fact into account.

The study of Śaṅkara has to be critical than sympathetic. The traditional reverence for Śaṅkara, and the deified position he occupied in the *Advaita* lineage, shall not compromise or constrain the kinds of questions that might be addressed to him. The critique has to take note of the inconsistencies and weak points of *Śāṅkaravedāntic* system, not merely to find fault with it, but rather, to look for its potential to become more reasonable and meaningful so that it might adequately serve the integrity of the humanity and the world at large.

Critical study on Śaṅkara, or any thinker for that matter, has to take into account the fact that no ideologies are history-free. One cannot be inattentive to the reasons why some ideas take root or why some of them get eclipsed in a particular culture and society in a particular historical period. The reasons always have cultural, historical, political and religious influences. Study on Śaṅkara, totally disconnected from its historical context, will be incomplete. But, at the same time, it has to take notice of how the thinker, by making attempts to transcend the historical influences, remains inadmissible to be jailed by such contexts. Some of the social and cultural practices are sometimes ignored or differently interpreted so as to bring up his priorities of values and ideologies.

Śaṅkara as an interpreter might not be prejudice-free. For instance, it is possible that his life as a *sannyāsi* might influence his interpretation; which would have a different nuance if he were a householder. He was not giving mere word-to-word interpretation to the text, but had his own priorities and agendas which he has skilfully expressed through his interpretive works. Understanding him requires recognising his hermeneutical prejudices and agendas with which he responded to the theological, moral and social issues.

A sound study on *Śāṅkaravedānta* has to recognise the nature of Śaṅkara's textual works as dialogical and pedagogical. On the one hand, he was responding to the existing philosophical and theological ideas which were different than his own, and on the other hand, he, through them, was giving insight to the *Vedāntic* aspirant on the right means for the enlightenment. His ideas have to be understood from within the dialogue-context: to whom was he speaking and to which question was he answering. Therefore, without grasping his fundamental and essential teachings which he held uncompromisingly, if an enquirer culls out some of the dialogue-parts, he/she will get only a distorted picture of *Śāṅkaradarśana*.

Ananalysis on Śaṅkara, which is creative and critical, has to serve as a guideline and inspiration for the present-day *Advaitins* to enter into dialogue with, and respond to the various traditions, ideologies, problems, needs and concerns of today. The dialogue partners of the present *Śāṅkaravedāntin* is not the same as that of Śaṅkara. The insights of *Śāṅkaravedānta* have to be critically evaluated and constructively explained in order that it might be relevant and creative. If not, *Advaita* which has been a living tradition by being studied and practised up to this day, will cease to be so, and will no more be meaningful for the world.

Keeping all these in mind, the present study makes an attempt to critique *Śāṅkaravedāntic* response to the problem of excluding *śūdra*s from the quest for *Brahman*. It takes Śaṅkara's interpretation to *Apaśūdrādhikaraṇam*—the portion or *adhikaraṇam* comprising five *sūtra*s of *Brahmasūtra* of Bādarāyaṇa (BS Bh 1.3.34–38)—as the key text. This text is significant because it is here Śaṅkara directly deals with the issue of *śūdra*-exclusion and his *bhāṣya* on *Brahmasūtra* is considered as one of his authentic works by all the scholars.

Śāṅkaravedāntin and the Exclusivism Today

The world today appears to be a wounded and fragmented one. World-peace is seriously threatened by the exclusive ideologies and practices which remain as the significant cause for and consequence of placing world in need of healing.

Exclusions are of diverse types and they vary in their intensity. Exclusion may be from the right to study, right to use the common spaces, right to free expression, etc. All these forms involve exploitation, denial of human dignity, deprivation of privileges and rights, violation of human freedom and equality. In addition to these forms of exclusion, the present Indian population in a special way experiences exclusions based on religion and culture. Indian nationalism and patriotism sometimes take extreme forms wherein the Indian culture is identified with Hindu culture. It seems that the question, who is an Indian, is treated in synonym with who is a Hindu. Such ideologies have become a political strategy and have gained power and authority. Its negative impacts—the tendency to look down upon some groups, to keep them excluded, and to deny their fundamental rights on the basis of religion, culture, caste, gender, etc.—have gained momentum. Some groups who propagate these consider themselves to be the legitimate spoke persons of Indian culture and religion, and condemn any ideas and practices other than theirs. This is done through silencing the dissenting voices through violence, banning some academic scholarly works, hijacking the mass media, and so on.

Social exclusion is as old as Vedic times; only the form and criteria get changed. Exclusion of *śūdra* from *brahmajijñāsā* is not an issue merely concerned about a specific group called '*śūdra*' and it is not about a particular form of exclusion. It is a specimen for the problem of exclusion in general. The '*śūdra*' could stand for any group of people who suffer from exclusive practices. In any system of democracy, which emphasizes the numerical superiority, it is always possible that the right of the minority is taken away by the decision of the majority. Political, social, religious, and cultural spheres contribute in their own way to the weaving of exclusive policies where the rights of the marginalised are robbed away. Today's '*śūdra*', the excluded, and the 'upper caste', i.e., those mainstream hegemonic systems which exploit the poor, are to be identified.

In this context, a critical enquiry into Śaṅkara's treatment of the problem of *śūdra*-exclusion is relevant. If this great thinker, who is from within the Hindu fold, and his celebrated text *Brahmasūtra Bhāṣya* could give scope for inclusive thinking, then it would become an eye-opener and a corrective force for exclusivism, especially for those ideologies which perpetuate the exclusion of non-Vedic and non-Indian traditions and cultures. The focus on exclusion from *brahmajijñāsā,* is significant because it involves deprivation, not merely from any mundane benefits but from the very possibility of self-realization which is considered to be ultimate human goal. Added to this, such discrimination and injustice is based merely on caste, gender, and social status. The issue is all the more acute if this is considered to be sanctioned by *Brahmasūtra Śāṅkara Bhāṣya*, one of the popular theological and philosophical texts of Indian wisdom, and thereby the veracity and integrity of the text and its truth is at question. Therefore, a proper study on this issue is in place in this modern world in which there are also authentic seekers who search for self-realizing experience, and many people—traditional, non-traditional, national, international, and those from various caste, race and culture—hope to find it in Indian wisdom.

Textual Responses to *Śūdra*-Exclusion: Literature Review

Śaṅkara is not the first one, and his *bhāṣya* on *Brahmasūtra* is not the first text which took up the issue of *śūdra*-exclusion. It has a long history going back to Vedic times and reaching up to the present century.

Vedas have explicit mention of underestimating *śūdra*s. Later texts of the tradition, especially Dharmasūtras, interpreted them as strict exclusion from Vedic learning and religion. At least from the Upaniṣadic time onward, from within and without the tradition, there were social and textual reactions against this. Upaniṣads have tried to be inclusive but the later traditions generally took the same lead of Dharmasūtras, perhaps with some variations.[2] Buddhism, Jainism, and *Bhakti* Movements reacted against such exclusions and consequent exploitations. These traditions, anyway, did not oppose and overturn the *brāhmaṇic* ones, but developed as parallel systems. In the *brāhmaṇic* traditions *śūdra*-exclusion continued as social practice and the texts upheld it.

After Śaṅkara, thinkers and social reformers have taken up this theme. The thinkers immediately after Śaṅkara generally took the lead of *Apaśūdrādhikaraṇam*. Rāmānuja and the succeeding age of *brāhmaṇic* tradition became stricter on this matter than Śaṅkara. We find Rāmānuja criticising Śaṅkara for becoming lenient on exclusion.[3] In later periods, from the nineteenth century onward, the thinkers both from within and without the *Advaitic* tradition, through their social

---

[2] A study on *śūdra*-exclusion in the major texts of *brāhmaṇic* tradition (Vedas, Upaniṣads and Dharmasūtras) is undertaken in the second chapter of this dissertation.

[3] The position of Rāmānuja and Madhva on *śūdra*-exclusion is studied in the third chapter (3.1) of this dissertation.

and textual works, have made critical responses to the exclusion and consequent exploitations on the basis of caste and other human made laws. Some of the important figures are Sāvitrībhāī Phūle, Caṭṭampiswāmikal, Nārāyaṇaguru, Vivekānanda, Aurobindo, Ambedkar and so on. From among them Caṭṭampiswāmikal (1853–1924), who followed the Vedic tradition, and his work *Vedādhikāranirūpaṇam* is noteworthy. This text takes up exactly the issue of *śūdra*'s ineligibility for Vedas and touches up on *Apaśūdrādhikaraṇam*. The author argues strongly that this prohibition has no base in the Vedas. He shows the examples of Jānaśruti who had Vedic knowledge from Raikva (Ch U 4.1–3) and Satyakāma from Gautama (Ch U 4.4–9) as the *śruti* examples for eligibility of *śūdra* for knowledge. He considers prohibition to learn Veda is against *dharma* and equalises it with denying food to the hungry, and thus, he affirms, anyone who is desirous of Vedic knowledge has to be imparted with it. He criticises *Apaśūdrādhikaraṇam* of *Brahmasūtra,* especially the interpretation given to it by Śaṅkara, by arguing that this particular text is misinterpreted so as to advocate *śūdra*-exclusion.[4]

A critical study on *Advaita*, focusing on Śaṅkara's original works, took momentum from twentieth century onward. There were attempts to distinguish Śaṅkara's teachings from the general *a-dvaitic* understanding of the tradition. Scholars such as Anantanand Rambachan, Arvind Sharma, Srinivasa Rao, and Richard De Smet are some of the important figures. Srinivasa Rao, in his article "Two Myths in

---

[4] Srī Caṭṭampiswāmikal, *Vedādhikāranirūpaṇam* (http://hinduebooks.blogspot.com, 2010), 27, 37–53, 75. https://archive.org/details/VedadhikaraNirupanam-ChattampiSwamikal-Malayalam (accessed February 20, 2017).

Advaita" argued that the general understanding of *Advaita* tradition that the world is an illusion was not Śaṅkara's teaching but rather a post-Śaṅkara development.[5] This gave light to the inclusive feature of *Śāṅkaravedānta* on socially engaged *Advaitin* besides the normally accepted contemplative character of *Advaita.* Roger Marcaurelle through his work, *Freedom through Inner Renunciation*, gave an inclusive understanding of Śaṅkara's concept of *sannyāsa* and argued even *śūdra* could take it up.[6] Prabhakara Rao's article "Inconsistencies in the *Brahmasūtra* and *Śāṅkarabhāṣya*: With Special Reference to the Competence of *Śūdra*" pointed out that the claim of *Apaśūdrādhikaraṇam* to exclude *śūdra* from Vedas remains inconsistent.[7] For Michael Comans and Padurang Vaman Kane, Śaṅkara had to favour the exclusion because of the reasons related to his context.[8] Satchidananda Murty has stated that in the Vedas there are no injunctions on exclusion of *śūdra*s neither from salvation nor from Vedas.[9] For Anantanand Rambachan, *Advaita* can go beyond *varṇa* and

---

[5] Srinivasa Rao, "Two Myths in Advaita," *Journal of Indian Philosophy* 24, no. 3 (June 1996): 265–279.

[6] Roger Marcaurelle, *Freedom Through Inner Renunciation: Śaṅkara's Philosophy in a New Light* (New York: State University of New York Press. 2000), 11–40, 137–158.

[7] M. Prabhakara Rao, "Inconsistencies in the *Brahmasūtra* and *Śāṅkarabhāṣya*: With Special Reference to the Competence of *Śūdra*," *Journal of Indian Council of Philosophical Research* 19, no. 2 (April–June 2002): 139–155.

[8] Michael Comans, *The Method of Early Advaita Vedānta: A Study of Gauḍapāda, Śaṅkara, Sureśvara and Padmapāda* (Delhi: Motilal Banarsidas, 2000), 317; Pandurang Vaman Kane, *History of Dharmaśāstra: Ancient and Medieval Religious and Civil Law in India,* vol. 2, pt. 1 (Poona: Bandarkar Oriental Institute, 1941), 155.

[9] Satchidananda Murty, *Vedic Hermeneutics* (New Delhi: Shri Lal Bahadur Shastri Rashtriya Sanskrit Vidyapeetha, 1993), 15.

āśrama restrictions for its ethics is primarily based on the four virtues of *sādhanacatuṣṭaya*, which have universal scope. He questions the significance of caste divisions in a tradition that proclaims the identity and sameness of the self in all beings. For him it is the role of *Advaita* tradition to take the lead in the repudiation of the discrimination and exploitation based on caste and gender.[10]

The Present Study: Hypothesis and Structure

The preceeding textual contributions in the field of *Śāṅkaravedānta*, though have tacitly made some contributions to the inclusive interpretation of *Śāṅkaradarśana,* have not focused on the inclusive potentials of it in the background of exclusion and the related exploitations, by making a critical study on Śaṅkara's interpretation on *Apaśūdrādhikaraṇam* which is the key text that would speak wether *Śāṅkaradarśana* is exclusive or inclusive. Though some of them have argued that the *śūdra*-exclusion which is explicit in *Apaśūdrādhikaraṇam* is incosistent with *Advaita* philosophy, they have not carried forward it with the questions such as:why inspite of being so, Śaṅkara had to go on with explicit statement on exclusion; is exclusion the final word in *Śāṅkaradarśana;* how far its inclusive potentials can be explored.

The present study brings the preceding scholarships on a single platform of critiquing *Śāṅkaravedānta* on the issue of exclusion of *śūdra* from *brahmajijñāsā*. For this purpose the text *Apaśūdrādhikaraṇam* from *Brahmasūtra Śāṅkara Bhāṣya*

---

[10] Anantanand Rambachan, *The Advaita Worldview: God, World, and Humanity* (Albany: State University of New York Press, 2006), 27–29; Anantanand Rambachan, "Rethinking *Advaita*: Who is Eligible to Read *Advaita* Texts?" *Journal of Hindu-Christian Studies* 22 (2009): 8–13.

is taken. This particular text is important as far as the theme under discussion is concerned. Because: 1) this is considered as one of the authentic works of Śaṅkara and 2) it is here he explicitly discusses on the issue of *śūdra*-exclusion 3) a critique on it, in view of probing inclusion-exclusion issues and concerns of Śaṅkara, is so far not adequately carried out. This present study is primarily a critique. Critiqing a particular philosophy or text is not merely to find fault with, but it consists in analysing the strong and weak aspects of it and in exploring its further potentials and possibilities that it might become more meaningful and integral. Respecting the spirit of true critique, this dissertation attempts at critiquing *Śāṅkaravedānta* on the issue of *śūdra*-exclusion basing on the text *Apaśūdrādhikaraṇam*.

This research hypothesises, *Śāṅkaravedānta* is inclusive: a closer reading of *Śāṅkaravedānta* reveals that it is non-exclusive, and the inclusivism implied in it can be explored in the light of a critical re-reading of *Apaśūdrādhikaraṇam*. It critiques Śaṅkara's position on *śūdra*-exclusion and looks for its inclusive possibilities. The study presumes that the inclusive insights of *Śāṅkaravedānta* can be enriched and carried forward as the light for the present context of exclusivism. It argues, a true Ś*āṅkaravedāntin* with his/her non-dual insight becomes inclusive in his/her thinking and attitude, and therefore, is a pro-subaltern.

This dissertation is divided into five chapters. The first chapter consists in making the idea of *brahmajijñāsā* clear, unearthing the text *Apaśūdrādhikaraṇam*, expounding the social impacts of exclusion, and then connecting these under *Śāṅkaravedāntic* treatment on *śūdra*-exclusion. This chapter introduces and expounds the research problem. The second chapter is a historical analysis: how the group called *śūdra*s were formed, and how the texts which preceded Śaṅkara's works treated the issue of exclusion. In the third chapter the text *Apaśūdrādhikaraṇam* is taken for a critical analysis. It brings out how the text is inconsistent and weak in its arguments favouring exclusion. The next chapter opens up the curious question, why Śaṅkara, in spite of being inconsistent, held the exclusive norms. It observes Śaṅkara's dilemma: he does not openly agree with the inclusion of *śūdra*s, but at the same time leaves a lot of scope for their inclusion, making his program for salvation universal. The reasons for such dilemma are explored here. The final chapter, in its first part makes a critical response to his reasons for exclusion. Those are viewed through the lens of essentials of *Śāṅkaravedānta* which is inclusive and universal in their theoretical scope and practical application. The second part of this chapter joins hands with applied *Advaita* or practical *Vedānta*. Admitting the fact that a detailed exposition on the proposals for practising *Advaitic* inclusivism in concrete situations is beyond the scope of this study, it takes up some of the issues related to exclusion. From the insights on inclusivism received from the preceding study, it invites *Śāṅkaravedāntin*s to enter into dialogue with some of the ideologies, issues and concerns that might perpetuate exclusivism and to respond to them creatively and meaningfully.

The aid for this study, in the form of bibliography, which isgiven at the end, will provide the reader to have better exposure into the related textual studies. The words that occur frequently have been included in the glossary. All the non-English words are transcribed with diacritics to facilitate their correct articulation. They are italicized, but with the exception of names of persons, places, terms referring to the groups of texts—such as Dharmasūtras and Purāṇas—and some names which are commonly used in English language, e.g., Veda and Aryan.

The present study, which is predominantly analytical, critical and contextual, attempts at an inclusive understanding of *Advaita.* It tries to bring into light the potential of the fundamental teachings of Śaṅkara to go beyond the discriminations and exploitations based on caste, gender, social class, culture, nationality, etc. This study which explores the inclusive possibilities of *Śāṅkaravedānta* might become a contribution to the mission of the *Advaitins* to become part of the healing process of the world today which is wounded by the exclusive strategies and practices.

CHAPTER 1

BRAHMASŪTRA BHĀṢYA OF ŚAṄKARA AND THE PROBLEM OF EXCLUSION: AN EXPOSITION

Introduction

Every concept has a specific meaning according to its use in a particular context. Understanding this meaning becomes richer when it is attented from within the context of its use. A study of a concept or an idea depending only on its general understanding will make it limping.

In order to make an analysis on the problem of exclusion from *brahmajijñāsā* in *Śāṅkaravedānta*, the specific meaning and use of the term *brahmajijñāsā*, the concept of exclusion, and the social problems related to it are to be explored. In addition to this, the context in which this theme has come up in the *Vedāntic* texts of Śaṅkara has to be looked into. For this purpose, the text which should come to the prime consideration is Śaṅkara's *bhāṣya* (interpretation) on *Brahmasūtra*. Because among the many works traditionally attributed to Śaṅkara, the authorship of *Brahmasūtra Bhāṣya* is undisputed, and thus, it is even considered as the standard by means of which the authenticity of other works attributed to Śaṅkara could be measured.[11] From *Brahmasūtra Bhāṣya* of Śaṅkara, *Apaśūdrādhikaraṇam,* which is the set of five aphorisms, is chosen for a critical study because it is in this text Śaṅkara explicitly deals with the issue of *śūdra's* eligibility for learning Veda and thus to take up *brahmajijñāsā*. Therefore,

[11] Sengaku Mayeda, introduction to *A Thousand Teachings: The Upadeśasāhasrī of Śaṅkara* (Tokyo: University of Tokyo Press, 1979), 6.

an in-depth study on the exclusion of *śūdra*s from *brahmajijñāsā* in *Śāṅkaravedānta* needs a probe into the textual setting of *Apaśūdrādhikaraṇam* within *Brahmasūtra Bhāṣya*, so that how and why this idea is reasonably fitted into the text will be clear.

Exclusion, with its various social dimensions, is a concept which is very much on the platform of discussions today. It is significant, because it often becomes inhuman by undervaluing the worth of human person. This chapter explains the concept *brahmajijñāsā* and explores the social problem of exclusion with a special emphasis on the gravity of it in the *brāhmaṇic* tradition. The practice of exclusion, in this tradition, was mainly based on caste and it effected barring certain social groups from education and freedom of religion and thus from self-realization, the liberation. This chapter also introduces *Apaśūdrādhikaraṇam* in view of exploring its textual context within *Brahmasūtra Bhāṣya* of Śaṅkara so that it would serve as an adequate prelude in understanding the mind of Śaṅkara, the great *Vedāntin* on the issue of exclusion from *brahmajijñāsā*.

1.1 *Brahmajijñāsā*

Athātobrahmajijñāsā, (अथातोब्रह्मजिज्ञासा) "then, therefore, the inquiry unto *Brahman*," is the first aphorism (*sūtra*) of Bādarāyaṇa's *Brahmasūtra* (BS 1.1.1), which is known as *jijñāsādhikaraṇam* (जिज्ञासाधिकरणम्). The word *atha* (अथ) means 'then'. This word is used in the sense of 'sequence' and not 'commencement' (BS Bh 1.1.1)[12] and it implies that the inquiry of *Brahman* should precede something. This suggests that there are some prerequisites to have a fruitful search for *Brahman*. The word *ataḥ* (अतः) means 'therefore' and it shows that there is a reason why one should take up the inquiry. The reason is revealed in the Veda itself, that the highest aim of human life is realized by the knowledge of *Brahman.*[13] It is obvious from the texts such as, 'he who knows *Brahman* attains the highest' (Ta U 2.1). It is the reason (therefore) why one has to undertake the enquiry of *Brahman* (BS Bh 1.1.1).

1.1.1 Meaning and Implications of the Term

Śaṅkara uses the term '*brahmajijñāsā*' to mean the enquiry or the quest for *Brahman*. The word *jijñāsā* (जिज्ञासा) is a noun from the root word *jñā,* (ज्ञा) 'to know',[14] prefixed with *ji* and suffixed with *sa.* The word *ji* (जि) literally means 'to win or to acquire'.[15] The word *sa*has its root in *san* (सन्) 'to wish to acquire'.[16] Thus the word *jijñāsā* stands for 'desire to know';[17]

---

[12] तत्राथशब्द आनंतर्यार्थः परिगृह्यते, नाधिकारार्थः, ब्रह्मजिज्ञासायां अनधिकार्यत्वात् । (BS Bh 1.1.1) Cf. Śaṅkara, *Brahmasūtra with Śāṅkarabhāṣya*, ed. Ministry of Education, India (Delhi: Motilal Banarsidas, 1964), 3.

[13] Richard De Smet, "The Theological Method of Śaṃkara" (PhD diss., Pontificiae Universitatis Gregorianae, Rome, 1955, typewritten, unpublished), 78.

[14] Moniner Moniner-Williams. *A Sanskrit-English Dictionary: Etymologically and Philologically Arranged* (1899; repr., Delhi: Motilal Banarsidass, 2005), s.v. "*jñā.*"

[15] Moniner-Williams, *A Sanskrit-English Dictionary*, s.v. "*ji.*"

[16] Moniner-Williams, *A Sanskrit-English Dictionary*, s.vv. "*sa,*" "*san,*" "*āśā.*"

[17] Moniner-Williams, *A Sanskrit-English Dictionary*, s.vv. "*jijñāsana,*" "*jijñāsā.*"

and it means 'an ardent or earnesrt desire to know'.[18] Such desire, according to Śaṅkara, aims at a result and it is realisation (of *Brahman*).[19] Since it is a verbal noun, it retains the vigorous meaning of a verb as a process which is most creative. Therefore, *jijñāsā* should not be understood merely as a 'pure wish to know' but it is the dynamic effort of the aspirants making use of all their abilities and faculties—physical, psychical, moral and intellectual—for knowledge.[20]

The desire for knowledge which is dynamic and vibrant must have an aim. The purpose or the end of such desire has to be looked into. Indian scriptures suggest mainly four kinds of ends: sensuous pleasure (*kāma*), worldly goods (*artha*), moral virtues (*dharma*) and liberation (*mokṣa*). By the time of Śaṅkara, it had become generally accepted that *mokṣa* alone could be the supreme end of a person.[21] The word *jijñāsu* (the one who desires to know)[22] is derived from the term *jijñāsā* (the desire to know). This word is very much related to

---

[18] K.L. Seshagiri Rao and Kapil Kapoor, eds., *Encyclopedia of Hinduism* (New Delhi: India Heritage Research Foundation and Rupa, 2010), s.v. "*jijñāsā.*" *Jijñāsā,* from the literal point of view, is an earnest desire to win in the acquiring of knowledge; this could be understood as a 'quest for knowledge'.

[19] ज्ञातुमिच्छा जिज्ञासा।अवगतिपर्यतं ज्ञानं सन्वाच्याया इच्छायाः कर्म फलविषयत्वादिच्छायाः।

(*Jñātumicchā jijñāsā. Avagatiparyantam jñānam sanvācyāyā icchāyāh karma phalaviṣayatvādicchāyāh*) (BS Bh 1.1.1). Cf. Śaṅkara, *Brahmasūtra with Śāṅkarabhāṣya*, ed. Ministry of Education, India, 4.

[20] Richard De Smet, "From Catholic Theology to Śāṅkara Vedānta and Return with Fr F.X. Clooney," in *Understanding Śaṅkara: Essays by Richard De Smet,* ed. Ivo Coelho (Delhi: Motilal Banarsidas, 2013), 406; De Smet, "The Theological Method of Śaṃkara," 79-80.

[21] De Smet, "The Theological Method of Śaṃkara," 81.

[22] Moniner-Williams, *A Sanskrit-English Dictionary*, s.v. "*jijñāsu.*"

the word *mumukṣutvam* (मुमुक्षुत्वं, the intense desire for *mokṣa*). *Mumukṣu* is the one who intensely desire *mokṣa*. In other words, *jijñāsu* is a *mumukṣu*.[23] For Śaṅkara, the end of the desire is *mokṣa* or liberation, achieved through the knowledge of Vedic scriptures, and this is *brahmajñāna* or *ātmajñāna*[24] (BS Bh 1.1.1; Ta U 2.1).

The enquiry is for the realisation of *Brahman* and the knowledge of which is liberation. The word *Brahman* is derived from the root *bṛh* (बृह्) ('to grow' or 'to burst forth') which at first meant prayer.[25] *Brahman* as prayer is what manifests itself in audible speech. From this understanding, later, its philosophical significance must have derived. Therefore, in the Upaniṣads this term indicates the primary cause of the universe—what burst forth spontaneously in the form of the nature as a whole and not as mere speech only.[26] Gradually the word *Brahman* began to mean the Absolute which is the ultimate cause of every reality. Upaniṣads has

---

[23] Anantanand Rambachan, *Accomplishing the Accomplished: The Vedas as a Source of Valid Knowledge in Śaṅkara* (Honolulu: University of Hawaii press, 1991), xi.

[24] For Śaṅkara, *brahmajñāna* (knowledge of *Brahman,* the Absolute) or *ātmajñāna* (knowledge of the self or self-realization) are identical with liberation.

[25] Moniner-Williams, *A Sanskrit-English Dictionary*, s.vv. "बृह्," "ब्रह्मन्"

[26] M.Hiriyanna, *Outlines of Indian Philosophy* (London: George Allen & Unwin, 1958), 54.

According to Gambhirananda, the word *Brahman* is from the root *bṛṁh* means growth, and the suffix *man*, added to it, signifies an absence of limitation (in expanse). So, *Brahman* derivatively means that which is absolutely the greatest. Eternality, etc. follows as a matter of course from this limitlessness. Cf. Śaṅkara, *Brahmasūtra Bhāṣya of Śri. Śaṅkarācārya*, trans. Swami Gambhirananda (1965; repr., Kolakata: Advaita Ashrama, 2013), 12n32.

made it clear that this *Brahman* is *Ātman* which is the very inner self of human being.[27]

Thus *brahmajijñāsā* is the creative and dynamic enquiry for *Brahman* or *Ātman* or for self-realization which is the supreme end of every human being (*mokṣa*), and which involves not an intellectual enquiry alone but the conversion or transformation of the whole person as the prerequisite for attaining the knowledge of *Brahman*.[28]

1.1.2 Eligibility for *Brahmajijñāsā*

In *Athātobrahmajijñāsā*, the first *sūtra* of *Brahmasūtra,* the word '*atha*' (then) imputes some prerequisites for taking up the enquiry for *Brahman*. Since *brahmajijñāsā* calls for a transformation of the aspirant, and since self-realizing knowledge is through Vedic scriptures, taking up of *brahmajijñāsā* presupposes certain qualities in the aspirant, both internal and external.

Brahmajijñāsā, the enquiry for *Brahman*, results in self-realization. For Śaṅkara this knowledge of *Brahman* is possible through sacred scriptures, *śruti*[29] (BS Bh 1.1.2; 2.1.31). The proper and direct discipline for realizing *Brahman*

---

[27] M.Hiriyanna, *Outlines of Indian Philosophy*, 55.

[28] Richard De Smet, "Language and the Knowledge of the Absolute According to Śaṅkara," in *Understanding Śaṅkara,* 68.

[29] The sacred scriptures of Hinduism are divided in to two: *Śruti* and *smṛti*. *Śruti* literally means 'what is heard'. These are body of directly received knowledge enshrined in Vedic texts, and are Vedas and Upaniṣads. These are considered authorless and eternal. *Smṛti* literally means 'what is remembered,' and are the texts which have comparatively later origin and are authored; for example, *Bhagavadgītā*, *Manusmṛti*, etc. See Rao *Encyclopedia of Hinduism,* s.vv. "*Śruti,*" "*Smṛti.*"

involves: listening to *śruti* from an appropriate teacher (श्रवण, *śravaṇa*), reflection and rational personalization on what is heard (मनन, *manana*) and meditating on the word that is heard and reflected (निदिध्यासन, *nididhyāsana*) (BS Bh 1.1.2; 1.1.4; Bṛ U 2.4.5). This triple process for the acquisition of *brahmajñāna* is described in *Bṛhadāraṇyakopaniṣad* on the occasion of Yājñavalkya's instruction to his wife, Maitreyī. "The self my dear Maitreyi, should be realized—should be heard of, reflected on, and meditated upon. By the realization of the self, my dear, through hearing, reflection and meditation, all this is known" (Bṛ U 2.4.5; 4.5.6; BS Bh 1.1.2).[30]

The task of *śravaṇa* is to acquaint the aspirant with the declarations of *śruti*, strictly under the guidance of a proper teacher.[31] It includes: listening, repeating and learning the sacred texts; having a linguistic and grammatical understanding of the meaning of the text. This study is exegetical by making use of all rational faculties.[32]

Knowledge gained during *śravaṇa* however, is not self-certifying and, therefore, is incapable of conferring freedom. It is indirect and lacks conviction. *Manana* is

---

[30] आत्मा वा अरे दृष्टव्यः श्रोतब्यो मंतब्यो निदिध्यासितव्यो मैत्रेय्यात्मनो वा अरे दर्शनेन श्रवणेन मत्या विज्ञानेनेदं सर्वं विदितम्॥ (Bṛ U Bh 2.4.5) Cf. Śaṅkara, *Īśādidaśopaniṣadaḥ: Ten Principal Upanishads with Śāṅkarabhāṣya*, ed. Ministry of Education, India (Delhi: Motilal Banarsidas, 1964), 141.

[31] From the point of *brahmajijñāsā*, *śravaṇa* means hearing, understanding Vedic word. The good teacher is a pedagogue, and is the one who teaches according to the capacity of the pupil, inviting doubts in the form of questions from the aspirant. See De Smet, "The Theological Method of Śaṃkara,"159.

[32] Richard De Smet, "The Fundamental Antinomy of Sri Śaṅkarācārya's Methodology," in *Understanding Śaṅkara: Essays by Richard De Smet,* ed. Ivo Coelho (Delhi: Motilal Banarsidas, 2013), 76.

personal reflection on what is learnt; intended to remove all doubts which might have arisen about the validity of what aspirants have apprehended during *śravaṇa*. Here the disciples make themselves clear on the inner rationality of what is learnt, and they confront all the possible objections inspired from the other *pramāṇas* so as to show that it can never be contradicted. *Manana* releases and relieves knowledge from doubt.[33] When both inner rationality and complete non-contradiction are secured, full credibility and the completion of *manana* are obtained.

Even at this stage of the process, knowledge is still inadequate. After *manana* one undertakes the practice of *nididhyāsana* (contemplation)[34] which eventually provides with a direct experience of what is gathered as a possibility in *śravaṇa* and reasoned over in *manana*.[35] This consists in abiding constantly in *Brahman*/*Ātman*, bearing in mind that It is all and nothing else is really existent (BG Bh 6.25). It is beyond reasoning and actions (Uapd 1.18.9–21; 1.18.105–108; 1.18.222). Śaṅkara sheds light on this triple process when he writes: "The disciple having been told so by the teacher, sat in

---

[33] Rambachan, *Accomplishing the Accomplished*, 107.

[34] The word often used for this final stage of liberation is '*nididhyāsana.*' It is combination of four words. '*ni*', '*di*', '*dhy*', and '*āsana*'. '*Āsana*' means the comfortable *yoga* posture (bodily) to be adopted for undisturbed mediation, '*dhy*' means the intellect which is to be fixed itself exclusively, '*di*' with ever-renewed intensity (as implied by this repetitive prefix '*di*'), '*ni*' upon the truth previously ascertained. Thus, this word implies fixing the intellect with ever renewed intensity upon the truths already ascertained in a posture which is conducive for it. See Richard De Smet, "The Dynamics of Contemplation According to Śaṅkarācārya," in *Understanding Śaṅkara: Essays by Richard De Smet,* ed. Ivo Coelho (Delhi: Motilal Banarsidas, 2013), 290.

[35] De Smet, "The Dynamics of Contemplation According to Śaṅkarācārya," in *Understanding Śaṅkara,* 287.

solitude with his mind concentrated, deliberated on the traditional teaching as imparted by the teacher together with its purport, ascertained it by a process of reasoning, made it a matter of personal experience, approached the teacher, and said 'Now *manye*, I think; (Brahman) is *viditam*, known'" (Ke U Bh 2.1 p. 62).[36]

The triple *śruti* process—*śravaṇa*, *manana* and *nididhyāsana*—are interdependent.[37] "When this three are combined, then true realization of the unity of Brahman is accomplished, not otherwise—by hearing alone" (Bṛ U Bh 2.4.5 p. 247).[38] But to get initiated in this triple process Śaṅkara is very particular that the aspirant must be prepared to it: social, moral and intellectual preparations are demanded as a prerequisite for *brahmajijñāsā*. These prerequisites could be

---

[36] Direct quotes from Ke U Bh of Śaṅkara (translation), throughout this dissertation, are given page number followed by 'p.' Page numbers are from: Śaṅkara. *Eight Upaniṣads with the Commentary of Śaṅkarācārya*, vol. 1. Translated by Swami Gambhirananda. 1957. Reprint, Kolkata: Advaita Ashrama, 2013.

[37] Rambachan, *Accomplishing the Accomplished*, 44; Richard De Smet, "Theological Method and Vedānta," in *Understanding Śaṅkara: Essays by Richard De Smet,* ed. Ivo Coelho (Delhi: Motilal Banarsidas, 2013), 103. "In short, 'I don't know' is removed by *śravaṇa*; 'I don't understand' is removed by *manana*; 'I don't experience, is removed by *nididhyāsana.*" Swami Advaitananda, "The Journey of a Seeker," in *Advaitāmṛtam*, ed. Sandhya Sundar and Dilip Kumar Rana (Ernakulam: Chinmaya International Foundation, 2015), 217.

[38] यदैकत्वमेतान्युपगतानि तदा सम्यग्दर्शनं ब्रह्मैकत्वविषयं प्रसीदति, नान्यथा श्रवणमात्रेण । (Bṛ U Bh 2.4.5) Cf. Śaṅkara, *Īśādidaśopaniṣadaḥ,* ed., Ministry of Education, India, 142.

Direct quotes from Bṛ U Bh of Śaṅkara (translation), throughout this dissertation, are given page number followed by 'p.' Page numbers are from: Śaṅkara. *Bṛhadāraṇyaka Upaniṣad with the Commentary of Sankaracarya*. Translated by Swami Madhavananda. 1934. Reprint, Kolkata: Advaita Ashrama, 2015.

classified as internal (the group of qualities which demand the personal, inner transformation) and external (those socio-cultural environment which makes this transformation possible).

1.1.2.1 Internal Prerequisites

The internal qualities that are necessary in order to take up the study of the scriptures are the four mental practices or disciplines (साधनचतुष्टय, *sādhanacatuṣṭaya)* which Śaṅkara gives in the very first aphorism of his *Brahmasūtra Bhāṣya* (BS Bh 1.1.1).[39] They are as follows:

1) *Viveka*: Discrimination between the eternal (*nitya*) and non-eternal (*anitya*). This implies the necessity of an alert and discriminating intellect (Ka U 1.3.4–9; 1.3.12–14).
2) *Vairāgya*: This is non-attachment to the results of one's actions here or hereafter.
3) *Śamadamādisādhanasampatti*: accomplishment of qualities such as *śama, dama*, etc. referred to as the wealth of six disciplines. They are: *śama, dama, uparati, titikṣa, samādhāna,* and *śraddhā* (BS Bh 3.4.26; Bṛ U 4.4.23). *Śama* is defined as mental control. *Dama* is control or restraint of the sense organs and the organs of action. *Uparati* is withdrawal and seems to differ little from *śama* and *dama* but would seem to indicate the actual state of quietness achieved by the

[39] तस्मात्किमपि वक्तव्यमं यदनंतरं ब्रह्मजिज्ञासोपदिश्यत इति। उच्यते—नित्यानित्यावस्तुविवेकः, इहामुत्रार्थभोगविरागः, शमदमादिसाधनसंपत्, मुमुक्षुत्वम् च। (BS Bh 1.1.1) Cf. Śaṅkara, *Brahmasūtra with Śāṅkarabhāṣya*, ed. Ministry of Education, India, 3–4.

practice of the both.[40] *Titikṣa* is fortitude which is the patient endurance of suffering; cheerful accommodation of pleasant and unpleasant experiences occurs in one's life. *Samādhāna* is single-pointedness of mind. It is the ability to focus one's attention upon the object of inquiry until the end is attained. *Śraddhā* is faith in the authority of *śruti* and the teacher who unfolds it.

4) *Mumukṣutvam*: it is a burning desire for *mokṣa*. Unless there is a deep earnestness and sincerity of purpose, efforts will be mediocre.

These virtues are interrelated, i.e. the acquisition of one often pre-supposes and implies the other.[41] A *brahmajijñāsu* (the one who has taken up *brahmajijñāsā*) has to carefully cultivate these virtues as *sādhana* or spiritual discipline. For a *brahmajñāni*, these become an expression and spontaneous characteristic mark of self-realisation.[42]

1.1.2.2 External Prerequisites

Śaṅkara specifies certain qualifications in the aspirant which make cultivation of internal moral virtues easily possible. Among them, the important one is that the aspirant must be a renunciant (*sannyāsi*) (BS Bh 3.4.17; 3.4.20; Upad

---

[40] Rambachan, *Accomplishing the Accomplished*, 90.

[41] Rambachan, *Accomplishing the Accomplished*, 88.

[42] Rambachan, *The Advaita Worldview*, 20–21. "As far as the aspirant is concerned, it is not the perfection of these qualities which is demanded. In fact, such a perfection is not possible without *brahmajñāna*, when these qualities are spontaneously manifest. What is required is a disposition toward and a relative mastery of the fourfold means. As the inquiry proceeds and understanding grows, the qualities emerge in a new depth and profundity." Rambachan, *Accomplishing the Accomplished*, 88.

2.1.2). Only the one who has completed the initial study of Vedas was permitted to adopt *sannyāsa* mode of living. To get initiated to the Vedic study the investiture of the sacred thread is a must. For this the aspirant must be a male member from any of the three upper castes—*brāhmaṇa* (priest) *kṣatriya* (warrior aristocrat) and *vaiśya* (cultivator and the trader). Demand for these requirements excludes *śūdra*s, women, householders, etc. from the program of liberation (BS Bh 1.3.34; 1.3.38).

The eligible aspirant—with both internal and external pre-requisites—gets into the proper *Vedāntic* training under the guidance of an appropriate teacher through the triple process of *śravaṇa*, *manana*, and *nididhyāsana*. *Brahmajijñāsā* which involves dynamic and adequate attempts for self-realisation cannot be a sudden urge of an individual thirsty for knowledge. One may grow in this desire and enquiry by means of scriptures. It is the expected result of learning the sacred Vedas.[43] It springs from the traditional ground of unquestioned faith in the Vedas and is awakened 'through the grace of the merciful *guru*' (Bṛ U Bh 4.4.15) to those who are eligible for it with both internal and external qualities. The nature and scope of these prerequisites are very much contributing to examine the exclusivism and inclusivism in the program of *brahmajijñāsā* according to Śaṅkara.

1.1.3 Possibility of *Brahmajijñāsā*: Antinomy of Śaṅkara

Brahmajijñāsā—which is the enquiry for *Brahman* and for which Śaṅkara has given means to achieve—is faced with some theoretical problems questioning the very possibility of

[43] De Smet, "The Theological Method of Śaṃkara," 78.

it. From the larger context of Śaṅkara's *Advaita* it is possible to doubt whether such an enquiry is possible at all. Śaṅkara is aware of the problem and has dealt with the same.

One of such problems is dealt in the interpretation and explanations that are given for the first aphorism of the first chapter of *Brahmasūtra* (BS Bh 1.1.1). The opponent suggests, if *Brahman* is familiar and known, It need not have to be deliberated for the sake of knowledge. If *Brahman* is unfamiliar and unknown, any deliberation on *Brahman* will be futile. For this, the answer of the *Vedāntin* is, *Brahman* does exist and *Brahman's* existence is known. The existence of *Brahman* is well known from the fact of Its being the Self of all: for every person feels that one's Self exists, and never feels one does not exist. But there is conflict about the distinctive nature of the Self. For example, some schools of philosophical thought recognize body alone to be the Self; some say that it is momentary consciousness; still others believe that there is a soul separate from the body which transmigrates, and is the agent (of work) and the experiencer (of results). In this way there are many views depending on logic and texts. If one accepts any one of these views without examination, one is liable to be deflected from emancipation and come to grief. Thus deliberation on *Brahman* is needed by ascertaining the meaning of the Upaniṣads with the help of reasoning which will lead to emancipation through knowledge (BS Bh 1.1.1).

Upaniṣads have presented the difficulty that *Brahaman* cannot be known using the *pramāṇas* (Ta U 2.4; Ke U 1.3). Śaṅkara also agrees the same: only that which can present itself to the senses as an object can be known; the principle of knowing in the knower cannot be known just as the principle of burning in the fire cannot be burnt (Ke U Bh 2.1).

Objectification, which is the human way of sense knowledge, cannot be applied to *Brahman* for It is a subject too subtle to be apprehended as an object (Ka U Bh 1.1.21). But, at the same time, *Brahman* is not absolutely unknowable because the testimony of *śruti* and those who had this knowledge indicate the possibility of it (Ka U Bh 12–15).[44] The underlying paradox in Śaṅkara is: for him, the Real is the non-dual Absolute, and knowing which is *Vidyā*. But all the human knowledge which is in the realm of this world which is not real, is not knowledge proper (*avidyā*). All human attempts to know the non-dual reality are from this world of duality and the consequent knowledge cannot be *Vidyā*. Richard De Smet, one of the prominent *Advaitins*, has summed up the antinomy as follows:

> Whatever is not the perfectly simple realization of the Absolute is not *Vidyā*, but *avidyā*, hence, *Brahmajijñāsā* itself and all its means are *avidyā*; now, no form of *avidyā* (and no combination of any privileged forms of it can ever cause *Vidyā*, which is ever existing and can never be caused; and still *Brahmajijñāsā* is painstakingly undertaken and proposed to the disciple as if it were the real means of extinguishing *avidyā* and thus causing the manifestation of *Vidyā*.[45]

The possibility of *Vidyā* presupposes transcendence from *avidyā* to *Vidyā*, duality to non-duality, unreality to

---

[44] According to Rambachan, "Śaṅkara generally interprets Upaniṣad texts that speak of unknowability of *brahman* in two ways. He interprets some of these texts as refuting the possibility of knowing *brahman* as an object, while other are seen as emphasizing the exclusivity of the Upaniṣads as the valid means of knowledge." Rambachan, *The Advaita Worldview*, 56.

[45] De Smet, "The Fundamental Antinomy of Sri Śaṅkarācārya's Methodology," in *Understanding Śaṅkara*, 78.

Reality. How this can be possible? Its possibility or impossibility determines the answer for the question, whether *brahmajijñāsā* is possible at all? Śaṅkara is aware of this antinomy and gives solutions to it:

1) For Śaṅkara this world is not completely unreal as barren women's son, and secular knowledge is not completely *avidyā* as contradictory to *Vidyā*.[46] But, compared to ultimate reality and ultimate knowledge, the reality of this world is less real and the knowledge is incomplete.
2) An analysis of the process of ordinary cognition and human knowledge reveals the presence of an ultimate knower, which makes the knowledge of an object and 'knowledge of the knowledge' of that object possible. If not, the chain of knowledge would go on *ad infinitum* and knowledge would become impossible. But the knowledge is possible, and there is the ultimate knower which *Advaita* terms as witness consciousness and which is *Ātman* (BG Bh 2.16; Bṛ U Bh 4.3.7). "Hence every ordinary cognition, though it is *avidyā*, implies the direct knowledge of being (*sat*), *Ātman*, and *jñāna* which, when seen as one, constitute the supreme *vidyā*. There is, therefore, a link or a kind of passage between *avidyā* and *Vidyā*"[47]

---

[46] A sincere search confronts with the limits of knowledge, wealth, pleasures, etc. of this physical existence. Every finite search for knowledge carries an implied underlying quest for the infinite. See Rambachan, *The Advaita Worldview*, 10–14, 16.

[47] De Smet, "The Fundamental Antinomy of Sri Śaṅkarācārya's Methodology," in *Understanding Śaṅkara*, 80. Self-ignorance is not the complete absence of the knowledge about the self. It is the incomplete knowledge of the self that causes its misapprehension. See Rambachan, *The Advaita Worldview*, 53.

3) Scriptural words have the power to go beyond their primary meaning (dictionary meaning) to the supreme meaning (*paramārtha*) by means of analogical understanding of words. This, for Śaṅkara, is the *lakṣaṇā* theory of meaning. The importance of *lakṣaṇā* is that it provides a bridge for our weak intellect to cross over the abyss between the finite and the infinite or between *avidyā* and *Vidyā*.[48]
4) Though, through *pramāṇa*, by way of objectification, one cannot know the Absolute, it is not impossible that it be 'realized' through the direct intuition.[49] The transcendental experience at the final point of realization which is trans-empirical and trans-rational makes possible the leap from this worldly *avidyā* to Supreme non-dual *Vidyā*.

Theoretically these could suggest that the realization of the Absolute which is non-dual is possible from the world of duality. Now coming to the practical side of *brahmajijñāsā*, the question is how to achieve this realization? For Śaṅkara it is only through the scriptures (*śruti*)—through *śravaṇa*, *manana* and *nididhyāsana*. When he comes to the practical guidelines on undertaking *brahmajijñāsā*, by means of *śruti*, its all-inclusive nature and exclusive aspects come in conflict with.

---

[48] Richard De Smet, "Śāṅkara Vedānta and Christian Theology," in *Understanding Śaṅkara: Essays by Richard De Smet,* ed. Ivo Coelho (Delhi: Motilal Banarsidas, 2013), 395.

[49] Richard De Smet, "Language and Knowledge of the Absolute According to Śaṅkara," in *Understanding Śaṅkara*: *Essays by Richard De Smet,* ed. Ivo Coelho (Delhi: Motilal Banarsidas, 2013), 47.

1.2 *Apaśūdrādhikaraṇam* within *Brahmasūtra Bhāṣya*

Apaśūdrādhikaraṇam is the set of five aphorisms (*sūtra*s) which deal with the eligibility of *śūdra* for Vedic study. This consists of *sūtra*s 34–38 inclusive, from the third section constituting ninth topic of the first chapter of *Brahmasūtra,* i.e. BS 1.3.34–38. *Brahmasūtra* is an attempt done to systematize the ideas of Upaniṣads and this great task is ascribed to Bādarāyaṇa. This is one among the three basic texts of *Vedāntic* philosophy; the other two are *Bhagavadgītā* and Upaniṣads. It is mainly through the interpretations given to *Brahmasūtra, Vedāntic* thinkers have brought out their philosophy. Śaṅkara's non-dualistic interpretation is considered to be the earliest one of those extant today. His interpretation to *Apaśūdrādhikaraṇam* is unique in understanding his position on the possibility of *śūdra* for *brahmajijñāsā.*

1.2.1 *Brahmasūtra*

Upaniṣads do not contain any ready-made consistent system of thought. There are statements which would imply contradictions. Hence the necessity of systematizing the thoughts of the Upaniṣads arose. *Brahmasūtra* is such an attempt, and the authorship of it is ascribed to Bādarāyaṇa. He was not the first/only one who has made attempts to systematize the Upaniṣadic thoughts[50] but his is the most

[50] From Bādarāyaṇa itself we find that there were other great persons and the schools of thought. We find the names of Auḍulomi (BS 1.4.21; 3.4.45; 4.4.6), Kāśakṛtsna (BS 1.4.22), Bādari (BS 1.2.30), Jaimini (BS 1.2.28; 1.2.31; 1.3.31), Kārṣṇājijni (BS 3.1.9), Āśmarathya (BS 1.2.29; 1.4.20) and others mentioned.

systematic and probably the best.[51] This work is known in different names: it is known as *Brahma-sūtra* (since it deals with ultimate realty, the *Brahman*); *Vedānta-sūtra* (since it is the aphoristic text on Upaniṣads which are also known as *Vedānta*, the '*anta*', end of the Vedas);[52] *Śārīraka-sūtra* (since it is concerned with the nature and the destiny of the embodied soul); *Bhikṣu-sūtra* (since it is considered that those who are most competent to study it are the *bhikṣus,* the monks or *sannyāsins*). All the later *Vedāntic* schools hold this work to be the great authority and every new school starts with a fresh commentary on it.[53]

1.2.1.1 *Sūtra* Form of Composition

Brahmasūtra, the systematic treatise on the Upaniṣadic thoughts, is composed in short aphorisms called *sūtra*s. The word '*sūtra*' (सूत्र) is derived from the root '*siv*' (सिव्), to sew, and means 'thread',[54] or in the textual context, a more or less short thread of sounds (a *sūtra* can consist of even a single word) conveying meaning in a condensed form.[55] It is understood as:

---

[51] Swami Vireswarananda, trans., *Brahma-sūtras* (Calcutta: Advaita Ashram, 1962), v.

[52] Upaniṣads are the final literary portion of Vedas. They represent systematic philosophic formulation of Vedic ideals, and therefore, taken to be the flowering of Vedic thought. Thus, to the literal sense they are *Vedānta*; the end and the aim of Vedas. But popularly the title *Vedānta* is given to the later interpretations and explanations of the Upaniṣads and the various philosophical schools developed based on Upaniṣads, *Bhagavadgītā,* and *Brahmasūtra*.

[53] Vireswarananda, *Brahma-sūtras*, v.

[54] Moniner-Williams, *A Sanskrit-English Dictionary*, s.vv. "*siv*," "*sūtra*."

[55] Julius Lipner, *The Hindus: Their Religious Beliefs and Practices* (London: Routledge, 1994), 81.

"Concise, indicative of the (various) senses, composed of few letters and words, replete with sense, such are what the wise ones call '*sūtra*'."[56] They are intended as memory-aids to long discussions on any topic which the students have already gone through with their teacher. They are like short hand notes of the teaching of the preceptor to the pupils. The thoughts, while forming them as *sūtras*, were very much condensed, packed with meaning, for much was taken for granted.[57] Therefore, they are not intelligible without a commentary.

'*Sūtras*' which are considered as the vehicle of the ancient wisdom attests to the fact that such wisdom has traditionally been transmitted orally, and it facilitates such transmission. It is far easier to remember a *sūtra* or collection of *sūtras* than a text,[58] and therefore, it is typical memory device. Further, the *sūtra* points to the fact that *brāhmaṇic* wisdom was more or less safeguarded and transmitted as such; because the wisdom in the form of *sūtra* could be unlocked only in appropriate circumstances and only to those who are eligible and prepared to receive it.[59]

1.2.1.2 Date and Authorship

Śaṅkara in his *Brahmasūtra Bhāṣya*, tacitly but decidedly ascribed the authorship of *Brahmasūtra* to Bādarāyaṇa (BS Bh 3.4.1–17; 3.4.40). About Bādarāyaṇa very little are known. Tradition however identifies him with Vyāsa, the author of the *Mahābhārata*. Śaṅkara, in his commentaries

---

[56] De Smet, "The Theological Method of Śaṃkara," 76; Vireswarananda, *Brahma-sūtras*, iv.

[57] Vireswarananda, *Brahma-sūtras*, iii.

[58] Lipner, *The Hindus*, 81.

[59] Lipner, *The Hindus*, 81.

refers to Vyāsa as the author of the *Mahābhārata* and Bādarāyaṇa the author of *Brahmasūtra*. Perhaps to him these two personalities were different. His followers, Vācaspati, Ānandagiri and others identify Vyāsa and Bādarāyaṇa, while Rāmānuja and other commentators attribute it to Vyāsa.[60] Why and how this change has come is not conclusively known. S. Sankaranarayanan, one of the famous Indology scholars, offers probable reasons.[61] Important reasons could be to extol the founder of *Vedānta* on high at the level of Vyāsa[62] and to serve the purpose of propaganda and the furtherance of *Vedāntic* system so that the prestige of *Vedāntadarśana* (philosophy or ideals of *Vedānta*) could grow manifold.[63]

Assuming all the possibility that Bādarāyaṇa and Jaimini were contemporaries[64] and that Jaimini lived in the

---

[60] Vireswarananda, *Brahma-sūtras*, v.

[61] S. Sankaranarayanan, "Bādarāyaṇa and Vyāsa as Authors of the Brahmasūtra—A Historical Analysis," *Brahmavidya: The Adyar Library Bulletin* 67 (2003): 91–146.

[62] Non-*Vedāntic* schools claimed their founders of thought as *sarvajñās* (knowing everything) and incarnations of Viṣṇu. But the *sūtrakara* (the author/compiler of the *sūtras*) of *Vedānta*, Bādarāyaṇa had no such claim. It is possible in that age the *Vedāntins* too might have felt that the status of their *sūtrakāra* was lower when compared to that of their mighty rivals. Thus, for them it was fitting that the *sūtrakāra* of the *Vedānta*, who has refuted all other non-*Vedāntic* schools should excel the other founders of philosophy. So, the post-Śaṅkara *Vedāntins* must have gone a step further by honouring Vyāsa himself as the *sūtrakāra*. See Sankaranarayanan, "Bādarāyaṇa and Vyāsa as Authors of the Brahmasūtra," 119.

[63] Sankaranarayanan, "Bādarāyaṇa and Vyāsa as Authors of the Brahmasūtra," 119.

[64] In his *Brahmasūtra*, Bādarāyaṇa refers to Jaimini's views as many as eleven times. But excepting in one instance (3.4.40), as Śaṅkara shows, Bādarāyaṇa rejects them all. On the other hand, in his *Mīmāṁsāsūtra* Jaimini is found citing the views of the Bādarāyaṇa five times, and accepting them all with due reverence. The tradition takes this

Śrautasūtra period, some scholars have suggested the authorship of the *sūtra*s at sometime around 500 BCE. At the other extreme, H. Jacobi has estimated it between 200 and 450 CE.[65] But Dasgupta and Radhakrishnan basing on the fact that *Brahmasūtra* refers to almost all other Indian systems assume that its date cannot be very early and estimates its composition during the second century BCE.[66] Perhaps the only conclusive remark that can be made is, while the precise date of *Brahmasūtra* is uncertain, and is the subject of considerable disagreement, all agree that it represents one of the earliest attempts at systematizing the unsystematic contents of a body of scripture, and as such, holds a unique position in the Vedic textual tradition regardless of its exact date of authorship.[67]

1.2.1.3 Structure of *Brahmasūtra*

The stature in which Bādarāyaṇa's *Brahmasūtra* is held is based on the two fold greatness of the work: that is, greatness in both content and form. The content is outstanding as it represents the first comprehensive statement in a

---

strange feature as indicative of the fact that Bādarāyaṇa must have been the revered teacher of Jaimini. Since there are cross references it is very much likely that they are contemporaries. See Sankaranarayanan, "Bādarāyaṇa and Vyāsa as Authors of the Brahmasūtra," 120–121.

[65] H. Jacobi, "The Dates of the Philosophical Sutras of the Brahmins," in vol. 2 of *Studies in the History of Philosophy: An Anthology of Articles by Scholars Eastern and Western*, ed. Debiprasad Chattopadhya (Culcutta: K.P. Bagchi, 1978), 54–87.

[66] Surendranath Dasgupta, *A History of Indian Philosophy*, vol. 1 (Cambridge: Cambridge University Press, 1922), 418; S. Radhakrishnan, *The Brahma Sūtra: The Philosophy of Spiritual Life* (London: George Allen & Unwin, 1960), 22.

[67] George C. Adams, *The Structure and Meaning of Bādarāyaṇa's Brahma Sūtras: A Translation and Analysis of Adyāya I* (Delhi: Motilal Banarsidas, 1993), 9.

systematic manner of the vast corpus of Vedic thought. However *Brahmasūtra* is also outstanding in the form by which that content is expressed.[68] Bādarāyaṇa takes the vast body of scripture and organizes it into an exquisite work of order and symmetry attempting to bring order into the disorder of the multitude of different Upaniṣadic speculations.

The largest division of work is into four main *adhyāyas* (chapters). There is universal agreement among all the commentators that Bādarāyaṇa divided his work into these four main *adhyāyas*. The first two *adhyāyas* deal with *Brahman* as It is in Itself, the last two, with *Brahman* as the goal of human existence. More specifically, the first *adhyāya* is named as *Samanvaya* (समन्वय, harmony or order). It is reconciliation through proper interpretation, i.e. attempts to reconcile the different Upaniṣadic doctrines on the nature of *Brahman*. The second *adhyāya* is *Avirodha* (concord or non-conflict). Here Bādarāyaṇa discusses the objections that might be raised against the ideals of *Vedānta*. It shows how the *Vedāntic* philosophy withstands the challenges of other schools of thought such as, Buddhism, *Nyāya*, *Sāṁkhya*, etc. Third *adhyāya* is *Sādhana* (*mārga* or spiritual practice), and it deals with the ways or means for liberation. Fourth *adhyāya* is *Phala* (fruit or result), which focuses on the nature of liberation and attainment of *Brahman*.

From the *adhyāyas* Bādarāyaṇa extends the symmetry of the *sūtra*s even further by dividing each chapter into four *pādas* (sections). As with the *adhyāyas*, all commentators agree in dividing the work into four *pādas* per *adhyāya*, or total of sixteen *pādas*. Each *pāda* is further divided into a series of

---

68 Adams, *The Structure and Meaning of Bādarāyaṇa's Brahma Sūtras,* 12.

adhikaraṇas (topics) each of which is composed of several *sūtra*s. The *adhikaraṇas* are often arranged in a systematic manner, with one topic logically leading to the next. Each *adhikaraṇa* was based on a particular text of revelation, known as *viṣaya vākya* (topical text). Among the major commentators, there is a close, but not complete, agreement regarding the number of *adhikaraṇas* composing each *pāda*, and the number of *sūtra*s composing each *adhikaraṇa*. Śaṅkara, for instance, identifies 191 *adhikaraṇas* and 555 *sūtra*s, while Rāmānuja identifies 156 *adhikaraṇas* and 545 *sūtra*s, for Madhva, 223 *adhikaraṇas* and 564 *sūtra*s.[69]

With this division of *sūtra*s into *adhyāyas*, *pādas*, and *adhikaraṇas, Brahmasūtra* can be seen as a work in which the content is presented in accordance with a specific form, thereby imposing some order to the vast body of Vedic literature. While the commentators disagree on the precise division of the *sūtra*s, all agree that it is work of an exceptional order and symmetry.[70]

1.2.1.4 Different Interpretations on *Brahmasūtra*

A question may be raised how the same work could give rise to different interpretations forming various *Vedāntic* schools. The reasons are many. In the first place, the brevity of

---

[69] The references used in determining the number of the *sūtra*s are: Śaṅkara. *Brahmasūtra Bhāṣya of Śri. Śaṅkarācārya*. Translated by Swami Gambhirananda. 1965. Reprint, Kolakata: Advaita Ashrama, 2013; Rāmānuja. *The Vedānta-sūtras with the Śri-Bhāshya of Rāmānujāchārya*. Translated by M. Rangacharya and M.B. Varadaraja Aiyangar. Madras: The Educational Publishing, 1964; Madhva. *The Brahmasūtras: With English Translation of Madhva Bhāṣya*. Translated by S. G Mudgal. Mumbai: Archish Publications, 2005.

[70] Adams, *The Structure and Meaning of Bādarāyaṇa's Brahma Sūtras,* 12.

the *sūtra*s leaves much to be supplied by the commentators, and in the absence of a universally accepted unbroken tradition each is free to do this according to each one's pre-conceived ideas. Sometimes even without supplying anything the same *sūtra* is capable of being interpreted differently and even conveying quite the opposite meaning by the mere shifting of the stops (e.g. Śaṅkara and Rāmānuja on 3.2.11). Again, while there is a tradition which is accepted more or less by all as regards the arrangement into *adhyāyas* and *pādas*, there is no such accepted tradition as regards the division into *adhikaraṇas.* An *adhikaraṇa* may run to more than one aphorism. In such cases, the first one is the main and the subsequent ones are secondary. The number of aphorisms differs because the commentators take sometimes two aphorisms as one and vice versa.[71] Besides this there is nothing authoritative to guide as to which *sūtra*s form the *pūrvapakṣa* or the prima facie view and which give the *siddhānta* or the author's view. Again, often the *sūtra*s do not give any reference as to which texts of the scriptures are being discussed and as a result the commentator is free to select any texts from that vast repertory, so much so that it often happens that different commentators see different topics discussed in the same set of *sūtra*s. Added to all this is the difficulty that sometimes Bādarāyaṇa is often silent as regards his own decision and that on fundamental questions. He merely gives the view of different *Vedāntin*s and ends the topic.

There are at least ten significant interpretations to *Brahmasūtra.* Among them the chief systematic interpretations and the school that have a large following are: Śaṅkara (788–

[71] Rao, *Encyclopedia of Hinduism*, s.v. "*BrahmasūtraBhāṣya.*"

820 CE), the exponent of *Kevalādvaita* or absolute non-dualism; Rāmānuja (1017–1137 CE), the exponent of *Viśiṣṭādvaita* or qualified non-dualism; Nimbārka (1250 CE), the exponent of *Bhedābhedavāda* or the theory of difference and non-difference; Madhva (1238–1317 CE), the exponent of *Dvaita* or dualism; and Vallabha (1479–1544 CE), the exponent of *Śuddhādvaita* or pure non-dualism.[72]

1.2.2 The Textual Structure of *Brahmasūtra Bhāṣya* of Śaṅkara

Among all the expositors of *Brahmasūtra*, Śaṅkara's is the earliest of the extant commentaries.[73] Though more than hundred works—commentaries, expositions and poetry—are attributed to Śaṅkara most of them are not accepted as authentic. But *Brahmasūtra Bhāṣya* is considered to be the most authentic masterpiece of Śaṅkara. Śaṅkara's *Bhāṣya* is celebrated for its lucidity and depth. The other commentaries and the schools of thought that have come after Śaṅkara developed either as a criticism or as a response to Śaṅkara. They differ from certain points, but all of them have been influenced by Śaṅkara's commentary which has served as a model.[74] Śaṅkara has arranged all the *sūtra*s of *Brahmasūtra* into four *adhyāyas*. Each *adhyāya* has four *pādas* each. Each *pāda* has number of *sūtra*s and they are arranged under various

---

[72] Radhakrishnan, *The Brahma Sūtra*, 26; Rao, *Encyclopedia of Hinduism*, s.v. "*Brahmasūtra Bhāṣya*"

[73] George Thibaut, introduction to *The Vedānta-Sūtras with the Commentary by Śaṅkarācārya*, vol. 34 of *The Sacred Books of the East* (Oxford: The Clarendon Press, 1890), xiv.

[74] T.M.P. Mahadevan, foreword to *Brahmasūtra Bhāṣya of Śri Śaṅkarācārya*, translated by Swami Gambhirananda (1965; repr., Kolakata: Advaita Ashrama, 2013), xii.

adhikaraṇas. An *adhikaraṇa* responds to the initial, exegetically framed question exploring its various implications. It elaborates the initial doubt in all its logical and rhetorical possibilities, and follows set of positions, counter-positions, distinctions, refinements and conclusions, all of which together constitute the *adhikaraṇa*.[75] Joining with the method of *Mīmāṁsakas*, the discussions in the *adhikaraṇas* are in the form of dialogue. The structure of these dialogues shows certain characteristic features by means of which the ideas of the author are explained. Those factors are as follows:[76]

1) *Viṣaya* (topic): the subject matter taken up for the discussion which is the theme of the Upaniṣads.
2) *Saṁdeha/saṁśaya/viśaya* (doubt): the author raises any possible doubts or questions regarding the matter.

---

[75] Francis X. Clooney, *Theology After Vedānta: An Experiment in Comparative Theology* (New York: State University of New York Press, 1993), 47.

[76] The five factors given below are explained in Rao, *Encyclopedia of Hinduism*, s.vv. "*Brahmasūtra,*" "*Brahmasūtra Bhāṣya*." But some scholars like Francis X Clooney slightly differ on these five aspects in the discussions conducted through *adhikaraṇas*. His observation runs as: "Adhikaraṇas traditionally include these five moments: i. a topic (*viṣaya*), usually defined by reference to a problematic text; ii. a doubt (*saṃdeha*) is usually expressed as an either / or, recognizing two ostensibly possible courses of interpretation; iii. the first, adversarial position (*pūrvapakṣa*), will eventually superseded—though only after being thoroughly understood—and is usually portrayed as involving a misreading of the text in question; iv. a consequent position (*uttarapakṣa*) which responds to the objection (*pūrvapakṣa*) with a correction that at least partially rectifies the adversarial position; v. the 'final proven' position (*siddhānta*), a conclusion that resolves the initial doubt." See Clooney, *Theology After Vedānta,* 47.

3) *Saṁgati* (relevance): the harmony with the sections under discussion is brought out in view of highlighting the use and relevance of the conclusion.
4) *Pūrvapakṣa* (earlier view): it is the *prima facie* argument concerning it. The views of the schools of thought, which might oppose *Vedāntic* interpretation, are placed. It shows the text's openness to the other opposing views.
5) *Uttarapakṣa* (later view) or *Siddhānta* (theory): the refutation of the other opposing views with sound arguments and stating the finally established conclusion which is the result of the sound argument.

Śaṅkara's division of *sūtra*s into various *adhikaraṇas* within the *pāda* and *adhyāya* is as follows:

***Adhyāya* (Chapter)**	***Pāda* (Section)**	**Number of *adhikaraṇa* (Topics)**	**Number of *sūtra*s (Aphorisms)**
Chapter 1 *Samanvaya* (Reconciliation through Proper Interpretation)	Section 1	11	31
	Section 2	7	32
	Section 3	13	43
	Section 4	8	28
Chapter 2 *Avirodha*	Section 1	13	37

(Non-contradiction)	Section 2	8	45
	Section 3	17	53
	Section 4	9	22
Chapter 3 *Sādhana* (Spiritual Practise)	Section 1	6	27
	Section 2	8	41
	Section 3	36	66
	Section 4	17	52
Chapter 4 *Phala* (Result)	Section 1	14	19
	Section 2	11	21
	Section 3	6	16
	Section 4	7	22
4 *Adhyāyas* in total	16 *Pādas* in total	191 *Adhikaraṇas* in total	555 *Sūtras* in total

1.2.3 The Themes Dealt in the Four Chapters of *Brahmasūtra Bhāṣya*

Śaṅkara begins his BS Bh—before starting with interpretation of *sūtra*s—with an introduction where he makes clear the concept *adyāsa* (superimposition),[77] which is an important tool for explaining *Advaitic* metaphysics, especially interfacing the nature of reality as non-dual and the phenomenal plurality of the world. Superimposition is explained as the cognition of something as some other thing and this is considered by learned as *avidyā*, nescience (BS Bh 1.1.1).

The first chapter, *Samanvaya,* reconciliation through proper interpretation, has proved that all the *Vedāntic* texts taken as a whole have their purport *Brahman*, the non-dual reality.[78] The texts unanimously teach that *Brahman* is the only cause of the origin of the universe and is the Self of all. Those passages of the Upaniṣads where the clear mention is made of *Brahman* or *Ātman* do not present any difficulty. But there are other passages in which other terms are used—terms which do not normally mean *Brahman-Ātman*. In such cases the meaning should be construed from the context. For instance, *ākāśa* means ether. But in the text, BS 1.1.22, it is stated that all things

---

[77] Superimposition (*adhyāsa*) is false attribution. It is the appearance, of one thing, in another thing previously perceived in the form of memory. It is ignorance (*avidyā*); attribution of the qualities of one thing upon another (Upad 2.2.51), for example, mistaking rope for snake. Here when one sees a rope, the qualities of a snake are superimposed upon the rope due to the memory of the snake which is perceived previously. It is mutual superimposition of *Ātman* and non-*Ātman* such as body, the senses, and inner organ (BS Bh intro.). See Mayeda, introduction to *A Thousand Teachings*, 77.

[78] Mahadevan, foreword to *Brahmasūtra Bhāṣya of Śri Śaṅkarācārya*, vi.

come out of *ākāśa* and get resolved into it. Here the expression *ākāśa* obviously means *Brahman*, which is the ground of the universe. To prove this fact various Upaniṣadic passages which deal with *ākāśa* are brought into the discussion (Ch U 1.9.1–2; 3.14.3; 8.14.1; 4.10.5; Bṛ U 3.9.28; 5.1). From the context and use of the word *ākāśa* it is proved that it indicates *Brahman*; not the ether, one of the elements. BS 1.1.23 takes up the Upaniṣadic question 'which is that deity?' the answer given is *prāṇa* (Ch U 1.11.4–5). Here the term '*prāṇa*' cannot be conveying the meaning of vital air but it indicates *Brahman* because all beings are said to merge in it (BS Bh 1.1.23). In all such cases, what determine the meaning of a term is not the ordinary usage, but the context and the construed meaning of the related texts (BS 1.2.10; 1.4.19). The *Bhāṣya* makes it clear that the "*Vedāntic* texts harmoniously teach *Brahman* as the plenary reality, the world ground which is of the nature of consciousness and is the supreme object of meditation, and which is the final end to be realized."[79]

The second chapter, *Avirodha*, non-contradiction, discusses the objections that may be raised against the metaphysics of *Vedānta*. It has been explained why the views of the other systems of thought should be ignored. For example, *Sāṁkhya* argues that the principle of matter which is called *pradhāna* or *prakṛti* is the cause of evolution. But *Vedāntin* argues *prakṛti* of *Sāṁkhya* which is inert or non-intelligent cannot be the cause of the universe which has a design and purpose (BS Bh 2.2.1–6). For *Vaiśeṣika* system atoms are the cause of everything and it traces the world to primary atoms which are part-less, and posits *adṛṣṭa* (an

---

[79] Mahadevan, foreword to *Brahmasūtra Bhāṣya of Śri Śaṅkarācārya*, vi.

unseen power) responsible for bringing the atoms together and separating them. But, whether it is located in the atoms or in the souls, the unseen potency cannot move the atoms because it is unintelligent even as the atoms are. In addition to this, *Vaiśeṣika* system fails in holding and explaining how from the part-less atoms, the things of the world with parts arise (BS 2.2.11–17). This chapter shows that the non-*Vedāntic* views are contradictory and cannot explain the Upaniṣadic reality proper.

The third chapter, *Sādhana* (Spiritual Practice) discusses the means to release. The souls are non-different from *Brahman*. Because of ignorance it imagines that it is different. When ignorance is removed through knowledge, the soul realizes the truth of non-difference (BS Bh 3.2.26). The scriptures suggest meditations for enabling the soul to realize its non-difference from *Brahman*. The meditations have one and the same purpose (BS Bh 3.3.1). Practising any one of them will lead one to the goal (BS Bh 3.3.59). The meditations are on *Saguṇa Brahman* (qualified *Brahman*) and therefore, the one who practises them goes, after death, along the path of the gods, and eventually secures release (BS Bh 3.3.29). It is only the knower of *Nirguṇa Brahman* (non-qualified *Brahman*) does not go along any eschatological path; he attains *Brahman* here. *Sannyāsa* (the renunciant mode of life-stage) is recognized as the most adequate means for the realization of *Brahman*. *Sannyāsins* have no need to perform the rituals; they are eligible to pursue the path of knowledge. They have no other obligation such as tending the fires (BS Bh 3.4.25). To attain realization, detachment and other virtues such as calmness, equanimity, self-control, etc. are suggested (BS Bh 3.4.27). Those who have grown in these virtues, and if they properly listen, reflect and meditate on the scriptures, ignorance will be removed. This state of release is nothing but *Brahman* (BS 3.4.52).

The last chapter of *Brahmasūtra* is on *Phala*, the fruit or result. The one who follows the path of knowledge gains release in this very life (BS Bh 4.2.12). Through the realization of *Brahman* one is freed from all sins (BS Bh 4.1.13). The one who is released in this life is called a *jīvanmukta*. His body continues till the *prārabda* lasts. *Prārabda* is the *karma* which has begun to fructify and is responsible for present body. The knower of *Brahman* realizes the absolute non-difference from *Brahman* (BS Bh 4.2.16). When one has gained release there is no more return to the cycle of birth and death (BS Bh 4.4.22).

1.2.4 The Textual Context of *Apaśūdrādhikaraṇam* (BS Bh 1.3.34–38)

Apaśūdrādhikaraṇam (अपशूद्राधिकरणम्) (*apa-śūdra-adhikaraṇam*) is the ninth *adhikaraṇam* comprising of five *sūtra*s from the third *pāda* of the first *adhyāya* of *Brahmasūtra*. The term '*apa*' is a prefix used with nouns and verbs and it means 'away or off'. When prefixed to nouns it may sometimes give negative meaning.[80] Here the name *apaśūdrādhikaraṇam* is significant because this *adhikaraṇam* speaks about those characters of the scriptures—Jānaśruti, Satyakāma Jābāla, Vidura and Dharmavyādha—who have gained salvific knowledge and who were not from upper caste, but from the lowest rank of the society, probably *śūdra*s. But *sūtra*s of this *adhikaraṇam* try to prove that they are not in fact *śūdra*s, but

[80] For example, *bhī* means 'fear'; *apa-bhī* means 'fearless'. See Monier-Williams, *A Sanskrit-English Dictionary*, s.v. "*apa.*" Therefore, *apa-śūdra* could be taken as non-*śūdra* or a pseudo-*śūdra*.

pseudo *śūdra*s. This *adhikaraṇam* establishes that *śūdra*s are not eligible for Vedic study.

1.2.4.1 Thematic Structure of Third *Pāda* of First *Adhyāya* (BS Bh 1.3)

The general trend of the first *adhyāya*, *Samanvaya*, is reconciliation through proper interpretation which means to prove that the various Upaniṣadic passages, even though some of them appear to be contradicting, have one and the same purport as far as the ultimate reality is concerned and that is *Brahman*, the pure consciousness and the non-dual reality.[81] The third *pāda* of the first *adhyāya* has altogether forty three *sūtra*s which are arranged under thirteen *adhikaraṇas* and they also deal with this same theme and are consistent with the theme of the chapter to which they belong. The thematic arrangement of all the forty three *sūtra*s into nine *adhikaraṇas* in the third *pāda* of the first *adhyāya* can be shown as below:

Adhikaraṇam	***Sūtras* Contained**	**Theme**
Adhikaraṇam 1 (*Dyubhvādyadhikaraṇam*)	1–7	Proves that within which the heaven and earth are woven (Mu U 2. 2.5) is *Brahman*.
Adhikaraṇam 2 (*Bhūmādhikaraṇam*)	8–9	*Bhūman* referred to in Ch U 7.23–24 is *Brahman*.

[81] Mahadevan, foreword to *Brahmasūtra Bhāṣya of Śri Śaṅkarācārya*, vi.

Adhikaraṇam 3 (*Akṣarādhikaraṇam*)	10–12	The imperishable in which, according to Bṛ U 3.8.7–8, the ether is woven is *Brahman*.
Adhikaraṇam 4 (*Īkṣatikarmavyapadeśādhikaraṇam*)	13	The highest person who is to be meditated upon with the syllable *OM*, according to Pr U 5.5 is not the lower but the higher *Brahman*.
Adhikaraṇam 5 (*Daharādhikaraṇam*)	14–21	Discusses the question whether the small space/ether within the lotus of the heart mentioned in Ch U 8.1.1 is the elemental ether or the individual soul or *Brahman*; the last alternative is finally accepted.
Adhikaraṇam 6 (*Anukṛtyadhikaraṇam*)	22–23	Discusses about the light mentioned in the Mu U 2.2.10 and Ka U 2.2.15 as that which shines everything; whether it is some natural lustrous matter or the conscious Self. Śaṅkara shows that it is nothing material but *Brahman* itself.

Adhikaraṇam 7 (*Pramitādhikaraṇam*)	24–25	The being (*puruṣa*) of the size of a thumb that resides in the heart within the body mentioned in Ka U 2.1.12–13 is not the individual soul but *Brahman*.
Adhikaraṇam 8 (*Devatādhikaraṇam*)	26–33	Not the human beings alone but gods also are eligible for *Brahman*-knowledge.
Adhikaraṇam 9 (Apaśūdrādhikaraṇam)	34–38	On the basis of Scriptural prohibition *śūdra*s have no right to have salvific knowledge through Vedas.
Adhikaraṇam 10 (*Kampanādhikaraṇam*)	39	Proves that the *prāṇa* in which everything trembles, according to Ka U 2.3.2 is *Brahman*.
Adhikaraṇam 11 (*Jyotiradhikaraṇam*)	40	The light mentioned in the Ch U 8.12.3 is Supreme *Brahman*.
Adhikaraṇam 12 (*Arthāntaratvavyapadeśādhikaraṇam*)	41	The *ākāśa* (space) mentioned in the Ch U 8.14.1 is not material space but *Brahman*.

Adhikaraṇam 13 (*Suṣuptyutkrānty-adhikaraṇam*)	42–43	Discusses on the *vijñānamaya*: he who consists of knowledge, mentioned in Bṛ U 4.3.7 is whether the individual soul or Supreme *Brahman*. Śaṅkara argues it to be Supreme *Brahman*.

1.2.4.2 Thematic Sequence of *Apaśūdradhikaraṇam* (BS Bh 1.3.34–38)

The seventh *adhikaraṇam*, the *Pramitādhikaraṇam*, in the third pada of first *adhyāya* (BS Bh 1.3.24–25) decides that the *puruṣa* (Being) that is explained as the measured one as of the size of a thumb residing in the heart mentioned in Ka U 2.1.12 is not the individual soul, but *Brahman*. Here the opponent opinions that the Supreme Self is infinite and beyond time and space and cannot be said to be of the size of a thumb. Therefore, it must be the individual soul identified with intellect which is mentioned here as having the size of the thumb. But the next *sūtra* of the same Upaniṣad, Ka U 2.1.13, is stated by the *Vedāntin*, as: "The *puruṣa*, who is of the size of a thumb, is like a light without smoke. He is the ruler of the past and the future. He exists today and he will exist tomorrow. This is That." Since the one who resides in the heart is mentioned as the one who is the ruler of the past and future, it cannot be the individual transmigratory self but it indicates *Brahman*. Besides, the context of the above said Upaniṣdic passage is the answer given to Naciketas on his question of what is that entity which is beyond virtue and vice, cause and effect and past and future. Thus the mention can be only of *Brahman*. The doubter again asks how is the all-pervasive Supreme Self be mentioned as possessed of size? The answer is given: just like the space in fact is infinite but the space within the section of a bamboo can be spoken of as being a cubit in length. So from the point of view of the existence within the heart, it can be asserted that though the Supreme Self is all pervasive, It has the size of a thumb. But then the opponent brings another problem on the mention of the size of a thumb 'within the heart'. Hearts have no definite size and it differs from creature to creature. So the size of a thumb within the heart is ambiguous. Now, the problem is, can the mention of heart and that the *Brahman* as the size of thumb be a sufficient logical designation for *Brahman*. The answer of the *Vedāntin* is that here the mention is of the human heart, not that of any creatures. Because, the scripture is concerned about human beings and the scripture postulates the competence of human beings as they are not debarred from the *brahmajñāna* (knowledge of *Brahman*) and consequent realization.

Now the next, the eighth *adhikaraṇam*, the *Devatādhikaraṇam* (BS Bh 1.3.26–33) is in fact a continuation of the discussions of the previous *adhikaraṇam*. It has been already said that the Upaniṣadic text about the size of a thumb stands justified in relation to the human heart for the scriptures being concerned with human beings. Here, in this *adhikaraṇam*, the discussion is; is it only human beings are qualified for knowledge? *Vedāntin* makes it clear not the human beings alone but gods also are eligible for *Brahman*-knowledge. Their competence depends on that they can desire for realization of *Brahman*, they can have the ability and there is no scriptural prohibition.

Coming to the next, the ninth *adhikaraṇam*, the *Apaśūdradhikaraṇam* (BS Bh 1.3.34–38) is continuation from the previous discussion. It is to clarify if the competence of the gods are ascertained on the proved grounds, basing on those same grounds can all the human being—especially *śūdra*s—be considered eligible for *Brahma-vidyā*. The text places the intention of this *adhikaraṇam* as follows:

> It may be argued that, even as any hard and fast rule about the competence of men alone is denied and the competence of the gods as well for different kinds of knowledge is upheld, similarly by denying any monopoly of qualification by the three classes of the twice born alone, the *śūdras* also may be accepted as qualified. In order to remove such an assumption is begun the present topic (BS Bh 1.3.34 p. 229).[82]

The answer to the question of eligibility of *śūdra* is negative. Though *śūdra*s can have the desire and other eligibility, unlike the case of gods *śūdra*s are prohibited by the scriptures. Thus

---

[82] यथा मनुष्याधिकारनियममपोद्य देवादीनामपि विद्यास्वधिकार उक्तस्तथैव द्विजात्यधिकारनियमापवादेन शूद्रस्याप्याधिकारः स्यादित्येतामाशंकां निवर्तयितुमिदमधिकरणमारभ्यते । (BS Bh 1.3.34) Cf. Śaṅkara, *Brahmasūtra with Śāṅkarabhāṣya*, ed. Ministry of Education, India, 106.

Direct quotes from BS Bh of Śaṅkara (translation), throughout this dissertation, are given page number followed by 'p.' Page numbers are from: Śaṅkara. *Brahmasūtra Bhāṣya of Śri. Śaṅkarācārya*. Translated by Swami Gambhirananda. 1965. Reprint, Kolakata: Advaita Ashrama, 2013.

the discussion concludes "a *śūdra* has no right to knowledge through the Vedas" (BS Bh 1.3.38 p. 234).[83]

1.2.4.3 *Apaśūdrādhikaraṇam*: A Digression from the Main Theme of the Chapter

Eighth and ninth *adhikaraṇas* are a digression from the main theme of the first chapter and the third *pāda* of which these *sūtra*s belong.[84] The theme running all through the first chapter is establishing that the purport of various Upaniṣadic statements is *Brahman*. In the seventh *adhikaraṇa* (*Pramitādhikaraṇam*; BS Bh 1.3.24–25) the same is aimed at and the discussion is on the *puruṣa* of the size of a thumb residing in heart mentioned in Ka U 2.1.12–13 is whether the individual soul or Supreme Self. *Vedāntin* affirms it to be the Supreme Self.

But then begins a deviation from the discussion. The opponent raises the issue that can the Supreme Self which is all pervasive be said to be having a limited size. The *Vedāntin's* answer is that though the Supreme Self which transcends all the limitations cannot be said to be having a limited size, but from the point of its existence in the heart, it might be said to be so. But the following verse of the same Upaniṣad asserts that this *puruṣa* which is of the size of a thumb is the ruler of past and future. Thus this can be the Supreme *Brahman* alone.

---

[83] वेदपूर्वकस्तु नास्त्यधिकारः शूद्राणामिति स्थितम् ॥ (BS Bh 1.3.38) Cf. Śaṅkara, *Brahmasūtra with Śāṅkarabhāṣya*, ed. Ministry of Education, India, 108.

[84] Thibaut, introduction to *The Vedānta-Sūtras with the Commentary by Śaṅkarācārya*, xxxvii.

Now the opponent's next question takes the discussion further away from the main theme of the whole *adhyāya* and *pāda*. The next issue raised is that the *puruṣa* is mentioned as being the size of a thumb residing in the heart; does this mean human heart or other than human. *Vedāntin* affirms it to be human, for 'the scripture being concerned with the human beings' because human beings are able, desirous (of results), and not debarred and there are texts about initiation with the sacred thread' (BS Bh 1.3.25).

Vedāntin gives a further clarification that it is not human beings alone but beings higher than they are also qualified for knowledge. Thus the next *adhikaraṇam*, the eighth (*Devatādhikaraṇam*; BS Bh 1.3. 26–33) establishes that gods are eligible for knowledge. For they can have hankering for liberation, ability, and are not debarred by scriptures.

The next, the ninth *adhikaraṇam*, (*Apaśūdrādhikaraṇam*; BS Bh 1.3.34–38) is aimed at removing any assumption that *śūdra* also might be accepted as qualified. Since there is all the possibility of thinking in this way, clarification and explanation are needed. The opponent asks, since *śūdra* also can have all the necessary qualifications—aspiration and ability—which the gods are said to have for the *Brahman*-knowledge *śūdra* also must be eligible for salvific knowledge (BS Bh 1.3.34). But *Vedāntin* makes it clear that though *śūdra* can have all other qualities for *Brahman*-knowledge unlike gods they suffer from scriptural prohibition.

The next *adhikaraṇam*, the tenth, begins with the statement "the side issue about the competence is concluded"

(BS Bh 1.3.39 p. 234).[85] Thus it is clear that the preceding *adhikaraṇas*, eighth and ninth which discuss on the eligibility of gods and *śūdra*s respectively are a digression from the main theme: Upaniṣadic texts taken as a whole have their purport *Brahman*, the non-dual reality.

1.3. Exclusion and *Śāṅkaravedānta*

Excluding certain group of people from their rights is not a recently developed social phenomenon. Its history goes back to the Vedic times. *Brāhmaṇic* scriptures show indications of excluding *śūdra*s, the lower caste, from learning Vedas and from sacrificial religion of the Vedas. This exclusion continued in its varying intensity. *Vedāntic* writings also show the strong feeling of excluding *śūdra*s from the Vedic study leaning heavily on the justification that it is mandatory in the Vedic scriptures. Why Vedic scriptures have made it mandatory needs a historical study, and it shows various factors which contributed to the exclusion of *śūdra*s. Since from the later phase of Vedic times the reason for exclusion has become their birth in particular caste. Excluding *śūdra* from Vedic study would imply limiting the scope of *brahmajijñāsā* and excluding them from the means for attaining self-realization, the liberation. Śaṅkara, the *Advaitavedāntin* also is not free from this charge of exclusion. *Advaitic* metaphysics of non-duality gives little scope for upholding such division and exclusion on the basis of birth and other human-made laws. In spite of being inconsistent with his philosophical doctrine of *Advaitic* unity, Śaṅkara manages to

---

[85] अवसितः प्रासंगिकोऽधिकारविचारः । (BS Bh 1.3.39) Cf. Śaṅkara, *Brahmasūtra with Śāṅkarabhāṣya*, ed. Ministry of Education, India, 108.

assert that *śūdra* is not fit for Vedic study. The exclusionary mandate of barring *śūdra* from Vedic study puts inclusive and universal nature of *Advaitic* metaphysics in difficulty.[86]

1.3.1 Exclusion: The Social Fact

Exclusion, in its dictionary meaning,is the action of excluding which can be understood in various senses: shutting from a place, a society, etc. debarring from privilege, omitting from a category, from consideration etc.[87] "The term 'social exclusion' can be defined as a process by which certain collectivity or group or individuals are denied access to social, economic, and political rights by a dominant group or groups. By doing so, the dominant group keeps out the other groups from being part of their own."[88] This exclusion is not only a process but also a state of condition of being the 'outsider', the 'other', the 'excluded'.[89] It implies also the denial of human dignity, and of constitutional and human rights.[90]

Social exclusion in its ideological and academic level had its beginning in Western Europe, particularly in France in the 1970s to tackle the ever-increasing crisis of industrial capitalism in the context of a welfare state. The concept was

---

[86] Who is a '*śūdra*' for *Brahmasūtra Bhāṣya* and exactly from what he/she is excluded are taken for study in the coming chapters, especially in the 4th chapter of this dissertation.

[87] *The Oxford English Dictionary*, 2nd ed., s.vv. "exclude," "exclusion."

[88] Vivek Kumar, "Towards an Epistemology of Social Exclusion: A Critical Perspective," in *Marginality, Exclusion and Social Justice*, ed. Ashish Saxena (Jaipur: Rawat Publications, 2013), 64.

[89] Jeebanlata Salam, *Social Exclusion and Education* (New Delhi: Indian Social Institute, 2004), 9.

[90] Prakash Louis, "Social Exclusion," *Social Action* 58, no. 4 (October–December 2008): 344.

developed also as a reaction to the narrow money and income oriented economic approach to deal with the large group of unemployed people in the industrialized nations of Western Europe who could not participate in the normal activities of the society. Since then, the concept gradually crossed the European borders and by 1990s reached the developing nations of the world with the efforts of the United Nations agencies[91] and it has achieved a wider meaning.

The most startling scene in today's social scenario is the systematic exclusion of many groups from human and fundamental rights.[92] These rights of the people are related to their protection from any form of discrimination and exploitation, promotion of their personality and interests, accordance of equality and justice to them, and restoration of their dignity and respect. People equipped with better resources have easy access to these rights. But, those who are vulnerable and have remained traditionally exploited, degraded and deprived of their access to the existing socio-economic resources, need their human rights to be accorded to them by the state or society of which they are the inherent part.[93] Some groups in the society such as women, children, minorities,

---

[91] Abhijit Guha, "'Social Exclusion': A Sceptical View," *Journal of the Indian Anthropological Society* 42, no. 3 (November 2007): 287.

[92] Human rights are generally understood as those rights which are the most essential for every human being, irrespective of race, caste, ethnic affiliation, gender, age, creed and so forth. The fundamental rights are the rights provided to individuals or citizens of a country to make the best use of their freedom within their legal constitutional framework. See Nandu Ram, "Marginalized Groups and the State of Human Rights in India," in *Marginality, Exclusion and Social Justice*, ed. Ashish Saxena (Jaipur: Rawat Publications, 2013), 41–42.

[93] Kumar, "Towards an Epistemology of Social Exclusion," in *Marginality, Exclusion and Social Justice*, 29.

indigenous people, transgender, refugees, etc. could be identified as marginalized groups who are deprived of their rights and are at the risk of social exclusion. The institutionalization of their exclusion from larger socio-cultural and political processes implies their isolation from the mainstream of any society. Such exclusions are fundamentally rooted to the socially constructed hierarchies, underpinned by powerful dogmatic religiosity. The social process of exclusion undermines the ethical values of equality, freedom and respect for human dignity. Such exclusion is the cause and consequence of marginalization of certain social groups forming the subalterns pushing them to the peripheries by the mainstream core of the society.

Social exclusion addresses multiple aspects of being excluded and the consequences that arise out of it.[94] Exclusion can take place in very many areas. It could be: barring from access and control over resources, opportunity for education, health care, housing, public amenities, recreational faculties and spaces, basic needs and so on; denial of freedom for social interaction and access to social spaces, right to representation and participation in social, economic, political and cultural aspects of society and polity; prohibition of the right to mobility, right to practise one's religion and the right to organize and mobilize. Exclusion could be in the form of various types of prohibitions on holding ideologies and in curtailing the freedom for expression through print and social medias and also various restrictions laid on the free academic endeavours through bans, censors and other restrictions. Further, exploitation of the nature causes exclusion of the poor

---

[94] Louis, "Social Exclusion," 343.

from their right for natural resources (such as healthy air, water, etc.) and the denial of the life-supporting environment at large. The poor and the marginalized are on the front line among those who have to suffer the pathetic effects of the overuse and misuse of nature, because they are directly exposed to the nature and they cannot afford to have costly means to fight against the contaminated nature.

Taking the specific case of the Indian social scenario, it is moving fast in its track of excluding and marginalising the poor minority. The spirit of inclusion, accommodation, understanding, tolerance, and so on, to which India was known has come down very much in this present time. Considering one particular religion, culture and ideology as supreme and then, either reducing some others to it by discarding the unique features of those, or excluding and alienating some others, seems to be the very underlying mood of exclusion in India from the present socio-political point of view. It is very clear from silencing the dissenting voices through physical violation, brutal murder, threat, etc., curtailing the freedom of expression, banning the intellectual and literal studies and resultant works, etc. The very national identity of an Indian is at crisis, for they are to face the question 'who is an Indian' and the answer to which is being defined by the master culture/religion/ideology. It has come to the point that the supremo determines what to eat, what to speak, what work or job to be undertaken for lively hood, etc. The authoritarian spirit of domination is almost palpable as 'the 'other' may live here as 'We' determine and under 'Our mercy'. Though there are some movements against exclusion and for promoting inclusion, those are still to get momentum with solid philosophy, ideology, motivation, and with robust *modus operanti*.

A change in the ideologies of exclusion and its practices is highly resistant because it is intimately and inherently related to systems of domination and oppression.[95]Those who exclude and dominate the other may not easily initiate any change in this structure. In order to respond to the exclusions one needs to be aware of various forms of exclusion, the evils implied in it and the ideologies boosting them from behind. However, the response to the exclusion cannot be a passive exercise. Inclusion has to address the outcomes of exclusion and work out mechanisms for inclusion.[96]

1.3.2 Exclusion: The Problem

The differences which are peculiar to each individual, culture and society contribute very much in determining their identity and make each of them unique. An individual or society is considered acquiring certain integrity if such differences are recognized and accepted. Respect for the 'otherness' of the other guarantee the value of equality that consists in providing equal opportunity for all, respect for the dignity of every person, etc. which are considered as the values of great importance in both sacred and secular fields. But when the differences of the other are looked down upon, and are considered to be inferior flouting the values of equality then the very differences become a problem which leads to the exclusion of some groups by dominant groups from their basic human rights. The exclusion, when it is based on some human-

[95] Louis, "Social Exclusion," 345.
[96] Louis, "Social Exclusion," 352.

made laws, customs, taboos, systems and ideologies, becomes part of systematic exploitation of the groups whom the dominant group considers to be inferior.

Studies on subaltern groups and the social issue of exclusion have been promoting a very problematic idea of 'differences'. "It is problematic because in the world outside the academy, differences show in murderous ethnic conflict and continued inequalities among and within societies, classes and gender."[97] Interfacing the value of equality with the difference and uniqueness needs a careful handling. Social exclusion can take place on ascribed statuses such as caste, race, gender, etc., or achieved statuses such as class, occupation, education, etc. An individual or group or groups may be excluded on multiple pretexts such as religion, gender, regional, linguistic identity, and so on. All the excluded groups do not share single common deprivation; one may share multiple deprivations different from the other. In the same way, all exclusions need not be equally grave. There could be certain exclusion which is quite natural as there are certain natural inequalities.[98] Inequality can be distinguished in terms of whether they are inequalities of life chance, of outcome or of access, and are also differentiated as to whether they are just or unjust, avoidable or unavoidable, natural or artificially

---

[97] Vinay Bhal, "Relevance (or Irrelevance) of Subaltern Studies," *Economic and Political Weekly* 32, no. 23 (June 1997): 1341.

[98] Nature presents us with differences or potential differences. With human beings these differences do not become inequalities. Differences become inequalities only with the application of scales; socially and culturally constructed criteria of discrimination. See Andre Beteille, *The Idea of Natural Inequality and Other Essays* (Delhi: Oxford University Press, 1983), 8.

sustained.[99] Thus equality as a value could be better articulated as the equal opportunity in all the common spaces respecting the individual uniqueness. This implies respect for human dignity and individual freedom which would accord justice, and thus, the integrity of every human person and the society at large. The nature and seriousness of the exclusion differ according to the number and the fundamental character of the values deprived and the ethical reasonableness of the criteria by which the exclusion is made. Further, it very much depends on from what, and on what criteria the exclusion is.

Celebrating mere difference leaving no scope for a better future for the oppressed becomes ineffective. Sometimes it can happen that the subaltern people are told to be different—by belonging to the indigenous culture, tradition, etc.—is natural and that they should live with it and celebrate it. But this sometimes takes a neutral stand on the fact of deprivation by taking it to be a part of being different.[100] Every sphere of subaltern studies becomes relevant if it contributes to an emancipatory politics.[101] Planning for inclusive ideologies and practices which are appropriate to the contexts of exclusions is important. It is not enough to focus on the exclusions of underprivileged groups arising out of society's built-in normative order, e.g. exclusions based on caste, race, religion and other elements from the viewpoint of equality of opportunity for every citizen. But the exclusions caused by the capitalist system and the globalizing forces are to be considered seriously. The exclusions due to: technological

---

[99] Kumar, "Towards an Epistemology of Social Exclusion," in *Marginality, Exclusion and Social Justice*, 2.

[100] Bhal, "Relevance (or Irrelevance) of Subaltern Studies," 1342.

[101] Bhal, "Relevance (or Irrelevance) of Subaltern Studies," 1343.

improvements in the industrial sector which increases unemployment rate; displacement of groups of people due to unsustainable developments causing internal refugees; religious and ideological fundamentalism which threats human security and limits freedom of expression; policy caused exclusions such as land acquisition law—which excludes the numerous agricultural workers from receiving any compensation; leaving the displaced dalits and tribals without any protective provision, etc.—are to be taken for serious consideration.[102] The caste based exclusions in India cannot be explained without looking into its relations with class and power. So every form of exclusion has cultural, social, political and religious issues under it. Unless the theories, policies and praxis in view of treating the issue of exclusion which has become a festering wound of the society are not attended with due importance they become peripheral and ineffective in reaching out to the core of the problem.[103]

1.3.3 Caste System and the Exclusion in Ancient Hinduism

The exclusion in the ancient Hinduism was mainly based on caste: the hierarchical system of caste with the *brāhmaṇa* at the top and then *kṣatriya*, *vaiśya* and *śūdra*, the fifth being the untouchable, and therefore beyond the pale. Exclusion and discrimination are obvious consequence of this system. The idea of 'untouchability' which is related to the laws of purity and pollution added additional dimensions to the social discrimination. Due to these the excluded were

[102] Guha, "Social Exclusion," 288–289.
[103] Guha, "Social Exclusion," 290–291.

prohibited from participation in several social activities.[104] The ascribed features of the caste and its superior-inferior nature and the exclusions were justified on the religious grounds through sacred texts and religious philosophy. In fact, it was the upper caste males above the poverty line who enjoyed most privileges.

The lower caste was excluded in many ways and from many rights. They were not allowed to learn Vedas; they were prohibited to receive the rite of initiation into Vedic study (*upanayana*)[105] and to wear the sacred thread. This is to say, their right to education—to read and write—was denied because Vedic education was the only form of formal education of that time. Exclusion from education had far reaching consequences. The right to perform Vedic sacrifice was denied to them for it was reserved only for those who have learned Vedas. So they are excluded from the freedom of

---

[104] Sukhadeo Thorat and Narender Kumar, eds., *B. R. Ambedkar: Perspectives on Social Exclusion and Inclusive Policies* (New Delhi: Oxford University Press, 2009), 9.

[105] *Upanayana* means rite of initiation. Literally this word means 'leading or taking near' i.e. 'leading the disciple to the *guru'* (*upa*, near; *nayana*, leading) or 'providing an additional eye' (of knowledge and wisdom) (*upa*, additional; *nayana*, eye). It meant 'introducing the novice to the stage of student-hood'. See RV 10.109.5. Therefore, the word *upanayana* can be explained in two ways: (1) taking (the aspirant) near the *ācārya* and (2) that rite by which the aspirant is taken to the *ācārya*. The first sense appears to have been the original one and when an extensive ritual came to be associated with *upanayana* the second came to be the sense of the word. The main component of this rite is the ceremony of wearing sacred thread. It is usually performed on the male members of the three upper castes. By this ceremony they become twice-born, and get initiated to the first of the four *āśrama*s, the *brahmacarya* which is the stage of student-hood. It is initiation to the study of Vedas. See Kane, *History of Dharmaśāstra,* vol. 2, pt. 1, 269; Rao, *Encyclopedia of Hinduism*, s.v. "*Upanayana.*"

religion. Among the four ends of human life—*puruṣārthas*: *dharma* (righteousness) *artha* (wealth) *kāma* (desire or happiness) and *mokṣa* (liberation)—they were denied of *mokṣa*. They had access neither to Vedic knowledge nor to Vedic rituals which were considered to be the only means for liberation, and therefore, were deprived of the possibility of liberation of their soul, and could not get rid of the cycle of death and birth. They might achieve salvation not in this birth but in the next birth if they were born as a member of upper caste for which they had to be faithful to their caste duties in this birth. Thus *brahmajijñāsā* was limited to the upper caste men alone; *śūdra*s and women were denied the means for self-realization, i.e. liberation. Among the four stages of life—*āśrama*s: *brahmacarya* (student-hood) *gṛhasta* (house holder), *vānaprastha* (forest-dweller or hermit) and *sannyāsa* (renunciant)—*śūdra*s were allowed only to have *gṛhasta*. Because all the other three *āśrama*s needed Vedic study and it was reserved for the upper caste.

Those who were of lower rank, due to the laws of untouchability were deprived of the right for free interaction and were denied the right to use common spaces. Exclusion defines boundaries between groups, locates the different social groups in a hierarchy and regulates and guides their interaction.[106] The lower class were deprived of the freedom of occupation. They could not save wealth and thus were deprived of the right to property. If violated they had to face penal actions, excommunication, boycott, or even death penalty. Thus the consequences of the caste system were exclusion, discrimination, denial of equal rights and subordination of one

[106] Louis, "Social Exclusion," 345.

by another caste.[107] The causal effect of such processes resulted into segregation, shutting up, denial of access and disconnection of these people from the wider socio-cultural, political realms and easily succumbed to the economic, political social and cultural frame of reference set by the dominant groups.[108]

The only criterion for such exclusion and deprival was that *śūdra*s were born as members of lower caste. But while determining the status of a caste to be inferior various factors played their role since from the historical beginning of caste system. Poverty, non-practise of certain religious practices, non-acceptance of religious texts, ignorance of Sanskrit language, place of residence—for example, sometimes forest-dwellers are considered inferior—disagreement to getting conformed to the dominant culture, different food habits, etc. are some of them.

1.3.4 *Śūdra*-Exclusion: The Problem in Śaṅkara

The exclusive ideologies and practices of the ancient Hinduism have come down to the *Vedāntic* times too. The *Vedāntic* thinkers have taken up the topic whether *śūdra* is eligible for Vedic knowledge. The great *Advaitic* teacher Śaṅkara follows the tradition of excluding *śūdra*s from Vedic study. In *Apaśūdrādhikaraṇam* (BS Bh 1.3.34–38) he makes clear that *śūdra* has no right to Vedic learning. This reserves salvific knowledge to those upper caste males; they alone can be eligible for the Vedic learning and others are outsiders in this regard. Exclusion becomes aggravated as Śaṅkara holds that the valid means for *brahmajijñāsā,* the enquiry for

---

[107] Thorat, *B. R. Ambedkar,* 10.

[108] Salam, *Social Exclusion and Education*, 9.

Brahman, is *jñānamārga* (way of knowledge)—through *śravaṇa, manana* and *nididhyāsana* of *śruti* (BS Bh 1.1.1; 1.1.2; 1.1.4). This implies one cannot take up *brahmajijñāsā* without exposure to Vedic scriptures, and so, it is beyond the reach of many such as *śūdra*s, women, etc.

In addition to this, for Śaṅkara, the *āśrama* (life-stage) which is conducive for the fruitful search for *Brahman* is *sannyāsa* (BS Bh 3.4.17; 3.4.20; Upad 2.1.2). This would mean knowledge of *Brahman* is reserved only for the elite upper caste male renouncer and it disqualifies many: householders, *śūdra*s, outcastes, women, and those who have not included in any of the four *āśrama*s, such as widower. Thus the means for liberation is limited and many are deprived of the right for it. Access to *brahmajijñāsā*, by qualifying both internal and external prerequisites becomes difficult, as a matter of fact, those get qualified for *brahmajijñāsā* are so rare.[109] For Śaṅkara, there is but "one in a thousand"(Bṛ U Bh 4.4.12 p. 512)[110] or but "some rare one among many people" that attains *jñāna*, as experience shows (BG Bh 13.2 p. 509).[111] In fact, exclusion from *brahmajijñāsā* becomes grave for it implies barring one from the possibility of self-realization, the fulfilment, and therefore, from achieving the very purpose of human life.

---

[109] De Smet, "The Fundamental Antinomy of Sri Śaṅkarācārya's Methodology," in *Understanding Śaṅkara*, 76.

[110] अत्मानं स्वं परं सर्वप्राणिमनीषितज्ञं हृत्स्थमशनायादिधर्मातीतं चेद्यदि विजानीयात्सहस्त्रेषु कश्चित्। (Bṛ U Bh 4.4.12) Cf. Śaṅkara, *Īśādidaśopaniṣadaḥ,* ed., Ministry of Education, India, 293.

[111] Direct quotes from BG Bh of Śaṅkara (translation), throughout this dissertation, are given page number followed by 'p.' Page numbers are from: Śaṅkara. *Bhagavad Gītā with the Commentary of Śaṅkarācārya*. Translated by Swami Gambhirananda. 1984. Reprint, Kolkata: Advaita Ashrama, 2014.

The above discussed *Śāṅkaravedāntic* norm of *śūdra*-exclusion is very hard to harness with its metaphysics of non-duality which gives a lot of theoretical strength for the universality of liberation. The *Advaitic* tradition affirms that all beings are identical, at the most fundamental level of self, with the infinite *Brahman*. It points to the all-inclusivism of *Advaita*. The fundamental human problem that Śaṅkara understands is ignorance of this basic identity, and this problem is universal in nature. This is not merely the problem of a few or of a particular tradition but of all humanity. The solution Śaṅkara offers to this problem also must be for all and not for a selected few. *Advaita* is an excellent example of an Indian tradition making explicit universal claims about the human condition and its resolution.[112] For Śaṅkara, the knowledge of *Brahman* is possible for all who desire it. Answering a doubt as to whether the statement, 'I have realized it myself' means that only one person ever obtained knowledge of *Brahman*, Śaṅkara replies that it is not so, "that the knowledge of Brahman is accessible to all" because *śruti* states that it to be so(Bṛ U Bh 4.4.8 p. 509).

Though in theory Śaṅkara's philosophy would stand for inclusivism but when coming to the practical side of how to achieve the liberation he affirms*jñānamārga*, through listening, reflection and contemplation of *śruti*. Besides this, *sādhanacatuṣṭaya*, the internal prerequisites for *brahmajijñāsā*is of universal nature open to all but the external such as *sannyāsa*, non-*śūdratva*, etc. are very much based on caste and life-stage discriminating people to be *śūdra*, women, householder, etc.[113] Thus *Śāṅkaravedānta* tradition on the one

[112] Rambachan, "Rethinking *Advaita*," 9.
[113] Rambachan, "Rethinking *Advaita*," 9.

hand makes universal claims and keeps *brahmajijñāsā* open to all; on the other, it is restricted to a few who can qualify the requirements and limits the access on the basis of restricted criteria, such as caste or gender or stages in life. This exclusion-inclusion dilemma has triggered the ethical consciousness of justice and equality of the modern times with relevant questions. Is the Vedic revelation is for all the humanity or for a few? Who can study and teach Vedic scriptures (since the scriptural source of *Advaita* is primarily Vedic texts of Upaniṣads)or who can have authority (*adhikāra*) to speak for *Advaita?* If it is only for the upper caste males who belong to the Vedic tradition alone, the Vedic scholars and their erudition and contribution from 'outside' the tradition, such as women scholars, scholars from other religion such as Christianity or Islam, from western nations and so on are to be neglected. Further, questions in this regard could be: How far *Śāṅkaravedānta* is open to other traditions with regard to *brahmajijñāsā*? Does Śaṅkara give space for aspirants taking up *brahmajijñāsā* from all walks of life, from different tradition, faith or culture? These are some of the important issues to which *Śāṅkaravedānta* has to respond. Before considering these problems, a thorough understanding on what exactly was the mind of Śaṅkara when he restricted the entry to *brahmajijñāsā,* is inevitable. For this purpose a critical study on *Apaśūdradhikaraṇam*of*Brahmasūtra Bhāṣya*can serve as the key.

Conclusion

The social problem of exclusion is crucial with its multifaceted effects and it undermines the values which keep every person and society moving towards its growth into maturity and integrity.The problem of exclusion which is wide, touching various areas of society, is narrowed down, for the purpose of this study, to the case of *śūdra*-exclusion in the *brāhmaṇic*tradition, especially in *Śāṅkaradarśana*. Here the exclusion is very much based on one's birth, and consists in the ineligibility for Vedic learning. Though the study focuses on this specific issue, the ideologies and attitudes derived from it can have wider applications affecting the various forms of exclusions.

Study of Vedic scriptures were very pivotal to the ancient Hindu community for two reasons: (1) those who did not know Vedas were considered very much inferior in the society, and at the same time, those were considered inferior in the society through some human made criteria such as caste, gender, poverty, etc. were not permitted to learn Vedas; (2) one could achieve salvation only through the Vedic learning and rituals; the denial of access to the scriptures meant denial of *brahmajijñāsā* which is the desire and also the wholehearted attempts for attaining *Brahman*, i.e.achieving self-realization or the meaning of life. When the access to the scriptures is limited only to the upper caste males it excludes many such as *śūdra*s and women from the possibility of self-realization.

Advaitic non-dualism, which advocates all-inclusive universalism at the fundamental level of all human beings, is not free from the charge of restricting Vedic study, which is the means for self-realization, to the upper caste males alone. This is mainly because, for Śaṅkara, *jñānamārga*which is the means for *brahmajijñāsā* involves knowledge of the Vedas, and *sannayāsa* as the most suitable disposition for the acquisition of this salvific knowledge. This will keep many groups such as, householder, women, *śūdra*, widower, etc. excluded for they are without the knowledge of Vedas, in the sense that, they either do not have or are prohibited from having it, and are not able to take up *sannayāsa* for it need getting initiated into Vedic learning. Such exclusion remains as a major setback to the consistency and greatness of *Śāṅkaravedānta* and places it under the charge of elite monasticism. To understand Śaṅkara's position on this issue, the study has to be two dimensional: (1) for Śaṅkara, are Vedic scriptures the only means for salvation? and (2) is *sannyāsa* alone the suitable *āśrama* for *brahmajñāna*?

Apaśūdradhikaraṇam in *Brahmasūtra Bhāṣya* of Śaṅkara is an important passage to understand the mind of Śaṅkara in this regard, especially on the issue of *śūdra*s'exclusion. This is because*Brahmasūtra Bhāṣya* is the most accepted authentic work of Śaṅkara and *Apaśūdrādhikaraṇam* directly takes up the discussion on the topic whether *śūdra*s can study Veda and achieve self-realization. Taking this *adhikaraṇam* as the key, an analytical and critical study of it will shed better light to understand why Śaṅkara held the restrictions at the risk of placing himself in the dilemma of exclusion and inclusion. It will also be great help in assessing how far *sannyāsa* and Vedic scriptures—which contribute very much in determining the inclusive/exclusive nature of *Śāṅkaradarśana*—are necessary for *brahmajijñāsā*. Besides this, the textual context of this *adhikaraṇam*—which is theological and philosophical—in which the discussion occur also has to be looked into for a clear understanding of the issue. All these, in the course of exploring the non-exclusory scope of *Śāṅkaravedānta*, are aimed and attempted in the following chapters.

CHAPTER 2

HISTORY OF EXCLUSION IN THE TEXTUAL TRADITIONS OF INDIA

Introduction

Exclusion of *śūdras*from Vedic knowledge has a long history which goes back to *Ṛgvedic* times. A proper understanding of the same in the later *brāhmaṇic* texts of *Vedānta* needs a socio-historical analysis of the origin and evolution of this particular idea and its actual social practices.

No ideologies are history-free. Ideology speaks of and from a social order and ideas can be used to justify or challenge a particular order. Often history can explain why some ideas take hold of and spread while others do not; ideas take root only when they become important to people at a particular time.[114] According to Romila Thapar, one of the prominent historians, "to study ideology without its historical context is to practice historical hydroponics, for ideas and beliefs strike roots in the humus of historical reality."[115] The interaction between society and ideology takes different expressions—such as religious practices, literary texts of both religious and non-religious, polity of the society, education, etc.—with varied patterns. To insist always on the primacy of one over the other is to deny the richness of the understanding of a particular ideology.

An ideology which took shape in a particular society with its theoretical and normative expressions through the

---

[114] Wendy Doniger, *The Hindus: An Alternative History* (Oxford: Oxford University Press, 2009), 21.

[115] Romila Thapar, *Cultural Pasts: Essays in Early Indian History* (New Delhi: Oxford University Press, 2000), 85.

various texts of the time need not necessarily be the actual practice in its every detail. Much of the early history of India was reconstructed almost entirely from the then Sanskrit texts, and reflected views and ideologies associated with their authors. Many of these works were texts on religion and manuals of ritual, authored by the *brāhmaṇas* generally adhering to *brāhmaṇical* theories of society irrespective of whether or not they had widespread social applicability. For example, caste as described in texts such as Dharmaśāstras is referred to a hierarchy of ritual status creating a closed stratification of society, apparently imposed from an early period and thereafter preserved almost intact for many centuries. The lower castes were seen from the perspective of the upper caste *brāhmaṇa* authors of the texts. Yet the actual working of caste in Indian society permitted many variations, in accordance with the local conditions, which the authors of the Dharmaśāstras were reluctant to admit.[116]

Ideologies are never static. The same ideology takes different interpretations and practices from society to society as the time changes. In the same way meanings very often do not stem from just the vocabulary but require familiarity with the cultural context of the word.[117] There is all possibility that the practice of exclusion of *śūdra*sand even the meaning of the very word '*śūdra*' undergo changes from what it had at the time of its origin. Thus a study on the exclusion of *śūdra*s has to be two dimensional: on the one hand it should focus on texts of the time, on the other, it should give attention to the historical enquiry into the context of the evolution of the

[116] Romila Thapar, *Early India: From the Origins to AD 1300* (California: University of California Press, 2002), 10.

[117] Thapar, *Cultural Pasts*, 86.

concept. Such study will throw light into the better understanding of*Vedāntic* discussion on the issue of *śūdra*-exclusion from Vedic knowledge.

2.1 Categories of Societies in Ancient India

Indian sub-continent had been the habitat of many societies, ranging from those with a relatively simple organization to others with more complex organizations. It is often in the context of such differing societies that the patterns of Indian culture were formed.[118] The categories of societies could be listed as hunter-gatherers, pastoralists, peasants, and townsmen. This categorization does not mean that they were strictly separated from each other or they were placed in an evolutionary order, one following the other. There were overlaps and changes alongside the socio-economic, geographical and historical change that the region underwent. But one thing is clear the hunter-gatherers had minimal social organizations and structures and it becomes more complex as it passed on to pastoralists, peasants and townsmen.[119]

Hunter-gatherers lived by hunting animals for food and other requirements. Their societies were organized in clans with a chief, and the larger unit which comprises many clans, was a tribe.[120] The aboriginal tribes of India could be included in this type. In the course of time when the agrarian peasant groups emerged, when the cultivators began to clear the forests and start cultivating the land, the existing hunter-gatherers

---

[118] Thapar, *Early India,* 54.

[119] Burton Stein, *A History of India* (New Delhi: Oxford University Press. 1998), 45–47.

[120] Vincent A. Smith, *History of India* (Oxford: Oxford University Press, 1958), 24.

understandably resorted to a ferocious defence of their territory.[121]

Another category was that of pastoralists—shepherd groups—who were nomadic in nature. It does not mean that the hunter-gatherers took an enbloc shift from hunting to pastoralism; many continued to be hunters.[122] Pastoral grouping of the society encouraged the possibilities of migration and exploitation of new grazing grounds, and therefore, involved history of movements of the people. Among the pastoralists, membership of a tribe generally included those claiming common grazing grounds, common ancestor, common language and customs, as well as rituals.[123] Pastoralists from central Asia intervened from time to time in the history of India, often because of disturbances in central Asia that resulted in migrations and incursions or invasions further south. Such disturbances are thought to have led indirectly to the arrival of the Indo-Aryan speakers. But other pastoral groups within the subcontinent were also important. During this period in the clan or tribe organization the chief was invested with more power. The chief protected the group from enemies and led the raids in view of capturing the wealth of the other clans or tribes. It could be considered as a seminal form of a powerful monarch that developed in the later period. Among the pastoralists there were enslaved persons who had

---

[121] It is possible that the descriptions of those outside the pale of caste society—demoniac figures which the religious texts of Vedic period mention as inhabiting the forest, such as *rākṣasas*—could be these forest-dwellers. See Thapar, *Early India*, 57.

[122] Smith, *History of India*, 25.

[123] Thapar, *Early India*, 58.

been captured after a raid or those who were not the members of the clan.[124]

Then the ancient India found the emergence of peasant communities; a shift from pastoralism to agriculture,[125] whereas many clans or tribes retained their pastoral life. From the socio-economic point of view pastoralists and agricultural peasants co-operated each other but pastorals were often counted inferior to agriculturalists.[126] Surplus food fed non-producers, and therefore, elite priests, soldiers and traders became viable.[127] When the community became agrarian it needed organized labourers. Divisions in the society became more evident mainly on the basis of poverty and occupation. To ensure the availability of manual labourers, lineage was emphasized as the criteria for deciding to which class one belonged. Mobility, especially the upward mobility—for getting included in the higher class—was made very strict.

The growth of the Indian society further moved to the formation of townships. The genesis of towns varied: some began as administrative centres, with a focus on the location of the treasury where the tribute was brought; some as centres of craft production more specialized than in villages; some as pilgrim centres; and some as centres of commercial exchange. The heterogeneity of urban life distinguished it from the village. Towns were closely packed settlements with populations larger than in a village. Sanskrit culture came to be

---

[124] Thapar, *Early India*, 58.

[125] Burjor Avari, *India: The Ancient Past; A History of the Indian Sub-Continent from c.7000 BC to AD 1200* (London: Routledge, 2007), 12, 70.

[126] Avari, *India*, 28–29.

[127] Thapar, *Early India*, 60.

city-based and the 'man-about-town' was the central figure in many writings.[128]

2.2 Social Context of the Formation of Caste System

The categories of societies and their formation involve very much into the process of social organization called 'caste' system that is fundamental to the understanding of Indian society. The word, as used in modern European languages, comes from a root '*castus*' (Latin) and '*casta*' (Portuguese) meaning 'pure' and reflects the application of what is termed as *varṇa*, a concept now often translated as ritual status.[129] *Varṇa* is an order dividing society into four groups arranged in a hierarchy—the *brāhmaṇa* (priestly class), *kṣatriya* (*rājanya* i.e. ruling/warrior class), *vaiśya* (cultivator and the trader) and *śūdra* (servile/labourer class). The division was mainly based on the following:

1) Marriage and lineage functioning through endogamous kinship relations. Such kinship groups were known as *jāti*.
2) The division of labour which eventually took the form of service relationships.
3) The idea of pollution where some groups are regarded as ritually pure, others less so and yet others totally impure or polluting.

---

[128] Thapar, *Early India*, 62.

[129] The word *varṇa* means 'color' or 'light'. This word is associated with groups of people having a skin of a dark or fair color. In the *Ṛgvedic* period Aryans and *dāsas* were the two opposing camps and both were designated '*varṇas*' on account of the color of their skins. Later, this word began to get the connotation of caste. See Kane, *History of Dharmaśāstra*, vol. 2, pt. 1, 25.

4) Living settlements in particular geographical locations. For instance, those who lived in the forests were given a low status.
5) Speaking or non-speaking of particular language. Those speaking a non-Indo-Aryan language were frequently given a low rank and sometimes described as *mḷeccha.*[130]

All these factors could have been there in some way or other, in some degree even in the early phase of ancient Indian societies which were more organized in the later period.[131]

As a seminal to the caste system, even among the hunter-gatherers, there must have been some kind of disparity between the clans. Even in a single tribe, which is a cluster of many clans, it is possible that there existed some non-egalitarianism in the form of unequal access to economic resources. In addition to this, there could have been local endogamous groups (*jāti*) which is a delimited group by way of residence and kinship with important corporate functions, intermarriage, common status, traditional occupation, etc. These forms of non-egalitarian social forms must have continued and increased in the pastoralist communities. With the emergence of Vedic culture the already existing divisions in the society received an ideological legitimation with the ideal of *varṇa* which underlined hierarchy, occupation and

---

[130] It is a noun—from the root *mḷech*, 'to speak indistinctly'—used by the Vedic Aryans and in the subsequent *brāhmaṇical* discourses, to designate foreigners. By definition they spoke languages other than Sanskrit, but more widely they were beyond the pale of Aryan fold. See W. J. Johnson, *Dictionary of Hinduism* (Oxford: Oxford University Press, 2010), s.v. "mleccha." See also Moniner-Williams, *A Sanskrit-English Dictionary*, s.v. "mlech."

[131] Thapar, *Cultural Pasts*, 317.

purity. Various *jātis* and other divisions in the society were grouped under four classes under the title*varṇa* or caste.[132]*Varṇa* status would follow with such groups performing rituals, and observing, at least in theory, a hierarchy according to certain prescribed rules—determined by those controlling the religious ideology—and accepting notions of purity and pollution among the castes. Many clans and tribes were accepted into higher *varṇa*s whereas many were relegated to lower ones. *Brāhmaṇas* were considered most pure and others in descending order to the most impure, the untouchables. This inclusion and exclusion was not very strict in the beginning. The forest dwellers who were regarded as *mḷeccha*—those beyond the pale of the caste society—were given a caste status when they were converted into peasants or craftsmen, then they would become the part of acceptable hierarchy. Even the members of the same group—for example, *Ābhīras*[133]—were given different *varṇa* status, either *brāhmaṇa* or *śūdra*. It is only in the later period birth and lineage became very strict in excluding and including one in a

---

[132] Richard G. Fox, "Varna Schemes and Ideological Integration in Indian Society," *Comparative Studies in Society and History* 11, no. 1 (January 1969): 28; Thapar, *Early India*, 65. *Jāti* is a term which lays all emphasis on birth and heredity. *Varṇa*, at least originally, gave importance to social duties, of course, it was not without lineage. There is an opinion that *jāti* is a later origin, because the notion of *jāti* is not found in *Ṛgveda*. See Kane, *History of Dharmaśāstra,* vol. 2, pt. 1, 54. But Fox and Thapar are of the opinion that *jāti* as a kinship-lineage based system must have been there in the ancient society which was based on clan and tribe even much before the *varṇa* ordering done by Aryans. Later, when this ordering could not contain the varieties of groups formed again by inter-caste marriages the notion of *jāti* must have come to the forefront.

[133] Name of an ancient community whose primary occupation was tending the cattle. See Rao, *Encyclopedia of Hinduism*, s.v. "*Ābhīras*."

particular caste and also made the upward movement impossible.[134]

2.3 Who were *Śūdra*s?

In the context of the above discussion the question 'who were the people denoted by the word *śūdra*' is important. There are various suggestions on this matter:

1) *Śūdra*swere people drawn from the ranks of the colonized Harappans and other indigenous people.
2) They were those who had been disgraced or socially ostracized for some reasons, perhaps due to some non-*brāhmaṇic* practices.
3) They were the products of inter-tribal marriages which violated the *jāti* rules.[135]
4) *Śūdra* was an Aryan tribe came either much before Vedic Aryans or during the influx of Vedic Aryans as an inferior servile group.
5) *Śūdra* was a non-Aryan tribe that had come into India and was given the low status in Aryan society.[136]

Looking for a most probable hypothesis reveals that the formation of the group called *śūdra* had social and religious reasons and it was composed neither solely of Aryan nor of a non-Aryan people. There lies all the possibility of co-option and integration between Aryan and non-Aryan in the formation of the social group called *śūdra*.[137]

---

[134] Thapar, *Early India*, 65.

[135] Lipner, *The Hindus*, 92.

[136] Jayantanuja Bhandyopadhyaya, *Class and Religion in Ancient India* (New Delhi: Anthem Press, 2007), 37.

[137] Lipner, *The Hindus*, 92.

2.3.1 Aryans' Entry into India and the Formation of Indo-Aryan Culture

There are mainly two views regarding the coming of the Aryans into India. One is, Aryans came from somewhere 'out of India'.[138] This theory shows that they migrated originally from the Caucasus region through Iran and Afghanistan and continued to move in a south-eastern direction. This hypothesis has a corollary; the Aryan entry was a massive invasion and they caused the decline of Harappan civilization. But scholars have proved this to be very much unlikely. The Aryans came as migrants in small groups within a quite long span of time. There are other more probable reasons—natural calamities such as earthquake, flood, rivers changing their roots, etc.—for the decline of the Harappan civilization.[139]

Another opinion is that Aryans 'originated in India'.[140] They generally push back the date of Vedas to the beginnings of the Indus valley civilization, which they claim to be the oldest civilization of the world. But there are considerable archaeological and philological evidences against it.[141]

The more probable hypothesis could be, various groups of Indo-Aryan speakers gradually migrated—as a continuous process lasting for nearly a millennium after 2000 BCE—from

---

[138] Arvind Sharma, "Dr. B.R. Ambedkar on the Aryan Invasion and the Emergence of the Caste System in India," *Journal of the American Academy of Religion* 73, no. 3 (September 2005): 862.

[139] Doniger, *The Hindus*, 91; Thapar, *Early India*, 86–87.

[140] N. Kazanas, "Indigenism and the Collapse of Aryan-Invasion-Theory," *Brahmavidya: The Adyar Library Bulletin* 78–79 (2014–2015): 365–425.

[141] Avari, *India*, 61–66; Doniger, *The Hindus*, 94; Thapar, *Early India*, 105.

the Indo-Iranian broader lands and Afghanistan to north India, where they introduced their language. The racial identities of speakers of Indo-Aryan languages are not known. The word Aryan could mean a 'people who spoke Vedic Sanskrit' rather than a race.[142] Various Aryan groups as nomads must have kept coming to India even before the Vedic group of Aryans (the group that treasured Vedas and practised Vedic rituals) reached.[143] According to Burjor Avari, the historian:

> Groups of nomadic tribal people from eastern and southern Afghanistan started to migrate into the Indian sub-continent around 1700 BC; and their movement gained momentum with the arrival, about 1400 BC, of a particular group which called itself *Arya*, or noble. We sometimes call them the Rig-Vedic Aryans, because they brought with them the earliest portion of a collection of hymns, known as the *Rig-Veda*. … Other tribal groups of that period who did not call themselves *Arya*, also tend to be included by historians under the generic label of Aryans. … The Indo-Aryan culture that eventually emerged, more commonly known as the Vedic Culture.[144]

---

[142] Sharma, "Dr. B.R. Ambedkar on the Aryan Invasion and the Emergence of the Caste System in India," 848. In *Ṛgveda* the word 'Arya' indicate a group or class (ṚV 2.12.4; 1.179.6; 9.71.2; 3.34.9; 4.16.13; 9.41.1; 1.104.2). The fact that *Aryavarṇa* and *Dāsavarṇa* are spoken of indicates a group consciousness. See Sharma, "Dr. B.R. Ambedkar on the Aryan Invasion and the Emergence of the Caste System in India," 849.

[143] Stein, *A History of India*, 52; Thapar, *Early India*, 106. Since most of our knowledge of the Aryans comes from Vedic scriptures, Vedic Aryans are sometimes mistaken as the one and the only group reached in India.

[144] Avari, *India*, 60.

This nomadic entry was not a massive attack in military invasion but it was generally a peaceful one. However, there were occasional wars, subduing, compromises, accommodation, etc. Amalgamation of various cultures is evident in Vedas. The literary evidence of four Vedas indicates that when these were being composed, Aryans were constantly moving from one place to another in the face of stiff resistance from the local populations. They were expanding their habitat towards the eastern parts of North India, especially towards the Ganges plains.[145]

We can no longer regard the early first millennium as a period of Aryan conquest that resulted in the spread of a homogenous Aryan culture across northern India; nor can it be described as the articulation of an indigenous culture that was untouched by anything extraneous. When Vedic Aryans reached in India, it is very much likely that, there must have been already some Iranian-Afghanistan groups who were from the same linguistic and cultural stock and who possiblywere already very much incorporated into the indigenous culture.[146] Besides them, other non-Aryan people also must have arrived earlier and later to the Aryan group with their own language

[145] Bhandyopadhyaya, *Class and Religion in Ancient India*, 10.

[146] This is further clear from the *Rgvedic* attitude towards *dāsas*. Though the *Rgvedic* Aryans considered both *dāsas* and *dasyus* hostile, they were comparatively lenient and soft towards the *dāsas* than they for the *dasyus*. *Dāsas* are found not completely unfamiliar with the rituals and the language of the Aryans. This could possibly be a group which is from an earlier migration but got very much incorporated into the pre-Aryan culture. (Further explanations follow the succeeding part of this chapter).

and cultures.[147] According to Wendy Doniger, the famous Indology scholar, non-Vedic elements that appear in Vedic history shows the existence of at least the following cultures:

> (1) Stone age cultures in India long before the Indus are the foundation on which all later cultures built. (2) At some point, comes the *Adivasis*, the "original inhabitants" of India who spoke a variety of languages and contributed words and practices to various strands of Hinduism. It is impossible to fit them into a chronology or even an archaeology. Many of them were there long before the IVC [Indus Valley Civilization] and might have been a part of it; many of them had never been assimilated to Hinduism. Next come (3) the Indus civilization and (4) the village traditions that preceded, accompanied, and followed it, and after which came (5) the culture of Vedic people. Along the way, other language groups too, showed their presence, such as (6) the Tamils and other Dravidian speakers who might or might not have been a part of the IVC.[148]

---

[147] According to Burjor Avari, "Some of the groups have lived in India for countless millennia. Sometimes they are called the aborigines or adivasis. In the Stone Age they were the nomadic hunter gatherers or forest dwellers, and constituted the majority of the very small population that existed then in India. In the course of history, different ethnic groups separately developed their particular historical cultures in the diverse geographical terrains, such as mountain regions, river valleys and planes, deserts, coasts or forests. Ethnic groups also came from abroad, such as Aryans, Iranians, Turco-Afghans, Graeco-Macedonians, and Tibeto-Burmans, and to be absorbed into the ethnic admixture." Avari, *India*, 12.

[148] Doniger, *The Hindus*, 101.

2.3.2 Antagonism in *Ṛgveda*: Aryans vs *Dāsa*

In *Ṛgveda* we find mainly four groups—*dāsa*, *dasyu*, *paṇis* and *rākṣasas*—with whom Vedic Aryans were in conflict with.

There are indications of occasional conflicts and war between Aryans and *dāsas and dasyus*. *Dāsa* and *dasyus* are unlikely to be of the same fold.[149] Aryans were much more lenient and soft towards the *dāsas* than they for the *dasyus*. They followed a policy of ruthless extermination towards the *dasyus*, which, in the case of the *dāsas*, was tempered with moderation.[150]*Dasyus* wereconsidered as evil, not practising the Aryan observances, having some black magic, having different law or without law and are hardly human (ṚV 1.51.8–9; 1.101.2; 1.175.3; 4.16.9; 6.14.3; 10.22.8). It is notable that such adjectives were not given to *dāsas*. The combined term '*dāsa* and *dasyus'* are sometimes interpreted as 'slaves and robbers'; *dasyus* as cattle-thieves, lived in the forests or mountains,[151] of course, speaking probably a different language and having a different life style, which does not seem to be the case with *dāsa*.[152] This indicates that the two were not

---

[149] Sharma, "Dr. B.R. Ambedkar on the Aryan Invasion and the Emergence of the Caste System in India," 856.

[150] Ram Sharan Sharma, *Śūdras in Ancient India: A Social History of the Lower Order down to Circa A.D. 600* (Delhi: Motilal Banarsidas, 1980), 11. There are more references to the destruction or subjugation of the *dasyus* than of the *dāsas*. Though there is a mention of killing of individual *dāsas*, the 'slaughter of *dāsa'* is not mentioned but such mentions are there in the case of *dasyus* (ṚV 1.51.5–6; 1.103.4; 5.7.10; 7.5.6; 10.95.7; 10.99.7).

[151] Abhinas Chandra Das, *Ṛgvedic India*, rev. ed. (Delhi: Motilal Banarsidass, 1971), 117.

[152] T. Rengarajan, *Dictionary of Vedas* (Delhi: Eastern Book Linkers, 2004), s.vv. "*dāsa,*" "*dasyu.*"

identical. It is possible that *dāsas* could be an Aryan tribe that came into India much before Vedic Aryans and got incorporated very much into the indigenous culture, practices and worship. Since the *dāsas* shared language and some other elements of culture with *Ṛgvedic* people the latter followed a policy of conciliation towards them.[153]

Many Vedic passages show general hostility towards the people known as *paṇis* (ṚV 1.124.10; 1.182.3; 4.25.7; 4.51.3; 5.34.7; 6.13.3; 6.53.6–7). *Paṇis* in *Ṛgveda* denotes a person who is rich, but who does not give offerings to gods, or gifts to priests, and therefore is an object of intense dislike. *Paṇis* could be either rich aborigines who did not come into a lenient relation with the Aryans or fellow tribesmen of Aryans[154] who were greedy, accumulated wealth and did not share and were disliked by the common folk.[155]

The people who were called *rākṣasa* had different practices and culture other than Aryans and did not come in any friendly relation with Aryans. They disturbed them with occasional attacks, and by desecrating the sacrifice. This could be some groups of indigenous people who were hunter-gatherers living in the forests.

In addition to this, *Ṛgveda* makes mention of internal conflicts between the Aryan tribes themselves. There are many references indicating hostility among the Aryans themselves (ṚV 6. 33.3; 6.60.6; 7.83.1).

The reasons for warfare and conflicts with various groups were on the one hand religious and cultural, i.e.

---

[153] Sharma, *Śūdras in Ancient India*, 27.

[154] *Paṇis* are said to be a branch of the Aryan race who were merchants. See Das, *Ṛgvedic India,* 107.

[155] Sharma, *Śūdras in Ancient India*, 20.

difference in worship, speech, and other practices, on the other hand, economic; the nomadic Aryans coveted the wealth of their enemies accumulated in the settlements, for the possession of which there were regular warfare between them (ṚV 4.30.13; 5.40.6; 10.69.6). Thus the defeated group practically became impoverished and had no other go for their livelihood and had to be subservient to those who won the war.

Vedic Aryans in the beginning must have used the name *dāsa* in the sense of 'those to be treated violently'[156] to those earlier Aryan inhabitants who were very much adapted to local culture and who opposed the new Aryan wave. In the later period, to the term *dāsa* people such as *dasyus, rākṣasas* and *paṇis* must have been added and became a blanket term for all the antagonistic groups. Further in a later period the term '*dāsa*'—in the sense of 'slave'[157]—stood for those who were impoverished or reduced to subjugation on account of conflicts and raids[158] and were amenable to the Aryans. Thus *dāsas* and Aryans were the two opposing camps in the *Ṛgvedic* period.[159] The major distinctions between these groups were in the colour of their skins, in bodily appearance, in worship and in speech.[160]

---

[156] Sharma, *Śūdras in Ancient India*, 26. The root word *das* means 'to loose' or 'to throw'; *dās* means 'to hurt', 'to injure' or 'to kill'. See Jibananda Vidyasagar, *Śabda-Sāgara: Sanskrit-English Dictionary* (Varanasi: Chowkhamba Sanskrit Series office, 2002), s. vv. "*das*," "*dāsa*."

[157] The original meaning of the word *dāsa* in its Iranian context is 'man'; it is used in this sense in the Vedic names Divodās, 'divine man', Sudās 'good man'. It is in a later period it acquired a hostile and degrading connotation; and then the term began to represent 'servant'. See Rengarajan, *Dictionary of Vedas*, s.v. "*dāsa*"

[158] Sharma, *Śūdras in Ancient India*, 27.

[159] Kane, *History of Dharmaśāstra*, vol. 2, pt. 1, 25.

[160] Kane, *History of Dharmaśāstra*, vol. 2, pt. 1, 27.

2.3.3 Origin and Meaning of the Word *Śūdra*

The origin and meaning of the word *śūdra* remains obscure. There are some indications that there existed a tribe namely *Kṣudrakas* (M Bh 2.48.14). There are records of advance of Alexander against the tribe called *Sodroi* in fourth century BC.[161] This could be the tribe later known as *śūdra*. It is interesting to note that they were always bracketed with the *Ābhīras*, who spoke an Aryan dialect called *ābhīrī* (M Bh 6.10.45), which indicates that they, though remotely, were acquainted with the Aryan language. Further, *śūdra*sare never mentioned in the lists of the pre-Aryan people, such as *Drāviḍas*, *Pulindas*, *Śabaras*, etc. It is probable that *śūdra*s, like the *dāsas* were a people allied to the Indo-Aryan stock with inferior rank.[162] In the later Vedic period when the *varṇa* classification took place the word *śūdra* must have become a common name for all clans and groups, including *dāsas*, whom the Vedic Aryans considered inferior.

There were different attempts at etymological derivation of the term *śūdra*. One is found in the *Vedāntic* texts, where the word is divided into two parts *śuk*, 'grief' and *dra*, 'to rush'; which means 'the one who rushed into grief' or the 'grief rushed onto him'(BS Bh 1.3.34). In the Buddhist lexicon of the early medieval times *śūdra* became a synonym of *kṣudra*, meaning 'small or low', and on this basis it is suggested that *śūdra* is derived from *kṣudra*.[163] Both the derivations are unsatisfactory and the meanings are farfetched. They only suggest the inferior status of *śūdra*s in the society.[164]

---

[161] Sharma, *Śūdras in Ancient India*, 34.
[162] Sharma, *Śūdras in Ancient India*, 39.
[163] Thapar, *Cultural Pasts*, 382.
[164] Sharma, *Śūdras in Ancient India*, 44.

2.3.4 Inclusion and Exclusion: Clans and Tribes into *Varṇa* Status

In the later period of Vedas, the antagonistic situation gave way to some compromise and co-option of the many non-Aryans to the Aryan fold.[165] Some of the indigenous priests and ruling chiefs were included into the corresponding Aryan class of *brāhmaṇa* and *kṣatriya*. Some of the Aryans who were either poor or disliked by the mainstream Aryans for some reasons were regarded as the lower class. The various clans and tribes with manifold differences among them were brought under the theoretical framework of four classes—*brāhmaṇa, kṣatriya, vaiśya* and *śūdra*—on the basis of family lineage (*jāti*), ritual purity, poverty, occupation and other cultural differences such as language, area of habitation, food etc. Most of the vanquished *dāsas* and *dasyus* were integrated into Aryan society as *śūdra*s and relegated the status of manual workers whose duty was to serve the three 'upper' classes. A section of non-Aryans, of course, refused to submit them to Aryan imperialism, continued to fight, and retreated into the forests and mountains.[166]

From the above discussions it is obvious that either the views, that *śūdra varṇa* was made up of pre-Vedic non-Aryans or of Aryan people seem to be one-sided.[167] Thus the group which is later known to be *śūdra*s comprises both the Aryan and the non-Aryan fold; they were those made poor and

---

[165] Even in *Ṛgveda* we find Indra converting Aryans into *dāsas* and the relegation of Aryans into *dāsas* (ṚV 6.22.10; 10.49.3). See Sharma, *Śūdras in Ancient India*, 21–22; Bhandyopadhyaya, *Class and Religion in Ancient India*, 33–36.

[166] Bhandyopadhyaya, *Class and Religion in Ancient India*, 25.

[167] Sharma, *Śūdras in Ancient India*, 45.

impoverished; they had some familiarity with Vedic religion but did not get conformed to it. They differed in their food habits and other day-to-day practices mainly due to their poverty which the Vedic Aryans considered impure.

To the question, why the defeated, impoverished groups were incorporated into Aryan fold under the title *śūdra*, there could be mainly two suggestions:

1) The mainstream Aryans were more lenient towards them because many of them—unlike other groups, such as forest dwelling hunter-gatherers—could understand the Aryan language and were familiar with at least some of the Aryan religious and social practices. Thus from being enemies they were brought into friendly relations. This opinion puts the Vedic Aryans more on the positive side that they no longer wanted to exterminate this group through constant enmity and warfare but took them into their own fold, of course, giving a lower position—as menial workers and by excluding them from Vedic sacrifices.[168]
2) But there is a different phase of it. The *śūdra*s who were defeated, looted, and subdued were brought into the part of society only for the purpose of getting their service which was needed for the three upper classes.[169]

---

[168] Kane, *History of Dharmaśāstra*, vol. 2, pt. 1, 33. According to Kane a solemn religious recognition is given to this incorporation in the famous *puruṣasūkta* of *Ṛgveda* where *brāhmaṇa*, *kṣatriya*, *vaiśya* and *śūdra* are described as limbs of the same *puruṣa*, the creator.

[169] Bhandyopadhyaya, *Class and Religion in Ancient India*, 38. For Bhandyopadhyaya *Puruṣasūkta* which is a late composition of the *Ṛgveda* and is a conscious and deliberate ideological formulation

From the part of the subdued people they also must have accepted being in the Aryan fold, on the one hand, as a viable alternative for them instead of continuing with constant hostility, war and struggle which led them to abject poverty; on the other, as a privilege to get included in the Aryan fold. Besides this they, unlike the outcastes—such as forest-dwellers—acknowledged the authority of Vedas.[170] All these reasons must have played their own roles in the process of socialization.

Besides this inclusion and exclusion into four classes there were outcastes who remained excluded from the Aryan fold. These were groups of forest dwelling untouchables who had no affinity with the Aryans, got nothing to do with Vedas or sacrifice and did not want to get incorporated into the Aryan fold. The Aryans too did not mind getting them into their fold, but considered them highly polluting, even their very presence is to be avoided.

2.4 Exclusion of *Śūdra*s in the Vedic Period (1700–500 BCE)

The period of 1700–500 BCE is remarkable; it is now that the Aryan nomads in Punjab region composed *Ṛgveda* (1700–1500 BCE), later they moved towards the eastern India i.e. to Ganges Valley, during which the composition of *Yajur*, *Sāma* and *Atharva* Vedas (1200–900 BCE), composition of *Brāhmaṇas* (800–600 BCE) and *Āraṇyakas* (600–500 BCE) took place. An overview of the history of this period would

---

intended to legitimize and sanctify an oppressive and exploitive class structure that had already come to existence.

[170] Lipner, *The Hindus*, 55.

give a better picture of reasons and practice of exclusion of *śūdra*s during this period.

2.4.1 Social Context of Vedic Age

Social organizations during the early phase of Vedic period were very simple. People lived largely as cattle herders and then took a gradual shift to agriculture. They lived as small bands called clan. Membership in a clan was determined by common grazing ground and the kinship. When the need for protection and for social regulation became necessary, the most capable protector was selected as chief. The chief gradually began to assume privileges that were later incorporated into kingship.[171] Social structure by way of clan was greatly egalitarian. Many clans of homogenous nature in occupation and culture formed a tribe. Chief-ship began to be associated with territory, incorporating families settled in the villages, the wider clans and still larger unit of the tribe. Later on, these constituted the *janapada*—literally, the place the tribe places its foot—significantly named after the ruling clan. This could be either a single clan such as *Kekayas*, *Madras*, *Kurus*, and *Kosalas*, or a confederacy such as that of *Pāncālas*. A more complex confederacy involved in the coming together of the *Kurus* and the *Pāncālas*.[172]

2.4.2 *Śūdra*s in the Vedic Period

There are no indications of rigid exclusion of *śūdra*s in the earlier phase of the Vedic period. *Śūdra*s as a recognizable social class did not exist in *Ṛgvedic* period.[173] The word *śūdra*

---

[171] Thapar, *Early India*, 119.
[172] Thapar, *Early India*, 121.
[173] Bhandyopadhyaya, *Class and Religion in Ancient India*, 44.

does not occur in *Ṛgveda* except in the *puruṣasūkta*, which is believed to be a composition of *Atharvaveda* period (ca. 800 BCE) and was later interpolated into *Ṛgveda* (ṚV 10.90).[174] It states, *brāhmaṇa* emanated from the mouth of the primeval man, *kṣatriya* from his arms, *vaiśya* from thighs and *śūdra* from feet. Either it shows that *śūdra*s were supposed to belong to the same stock, and hence were a section of the Aryan community, or it represents an attempt to find a common mythical origin for the heterogeneous *brāhmaṇa* community.[175] Although, in *Ṛgveda,* the word *varṇa* is applied to Aryan and *dāsa*, it does not indicate any division of labour, which became the basis of the broad social classes of later times.[176] But, though not organized and not excluded with strict measures, there must have existed a servile group.

But, disregard for *śūdra* is evident in Vedas. While mentioning who can become the first husband of a woman, the names of the three upper classes are mentioned but *śūdra* is left out (AV 5.17.8–9). A hymn to *agni* prays for augmentation of the sacrificial power of the *brāhmaṇa*, the fighting power of *kṣatriya*, and the cultivating and trading power of *vaiśya* (Ta Sa 1.6.1), but *śūdra*s are not mentioned here. *Taittirīyabrāhmaṇa* declares that the members of various *varṇas* should formally take up the duties of the orthodox householder by lightning or 'installing' the sacred fires which they will use for all ritual purposes throughout their lives: the *brāhmaṇa* should install the fires during spring, the *kṣatriya* during summer, the *vaiśya* during autumn, the *rathakāra*[177]

---

[174] Kane, *History of Dharmaśāstra*, vol. 2, pt. 1, 27.

[175] Sharma, *Śūdras in Ancient India*, 33.

[176] Sharma, *Śūdras in Ancient India*, 20.

[177] The issue of the union of a *vaiśya* and a*śūdra* woman is regarded as *rathakāra.* See Sharma, *Śūdras in Ancient India*, 132.

during the rains. *Śūdra*s are not mentioned here (Ta Br 1.1.2.6–7).

There are also sharp comments on the low ranking of *śūdra*s. It is established that due to their low birth *śūdra*s are unfit for performing sacrificial offering (Ta Sa 7.1.1.6; Ta Br 3.2.3.9). *Śūdra*s are created from the feet of Prajāpati[178] without any God, and therefore, the lords of the house are their gods and they are to earn their living by washing feet (Ja Br 1.68–69).[179] In *Aitareyabrāhmaṇa*, *vaiśya* appears as the one to be oppressed, and *śūdra* as one to be beaten at the pleasure of the master (Ai Br 7.29). Unlike the members of the three higher *varṇas, śūdras* could not take part in the sprinkling ceremony on the occasion of *rājasūya* sacrifice[180] (Śa Br 5.3.5.11–14; Ta Br 1.7.8.7). A rite connected with the building of the fire alter, without which there can be no Vedic sacrifice, is explained as removing *agni* from *śūdravarṇa* (Śa Br 6.4.4.9).

But, exclusion of *śūdra*s was not altogether emphatic. There are also certain indications of concern for *śūdra*. *Śatapathabrāhmaṇa*, while dealing with the new and full moon sacrifices shows exclusion not of *śūdra*s but *rākṣasas*; and while mentioning four different forms of hymns which were to be chanted by various castes *śūdra* also is given a form of hymn (Śa Br 1.1.4.12). *Taittirīyasaṁhitā* registers a prayer for the glory of *śūdra*s (Ta Sa 5.7.6.4). "This is a sure indication

---

[178] Prajāpti is the 'Lord of Creatures' or the 'Creator God'. In Vedas this term is applied to *Indra*, *Savitrī*, *Soma*, *Hiraṇya* and other deities. See Rengarajan, *Dictionary of Vedas*, s.v. "*Prajapti*"

[179] Quoted in: Sharma, *Śūdras in Ancient India*, 49.

[180] *Rājasūya* sacrifice is a Vedic ritual performed by a *kṣatriya* king desirous of liberation. It requires three years of time and consists of various major and minor sacrifices. See Rao, *Encyclopedia of Hinduism*, s.v. "*Rājasūya Yajña.*"

that *śūdra* who took the place of the *dāsa* is here placed on the same level with the other three classes in the matter of the receipt of light from God."[181] *Yajurveda* makes a universal invitation to the study of Vedas: Vedas have been revealed for the benefit of all people, *brāhmaṇas*, *kṣatriyas*, *vaiśyas*, *śūdra*s and others of very low origin (ŚYV 26.1–2). A hymn from the same Veda includes prayer for *śūdra* together with other upper castes: give lustre to *brāhmaṇas*; give lustre to our kingly men; give lustre to our *vaiśyas* and *śūdra*s (ŚYV 18.48). The mention of *upanayana* (the rite of initiation to Vedic studies) is found in *Atharvaveda*, where the youth is initiated into a new life by the teacher, becomes a *brahmacārin* (the one who is the state of student-hood),[182] but there is no indications of *varṇa* (AV 11.5.3). *Atharvaveda* states that Veda is a universal scripture: the revealer of the Vedic knowledge declares that the revealer cannot be partial either to a *dāsa* or to an Arya. All those who follow the truthful commands will be saved (AV 5.11.3). It is stated in *Taittirīyabrāhmaṇa* that *vaiśya* was born of *Ṛgveda*, *kṣatriya* of *Yajurveda*, and *brāhmaṇa* of *Sāmaveda* (Ta Br 3.12.9.2). This obviously implies that *Atharvaveda* was meant for *śūdra*. It means that the *śūdra* was excluded from the acquisition of the orthodox Vedic knowledge but not of the other forms of knowledge.[183] *Śatapathabrāhmaṇa* also gives the same impression: the priest could instruct snake charmers, usurers, fishermen, bird-catchers, *niṣādas*, and *asuras*[184] many

---

[181] Kane, *History of Dharmaśāstra*, vol. 2, pt. 1, 34.

[182] The technical name of a student is *brahmacārin*. Upaniṣads have called him by the name *antevāsin* (Ch. U 3.1.5; 4.10.1; Bṛ U 6.3.7–12).

[183] Sharma, *Śūdras in Ancient India*, 75.

[184] The word *asura* literally means 'vigorous and mighty'. In Ṛgveda this word is used in the sense of both "godly" and "demoniac".

of whom seem to have belonged to *śūdravarṇa*. The subjects taught were *Itihāsas*, *Atharvaveda*, the art of the snake charming and demonology (Śa Br 13. 4.3.7–13; Ch U 7.1.1). The instance of Kavaṣa in *Aitareyabrāhmaṇa* provides a strong indication of *śūdra*s having knowledge and even taking part in the sacrifices. *Aitareyabrāhmaṇa* presents Kavaṣa as the child of a slave woman, a cheat and not a *brāhmaṇa*. The seers were to perform a sacrifice and they drove Kavaṣa away but later recognising his wisdom they brought him back. Even the hymns composed by him are included in *Brāhmaṇas* (Ai Br 2.3). *Kauṣītakibrāhmaṇa* also mentions this same instance of Kavaṣa (Ka Br 12.3).

As such in the beginning *śūdra* members of the disintegrated Aryan tribe may have continued to perform the initiation rites of the *upanayana* and the *brahmacarya* in the same manner as they performed several other rituals.[185] In the later periods the upper class became more sharply delineated from *śūdra*s[186] and these rites might have been reserved for the upper class alone.

Later this word began to mean those who are inimical to Gods and human beings. See Rao, *Encyclopedia of Hinduism*, s.v. "Asura".

[185] In the beginning of the Vedic period *dāsas* who were familiar with Aryan language and rituals might have access to Vedic rituals (at least of some of the Vedic traditions). Later more servile groups who had no familiarity with or less respect for rituals, but who became amenable to Vedic Aryans were added to them. As a group they were called *śūdra;* gradually exclusion also became stricter. See Katherine K. Young, "Śaṅkara on the Salvation of Women and *Śūdras,*" in *Goddesses and Women in the Indic Religious Tradition,* ed. Arvind Sharma (Leiden: Brill, 2005), 159; Sharma, *Śūdras in Ancient India*, 74.

[186] Doniger, *The Hindus*, 166.

2.4.3 Reasons for the Practice of Exclusion in Vedic Age

The exclusion of the *śūdra*s was not so total during the earlier period of Vedic age: rights and disabilities existed side by side. This could be counted as the decaying of clan and tribal features alongside growing *varṇa* distinctions. Since a considerable number of clans, which were later included in the group of *śūdra*s, were originally part of the Aryan community, they retained several Aryan rights, especially religious, in the beginning. But later, slowly the exclusion became strict and they were more and more divested of various social rights including right of education.[187] The reasons could be the following:

1) As the people moved from North West to more eastern direction (to the Gangetic plains) the source of the economy was greatly changed from pastoralism to agriculture and trade. Agricultural resources required not capturing and raiding but the availability of regular and co-ordinated labour. This intensified the need for keeping an increased number of manual workers disposed of many social rights. To ensure greater permanency of their availability *varṇa* system gave greater emphasis on lineage and thus checked the upward mobility of the occupation, thus one who is born from *śūdra* parents had always to be a *śūdra*, a manual labourer.[188]
2) The agriculture surplus was stored for the future and traded them to get other needs for a better life. Once the community achieved the food security there was

[187] Sharma, *Śūdras in Ancient India*, 314.
[188] Thapar, *Cultural Pasts*, 820.

greater possibility of (1) non-involvement of the upper class directly into the food production, and (2) the growth of other handicrafts and other occupations such as iron smith, carpenter etc. This facilitated the strict demarcation of the social class so as to block manual labourers from the change of occupation.

3) Vedic sacrifices became an affair of display and distribution of wealth. Those who accumulated wealth by raids and revenue, generally *kṣatriyas*, spent them for organizing sacrifices and distributed to the *brāhmaṇa* priests during sacrifice. In turn, priests did the rituals for them invoking blessings of gods especially for wealth, progeny and for protection from natural calamities.[189] Such mutual economic relation between the upper classes urged the lower classes to be producers; among which *śūdra*s*'* manual labour was enforced.
4) *Śūdra*s, on the one hand, could not afford to the sacrifices because they were poor and had no strict practice of Vedic learning for they were manual labourers; on the other hand, from the part of the upper caste, one of the effective means to block them from upward mobility of occupation was to deny them knowledge of Vedas. Consequently they were excluded from Vedic ritualism which required Vedic knowledge.
5) Vedic sacrifice, which became very elaborate by the time of *Brāhmaṇa* period, played a great role in the

---

[189] This could be partly a reason why greater social disparity occurred not in western Ganga valley but in eastern valley, by then the society was agrarian and rich. See Thapar, *Cultural Pasts*, 76.

stratification and exclusion of the lower caste mainly because of the sense of purity which took precedence in conducting a sacrifice.[190]

2.5 Exclusion of *Śūdra*s in the Upaniṣadic Period (500–100 BCE)

The classical Upaniṣads represent the flowering of Vedic thought. Upaniṣads are the end portions of Vedas and they are considered representing the central aim and meaning of the teaching of Vedas. Social and political contexts have very much to say how and why certain ideals of Upaniṣads differed from Vedic, and have developed and were widely accepted at a particular period of the history. Exclusion of *śūdra*s found in the texts of the time has to be examined through this optic.

2.5.1 Social and Historical Context of the Upaniṣads

The sixth century BCE witnessed a transition to a new historical scene in north India with the establishment of kingdoms, oligarchies and chiefdoms, and the emergence of towns. Attention was shifted from the north-west and Punjab to the Ganges plain, although the former area continued its

---

[190] To sacrifice is to 'make holy'; the word used is *yajña,* from the root *yaj*, 'to worship', 'to consecrate'. It carries the same meaning of converting the profane in to the sacred. Thus, the place selected was purified through certain rituals. The one on whose behalf the sacrifice is conducted (*yajamāna*) underwent moral and ritual procedures of purification and other preparations for sacrifice including keeping away from the daily activities. Thus, those who laboured and could not afford to these rituals were excluded. Exclusion from sacrifice implied exclusion from Vedic learning, for Vedic knowledge was a prerequisite for sacrifice. See Thapar, *Cultural Pasts*, 834.

activity. Permanent settlement in a particular area gave a geographical identity to a clan, or a confederacy of clans, and subsequently this identity was given concrete shape by its claiming possession of the territory then naming it after the ruling clan. By the mid-first millennium BCE the societies of northern India had moved a long way from the agro-pastoral communities of *Ṛgveda* and were now ensconced in the politically effective territories ruled by clan aristocracies or kings.[191]

In the sixth and seventh centuries BCE, there were initially four major kingdoms in north India including Bihar and Orissa, namely Avantī, Vasta, Kosala and Magadha. About the middle of the sixth century BCE, Magadha established its ascendency over the other kingdoms, and in ca. 545 BCE Bimbisāra became its king. Gautama, the founder of Buddhism, and Mahāvīra, the founder of Jainism, preached and died during the reign of Bimbisāra. Bimbisāra became the follower of the Buddha and propagated Buddhism in his kingdom. But he was killed by his son Ajātaśatru, who banned Buddhism and made its practice a punishable offence. After his death there was a short obscure period of confusion, until people are said to have appointed Śiśunga of indigenous non-Aryan origin as king. He was succeeded by his son, the black Kākavarṇa. Mahāpadma Nanda, who was born of *śūdra* mother, then captured power possibly by killing Kākavarṇa. He established the Nanda dynasty of the *śūdra*s, whose nine kings ruled 155 years. The Nanda dynasty was overthrown by Chandragupta Maurya, belonging to *Maurya* tribe—which is

[191] Thapar, *Early India*, 136.

lower in rank possibly from *śūdra* fold— reportedly with the help of Cāṇakya or Kauṭilya.

Meanwhile, during the sixth century BCE, north-western India became a part of the Achaemenid Empire.[192] Among the famous cities of the north-west was Takṣaśila. It rapidly became a cosmopolitan centre where Indian and Iranian learning got mingled, to which was later added knowledge from Hellenistic Greeks. Orthodox *brāhmaṇas* treated this region as impure since Vedic rituals were no longer performed. That Iranian and Vedic ideas and rituals had once been close seem not to have been remembered. Achaemeind ascendency in north-western India ended with the conquest of the empire by Alexander of Macedon ca. 330 BCE. Alexander could not invade the further eastern part of the land probably the strength of the Nanda army could be the cause.[193]

2.5.2 Texts During the Upaniṣadic Period

The textual scene of this period is remarkable for the Upaniṣadic texts, which are considered in-depth philosophical expressions of Vedic ideals. In addition to this, there was another set of texts called Śrautasūtras (dealing with elaborate sacrificial rituals), Gṛhyasūtras (dealing with domestic rituals) and Dharmasūtras (dealing with customs and social duties). It was during this time Buddhism and Jainism began to spread. The great epics of the *Mahābhārata* and the *Rāmāyaṇa* and philosophical systems such as *Pūrvamīmaṁsā*, *Vaiśeṣika* and *Nyāya* had their early beginning during this period. The last

---

[192] This is the First Persian Empire, founded by Cyrus the Great based in West Asia.

[193] Thapar, *Early India*, 158.

phase of this period could be marked with the emergence of Manu's *Dharmaśāstra* (*Manusmṛti*).

2.5.3 Upaniṣads: The Texts of Dissent

The Upaniṣadic texts show certain dissent from Saṁhitā and Brāhmaṇa texts. It was not a complete breakaway from Vedic ideals but gave a new emphasis and interpretations. The important one was a shift from ritualism to the acquisition of knowledge as the means for realization. We find *kṣatriyas* as teachers rather than *brāhmaṇas*.[194] The new doctrine required discipline, meditation and concern with the self alone and was a shift from ritual and religious duties, which required a high degree of specialization in *mantra*s and rites. It called for neither intermediaries (priests), nor deities, which therefore, gave greater openness as far as the possibility of self-realization was concerned.

2.5.4 Upaniṣads: The Pro-*Śūdra* Texts

Disgust for Vedic stratification and inhuman distinction between upper class and lower class was almost palpable in Upaniṣads. Among those who received Upaniṣadic teaching include those who would normally be excluded from Vedic ritual—those of uncertain social origin such as Satyakāma (Ch U 4.4.1–5) and woman such as Maitreyī, the wife of Yājñavalkya (Bṛ U 2.4.5; 4.5.6). The story of Satyakāma[195] indicates that the centrality of *brāhmaṇatva* was

---

[194] Thapar, *Cultural Pasts*, 814.

[195] Satyakāma who wanted to become a disciple of a teacher named Gautama Haridrumata is asked to identify his caste. He replied truthfully that he did not know his father, and his mother is of low caste. He was initiated and later became an authority on spiritual knowledge.

not essential for the reception of knowledge. The teachers also were not always the traditional *brāhmaṇas*. For example, Raikva, one of the Upaniṣadic teachers sits under his cart scratching himself and hardly behaves as would upper caste teachers (Ch U 4.1–2). Once the centrality of the ritual was denied, the reception of the traditional Vedic knowledge in view of sacrificial ritual and its strict exclusion of the lower class also were side-lined. It is stated in the *Bṛhadāraṇyakopaniṣad* that even the *caṇḍāḷas* and *pulkāsās*[196] cease to be as such in the world of the souls, where all the distinctions disappear (Bṛ U 4.3.22). The *Chāndogyopaniṣad* states that even a *caṇḍāḷa* is entitled to the leavings of the *agnihotra* sacrifice,[197] around which hungry children sit just as they sit round a mother (Ch U 5.23.4).

This tendency was carried forward by the reformation movements, such as Jainism and Buddhism, while the opposite tendency, which sought to impose increasing disabilities on *śūdravarṇa*, was continued by the compilers of Gṛhyasūtras and Dharamasūtras.

2.5.5 Buddhism and Jainism: Anti-*Brāhmaṇic* Religions

During this period Buddhism and Jainism, which professed a complete breakaway from Vedism, had their beginning which really challenged Vedic sacrificial religion and the oppression and exclusion of *śūdra*s. They pronounced

---

[196] *Caṇḍāḷas* and *pulkāsās* are outcastes. *Caṇḍāḷa* is son of a *śūdra* from *brāhmaṇa* woman and *pulkāsa* is son of a *śūdra* from *kṣatriya* wife. See Kane, *History of Dharmaśāstra*, vol. 2, pt. 1, 81 and 89.

[197] *Agnihotra* is a simple Vedic ritual performed daily by the head of the family and his spouse. It is daily worship of the sacred fire, oblation unto the fire-god. See Rao, *Encyclopedia of Hinduism*, s.v. "*Agnihotra*."

acceptance to *śūdra*s in imparting of knowledge. For the Buddha, just as the king or the owner of the royal domain should not appropriate all revenues to himself, so also a *brāhmaṇa* or a *śramaṇa*[198] should not monopolize all knowledge to himself. A teacher, even from a lower rank of society, is to be always respected. Early Jainism admitted to its monastic order members of all the *varṇa*s.[199] It is significant that the first woman disciple of Mahāvīra is said to have been a captured slave.

2.5.6 Political Power and Pro-*Śūdra* Attitude

From the political point of view, rulers during this time were mostly from the lower class and were supporters of Buddhism, which was favourable to *śūdra*s. Thus there could not have been state sponsored suppression of the *śūdra*s. There must be another political reason why they kept a soft corner for them. The peasant folk consisting of *śūdra*s is said to have occasionally resorted to migrations to express protest. This would not only disrupt the existing economy because of the desertion of villages and fields but would form new settlements if conditions were optimum beyond the boundaries of the kingdom which would become an alternative to the existing system.[200] In order to prevent this, rulers treated them diplomatically.

---

[198] A *śramaṇa* is the one who holds non-Vedic ideology or belongs to such religious groups. Buddhism and Janism are examples of such groups.

[199] Sharma, *Śūdras in Ancient India*, 147.

[200] Thapar, *Cultural Pasts*, 227.

2.5.7 Revival of *Brāhmaṇism*

Though Vedic tradition and culture were challenged by the new movements—such as Upaniṣadic Philosophy, Buddhism and Jainism—Vedic ritualism and its sacrificial religion also continued to exist side by side. There was no physical violence, revolution or strategic planning against Vedic *brāhmaṇism*. Vedic orthodoxy, hardened its defences. Rules and regulations discriminating those who were eligible and not to participate in the ritual use of the Vedas were drawn up in legalistic compilations called Śrautasūtras, Gṛhyasūtras and Dharmasūtras. The strict rules laid by these texts against those who revolted the caste system show the unrest in the social stratification and there must have been instances where people from lower rank were given Vedic knowledge.

In addition to this, there were ideological reasons why these texts could revive the caste system. The Upaniṣads forwarded the theory of *karma* and rebirth; the souls are to be reborn until they attain *mokṣa*, the final realization. Now, what should be the criteria to determine whether one is reborn to lower or higher level or to be released from the circle of rebirth? According to the *brāhmaṇa* authors of the Dharmaśāstras it was possible only by observing the *dharma* of caste. If one does not perform his/her *dharma* he/she would be born as lower animals or as people belong to the lower caste. "The explanation of social inequalities on the basis of transmigration could keep society under control of those who pronounced on conduct. The irrelevance of *varṇa* status in the new doctrine of the Upaniṣads was nullified by this explanation of social differentiation."[201]

---

[201] Thapar, *Cultural Pasts*, 825.

The emergence of new groups of people other than who are defined by *varṇa* status is another reason why the *brāhmaṇa* texts focused on caste norms. There were new migrant and invading groups such as Bactrians, Śakas, Parthians, etc. and also there were groups from inter caste marriages. Now the *brāhmaṇic* ideologues took it their task to include them somehow in the *varṇa* status, and to specify the rules regarding these matters.

2.5.8 Exclusion of *Śūdra* in the Texts of Śrauta and Dharmasūtras

The law-givers emphasized the anti-*śūdra* messages—for instance, *śūdra*s were born from the feet of God (Va Dh S 4.2; Ba Dh S 1.10.18.5–6); their duty was to serve the three higher *varṇa*s, and thus to maintain their dependents (Āp Dh S 1.1.1.1–7; Ga Dh S 10.54–57)—and imposed on them numerous social disabilities. *Kātyāyana Śrautasūtra* prescribes that all can perform Vedic rites except those who are deficient in a limb, not learned in the Vedas, impotent and *śūdra*s (Kā Śr S 1.1.3–5). Study, sacrifice and distribution of gifts were reserved only for the twice-born[202] (Ga Dh S 9.1) they can bear fruit only in the case of those who are not *śūdra* and do not indulge in wicked activities (Sa Śr S 26.1.6).[203] If *śūdra*s intentionally listen to Veda for committing to memory, then their ears should be filled with (molten) lead; if they utter the Veda their tongue be cut off; if they master the Veda their body

[202] The Three upper class—*brāhmaṇa*, *kṣatriya* and *vaiśya*—are known as twice-born (*dvija*). The first is physical birth. Through the rite of initiation to Vedic study which is called *upanayana* they are considered born again. Since *śūdra*s cannot have the rite of initiation they have only single birth.

[203] As quoted in: Sharma, *Śūdras in Ancient India*, 76.

should be hacked (Ga Dh S12.4–6). The initiated student was not allowed to talk to a *śūdra* (Dr Śr S 7.3.14). *Śūdra* should wash the feet of those students who have completed their course (Sa Śr S 19.4.13).[204] Vasiṣṭha declares that *śūdra* is a walking crematorium, one should not read in the neighbourhood of *śūdra* who is not worthy of receiving any advice or the contents of the law (Va Dh S 18.7–14).

Though *śūdra* was not admitted to *upanayana*, on the ground that it was a Vedic ritual, but the religious life of this time shows that certain sections of *śūdra*s such as *rathakāra*, were not always excluded from all Vedic rituals (Āp Śr S 5.3.19; 5.11.7). Gautama, however, quotes certain authorities who allow a *śūdra* to perform a select list of small Vedic sacrifices known as *pāka-yajñas* (simple domestic rites) (Ga Dh S 10.65). A passage from *Āpastamba*, however, favours the education of *śūdra* in Vedic literature. While stating that a student should pay fee to the Vedic teacher, he declares that the latter can accept it either from an *ugra*[205] or a *śūdra*, under all circumstances (Āp Dh S 1.2.7.19–21). This may indicate an earlier state of things, when a *śūdra* was admitted to Vedic education; but later this was denied to him. The mass evidence in favour of *śūdra* participation in Vedic sacrifice is more than counter balanced by the evidence against it. Jaimini, the author of *Mīmāṁsāsūtra*, quotes an old teacher Bādari as stating that Vedic sacrifice can be performed by members of all the four *varṇa*s (Ja Mī S 6.1.25–27). But he does not approve of this idea (Ja Mī S 6.1.33f) and thus seems to represent the dominant view of his age.

---

[204] Sharma, *Śūdras in Ancient India*, 76.

[205] The issue of the union of a *kṣatriya* and *śūdra* woman is known as an *ugra*. See Kane, *History of Dharmaśāstra*, vol. 2, pt. 1, 73.

2.5.9 *Śūdra* in *Manusmṛti*

Most of the direct information about the position of *śūdra*s during the later phase of Upaniṣadic period is derived from the law-book of Manu, which is ascribed to this period (ca. 100 BCE). Dharmasūtras were written when urbanization in the Ganges plain was upsetting the mores of Vedas, and the 'heterodox' sects were questioning *brāhmaṇical* norms. The *Manu Dharmaśāstra*, perhaps the most conservative of these texts, was compiled in the context of the period of the rule of the 'degenerate *kṣatriyas*'—those ruling kings even from lower rank—with the opening of the sub-continent to trade and new ideas.[206] It was a time when the *varṇa* divided society was marked by strong social conflicts and undermined by the activities of heretical sects and the incursions of the Bactrian Greeks, Śakas, Parthians, etc. Partly as a reaction to the pro-Buddhist policy of the political leaders and partly because of the advent of these new people, Manu tries to preserve *brāhmaṇical* society, by ordaining rigorous measures against *śūdra*s. The severity of the Dharmaśāstras was doubtless as a commentary arising from the insecurity of the orthodox in an age of flux.[207]

Manusmṛti reaffirms the old theory that *śūdra*s are ordained by God to serve the higher castes (MS 1.91; 8.410). They have no right for *saṁskāra*, purificatory rites (MS 10.126). The text reproduces the old injunction confining Vedic studies to the twice-born (MS 2.163–170; 10.4). The presence of *śūdra* is to be scrupulously avoided while the study of Veda goes on (MS 4.99). It ordains that nobody should give

---

[206] Thapar, *Early India*, 261.

[207] Thapar, *Early India*, 279.

advice to a *śūdra* or should explain a law to him (MS 4.80). In the religious sphere *śūdra* continued to be deprived of the right to Vedic sacrifice and Vedic knowledge (MS 4.80).

Manu lays down very severe punishments for *śūdra*s offending against the members of the superior *varṇa*s. Thus if *śūdra*s insult a twice-born with gross invective, they shall have their tongue cut out. If they arrogantly teach *brāhmaṇas* their duties, the king shall cause hot oil to be put into their mouth and ears (MS 8.270–272). These could be directed against the '*dharma*-preaching' learned *śūdras*, i.e. the Buddhist or Jain *śūdra*s and *śūdra*s who claim equality with the higher classes. It is difficult to say how far these laws were put into effect. Perhaps these may have been the suggestions of a fanatic and were rarely if ever put into practice.[208] There are strict disciplinary measures suggested to teachers instructing *śūdra*s. Manu provides that those who instruct *śūdra* pupils or learn from a *śūdra* teacher should not be invited at the *śrāddha*[209] (MS 3.156). It reveals that there were *śūdra* teachers and *śūdra* disciples, and Manu somehow accommodates them by giving the rule they have to be considered lower in status by excluding them from *śrāddha*.

2.6 *Śūdra* in the Post-Upaniṣadic Period (100 BCE–500 CE)

Post-Upaniṣadic period is important for the great epics of the *Mahābhārata* and the *Rāmāyaṇa* which received their final form during this time. Another popular literature of the time was Purāṇas. The emergence of *Śaiva* poets and *Vaiṣṇava*

---

[208] Sharma, *Śūdras in Ancient India*, 212.

[209] *Śrāddha* is an annual religious ceremony of the Hindus performed for the departed ancestors. See Rao, *Encyclopedia of Hinduism*, s.v. "*Śrāddha*."

saints popularizing the *Bhakti* Movements very much influenced the society. The *smṛtis* of Viṣṇu, Yājñavalkya, Nārada, Bṛhaspati and Kātyāyana are ascribed to this period. It is the time when *Pūrvamīmāṁsā* and other orthodox systems including various *Vedāntic* schools flourished.

2.6.1 Socio-Historical Setting of Post-Upaniṣadic Period

The Maurya dynasty rapidly disintegrated after Aśoka, who died around 232 BCE. The last Maurya King, Bṛhadrata, was killed by his *brāhmaṇa* commander-in-chief, Puṣyāmitra Śunga, who ascended the throne in 187 BCE and founded the Śunga dynasty. Puṣyamitra started resurrecting Vedic religion and *varṇa* system, triggering the state-led *brāhmaṇical* counter offensive against Buddhism, the atheist and rationalist movements, and the anti-Vedic immigrant communities. This pro-*brāhmaṇical* move continued through royal patronage and political activism under the Guptas from about the second century BCE to about the seventh century CE. During the Gupta era, which has been called by many historians the golden age of *brāhmaṇism*, and even afterwards, many big and small kings in both North and South India were actively engaged in implementing the injunctions of the Dharmaśāstras regarding the duty of the king to maintain the rigid hereditary occupational structure of *varṇa* system.[210]

2.6.2 Social Status of *Śūdra*

Social laws continued to be projected as rigid and the theories of *Manu Dharmaśāstra* were regarded as authoritative. Theoretically, the four *varṇa*s were precisely and

---

210 Bhandyopadhyaya, *Class and Religion in Ancient India*, 208.

clearly defined, with rules pertaining to their lawful activities and functions set out in the Dharmaśāstras. Yet in Practice there were many discrepancies. The sharpening of stratification at the theoretical level may have been a *brāhmaṇical* response to the more flexible attitude reflected.[211] The reasons for the relaxation in the social practice of *varṇa* system could be:

1) There were an increase in trade and the coming of the people from western and central Asia. It resulted in (1) relating with people of different customs and cultures and (2) taking up of new occupations other than that were allotted for each class. It became difficult to insist on *varṇa*, other than the category of the *brāhmaṇas*.[212]
2) The spirit of awakening by popular *Bhakti* Movements, Buddhism and Jainism challenged *brāhmaṇic varṇa* system.
3) The presence of *śūdra*s who became rich and owned land might have lightened the severity of discrimination.
4) Many more groups being added to the title of *śūdra*s who accepted at least in some degree the Aryan hierarchy and Vedic values, such as those with small income, the immigrant groups those not born into a caste based society and those forest tribes who became amenable.
5) The rise of Islam and Christianity which ignored *śūdra*-exclusion must have downplayed the popularity of *varṇa* distinction.

---

[211] Thapar, *Early India*, 260.

[212] Thapar, *Early India*, 260. The fluidity of an urban population was one reason for urban life being downplayed in the Dharmaśāstras.

As a reaction to these social facts *brāhmaṇism* hardened their rules. The higher classes were found increasingly tracing their descent and were organized on a lineage system. The kings in whatever *varṇa* they might originally belong claimed a lineage which is higher and respectful. Conducting the great Vedic sacrifice became a means for legitimizing their authority. *Śūdra*s had no lineage ancestry, only the *varṇa* of their individual parents determined their status and were looked down upon by those who claimed lineage origin; lineage became prominent in determining one's *varṇa*.[213]

2.6.3 *Śūdra* in Epics and Purāṇas

The great epics, the *Mahābhārata* and the *Rāmāyaṇa* and Purāṇas were professed to be having universal availability and *śūdra* had access to them. They show comparatively liberal attitude towards *śūdra*s. The *Mahābhārata* declares that all the four *varṇa*s ought to hear Veda (M Bh 12.328.49). Such injunctions are in sharp contrast to those of *Manusmṛti*, which placed very severe punishments in such cases. *Bhāgavatapurāṇa* says, as the three Vedas cannot be learnt by women, *śūdra*s and the *brāhmaṇas* (who are so only by birth), the sage Vyāsa composed the story of the Bhārata out of compassion for them (Bh Pu 1.4.25). The emphasis was turned towards good character rather than ritual sacrificial practices,

---

[213] Thapar, *Cultural Pasts*, 383.

as in the story of Dharmavyādha[214] in the *Mahābhārata* (M Bh 3.206.20–22).

But certain narratives show that these texts too did not make very substantial change from orthodox *brāhmaṇism* on imparting the knowledge to *śūdra*. For example, in the *Rāmāyaṇa* we find Śambuka who was killed by Rāma because he, being a lower caste, studied Veda (RN 7.64–67). In the *Mahābhārata,* Ekalavya had to cut his thumb as *guru dakṣiṇa*[215] because he did not belong to a higher class and consequently all his learned skills became useless (M Bh 1.123.10–39). As *śūdra*s could not be initiated into Vedic study, the only *āśrama* out of four that they were entitled to was that of the householder, *gṛhastāśrama* (M Bh 12.63.12–14). But in their liberal attitude they showed that *śūdra* is not completely denied of the knowledge necessary for a good moral life and they too can achieve liberation, not by the study of Veda and the practice of sacrificial religion but by the study of epics and Purāṇas, which contained very many quotes from Vedas.

2.6.4 *Bhakti* Movements: Anti-*Brāhmaṇic* Tendencies

The *Bhakti* Movements marked by *Vaiṣṇavism* and *Śaivism* became popular among common people. It was a reaction against formalistic Sanskrit culture and religious practice introduced to the elite circles, and a reluctance to be

---

[214] Dharmavyādha who is from the lower rank of society is pictured as the one who has acquired *brahmajñāna*. It is explained that he acquired *jñāna* not through Vedas but some other means.

[215] Some form of honorarium given to the teacher as an expression of gratitude for the education received.

subordinated to this culture.[216] The rituals and the claims of *brāhmaṇas* being close to gods were unacceptable as was the social exclusion of lower castes.[217]

Bhakti Movements offered *śūdra*s an option, and they could get rid of some religious disabilities imposed on them by the *brāhmaṇical* system. They offered salvific passage irrespective of one's eligibility to use Vedas ritually.[218] They emphasized moral virtues more than ritual practices. These movements explored the pro-*śūdra* nuances contained in Purāṇas. Among their founding saints and poets included women and *śūdra*s. The *Vaiṣṇava* texts never failed to emphasize the possibility of emancipation for women and *śūdra*s through pure devotion (BG 9.32; Bh Pu 7.7.54–55). Those who disregard *śūdra* devotees of Viṣṇu are condemned to hell; hence a wise person should not disregard even a *caṇḍāḷa* devotee of Viṣṇu (M Bh, Southern Edition 14.116.22). Like the members of the three higher *varṇas*, a *śūdra* devotee of Śiva is also promised salvation.[219] *Tāntrism*, which was connected with both *Vaiṣṇavism* and *Śaivism*, also did not recognize *varṇa* distinctions in matters of religion.[220] Vedic ritualism and the learning were bypassed with devotion, and these movements did not count it a point to speak for Vedic education for all.

---

[216] The role of the *bhakti* tradition in relation to Vedic *brāhmaṇism* was in many ways similar to that of the earlier sects of Buddhism, Jainism, *Cārvāka*, etc. during the Upaniṣadic period.

[217] Thapar, *Early India*, 355.

[218] Lipner, *The Hindus*, 57.

[219] Sharma, *Śūdras in Ancient India*, 309.

[220] Sharma, *Śūdras in Ancient India*, 309.

2.6.5 Later *Smṛti* Texts and *Śūdra*s

The *smṛtis* of Viṣṇu, Yājñavalkya, Nārada, Bṛhaspati and Kātyāyana constitute the main source for the study of the position of the *śūdra*s in this period. A characteristic feature of *smṛti* writings of this period is their *Vaiṣṇavite* leanings which liberalized the *brāhmaṇical* attitude towards *śūdras*. The earlier law-givers permitted arts and crafts to *śūdra*s only when they failed to earn their livelihood through the service of the three higher *varṇa*s, but this condition is now waved and handicrafts are included in the normal occupations of *śūdra*s.[221] Yājñavalkya states that an elderly *śūdra* deserves respect (YS 1.116). Unlike the early law-givers, he does not insist that *vaiśya* and *śūdra* guests should be made to work and then fed with the servants. Yājñavalkya shows the instances of educated *śūdra*s.[222] A passage of Yājñavalkya suggests the existence of the teachers of servants (YS 1.223).

2.6.6 *Mīmāṁsaka* Revival of *Brāhmaṇism*

During the post-Upaniṣadic period the ritual use of Vedas did not die out. *Yajña*-oriented religion, as practised by *Pūrvamīmāṁsakas*, was followed by *brāhmaṇa* upper caste minority. There were also *Vedāntin*s, (known as *Uttaramīmāṁsakas*) who took up the latter portion of Vedas—especially Upaniṣads—the *Bhagavdgītā* and *Brahmasūtra* of Bādarāyaṇa as their founding texts in building their *Vedāntic* philosophy. For *Vedāntin*s Vedic ritual was not to be abandoned altogether, rather, it was to be practised in the light of *Vedānta*, that is, as a stepping-stone to the more insight-

---

[221] Sharma, *Śūdras in Ancient India*, 262.
[222] Sharma, *Śūdras in Ancient India*, 283.

oriented religion of Upaniṣads. In any case, for both camps, Vedas were still the active, normative source of saving knowledge. The whole point of the *Vedāntic* enterprise was to claim the backing of *śruti* (as culminating in the Upaniṣads), and to this end *Vedāntic* theologians generally embarked on detailed exegesis of Upaniṣadic texts.[223] But it was almost normative for them to declare that *śūdra*s should not learn Vedas.

2.7 *Śūdra*s in South India: Spread of *Brāhmaṇism* and the Ideal of *Varṇa*

Towards the end of the first millennium BCE south India moved from pre-history into history and literary records reflecting historical events are available. The history of south India has been reconstructed from diverse sources: megalithic burials, inscriptions in Tamil *brahmi*[224] and Tamil poems of *Saṅgam* literature. Aśoka in his inscriptions refers to the people of south India as the *Coḷas*, *Ceras*, *Pāṇḍyas* and *Satyaputra*s. Reference to *brāhmaṇa* settlements begin around the middle of the first millennium. Migrants such as Buddhist and Jain monks used the avenues opened by the Mauryan administration. A historical study of the societies in South India proves that the idea of *śūdra* in the south differed from that of north India.

In south India, *Tirukuṛaḷ* and other Tamil narratives describe *brāhmaṇas*, kings, ministers, warriors, merchants, artisans, musicians, and ploughmen but not the four-*varṇa*

---

[223] Lipner, *The Hindus*, 58.

[224] *Brahmi* script was the earliest script used for writing Tamil.

system.[225] The *Saṅgam* poems refer to various occupations and leave nothing about social ordering of *varṇa*.[226]

The establishment of *brāhmaṇa* settlements in the South gradually introduced Sanskrit into the local language. More than language, the incorporation of deities and rituals took place, and this process went on.[227] This kind of incorporation made local recruitment to the *brāhmaṇa* rank inevitable, and adjustments also had to be made with the indigenous cultures. *Brāhmaṇa's* claim to be in communication with gods, their supposed ability to manipulate unseen powers, and their claim that they knew the correct *mantra* or formula to establish the well-being of the king were probably more convincing to the kings than other claims.[228] The Kings sought *brāhmaṇical* legitimation and support, and in turn they were given grants and gifts as land and areas for settlement.

Varṇa rules were introduced, but with limited success except among *brāhmaṇas*. The support for orthodoxy among the *brāhmaṇas* was probably related to their dependency on *velalas*, the other land owners and peasants, who were culturally distinctive, and whom the *brhāmaṇas* tried to subordinate by giving the status of *śūdra*s. But *velalas* who were land owners were also powerful.[229] The *velalas*, who in *varṇa* terms were often equated with *śūdra*s, were second in importance after the *brāhmaṇas*. The rest of the society was gradually shuffled into a caste hierarchy to the extreme of

---

[225] Stanley Wolpert, ed., *Encyclopedia of India* (Farmington: Thomson Gale, 2006),s.v. "Caste System."

[226] Thapar, *Early India*, 232.

[227] Thapar, *Early India*, 234.

[228] Thapar, *Early India*, 348.

[229] Thapar, *Early India,* 337.

highly polluting and who were debarred from entry into the temple.[230]

In the subsequent periods, the interaction of northern culture with that of the south, with the circuits of the traders, Buddhist and Jain monks and *brāhmaṇa* settlers, resulted in integration of the ideas and culture of north and south. The *brāhmaṇas* settled in the peninsula saw themselves as the keepers of what they regarded as sacrosanct Vedic tradition. Sanskrit becoming hegemonic language continued but its hegemony was not absolute, since the languages derived from Dravidian roots retained authority and were more widely used.[231] The rise and spread of the Vedic religion was very much challenged by the emergence of popular *Bhakti* Movements, *Vaiṣṇavism* and *Śaivism*. Division of the society and subjugation of some groups based on castes was largely opposed. Instead of elaborate Vedic sacrifice simple forms of worship, namely *pūja*[232] began to widespread.

There were attempts to bring the various modes of worship into one single fold giving them some ideological backing based on Vedic tradition. *Vedāntic* schools which spread during this period tried to take Vedic tradition out of ritualism. Their commentaries on Vedic corpus had encouraged discussions on and revitalizing the Vedic thought, but revitalization involved making changes in the orthodoxy.[233]

---

[230] Thapar, *Early India,* 389.

[231] Thapar, *Early India,* 348.

[232] *Pūjā* means worship or veneration or homage. It denotes the ritual worship of a deity in the form of an image. See Johnson, *Dictionary of Hinduism*, s.v. "*Pūjā*."

[233] Thapar, *Early India*, 349.

2.8 History of Exclusion: An Analysis

An analysis of the above discussions on the origin and development of *śūdra* and their exclusion will make this study profound. A reflection into the reasons for the exclusion in the initial phase of caste formation as well as the purpose of exclusion in its later stages will make this discourse more focused on understanding the position of Śaṅkara on the issue of exclusion of *śūdra*s as it is revealed in his *Brahmasūtra Bhāṣya.*

2.8.1 Rationale for the Exclusion

There are various justifications for the theory and practice of exclusion of *śūdra.* All of them might not be equally significant, but must have played their own role. These reasons for exclusion and its actual practice were subject to changes at various stages of history because some reasons might not have become reasonable and some practices not practical in a later period.

2.8.1.1 Exclusion as Exception

Exclusion could be seen from the point of view of exception given to *śūdra*s. The study of Vedas and practice of sacrifice and rituals were obligatory for the Aryan fold. *Śūdra*s were given an exemption from this. *Śūdra*s, as the servile group lacked Vedic Sanskrit as well as the intellectual acumen to learn and memorize Vedic *sūtra*s. In addition to this, Vedic sacrifice became very expensive that the poor *śūdra*s could not take it up. If the Vedic study and rituals were made compulsory for *śūdra*s it could become only a burden for them rather than a privilege. Therefore, they were exempted from these obligations.

Besides this, exclusion can be viewed as an initial step towards incorporation. The *śūdra*s were accepted into the mainstream society with some exclusion otherwise they would remain totally outside the social recognition and would be treated with hostility.

2.8.1.2 Exclusion and Religion

Some religious reasons could be found in the exclusion of *śūdra*s. Vedic words received a divine and the esoteric significance by the time of *Brāhmaṇa* period, and contributed very much in making Vedic learning exclusive.[234] Aryan theologians believed that Vedic words have a mysterious power if they were pronounced in an appropriate context with needed purity and with proper accent.[235] The slightest mistake in the pronunciation of Vedic *mantra*s would inevitably issue some disaster. The art of writing was not utilized for the purpose of preserving Vedic texts for a long time, and it was only orally transmitted to the posterity. As Vedic Sanskrit was not very familiar to *śūdra*s, it was feared that Vedic hymns would be transformed out of recognition, if they were transmitted orally in *śūdra* families from generation to generation. In the eyes of the theologians, this would be a

---

[234] G.K. Bhat, "Teacher-Pupil Relationship (In the Context of Upanishadic Literature)," *Annals of Bhandarkar Oriental Institute* 54, no. 1/4 (1973): 173.

[235] Vedic words were originally speech-acts which were used in relation with religion and the simple form of fire-cult. Later as the religious rituals became complex those Vedic speeches were deified with mysterious power to yield the needs of the reciter; "not everyone had equal access to that mysterious power of language." Madhav M. Deshpande, "Changing Conceptions of the Veda: From Speech-Acts to Magical Sounds," *Brahmavidya: The Adyar Library Bulletin* 54 (1990): 3–13, 26.

greatest disaster.[236] Later on, when female education began to lag behind and women as a class ceased to be educated in Sanskrit, it is remarkable that *brāhmaṇa* theologians declared them also, of all *varṇa,* unhesitatingly to be unfit for Vedic studies. Thus, theological animus or pride was not at the root of the exclusion of *śūdra*s and women from Vedic education. Nor did it amount to a total denial of religious education; for women and *śūdra*s were permitted to get religious enlightenment from the study of *smṛtis*, Epics and Purāṇas. Many of them became honoured preachers in medieval times.[237]

2.8.1.3 Exclusion and Exploitation

All the above said reasons could have played a role in the beginning when the *śūdra*s were excluded from Vedic study. In a later period they became tools for exploiting the poor working class namely *śūdra*s. As the community made a transition from pastoralism to agriculture it needed organized labour for which the upper class manipulated the manual labour of the lower class. In order to keep the food-producing working class, namely *śūdra*s, in eternal chains Dharmasūtras imposed almost inhuman disabilities on them and entrusted the state with the task of enforcing these disabilities. The most fundamental disability imposed on them was that of being debarred from any form of upward occupational mobility. For Manu, since the Supreme Lord created *śūdra*s as slave, they cannot become anything other than a slave in this life (MS 8.412–414). *Śūdra*s can move to a higher class, and thus can

[236] A.S. Altekar, *Education in Ancient India* (Varanasi: Nand Kishore, 1965), 46.

[237] Altekar, *Education in Ancient India,* 46.

improve their lot only in their next life, provided they remain faithfully and sincerely true to their duty of serving the other three classes in this life (MS 9.334–335). They were forbidden to accumulate wealth (MS 10.129). To ascertain their permanent availability lineage system was emphasized in determining one's caste.

Another major socio-economic disability which was imposed on the working class by the *brāhmaṇa* texts were the denial of the right to education. *Śūdra*s were forbidden to study, recite and even listen to Vedas (MS 3.156; 4.99; 10.127). Since Vedic education was the only available form of education before the expansion of the Epics and Purāṇas, the denial meant that the ruling class wanted the working class to remain subject to economic exploitation. But since this ignorance also made it difficult for them to understand and appreciate the great tradition of Vedic religion, the ruling class later adopted the strategy of pacifying them—and also to make them realize the greatness of Vedic tradition and to respect it—through oral instructions in Vedic and *brāhmaṇical* religion indirectly through the traditions of Epics and Purāṇas.[238]

Though *puruṣasūkta*, which is a late composition of the *Ṛgveda*, was understood as the solemn recognition that the Aryans gave to the poor defeated servile group into their fold, much more than this, it gave a conscious and deliberate ideological formulation intended to legitimize and sanctify an oppressive and exploitive class structure that had already come into existence.[239]

From the religious point of view, it was argued that the non-performance of various ceremonies and sacrifices was an

---

238 Bhandyopadhyaya, *Class and Religion in Ancient India*, 166.
239 Bhandyopadhyaya, *Class and Religion in Ancient India*, 38.

advantage to the *śūdra*s, who were free from the obligation of observing them. But what was advantageous to them became disadvantage because the dominant social outlook of those times condemned those who did not perform sacrifice and relegated them to a low social status.[240] When Vedic words were begun to be considered as mysterious and powerful, it gave increased importance and value to the teachings and was helpful to protect a mystery. But much more than protecting a mystery it helped to create a mystery. Secrecy is best understood as a strategy for concealing and revealing information. It is a tactic which functions to transform certain knowledge into a rare and valuable commodity, a rare resource, which in turn enhances the status and prestige of its possessor.[241]

2.8.2 Exclusion of *Śūdra* from the Study of Vedas: The Shift of Purpose

A historical study of the origin and development of *śūdra*-exclusion shows that the people denoted by the term *śūdra* and the practice of their exclusion were not always the

---

[240] Sharma, *Śūdras in Ancient India*, 135.

[241] Brian Black, *Priests, Kings, and Women in the Early Upaniṣads: The Character of Self in Ancient India* (Delhi: Motilal Banarsidas, 2014), 24. The composers of Vedic texts, which are primarily ritual, were priests. Meticulous oral preservation was backed by the theory that the sound was of fundamental importance and therefore a mispronunciation could render the purpose of the ritual ineffective. But this effected to serve another aim which was to limit the availability of the texts, for oral memorization was closed to those whom the priests wished to exclude. *Śūdra*s were, therefore, prohibited from even accidently hearing the Vedic hymns. Correct speech was considered the hallmark of the *brāhmaṇa,* and power lay in the sound of the recitation. See Thapar, *Cultural Pasts*, 197.

same from its origin to the *Vedāntic* times (fifth century CE). In the course of time many groups were added to, and many were taken to the higher class from the title '*śūdra*'. Social practice of exclusion too varied from place to place and from time to time; but the declaration that 'the *śūdra*s are not eligible for Vedic study' remained all throughout. The purpose of it has changed from its origin to the *Vedantic* thinkers.

Various kinds of non-egalitarian dimensions, based on lineage (*jāti*), leadership (chiefdom), sharing of common grazing ground, etc., were there in the clan based pastoral society of ancient India. Though this was not very much counted in terms of oppression, but in terms of privilege and responsibility, the fact is that the notion of high and low status existed. From the Vedic corpus—the ritual and theological texts of elite Aryans—we understand that the authors or the theologians envisaged all the different clans and groups could be ordered under four major classes and with the fifth as untouchables. This kind of ordering with its assignment of occupation, privileges, rights, and the laws concerning each class could be the norm which the elite among the Indo-Aryan group found to be ideal. In the course of time, this system was widely accepted and the later *brāhmaṇa* texts and the political power began to enforce it for various reasons.

To the question, who were the actual people denoted by the word *śūdra*, the answer could be: there were no ostensible homogenous group of people who were so marked always with the same criteria and who had claims of a common ancestor. Arya-*dāsa* dichotomy that we find in *Ṛgveda*, deriving from linguistic and cultural differences was later replaced by the Arya-*śūdra* dichotomy, where the main criteria were the use of Sanskrit and the observance of *varṇa* rules.[242] Besides this, poverty played an important role in excluding and including a particular group in to the higher or lower class. But these criteria kept on changing its emphasis from time to time. There were always occasions where some of the *śūdra*s moved to higher class by acquiring wealth, claiming noble genealogy, receiving the blessing of the priest, conducting great sacrifices, giving gifts to the priests, etc. By giving up eating meat, wearing sacred thread, and performing Vedic rituals and ceremonies like the *brāhmiṇas*, many *velala* castes in southern India were converted to *brāhmaṇism.*[243] The higher classes were sometimes relegated to *śūdra* status on account of their poverty, failure to follow the *brāhmaṇic* laws, etc.[244] Later, to the title '*śūdra'* were added the peasants, those who became poor and had no land, some of those clans which were once considered to be outcastes, some of the invading groups that came to India, and those who did not speak proper language, etc. Poverty became no longer an important factor in deciding one's status as *śūdra*; there were poor *brāhmaṇas* and wealthy *śūdra*s as well. One's conduct began to count very much for the social status, especially due to the influence of Buddhism,

[242] Thapar, *Cultural Pasts*, 862.

[243] Rao, *Encyclopedia of Hinduism*, s.v. "Caste, social aspects"

[244] The upper caste could 'lose caste' if they failed to live according to *dharma*. Certain kinds of *dhārmic* violation incurred 'loss of caste', e.g. some kind of killing (in particular, of a *brāhmaṇa*, or abortion), of sexual intercourse (particularly with one's *guru's* wife, or incest), of eating or drinking (e.g. the drinking of Alcohol by a *brāhmaṇa*), consorting with outcasts, etc. Being fallen means having lost: (i) the right to live according to the Veda-based rites and actions of the twice born; and consequently (ii) the fulfillment that results, in the hereafter, from such a life. But loss of caste was a terrible thing because of the social penalties it incurred which included isolation from one's community. See Lipner, *The Hindus*, 105.

Jainism and the *Bhakti* Movements. In South India, those whom the *brāhmaṇa* settlers called *śūdra* were land owners and wealthy. They were given the title only because *brāhmaṇas* found them with different religious practice than theirs and they did not accept the Aryan ritual practices. The term *śūdra* became a synonym for those who did not accept Vedic religion and ritual practices and became 'inferior' for those who did accept. The identification of a higher class or lower class was therefore, of a status that was modified from time to time by historical contingencies. It was neither homogenous nor a permanent ancestry.[245] Getting legitimized by Vedic authority became a matter of privilege and wider acceptance, and conducting Vedic sacrifice became a means for it.[246]

If we ask, what exactly are the texts by which the *śūdra*s were excluded, there is no such body of texts from which *śūdra*s were always strictly excluded from the very beginning up to now. Earlier, *śūdra*s had access to *Atharvaveda*. Only other three Vedas were debarred. *Pūrvamīmāṁsā* gave importance only to three Vedas—*Ṛg*, *Sāma* and *Yajur*. From among the portions of Vedas Upaniṣads were not considered as the part of Vedas (Ja Mī S 2.1.32–40).[247] Upaniṣadic philosophers, who gave importance to

---

[245] Thapar, *Early India*, 136.

[246] K.A. Nilakanta Sastri, *A History of South India: From prehistoric Times to the Fall of Vijayanagar*, 4th ed. (New Delhi: Oxford University Press, 2015), 134.

[247] Here while enumerating various parts of the Vedas Jaimini mentions only three Vedas and they are said to consist only of Mantras and Brāhmaṇas (Ja Mī S 2.1.32–40). There were even Vedists who held only the pre-*saṁhitā mantra*s or Saṁhitās alone constituted Veda, excluding other Vedic texts of Brāhmaṇas, Āraṇyakas and Upaniṣads.

knowledge rather than sacrificial ritual considered Vedas as not superior to their new teachings (Mu U 1.1.5; Ch U 7.1; 5. 3–10; 6.1; 3.5.4; Ta U 2.3). For them, the term 'Veda' meant those texts of the Vedic corpus except Upaniṣads. But later, the post-Upaniṣadic period considered Upaniṣads to be part of Vedic corpus and *śūdra*s were debarred from Upaniṣadic learning too.[248]

In addition to this, the reason for the exclusion is said to be the Vedic injunction to do so. Though there is derogatory attitude towards *śūdra*s, Vedas—the *śruti* texts—do not make any clear affirmation and exact command to keep *śūdras* away from Vedic knowledge. K. Satchidananda Murti, one of the famous Indology scholars states:

> Nowhere in the Saṁhitā-Brāhamaṇas or the Upaniṣadic portions is any caste, sex or race excluded from studying and benefiting from the Veda. The sentence "Women and Sūdras [*sic*] should not be taught the Veda" (*na strī śūdro vedam adhīyātām*), frequently cited by those who advocate prohibition of access to the Veda to lower castes and women, is not a Vedic text. Nor is the citation 'The Veda should not be studied by the Śūdra' (*Śūdreṇa nādhyetavyam*) in the Pūrva Mūmāṁsā [*sic*] Sūtra / Bhāṣya (VI. 1. 37–8) found anywhere in the Veda. (No one who has cited these two has found for them any loci in the śruti.)[249]

See R. N. Dandekar, "Vedic Literature: A Quick Overview," *Annals of the Bhandarkar Oriental Institute* 81 (2000): 1.

[248] Later on, Itihāsa-Purāṇas were accessible to *śūdra*s. But Upaniṣads considered them to be fifth Veda (Ch U 7.1.4).

[249] Murty, *Vedic Hermeneutics*, 15. Caṭṭampiswāmikal also states this fact. In Vedas there is neither prohibition of *śūdra's* Vedic learning nor reasonably validating statements on the prohibition. See Caṭṭampiswāmikal, *Vedādhikāranirūpaṇam*, 27.

There are *śruti* texts which say *śūdra*s are not eligible to perform sacrifices; but not from learning. There are occasions in the Vedas (AV 5.17.8–9; Ta Sa 1.6.1; Ta Br 1.1.2.6–7), while speaking about access to Vedas, the upper *varṇas* are instructed by calling out their name, but *śūdra*s are left out. This silence need not always be interpreted as strong denial and exclusion. It could be: usually the three upper *varṇas* did study and practise Vedic rituals so the instructions were given to them alone; or that *śūdra* as a recognizable social class might not be existing there at that time; or even from the part of *śūdra*s, there might not be great enthusiasm to get the right to learn Vedas and practice Vedic rituals rather they must be happy with the cessation of warfare and being accepted into the Vedic fold. Due to these facts it could be possible, for both the upper caste and for *śūdra*s as well, 'learning of a *śūdra*' might not be an issue to be discussed. Vedic Saṁhitās show comparatively clear pro-*śūdra* attitude. The neglect of this by the subsequent *brāhmaṇa* texts had certain socio-religious reasons which were not there before. The *smṛti* texts of this time made affirmative statements about the exclusion. But we should note, as we have seen, that there are also *smṛti* passages which maintain that the *śūdra*s are eligible for Vedic study (Āp Dh S 1.2.7.19–21; Ga Dh S 10.65).

To the point how complete was the exclusion from Vedic knowledge in its actual social practice gives diverse answers. The fact that the *smṛti* texts tightened instruction to debar *śūdra*s from Vedic study shows that in actual practice some of the *śūdra*s did study Vedas. Purāṇas and Epics were made accessible to *śūdra*s; but they contain a lot of quotations from Vedas, and it is believed that these could liberate *śūdra*s i.e. giving the same result as Vedas. Padurang Vaman Kane, the reputed scholar in Indian studies, makes an important observation on this regard:

> The śūdras had no right to study the Veda. But as a matter of fact the Purāṇas contain as exemplified above a good many Vedic mantras. It is stated in the Bhāgavata [1.4.25] 'women, śūdras and brāhmaṇas in name only are beyond the pale of the three Vedas; therefore the sage (Vyāsa) composed through compassion for them the Bhārata tale'. The Devibhāgavata states 'study of the Veda is not accepted for women, śūdras, and brāhmaṇas in name only and Purāṇas are compiled for the purpose of benefitting them'. From this it follows that in the case of śūdras the listening to the Bhārata was deemed to bring about the same results that the Veda does for *dvijas* and that even the śūdra may acquire the knowledge of the Self (and mokṣa) from the Bhārata.[250]

If debarring from Vedic knowledge was so strict even the access to Purāṇas and Epics also could have been barred.

The purpose of exclusion of *śūdra*s from Vedic knowledge—as a theory and as a norm advocated by the ritual and theological texts of the *brāhmaṇas*—has changed very much from its origin. Originally the purpose could be: an exception given to *śūdra*s, a religious intention for safeguarding the Vedic knowledge without faults, and the social reasons as a means for securing the food production of

[250] Kane, *History of Dharmaśāstra,* vol. 5, pt. 2, 921–922.

the community. But by the time of *Vedāntic* theologians the purpose of the norm that '*śūdra*s are not eligible for Vedic learning' suggests something more/other than its original aim. More than pointing out exactly who all are not eligible, it acquired a wider perspective which proposed those who cannot fulfil certain criteria of eligibility—as we have seen, the eligibility criteria kept changing in the various periods of history—shall not embark upon Vedic studies and those of such were titled as *śūdra*s. Added to this, by the time of *Vedānta*, Vedas were considered very much as a means for authentication. If certain ideas were explained by claiming their basis on Vedas, they had greater acceptance as legitimised by eternal wisdom and consequently constituting orthodoxy.[251] The norm of exclusion from Vedic study that occurs in the *Vedāntic* texts, which are theological treatise, has theoretical importance with certain theological purposes other than its meticulous social practice. Thus a proper assessment on the "connections between norm, fact and purpose"[252] is highly in place in understanding the exclusion of the *śūdra*s from Vedic knowledge.

Conclusion

The development of an ideology and its expressions in the texts are closely related to the then history. The idea of the exclusion of the *śūdra*s have originated and developed in Vedic tradition within a particular historical context. The questions

---

[251] Thapar, *Early India*, 309; Lipner, *The Hindus,* 62. Conducting Vedic sacrifices were also considered as a means for legitimising the political authority. See Lipner, *The Hindus,* 63.

[252] Francis X. Clooney, "Finding One's Place in the Text: A Look at the Theological Treatment of the Caste in Traditional India," *Journal of Religious Ethics* 17, no. 1 (Spring 1989): 20.

such as who were the people denoted by the title *śūdra*, what were the criteria for determining one's social status to be a *śūdra*, how strict and total was the exclusion, etc. might give different answers from time to time and from text to text. Exclusions and exploitations, where the weak minority groups such as the poor, migrants, etc. are looked down upon by the mainstream society will continue in their varied forms. This will form 'new *śūdra*s'for the present age. Thus exclusion of *śūdra* does not limit its application with the same group of people with the same title as '*śūdra*' were excluded from the same type of rights, by the same set of criteria by the upper class all throughout the history.

If the verbatim following of the exclusion of *śūdra*s from Vedic knowledge is stressed the questions such as, does Vedic norm of exclusion mean those traditionally considered *śūdra* alone to be excluded; or can out-castes—who are in a lower status than *śūdra*—learn Vedas, remain pertinent. Vedic norm of *śūdra*'s exclusion from Vedic knowledge, by the time of *Vedānta*, acquired theological significance more than a rigorous social practice. The emphasis here is that an unworthy shall not take up the scriptural studies, and stating anything contrary to it will be considered going away from the Vedic tradition. The theme which is located in *brāhmaṇical* scriptures and explained within their theological discourse cannot be studied solely from its social point of view, separating it from its theological and philosophical aspects[253] and this will be attempted in the following chapters.

---

[253] Clooney, "Finding One's Place in the Text," 1–2.

CHAPTER 3

POSSIBILITY OF A *ŚŪDRA BRAHMAJIJÑĀSU*: EXPLORING THE NON-EXCLUSORY SCOPE OF *APAŚŪDRĀDHIKARAṆAM*

Introduction

Exclusion of *śūdra*s has a long history reaching up to *Vedāntic* times. The reasons for such exclusion were mostly religious and social. Śaṅkara has taken up the same issue in his *bhāṣya* on *Apaśūdrādhikaraṇam* of *Brahmasūtra* (BS Bh 1.3.34–38) and makes his position clear when he concludes the discussion by stating: "But the conclusion stands that a Śūdra has no right to knowledge through the Vedas"[254] (BS Bh 1.3.38 p. 234). This would mean *śūdra*s cannot quest for *Brahman* because the quest, *brahmajijñāsā*, pre-supposes Vedic study (BS Bh 1.1.1),[255] and therefore, cannot have self-realization, the liberation. But this *śūdra*-exclusion is in need of explanation; the reasons for exclusion, given by Śaṅkara, are not without hiccups. They are liable to be deconstructed or at least can be proved to be unsound. Therefore, a critical study on *Apaśūdrādhikaraṇam* makes chinks in his armour of exclusivism.

Apaśūdrādhikaraṇam could be subjected to critical and analytical study mainly through four areas in view of bringing out its non-exclusory implications. First of all, a comparative

---

[254] वेदपूर्वकस्तु नास्त्यधिकारः शूद्राणामिति स्थितम् ॥ (BS Bh 1.3.38) Cf. Śaṅkara, *Brahmasūtra with Śāṅkarabhāṣya*, ed. Ministry of Education, India, 108.

[255] "The mere fact of the study of the Vedas cannot be the prerequisite sought for here, since this is a common factor (in both the cases of deliberation on *Brahman* and religious rites) (BS Bh 1.1.1 p. 7).

study of the *bhāṣya* on *sūtra*s of this *adhikaraṇam* with that of other prominent *Vedāntin*s reveals Śaṅkara is more on the side of inclusion. Secondly, a closer examination of the *śūdra* characters of Upaniṣads (Jānaśruti and Satyakāma) and of the *Mahābhārata* (Vidura and Dharmavyādha), who were with salvific knowledge and have come up in the *adhikaraṇam* in order to prove the exclusion, reveals that they bear inclusive impetus in their original context. The attempts to make them pseudo-*śūdra*s (*apa-śūdra*s) remain farfetched and unconvincing.

The major reason why Śaṅkara is very much understood as the champion of excluding *śūdra*s from salvation is his insistence on the path of knowledge, which Śaṅkara believed to be the means for salvation, and which involves both knowledge of Vedas (*śruti*) and renunciation (*sannyāsa*).[256] *Śūdra*s were without both these, in the sense that, they either did not have or were prohibited from having these. But in the last part of the *adhikaraṇam* (BS Bh 1.3.38) Śaṅkara admits the possibility of salvation through the ways other than *śruti* and *sannyāsa*, and he suggests that these could be bypassed through '*smṛti* (Itihāsas and Purāṇas)'[257] and the

---

[256] Katherine K. Young, "Śaṅkara on the Salvation of Women and Śūdras," in *Goddesses and Women in the Indic Religious Tradition,* 131.

[257] Itihāsas: (anecdotes) the narrative texts. The term is specifically applied to the two epics—the *Mahābhārata* and the *Rāmāyaṇa*.

Purāṇas: (mythologies) are the body of narrative texts. There are eighteen great Purāṇas and eighteen sub Purāṇas and some other minor Purāṇas.

Both these are often used combined (Itihāsa-Purāṇa) designating a huge body of narrative material which informs theistic Hinduism from a *brāhmaṇical* perspective and are considered part of *smṛti* textual tradition. These are sometimes designated also as fifth Veda. See Johnson, *Dictionary of Hinduism*, s.vv. "Itihāsa," "Purāṇa(s)."

'internal virtue of detachment' respectively. Therefore, the third section of this chapter looks into; for Śaṅkara, how far Vedas remain a necessary condition for *brahmajñāna*. Finally, an enquiry into *sannyāsa*—how Śaṅkara understood it and how it becomes indispensable for self-realizing *jñāna*—is attempted. This gives more light into his inclusive stance in the programme of salvation.

Discussions on the above aspects challenge alleging Śaṅkara as the one who has excluded *śūdra* from salvific knowledge. It could be the case that he is of the opinion of excluding them from Vedic study; but if *brahmajñāna* is possible through means other than Vedas, barring *śūdra* from Vedas does not preclude them from salvation. But Śaṅkara, in *Apaśūdrādhikaraṇam*, first makes the fort of exclusivism strong and later, as the discourse reaches in its conclusion, makes few openings for universal salvation making a *śūdra brahmajijñāsu*, at least in principle, not an impossibility. Therefore, exclusion of *śūdra* from *brahmajijñāsā*, according to Śaṅkara, needs explanation because it is not that exclusive as it could be taken.

3.1 Śaṅkara, the Inclusive *Vedāntin*: A Comparative and Analytical Exposition of *Apaśūdrādhikaraṇam*

A critical and comparative analysis of *Apaśūdrādhikaraṇam* throws better light into it, and to the inclusive stance of Śaṅkara. Such study on the *bhāṣyas* given to this *adhikaraṇam* by the great *Vedāntin*s, Śaṅkara, Rāmānuja and Madhva—representing the three schools of *Vedānta* philosophy with a large number of followers—reveals, among them Śaṅkara is more inclusive as far as the salvation of *śūdra* is concerned.

3.1.1 Difference in the Arrangement of the *Sūtra*s

For Śaṅkara and Madhva the discussion on *śūdra*-exclusion in *Apaśūdrādhikaraṇam* is comprised within the five *sūtra*s, thirty-fourth to thirty-eighth inclusive, in the first *adhyāya* of the third *pāda* of *Brahmasūtra Bhāṣya* (BS Bh 1.3.34–38). Rāmānuja has split *sūtra*s 35 and 38 into two and therefore, explains the same issue within seven *sūtra*s, BS Bh 1.3.33–39. Madhva's discussions are comparatively very short than Śaṅkara and Rāmānuja. The following chart makes clear the distribution of the *sūtra*s of *Apaśūdrādhikaraṇam* by the three *Vedāntin*s.

Śaṅkara	**Rāmānuja**	**Madhva**
Sūtra 1.3.34 *śugasya tadanādaraśravaṇā-ttadādrvaṇātsūcyat-ehi* (शुकस्य तदनादरश्रबणात्तदाद्रवणात्सूच्यते हि)	*Sūtra* 1.3.33 *śugasya tadanādaraśravaṇ-āttadādrvaṇātsūc-yatehi* (शुकस्य तदनादरश्रबणात्तदाद्रवणात्सूच्य ते हि)	*Sūtra* 1.3.34 *śugasya tadanādaraśra-vaṇāttadādrvaṇ ātsūcyate hi* (शुकस्य तदनादरश्रबणात्तदाद्रवणा त्सूच्यते हि)
Sūtra 1.3.35 *Kṣatriyatvagateśco-ttaratra caitrarathena liṅgāt* (क्षत्रियत्वगतेश्चोत्तरत्र चैत्ररथेन लिंगात्)	*Sūtra* 1.3.34 *kṣatriyatvagateśca* (क्षत्रियत्वगतेश्च)	*Sūtra* 1.3.35 *Kṣatriyatvagat-eścottaratra caitrarathena liṅgāt* (क्षत्रियत्वगतेश्चोत्तरत्र चैत्ररथेन लिंगात्)
Sūtra 1.3.36	*Sūtra* 1.3.35	*Sūtra* 1.3.36

saṁskāraparāmarś-āttadabhāvābhilāp-ācca (संस्कारपरामर्शात्तदभावाभिलापाच्च)	*uttaratra caitrarathena liṅgāt* (उत्तरत्र चैत्ररथेन लिंगात्)	*saṁskāraparā-marśāttadabhā-vābhilāpācca* (संस्कारपरामर्शात्तदभावाभिलापाच्च)
Sūtra 1.3.37 *tadabhāvanirdhāra-ṇe ca pravṛteh* (तदभावनिर्धारणे च प्रवृत्तेः)	*Sūtra* 1.3.36 *saṁskāraparāmar-śāttadabhāvābhil-āpācca* (संस्कारपरामर्शात्तदभावाभिलापाच्च)	*Sūtra* 1.3.37 *tadabhāvanird-hāraṇe ca pravṛteh* (तदभावनिर्धारणे च प्रवृत्तेः)
Sūtra 1.3.38 *śravaṇādhyayanār-thapratiṣedhātsmṛt-eśca* (श्रवणाध्ययनार्थप्रतिषेधात्स्मृतेश्च)	*Sūtra* 1.3.37 *tadabhāvanirdhār-aṇe ca pravṛteh* (तदभावनिर्धारणे च प्रवृत्तेः)	*Sūtra* 1.3.38 *śravaṇādhyaya-nārthapratiṣed-hātsmṛteśca* (श्रवणाध्ययनार्थप्रतिषेधात्स्मृतेश्च)
	Sūtra 1.3.38 *śravaṇādhyayanā-rthapratiṣedhāt* (श्रवणाध्ययनार्थप्रतिषेधात्)	
	Sūtra 1.3.39 *Smṛteśca* (स्मृतेश्च)	

3.1.2 Context and Reasons for Taking up Discussion on *Śūdras'* Eligibility

Devatādhikaraṇam (BS Bh 1.3.26–33) which precedes *Apaśūdrādhikaraṇam* discusses whether Gods are eligible for salvific knowledge. Śaṅkara asserts that Gods are eligible for knowledge. The reasons held are: (1) they can have hankering for liberation, (2) they can have ability, and (3) they are not debarred anywhere in the scriptures. After this, Śaṅkara begins with *Apaśūdrādhikaraṇam*, by giving reasons why the discussions on the eligibility of *śūdra* is undertaken. He raises all the possible arguments which support *śūdra*s' eligibility by placing those in the mouth of *pūrvapakṣin,*[258] the opponent. For Śaṅkara, in order to remove those doubts on *śūdra*s' eligibility for knowledge, which could possibly be caused by the arguments of the opponent, this *adhikaraṇam* takes up the discussion and he is prepared to refute *pūrvapakṣin*'s arguments (BS Bh 1.3.34).

The opponent's arguments,[259] as it is given by Śaṅkara (BS Bh 1.3.34) could be summarised as follows:

1) Just as Gods, whose competence for salvific knowledge is proved on their aspiration for liberation and their ability, *śūdra*s who also have both aspiration and ability, can be admitted to the knowledge.
2) The opponent quotes "*śūdra* is unfit for performing the sacrifice" (Ta Sa 7.1.1.6) and argues that the scriptural prohibition of *śūdra* is only for performing the sacrifice. Prohibition for sacrifice cannot be taken for the knowledge as well.
3) The narrative of Jānaśruti (Ch U 4.1–3)[260] where Jānaśruti is addressed as *śūdra* (Ch U 4.2.3, 5) and is

---

[258] *Pūrvapakṣa* is the earlier view or the opponent's view

[259] These could probably be also the arguments by the *dharma* preaching Buddhist monks and some other non-*Vedānta* teachers by which the *Vedāntic* disciples were challenged and confused.

[260] *Chāndogyopaniṣad* gives the narrative of Jānaśruti in its fourth chapter, sections (*khaṇḍa*) one (8 *sūtras*), two (5 *sūtra*s) and three (8 *sūtra*s) (altogether twenty-one *sūtra*s), i.e. Ch U 4.1–3.

imparted with knowledge[261] can be taken as *śruti* admitting *śūdra*'s competence for knowledge.

4) The *smṛti* texts also give examples for *śūdra* having the salvific knowledge as in the case of Vidura.[262]

The crux of these arguments is that the very reasons used for establishing the eligibility of Gods for knowledge can be equally applied to *śūdras* too. Just like Gods they also can have a desire for knowledge and ability for acquiring it. But only with regard to scriptural prohibition there may raise doubt. But the *śruti* texts (Ta Sa 7.1.1.6; Ch U 4.2.3, 5) and *smṛti* characters (Vidura and others) are given in support of *śūdra*.

Besides these, Rāmānuja adds one more: according to *pūrvapakṣin*, even if *śūdra* cannot read Vedas, they have Itihāsas and Purāṇas to which they are competent and the possibility of salvation is open to them (BS Bh 1.3.33). Rāmānuja prepares the ground, and in the course of the discussion he refutes this view.

The Upaniṣad mentions Jānaśruti with a second name Pautrāyaṇa which meant 'the great-grant son of Jānaśruta. See Paul Deussen, trans., *Sixty Upaniṣads of the Veda* Vol. 1, translated from German by V.M. Bedekar and G. B Palsule (Delhi: Motilal Banarsidas, 1980), 119.

[261] Jānaśruti was a king with great knowledge. Once he overheard two flamingos speaking about Raikva as the one who had greater knowledge than him. Desiring to acquire knowledge from him Jānaśruti reached him and made wealthy offering as gift. But Raikva called him a '*śūdra*' and refused to teach him (Ch U 4.2.3). Then again, he came with richer offerings including his daughter. This time he accepted him to teach. Then looking at the face of King's daughter he said "O *śūdra*, She will be the cause of my conversing with thee" (Ch U 4.2.5). Raikva taught him *samvarga vidyā* (meditation on merger).

[262] Vidura is a famous character spread throughout the *Mahābhārata*. His is a cursed birth given to god Dharma due to which he had to be born as a *śūdra*. The birth of Vidura is narrated in *Ādiparva* of the *Mahābhārata,* Chapters 90–101.

Madhva (BS Bh 1.3.34) gives only two reasons for having a discussion on *śūdra*-exclusion. When it is stated that the study of scripture is a subject to which all human beings are entitled (BS Bh 1.3.25, 26) it would equally apply to *śūdra*. Further, the case of Jānaśruti—who in spite of being addressed as *śūdra* is imparted with knowledge—is an *śruti* indication that *śūdra* can have knowledge. It is to clear the doubt caused by these two cases *bhāṣyakāra*[263] takes up the discussion on *śūdra*'s competence for knowledge.

3.1.3 Answering the *Pūrvapakṣin*: Reasons for *Śūdra*-Exclusion

Śaṅkara's answer to *pūrvapakṣin* and his disapproval of *śūdra*'s competence for salvific knowledge which is given in BS Bh 1.3.34 can be summarised as follows:

1) *Śūdra*s have no competence because they cannot study Vedas. One becomes competent for the things spoken of in the Vedas, after that person has studied Vedas and known these things from them.
2) There can be no reading of Vedas by *śūdra*s for the Vedic study presupposes investiture with sacred threads, which ceremony is confined to the three upper caste males.
3) *Śūdra*s may have aspiration but it cannot qualify anyone unless they have the ability. Mere ability in the ordinary sense alone cannot qualify; for scriptural ability is needed in the scriptural matter. But this scriptural ability is denied by the prohibition to right to study.

---

263 The author of the *bhāṣya*.

4) The text "*śūdra* is unfit for performing the sacrifice" (Ta Sa 7.1.1.6) has a common application; it suggests that *śūdra* has no right to knowledge as well, for the logic applies both ways. The reasons why *śūdra*s are excluded from sacrifice is the same for their exclusion from knowledge.
5) Taking the case of Jānaśruti: (1) it does not indicate a *śūdra* is educated with Vedic knowledge; because, indicatory mark become suggestive when it is stated logically. Since other scriptural passages state the opposite, this particular scripture remains contradicting them, and therefore, it is not a logically stated one; (2) even if Jānaśruti is taken to be a *śūdra*, he is taught only *samvarga-vidyā*,[264] and therefore, a *śūdra* is not qualified for all kinds of knowledge; (3) the word '*śūdra*' cannot be accepted in its primary sense as the member of fourth *varṇa*, because, its meaning can be construed from the context in some other way and it is a part of *arthavāda*[265] which is to be interpreted and

---

[264] Knowledge of the merger: it is Gautama's teaching given to Jānaśruti, in Ch U 4.3.1–4 that every element merge into their substratum, Air (*vāyu*) and breath (*prāṇa*).

[265] *Arthavāda* (eulogy) is one of the four parts into which Vedic texts are divided by *Mīmāṁsā*. The four major parts are: 1) Injunctions (*codana*, *vidhi*, *niṣedha*, *pratiśedha*); 2) Explanatory proclamations of the object or purpose (*arthavāda*); 3) Recitations during performance of a sacrificial act (*mantra*); and 4) Names (*nāmadheya*). According to *Mīmāṁsakas* injunctions are directly authoritative and *arthavāda* is authoritative only in so far as it serves as an auxiliary to injunctions. *Arthavāda,* even when not contradicted by other *pramāṇas* is not authoritative, as its sense is not complete in itself. See Rao, *Encyclopedia of Hinduism*, s.v. "*Arthavāda*."

understood in consistent with the logic of other injunctions.

The succeeding portions of the *adhikaraṇam* are elaboration of these arguments.

Rāmānuja refutes *pūrvapakṣin*'s arguments (BS Bh 1.3.33) mainly on three points:

1) *Śruti* prohibition for sacrifice applies to the prohibition for knowledge. Rāmānuja, maintaining his greater allegiance to *bhakti*, makes an important shift from Śaṅkara. For Śaṅkara, the whole discussion is on excluding *śūdra* from 'knowledge on *Brahman*' but for Rāmānuja it is from 'taking up meditation on *Brahman*'. For him, the capability of performing meditations on *Brahman* implies: (1) knowing the nature of *Brahman*, (2) knowing the due modes of meditation, and (3) knowing the requisite preliminaries of meditation, such as recitation of Veda, sacrifices, and so on. These are not available for *śūdra* because they are prohibited from studying Vedas.
2) According to Rāmānuja, Itihāsa-Purāṇas are not independent treatise and only confirm or support Vedas. They are allowed to *śūdra*s only for the sake of destroying their sins and not to prepare them for meditation on *Brahman*; not for salvific knowledge.
3) *Śūdra* persons with knowledge such as Vidura are to be understood as they had acquired their wisdom in their previous non-*śūdra* birth.

Madhva, without giving such elaborate reasons on why *śūdra*s are to be prohibited from salvific knowledge, enters into the interpretation of *sūtra* 1.3.34, and in the course of which he makes his points clear.

3.1.4 Jānaśruti: A Non-*Śūdra*

The case of Raikva addressing Jānaśruti as *śūdra* and then imparting him the knowledge is important because it is an instance from *śruti* texts (Upaniṣads)—not *smṛti*[266]—in favour of *śūdra*s' competence for Vedas. But for Śaṅkara (BS Bh 1.3.34), in this case of '*śūdra*-utterance', the word '*śūdra*' cannot be accepted in its primary sense as a member of fourth *varṇa*, but has to be interpreted as 'the one who is struck with grief (*śuk*)'.[267] Jānaśruti was engulfed with sorrow when he heard that the flamingos speaking about his having no knowledge of *Brahman* and then praising Raikva than him. As Jānaśruti reached Raikva, through his power of television, he could understand the grief of Jānaśruti. Therefore, this *śruti* passage is not an indication that born *śūdra* can have knowledge.

For Rāmānuja (BS Bh 1.3.33) too the appellation '*śūdra*' refers to his sorrow, not to his being a member of the fourth caste. In addition to this, he explains why Jānaśruti's gifts were denied for the first time and accepted later. For Raikva, the knowledge of *Brahman* might be imparted even without long attendance on the teacher, only if, Jānaśruti is liberal to the teacher to the utmost of his capability.

---

[266] Unlike *smṛti*, *śruti* is eternal, authoritative and canonical.

[267] Śaṅkara gives three variations of meaning: (1) Raikva approached towards that grief, (2) he was approached by that sorrow and (3) he rushed to Raikva because of sorrow. See Śaṅkara, *Brahmasūtra Bhāṣya of Śri. Śaṅkarācārya*, trans., Swami Gambhirananda, 231.

Madhva (BS Bh 1.3.34) follows the same argument on the *śūdra*-utterance of Raikva. For him, running towards Raikva, overcome by grief itself is the *śūdratva* (*śūdra*-hood) in Jānaśruti. He states, "This Poutrayana is not a Sudra (by birth). The state of being a sudra in his case consists in his rapidly betaking himself out of grief to (Raikwa)" (BS Bh 1.3.34).[268] *Śūdra*, therefore, here is not indicative of the caste of Jānaśruti, but it is indicative of the grief stricken mental condition of Jānaśruti.

3.1.5 Jānaśruti: A *Kṣatriya*

After proving Jānaśruti a non-*śūdra*, the *sūtrakāra*[269] proceeds to establish that he is a *kṣatriya*. For Śaṅkara (BS Bh 1.3.35), Jānaśruti's case cannot be an indication for *śūdra* acquiring knowledge.

The mention of Jānaśruti along with Abhipratārin, who is a *kṣatriya*, in the context of the same kind of knowledge, suggests that the former is a *kṣatriya,* because, usually equals are found to be mentioned together. The character Abhipratārin appears in the final section of Jānaśruti episode where instruction of the *samvarga-vidyā* occurs (Ch U 4.3). Now attempts are made to prove *kṣatriyatva* (*kṣatriya*-hood) of Abhipratārin. For this Śaṅkara quotes Ch U 4.3.5, "now then *brahmacārin* begged of Śaunaka of the line of Kapi and Abhipratārin, son of Kākṣasena, when they were being served on by the cook" (BS Bh 1.3.35 p. 231). Abhipratārin is mentioned together with Śaunaka who is in the line of Kapi. Kāpeyas are associated with Citraratha as it is obvious from a

---

[268] Madhva, *The Vedanta-sūtras with the Commentary by Sri Madhwacharya*, trans. S. Subba Rau (Madras: Thompson, 1904), 67.

[269] The author of the *sūtra*.

passage from *Tāṇḍya Brāhmaṇa* (20.12.5),[270] "the Kāpeyas made Citraratha perform this (*Dvirātra* sacrifice)." Since the people of the same lineage have the priests of a common descent, this show, Kāpeyas are of the line of Citraratha. Now, Citraratha's *kṣatriyatva* is proved using a text (anonymous), "From him issued one named Citrarathi who was a *kṣatriya* king" (BS Bh 1.3.35 p. 231–232).

Besides this, dispatching a *kṣattā*[271] for finding Raikva and having huge possession of riches indicate that Jānaśruti must be a *kṣatriya* king.

Rāmānuja splits what Śaṅkara considered as single *sūtra* (BS Bh 1.3.35) into two: BS Bh 1.3.34 and 1.3.35. *Sūtra* 1.3.34 offers proof for the *kṣatriyatva* of Jānaśruti from Ch U 4.1–2 and *sūtra* 1.3.35, from Ch U 4.3. In his *bhāṣya* on *sūtra* 1.3.34 Rāmānuja gives three reasons why Jānaśruti must be a king, and therefore, a *kṣatriya*: (1) Jānaśruti bestowed much wealth and food, (2) he is represented as sending his door-keeper to find Raikva, and (3) he bestows on Raikva many villages. In his *bhāṣya* for *sūtra* 1.3.35, taking the same lead as Śaṅkara, Rāmānuja proves Jānaśruti to be a *kṣatriya* connecting him with Citraratha, the *kṣatriya*. Rāmānuja concludes this discussion by affirming that the reason does not give any inferential proof to show the competence of *śūdra*.

---

[270] As given in: Śaṅkara, *Brahmasūtra Bhāṣya of Śri. Śaṅkarācārya*, trans., Swami Gambhirananda, 231.

[271] One born of mixed parentage—from a *śūdra* father and *kṣatriya* mother or of a slave woman—whose duty was to drive chariots, wait on princes, and so on. See Vettam Mani, *Purāṇic Encyclopaedia: A Comprehensive Dictionary with Special Reference to the Epic and Purāṇic Literature* (1964; repr., Delhi: Motilal Banarsidass, 1975), s.v. "*Ekādaśasaṅkaravarṇa*." See also Śaṅkara, *Brahmasūtra Bhāṣya of Śri. Śaṅkarācārya*, trans., Swami Gambhirananda, 232n50.

He, as an introduction to the next *sūtra*s states, "The next Sūtra declares that the non-qualification of the Sūdra proved by reasoning is confirmed by scripture and Smriti" (1.3.35).[272] For him all the succeeding *sūtra*s of this *adhikaraṇam* deal with scriptures confirming *śūdra*s' non-qualification for knowledge.

Madhva (1.3.35) gives only one single reason for Jānaśruti's *kṣatriyatva* which is completely different from Śaṅkara and Rāmānuja. For him Jānaśruti is related with *citraratha*; which is a chariot, which serves as a sign for *kṣatriya*. Madhva's explanation goes as:

> From the subsequent sentence, 'this is a chariot (drawn by) the mule,' which mentions 'Citraratha' connected with the king (as its owner) as a characteristic of Poutrayana, Pautrāyaṇa is understood to be a Kshatriya (and not a Sudra). The Brahmapurana says: The chariot to which a mule is yoked is called Chitra (i.e., Chitra Ratha). Further the Brahmavivarta purana says, "where there is (the study of) scripture, there only is the chariot; and where there is no study of scripture, there no chariot is (to be seen)." (BS Bh 1.3.35).[273]

3.1.6 Scripture on Purificatory Rites and Knowledge

BS Bh 1.3.36 brings out the scriptural evidence for the exclusion of *śūdra*s. Scripture testifies acquiring knowledge is preceded with sacred rites such as investiture with sacred

---

[272] Rāmānuja, *The Vedanta-Sūtras with the Commentary by Ramanuja*, trans. George Thibaut, vol. 48 of *The Sacred Books of the East* (1904; repr., Delhi: Motilal Banarsidas, 1971), 342.

[273] Madhva, *The Vedanta-sūtras with the Commentary by Sri Madhwacharya*, trans. S. Subba Rau, 67–68.

thread etc. For example: (a) Śa Br 11.5.3.13 "Him he vested with sacred thread." (b) Ch U 7.1.1 "Uttering the Sacred formula, 'teach me, venerable Sir', he approached." (c) Pr U 1.1 "They, who were adepts in the Vedas, adhered to the qualified *Brahman*, but were intent on an inquiry about the supreme *Brahman*, went to the venerable Pippalāda with sacrificial faggot in hand under the belief, 'this one will certainly tell us all about it'." (d) Ch U 5.11.7 is taken as a special case for it states "even without initiating them." Śaṅkara interprets this text and shows that some were exempted from the rite of initiation; but they were those who had it already. Scriptures also show the absence of purificatory rites for *śūdra*; such as (a) MS 10.4 "*śūdra* belongs to the fourth caste and has but a single birth." (b) MS 10.126 "*śūdra*s have no sins, nor are they fit for any purificatory rites." The argument is that to acquire knowledge purificatory rites are must; *śūdra*s are excluded from them; therefore, *śūdra*s can have no Vedic knowledge.

Rāmānuja (BS Bh 1.3.36) also explains this *sūtra* just as Śaṅkara. For him also there are two factors under consideration, the reference of rite of purifications in acquiring knowledge and the absence of them in the case of *śūdra*s. To prove this he uses all the scriptural quotes which Śaṅkara has used and he adds one of his own in view of proving the presence of purificatory rite for the acquisition of knowledge: "I (Haridruma Gautama) shall perform *upanayana* ceremony (the rite of initiation to Vedic studies) unto you (Satyakāma)" (Ch U 4.4).

Madhva (BS Bh 1.3.36) makes a different interpretation here. Since Vedic study must precede *upanayana* and *śūdra*s are not eligible for this they are not entitled to study Veda. Madhva states the women of higher calibre, even if they do have no rite of initiation, can have Vedic study. For him, 'if there is no *upanayana*, there is no right to study Veda', is a general rule. Even as the men have *upanayana*, women have marriage as a *saṁskāra*.[274]

3.1.7 Satyakāma: The Non-*Śūdra*

The next *sūtra*, 1.3.37 states the case of Satyakāma (Ch U 4.4.5).[275] Gautama, the teacher, initiated him on account of his truth-telling which is considered to be a sign of *brāhmaṇatva*.[276] For Śaṅkara and Madhva he was initiated only after his non-*śūdratva* was ascertained by the quality of speaking truth.

Rāmānuja on this *sūtra* (1.3.37) makes his explanation very short, even without stating the truth-speaking quality of Satyakāma. For him, Gautama was convinced that the one who wished to become his pupil was not a *śūdra,* and therefore, he proceeded to instruct him.

---

[274] *Saṁskāra* (sacraments) is the series of personal rites which an individual goes through during his/her life. This cycle, as it is reflected in *Gṛhyasūtra*s, begins at conception and ends at death. *Upanayana* and *vivāha* (marriage) are included in this series of rites. See Rao, *Encyclopedia of Hinduism*, s.v. "*Saṁskāra*."

[275] *Chāndogyopaniṣad* explains the narrative of Satyakāma in the fourth chapter under the sections (*khaṇḍas*) 4–9, comprising 23 *sūtra*s. Satyakāma is often second named with Jābāla, associated with his mother's name Jabālā.

[276] Satyakāma wanted to get formally initiated into the Vedic study. But neither he nor his mother knew who fathered him, and in which family line he belonged. Therefore, his caste status was not certain. He told this fact to his master Gautama Haridruma. On account his character of truth-telling he considered him to be a *brāhmaṇa* and accepted him for Vedic study.

3.1.8 *Smṛti* Prohibition on *Śūdra*

BS Bh 1.3.38 brings further reason why *śūdra*s shall not study Vedas. It is because *smṛti* prohibits them from hearing, studying and acquiring the meaning of the Vedas. Śaṅkara shows five *smṛti* passages which instruct *śūdra* not to hear, utter and memorise Vedas: (a) Ga Dh S 12.4, 'then should they happen to hear the Vedas, the expiation consists in their ears being filled with lead and lac' (b) Va Dh S 18.11–14, 'a *śūdra* is a walking crematorium. Hence one should not read in the neighbourhood of a *śūdra*' (c) Ga Dh S 12.4, 'chop off *śūdra*s' tongue if they should utter the Vedas, and cut the body into pieces if they should commit it to memory' (d) MS 4.80, 'knowledge is not to be imparted to a *śūdra*' (e) Ga Dh S 9.1, 'study, sacrifice and distribution of gifts are for the twice-born'. Prohibition for hearing Veda implies prohibition for studying and acquiring knowledge of Vedas. Then Śaṅkara proceeds with the case of the *Mahābhārata* characters Vidura and Dharmavyādha who belonged to *śūdra* caste but had salvific knowledge. For Śaṅkara, they had the knowledge due to their deeds of their past life and in this present life they are reaping the result of their knowledge which cannot be withheld. Then he states that all the four castes are competent for Itihāsas and Purāṇas. But the conclusion stands that a *śūdra* has no right for knowledge through Vedas.

Rāmānuja splits this *sūtra* (1.3.38) into two: 1.3.38 and 1.3.39. In 1.3.38 Rāmānuja deals with prohibition for hearing and studying Vedas. He evidences it with two scriptural passages. Among them one is the same which Śaṅkara has quoted, Va Dh S 18.11–14; and the other is an anonymous one, 'therefore a *śūdra* is a beast and is unfit to perform sacrifice'. For Rāmānuja, just like Śaṅkara, prohibition on hearing the

Vedas implies the prohibition of understanding and whatever depends on it.

Rāmānuja in the next *sūtra* 1.3.39, after restating the conclusion of the previous *sūtra* that 'it is a settled matter that *śūdras* are not qualified for meditations on *Brahman*' criticises the *Advaitic* view and places the reasons why *Śāṅkarites* does not and cannot have a legitimate platform to hold exclusion of *śūdras* from salvific knowledge. For him, *Advaitic* reasons for excluding *śūdra* remains ineffective and makes Upaniṣads defunct. The points of criticism are as given below:

1) *Advaitins* cannot logically hold that the Vedic texts to be the exclusive source of knowledge of the real nature of *Brahman*. One can acquire the knowledge that *Brahman* alone is real and everything else is falsely superimposed upon *Brahman,* from another person or from any other source. This is because: (1) knowledge of truth does not depend upon one's choice, and at once springs up in the mind even of an unwilling man as soon as the conditions for such cognitions are present; (2) error comes to an end through the knowledge of the true nature of things. Once the true knowledge is received, from whatever source it might spring, the error of a *śūdra* no less than of a *brāhmaṇa* comes to an end; (3) the one who has learnt Veda and received realisation can teach even a *śūdra,* because that person is beyond Vedic injunctions and prohibitions therefore, prohibition to teach Veda to a *śūdra* does not touch that person. If *śūdra*'s ignorance is not removed by the teaching of a realised person then it would be same with regard to a *brāhmaṇa*'s ignorance.

2) For *Advaita*, it is the steady meditation on Vedic sentences declaring the unity of *Brahman* and the Self, effects destruction of all impressions opposed to such unity. The effect is something visible in contrast to achieving *adṛṣṭa*, i.e. super sensuous transcendental effect. If the latter was the aim of meditation, according to Rāmānuja, there would be some meaning in excluding *śūdra*s from it.
3) For *Advaita*, *śūdra* can have the desire for knowledge through the means other than Vedic instruction and thereupon real knowledge may result from non-Vedic instruction. If so, exclusion form Vedas becomes least meaningful.
4) From the *Advaitic* point of view, it has to be admitted that the mere ordinary instrument of knowledge, i.e. perception and inference assisted by reasoning can reveal that the Real is non-differenced self-luminous intelligence and the objects of knowledge is superimposed upon the inner reality. Uninterrupted meditation on this inner reality can effect final release. Exclusion from scriptures does not come on the way.

In the next portion of the argument Rāmānuja tries to bring out his own arguments for the exclusion of *śūdra*s. Human beings, in the mundane existence, require receiving from somewhere the knowledge that this world is an error and the Reality is something different. It is Vedas which gives this knowledge and hence we cannot do without it. But this does not become an objection, because in criticising *Advaitic* view it is already pointed out that this knowledge can be achieved without the aid of Vedas. But then, for Rāmānuja, *Vedānta-*

texts enjoin devout meditation as the means of release (not the meditation on the knowledge). Such meditation has the effect of winning the love of the supreme spirit and is to be learned from scriptures only. The injunctions on such meditation refer to such knowledge only as springs from the legitimate study of the Veda on the part of the human duly purified by initiation and other ceremonies and is assisted by the seven means.[277] Pleased by such meditation, the supreme person bestows on the devotee the knowledge of it's true nature, dissolves thereby the ignorance. It is on this view, for Rāmānuja, the *sūtra* on non-qualification of *śūdra* holds good.

For Madhva this *sūtra*, BS Bh 1.3.38 exposes that *śūdra* is prohibited by *smṛti* from hearing, studying and understanding the meaning of the Vedas. Then he quotes Ga Dh S 12.4 as done by both Śaṅkara and Rāmānuja. For Madhva, *śūdra*s have no consecrated fire to be maintained, no sacrifice to be performed; therefore, they could not study the Vedas. It has been ordained that they should serve the three higher *varṇa*s only. He mentions the case of Vidura and others that they attained knowledge in their previous life; their case is different and should be treated as a special case than ordinary *śūdra*.

3.1.9 Highlights on the Comparative Study

From the above comparison and analysis few points are to be noted. All the three *ācāryas* agree on the exclusion of

[277] The seven means given by Rāmānuja in his BS Bh are: *viveka* (discernment), *vimoka* (tranquil mind; out of non-attachment to desire), *abhyāsa* (repetition), *kriya* (works; the performance of sacrifices), *kalyāṇa* (virtuous conduct), *anavasāda* (freedom from dejection), *anuddharṣa* (absence of exultation) (BS Bh 1.1.1).

*śūdra*s from the Vedic knowledge and the consequent liberation. But Śaṅkara's arguments seem to be weak. Rāmānuja leaves no stone unturned in criticising Śaṅkara on the point that he did not and his philosophy cannot support the exclusion. Among these three *Vedāntin*s, it is only Śaṅkara who agrees on the competence of *śūdra*s for Itihāsa-Purāṇas providing an opening for the salvation of *śūdra*s. Madhva omits the matter altogether and Rāmānuja argues against this position. Śaṅkara takes the case of Vidura and Dharmavyādha and states that they became eligible for knowledge due to the *karma*s of their previous life. Madhva also agrees with Śaṅkara on their knowledge, but for him, this is a separate case and need not have to connect with the general rule of *śūdra*-exclusion. From the comparative point of view Śaṅkara's reasons for exclusion seems to be less robust than the other two succeeding *Vedāntin*s; the reason could be that he is more pro-inclusive and open to universal soteriology.[278]

---

[278] One of the reasons for such comparatively relaxed position of Śaṅkara, from the sociological point of view, could be that he took it his task to revive the Upaniṣadic *brāhmaṇism* in the background of *Śaivism*, *Vaiṣṇavism*, Buddhism and Jainism, to which the low caste people were attracted, because these religions put no barrier of caste upon them and salvation was open to them. At the same time, he could not totally negate the *brāhmaṇical* system of caste. He maintained a mid-way between exclusion and inclusion. After Śaṅkara, by the time of Rāmānuja and Madhva, *brāhmaṇism* was comparatively established and gained momentum; especially in the context of the eclipse of Buddhism and Jainism which were the major challenge to *brāhmaṇism*. So, it is possible that they took a stricter stance. (See Kane, *History of Dharmaśāstra*, vol. 5, pt. 2, 922–926). But, at the same time, it is not that easy for them, from their *Bhakti-Vedānta* perspective, to support for *śūdra*-exclusion: how can God (*Viṣṇu* or *Śiva*) who is compassionate and all-loving be partial to his devotees?

Śaṅkara opens the *adhikaraṇam* and proceeds with the discussions underlining the impossibility of salvation of *śūdra*s because they cannot have access to Vedas and without which there could be no liberating knowledge. As the argument progressively reaches to its final part (BS Bh 1.3.38), Śaṅkara makes openings for *śūdra*s' salvation by admitting their competence for Itihāsas and Purāṇas. But he remains adamant on their ineligibility for Vedas. Therefore, he concludes the discussion: "But the conclusion stands that a *śūdra* has no right to knowledge through Vedas" (BS Bh 1.3.38 p. 234); it is not that *śūdra* has no right to knowledge anyway.

3.2 Pseudo-*Śūdra*s: Inclusive Features of the Characters in *Apaśūdrādhikaraṇam*

Apaśūdrādhikaraṇam mentions four characters from the scriptures to support the view it presents. Two of them, namely Satyakāma and Jānaśruti, are from Upaniṣads and the other two—Vidura and Dharmavyādha—are from the *Mahābhārata*. For Śaṅkara, though these characters appear as *śūdra* men of great knowledge, they are not *śūdra*s; he explains away their *śūdratva* and establishes that they are pseudo-*śūdra*s (*apa-śūdra*s). A closer look into the narratives where these characters occur, and an analysis of the very social and ideological context of the texts in which they are part, reveal these characters bear inclusive impetus as far as the salvific knowledge is concerned.

3.2.1 Upaniṣadic Characters in *Apaśūdrādhikaraṇam*

Brahmasūtra takes two narratives from *Chāndogyopaniṣad* in view of proving *śūdra's* ineligibility for knowledge: the narrative of Jānaśruti (Ch U 4.1–3) and

Satyakāma (Ch U 4.4–9). Upaniṣadic texts are subsequent development of the Vedic corpus after Brāhmaṇas. But it is unlikely that everything in the Upaniṣads were derived from Brāhmaṇas. The text was, at least in part, inspired by the circumstances of its own time.[279] An enquiry into the questions such as, why did the Upaniṣads develop out of Brāhmaṇas in such period of time, and what about the stuff that is not in Brāhmaṇas, will better reveal the significance of Upaniṣadic characters and what these narratives speak aloud.

3.2.1.1 From Vedas to Upaniṣads: A Look into the Ideological Shift

Upaniṣads are at one level philosophical discussions, but at another, they are embedded in the society in which they relate. The period of composition of the early and major Upaniṣads is generally taken as from eighth to sixth centuries BCE.[280] During this period trade flourished and towns were connected with trade routes. Commerce was facilitated by the rise of the prosperous kingdoms governed by *kṣatriya* clans. New ideas spread quickly and circulated freely. Students and thinkers moved over a wide geographical area in search of philosophical and theological debate, encountering new people and ideas from outside India.[281] There were already in existence at this time a number of ascetic movements that were non-Vedic, coming either from some indigenous pool of ideas or by critically responding to Vedas. These movements might

---

[279] Doniger, *The Hindus*, 20.
[280] Thapar, *Cultural Pasts*, 810.
[281] Doniger, *The Hindus*, 166.

have influenced Upaniṣads.[282] Upaniṣads must have become more popular and it is evident from the fact that the Sanskrit of Upaniṣads were more accessible, conversational and reader friendly which was not so in the case of Brāhmaṇa texts.[283]

Upaniṣads emerge out of earlier compositions, stemming from Vedic corpus—Saṁhitās and Brāhmaṇas—but with certain ideological deviations from these origins.[284] One of the major shifts that Upaniṣads took was the new interpretation given to the concept of *mokṣa*, the liberation. For Vedas, *mokṣa* meant enjoying the heavenly pleasures. But for the Upaniṣads it was getting liberated from the cycle of re-birth by achieving the realization of the *Ātman-Brahman*.[285] For the Brāhmaṇa texts, *mokṣa* was possible to anyone who knew the ritual, but Upaniṣads promised it to anyone who knew the teaching—a shift from the way of acting to a way of knowing;[286] from sacrificial ritualism (*yajña*) to the contemplative knowledge (*jñāna*).[287] This indicates a shift also in the theories of knowledge: "from the acceptance of the Vedas as revealed and as controlled by ritual to the possibility that knowledge could derive from intuition, observation, and

---

[282] Doniger, *The Hindus*, 184. A mixing of various cultures and ideologies especially those from the margins is almost palpable in Upaniṣads. See Thapar, *Cultural Pasts*, 809–827.

[283] Doniger, *The Hindus*, 167.

[284] Thapar, *Cultural Pasts*, 810.

[285] S. Radhakrishnan, trans., *The Principal Upaniṣads* (London: George Allen & Unwin, 1953), 51; Thapar, *Cultural Pasts*, 812.

[286] Doniger, *The Hindus*, 170.

[287] Israel Selvanayagam, *Vedic Sacrifice: Challenge and Response* (Delhi: Manohar Publishers, 1996), 103–118.

analysis."[288] Greater emphasis was given to the experiential knowledge and the function of intellect in acquiring it.[289]

The disciplines for achieving the liberation involved control over body and mind (*yoga*) and meditation (*dhyāna*); both required a form of life given to austerity. This makes each individual as central—other than priests, rituals and Vedas—who sought immortality through one's own effort which, therefore, gave it a universalism in the pursuit of *mokṣa.*[290] Sacrifices were relegated to an inferior position; the ritualism involved in it were reinterpreted ethically (*ātma yajña*).[291] Similarly, in several passages of Upaniṣads austerities, liberality, straight forwardness, *ahimsa* and truthfulness are put forward as equal to or superior to the actual performance of the ceremonial of sacrifice[292] (Ch U 3.17.4; Pr U 1.15; Mu U 1.2.11). Despite the fact that there was such a shift, Vedic ritual practice and sacrificial rituals were not suddenly discontinued but their role began to fade.[293] In elaborating on the means for liberation the term '*karma*' was differently interpreted by

---

[288] Thapar, *Cultural Pasts*, 811.

[289] Thapar, *Cultural Pasts*, 904.

[290] These ideological changes were the cause and consequence of breaking the nexus between *kṣatriyas* and *brāhmaṇas* as far as conducting sacrifice and other ritual matters were concerned. The rituals, and therefore, the priests, were no more necessary for the salvation. See Thapar, *Cultural Pasts*, 812–821.

[291] Radhakrishnan, *The Principal Upaniṣads*, 49; Selvanayagam, *Vedic Sacrifice*, 102–118.

[292] Kane, *History of Dharmaśāstra*, vol. 5, pt. 2, 918.

[293] Thapar, *Cultural Pasts*, 812. Veda and the performance of sacrifice were accepted in the Upaniṣads as preparatory; cleansing the mind of its lower passions and as making a person worthy of receiving the knowledge of the highest truth. Though their supremacy was denied but not altogether condemned. See Kane, *History of Dharmaśāstra*, vol. 5, pt. 2, 918.

Upaniṣads. Unlike Brāhmaṇa texts, which took 'renounce *karma*' to mean renouncing Vedic rituals, Upaniṣads understood it as renouncing the fruits of actions of all kinds.[294] During this period, the renunciant mode of life (*sannyāsa*) as the excellent disposition for *mokṣa* was given greater importance than that of householder (*gṛhasta*) and the ritual practices.[295]

The above mentioned ideological shift, by which the Vedic sacrificial rituals were subjected to a critique, contributed very much to loosening the rigidity of caste system; the spirit of universalism received acceleration.[296] Though Vedas did not lose its importance and respect altogether, the ritual knowledge of them was considered very much inferior. *Brāhmaṇa* supremacy was not unanimous and was questioned in various ways.[297] Upaniṣads both criticized the old ways of achieving the status of *brāhmaṇa* and also established new ways of becoming a *brāhmaṇa*;[298] the caste status was very much defined on character than by birth and lineage. Sarcastic reference to the greedy behaviour of priests

---

[294] Doniger, *The Hindus*, 186. Some of the non-Vedic traditions, e.g. Buddhism, also had accepted and popularized the meaning of *karma* as it is found in Upaniṣads.

[295] Paul Deussen, *The Philosophy of the Upaniṣads*, trans. A.S. Geden (Edinburgh: T & T Clark, 1908), 67.

[296] Selvanayagam, *Vedic Sacrifice,* 120; Radhakrishnan, *The Principal Upaniṣads*, 51.

[297] Doniger, *The Hindus*, 165; Radhakrishnan, *The Principal Upaniṣads*, 51.

[298] In Vedic texts, *brāhmaṇas* are defined by their participation in ritual, and the status of *brāhmaṇa* is established through family lines. In contrast, Upaniṣads show a number of non-traditional *brāhmaṇas* who earn their status through learning specific teachings and engaging in a different set of practices. See Black, *Priests, Kings, and Women in the Early Upaniṣads*, 16.

at the sacrificial ritual highlighted doubts about the ritual and its main actors (Ch U 1.12; Bṛ U 3.9.10–27; Mu U 1.2.9–13).

Another important feature is that these new ideas were explored often not by *brāhmaṇas* but by *kṣatriyas*. Even the learned among the *brāhmaṇas* are described as going to the *kṣatriyas* for instruction (Ch U 5.11.1; 5.3.7; Bṛ U 6.2.8).[299] Those who discoursed on the doctrine taught it either to their sons or to the selected pupils. Among the teachers included those who are not strictly with Vedic practices—for example, Raikva (Ch U 4.1–3)—and among the disciples included those who are not strictly and traditionally eligible, at least uncertain of caste and lineage like Satyakāma (Ch U 4.4–9) and also women like Maitreyī (Bṛ U 2.4; 4.5) and Gārgī Vācaknavī (Bṛ U 3.6; 3.8), the unmarried.[300] These new teachings, at least in its origin, developed under the patronage of *kṣatriya* kings. Later, *brāhmaṇas* took great interest in it and finally these teachings got incorporated into Vedic corpus, the *brāhmaṇic*

[299] Selvanayagam, *Vedic Sacrifice*, 124. Rāja of Kuru-Pāncāla explains to Śvetaketu that his father Gautama, though learned, is not familiar with all the aspects of the new teaching. Later we find Gautama is initiated into the teaching by Rāja. The Rāja says to the learned *brāhmaṇa* Gautama, "this knowledge has never in the past been vested in any *brāhmaṇa*, but I shall tell it to you (Bṛ U 6.2.8; Ch U 5.3.7). This is striking coming from the Rāja of the Kuru-Pāncāla, an area noted for its learned *brāhmaṇas* and frequently of the best sacrificial rituals (Bṛ U 3.1.1; 3.9.19). See Thapar, *Cultural Pasts,* 86.

[300] Remaining single meant 'not being included in any stages of life (*āśrama*)' and which was not a Vedic social practice. Gārgī is an Upaniṣadic indication for being included in any *āśrama* was not necessary to become a *jñāni*. In the same way the instance of Yājñavalkya, the great man of knowledge, who was a house holder, indicates formal *sannyāsa* as an *āśrama* was not a must for salvific knowledge. These throw some light on the openness of Upaniṣads on the universal soteriology.

texts, with ample references to other earlier Vedic compositions.[301]

3.2.1.2 Story of Jānaśruti and Raikva

The first two *sūtra*s of *Apaśūdrādhikaraṇam* (BS Bh 1.3.34, 35) speak about the case of king Jānaśruti and Raikva which is taken from Ch U 4.1–3. Śaṅkara makes great effort in his commentary to establish that this narrative does not give any indication of *śūdra* having Vedic knowledge.

Jānaśruti was a king with great knowledge[302] and reputed with his charitable works. Once he overheard two flamingos speaking about Raikva as the one who excelled in knowledge and was praise worthy than Jānaśruti. Then the king

---

[301] Deussen, *The Philosophy of the Upaniṣads*, 17–22. The interest of the *brāhmaṇas* in the new teaching which was attributed to the *kṣatriyas* and the inclusion of them in the *brāhmaṇical* texts must probably because:

(1) There must have been dissidents, even among *brāhmaṇas*, seeking alternative philosophies or those curious in exploring new ideas. Those attracted to asceticism might have supported such discussions. See Thapar, *Cultural Pasts*, 813.

(2) The new doctrines must be the natural result of various discussions conducted which must have become convictions of at least some of the *brāhmaṇas*. But for the *brāhmaṇas* to author a doctrine openly questioning the sacrificial ritual would, at this stage, have been an anomaly. At the same time, the doctrines which stimulated philosophical discussions would have required that it be recorded. Therefore, they must have taken the advantage of *kṣatriyas* as the spokespersons of new doctrines. See Thapar, *Cultural Pasts*, 87.

(3) Its inclusion may also partly have been an attempt to stem the heresies of the Buddhists and other sects. When the doctrine was appropriated by the heterodox teachers such as the Buddha, it could be maintained that even the roots of heterodoxy is extended to the Vedic tradition. See Thapar, *Cultural Pasts*, 87.

[302] The fact that he was able to understand the talk of the birds (flamingos) itself shows he was a person of great ability.

sent his attendants to look for Raikva. They found him under a cart scratching his itches. Desiring to acquire knowledge from him Jānaśruti offered six hundred cows, a necklace, and a carriage with mules and requested him, with veneration, for knowledge. But Raikva called him a '*śūdra*' and refused to teach him (Ch U 4.2.3). Then again he came with a thousand cows, a necklace, a carriage with mules, his daughter, and offered the whole village where Raikva stayed and then requested for knowledge. This time he accepted him to teach. Then looking at the face of King's daughter he said,'O *śūdra*, only by this face did you make me speak' (Ch U 4.2.5). Raikva taught him *samvarga vidyā* (meditation on merger).[303]

3.2.1.2.1 Jānaśruti: A Pseudo-*Śūdra*

Raikva, the great teacher, addresses Jānaśruti as *śūdra* and finally admits him to educate. Thus in the *Brahmasūtra Bhāṣya* of Śaṅkara, the opponent's argument is that this Upaniṣadic passage indicates that *śūdra* can acquire knowledge. But Śaṅkara argues against this. His arguments could be exposed as follows:

---

[303] The air (*vāyu*) is indeed the end of all. For when fire goes out, it goes into air. When the sun goes down, it goes into air. When the moon goes down, it goes into air. When water dries up, it goes into air. Air indeed consumes them all. So much is with reference to celestial beings, the *Devas*. Now with reference to the body: breath (*prāṇa*) is indeed the end of all. When a man sleeps, speech goes into breath, so do sight, hearing, and mind. Breath indeed consumes them all. These are the two ends, air among the Devas, breath among the senses (*prāṇa*) (Ch U 4.3.1–4).

1) Even if Jānaśruti is considered to be *śūdra*, he is imparted only with *samvarga vidyā*, which implies that *śūdra* cannot be qualified for all kinds of knowledge.[304]
2) Śaṅkara gives the etymology of the term *śūdra* by which Raikva addressed Jānaśruti. For him, the word is divided into two parts *śuk*, 'grief' and *dra*, 'to rush'; which means 'the one who rushed into grief' or the 'grief rushed onto him'. Since Raikva understood the grief-stricken state of Jānaśruti by his intuitive power he addressed him as *śūdra*.[305] Śaṅkara persuades for accepting this derivative meaning because: (1) conventional meaning is inadmissible because the scriptures prohibit and do not agree with a *śūdra* being qualified for knowledge, and (2) from the narrative it is clear Jānaśruti was struck by grief.
3) Śaṅkara attempts to prove that Jānaśruti was a *kṣatriya*, and therefore, this Upaniṣadic narrative does not prove the case of imparting knowledge to *śūdra*. Ch U 4.3.1–4 elucidates the *samvarga vidyā* which Raikva taught Jānaśruti. The following verses, Ch U 4.3.5–8, as the further explanation on the same, narrates an incident that took place in the life of Śaunaka Kāpeya and Abhipratārin Kākṣaseni.[306] Śaṅkara's argument is that

---

[304] कामं चायं शूद्रशब्दः संवर्गविद्यायामेवैकस्यां शूद्रमधिकुर्यात्, तद्विषयत्वात्, न सर्वासु विद्यासु। (BS Bh 1.3.34) Cf. Śaṅkara, *Brahmasūtra with Śāṅkarabhāṣya*, ed., Ministry of Education, India, 107.

[305] शुचमभिदुद्राव, शुचा वाभिदुद्रुवे, शुचा वा रैक्वमभिदुद्रावेति शूद्रः। (BS Bh 1.3.34) Cf. Śaṅkara, *Brahmasūtra with Śāṅkarabhāṣya*, ed., Ministry of Education, India, 108.

[306] Once while Śaunaka Kāpeya and Abhipratārin Kakṣaseni were being waited on at their meal, a religious student begged of them. They gave him nothing. He said: 'One god—who is he?—swallowed the four great ones, he, the guardian of the world. O Kāpeya, mortals see him not,

Abhipratārin Kākṣaseni is of the line of Citraratha who was a *kṣatriya* king. After proving the *kṣatriyatva* of Abhipratārin, Śaṅkara's reference to the case of Jānaśruti is: "Accordingly, the mention of Jānaśruti along with the Kṣatriya Abhipratārin, in the context of the same kind of knowledge, suggests that the former is a Kṣatriya; for equals are generally found to be mentioned together" (BS Bh 1.3.35 p. 232).

4) For Śaṅkara, the kingship and *kṣatriyatva* of Jānaśruti is evident also from the following points: (a) Jānaśruti possessed great riches which is evident from his offering made to Raikva and (b) like a king he had attendants and dispatches a *kṣāttā* in search of Raikva.

3.2.1.2.2 Jānaśruti and Raikva: Men of Knowledge from the Low Caste

The reasons given by Śaṅkara in favour of the non-*śūdratva* of Jānaśruti are farfetched and do not prove the fact adequately.[307] Kane is of the opinion that this Upaniṣadic

---

O Abhipratārin, though he dwells in many places. He to whom this food belongs, to him it has not been given.' Śaunaka Kāpeya, pondering on that speech, went to the student and said: 'He is the self of the Devas, the creator of all beings. His greatness is said to be great indeed, because, without being eaten, he eats even what is not food. Thus, do we, O Brahmacārin, meditate on that Being.' Then he said: 'Give him food'. They gave him food. Now these five (the eater *Vāyu* (air), and his food, *Agni* (fire), *Aditya* (sun), *Candramas* (moon), *Ap* (water)) and the other five (the eater *Prāṇa* (breath), and his food, speech, sight, hearing, mind) make ten, and that is the *Kṛta* (the highest) caste (representing the ten, the eaters and the food) [or the complete number] (Ch U 4.3.5–8).

[307] Caṭṭampiswāmikal clearly states that the *Brahmasūtra* and its various *bhāṣyas* have misinterpreted Jānaśruti-narrative of the Upaniṣads and have made all attempts to make Jānaśruti a *kṣatriya*. For him, the very fact of their vigorous attempts to prove the non-*śūdratva*

narrative indicates *śūdra* people of great knowledge. His opinion runs as below:

> In ancient times this prohibitions of Veda study was not so absolute and universal as the smṛtis make it. In the Chāndogya Upaniṣad IV.1-2, we have the story of Jānaśruti Pautrāyaṇa and Raikva where the latter addresses Janaśruti as śūdra and imparts to him the samvarga (absorption) *vidyā*. ... It is no doubt true that in the Vedāntasūtra (I.3.34) the word śūdra is explained not as referring to the class, but as meaning that sorrow (*śuc*) arose in Jānaśruti on hearing the contemptuous talk of the flamingos about himself and he was overcome (from *dru*) by that (i.e. śūdra is derived from *śuc* and *dru*). But this farfetched explanation had to be given because of the practice current in the times of the Vedāntasūtras that the śūdra is not entitled to study the Veda.[308]

Taking account of pro-margin concerns of Upaniṣads and their attitude in general on Vedas, rituals and *brāhmaṇa*'s authority, Śaṅkara's argument can find little support. Few points as response to Śaṅkara could be adduced.

1) Śaṅkara points out: 'even if Jānaśruti is considered to be a *śūdra* he is imparted only with *samvarga vidyā* and not the other *vidyās*'. It shows that there is at least one category of knowledge which could be delivered to the *śūdra*s; they are not completely devoid of knowledge. Further, Jānaśruti himself was a man of great knowledge and when he knew about the person having greater knowledge than him he desired that

---

of Jānaśruti itself points to the fact that in the original setting of this narrative, Jānaśruti must possibly be a *śūdra*. See Caṭṭampiswāmikal, *Vedādhikāranirūpaṇam*, 37–53.

[308] Kane, *History of Dharmaśāstra*, vol. 2, pt. 1, 155.

sublime knowledge. The narrative does not give any indication, and it is unlikely that Raikva kept the best part of knowledge for himself and taught a second category to Jānaśruti.

2) Raikva called Jānaśruti a '*śūdra'* for the first time when the offerings made by Jānaśruti was unsatisfactory for him (Ch U 4.2.3).[309] But when Jānaśruti came a second time with better offerings Raikva was happy with them, but even on this occasion he called him '*śūdra*' (Ch U 4.2.5).[310] So, we cannot say the term *śūdra* is used here as a contemptuous term as it is understood to be offensive for the higher caste to be addressed with

---

[309] In his *bhāṣya* on this Upaniṣadic passage, Śaṅkara mentions three reasons for Raikva's first-time *śūdra*-utterance: (1) overwhelmed by sorrow Jānaśruti hurried to Raikva and Raikva knew, through intuition, the grief-srticken state of Jānaśruti; (2) Jānaśruti approached Raikva like a *śūdra* who would try to get knowledge by offering wealth only, but not service; (3) Raikva called him a *śūdra*, out of anger because he had brought insufficient wealth (this third reason Śaṅkara presents not as his own but as 'some others say') (Ch U Bh 4.2.3)

[310] Śaṅkara in his Ch U Bh 4.2.5 downplays the significance of Raikva's second time addressing Jānaśruti as *śūdra*. For Śaṅkara: (शूद्रेति पूर्वोक्तानुकृतिमात्रं न तु कारणान्तरापेक्षया पूर्ववत् । Ch U Bh 4.2.5 Cf. Śaṅkara, *Īśādidaśopaniṣadaḥ,* ed., Ministry of Education, India, 194). "The word *śūdra* is only a repetition of its earlier use, but not having some other view as in the earlier case" Ch U Bh 4.2.5 p. 255. (Direct quotes from Ch U Bh of Śaṅkara (traslation), throughout this dissertation, are given page number followed by 'p.' Page numbers are from: Śaṅkara. *Chāndogya Upaniṣad with the Commentary of Śaṅkarācārya*. Translated by Swami Gambirananda. 1983. Reprint, Kolkata: Advaita Ashrama, 2015).

We should note, among the three reasons Śaṅkara gave in his Ch U Bh 4.2.3 for Raikva's *śūdra*-utterance for the first-time, the first two reasons remain the same even in the second time; only the third gets changed, for he brought more wealth. But still Raikva called Jānaśruti '*śūdra*'.

the term '*śūdra*'. Julius Lipner, the Indologist, brings an observation as:

> In the interest of maintaining an orthodox image, the classical Vedāntin theologians affected to be unhappy with the idea of a Brahmin revealing his Upanishadic secrets to a Śūdra. So, as theologians sometimes do, they resorted to exegetical legerdemain and tried to interpret *śūdra* not literally but metaphorically. But there is no call to do this. It seems clear that Raikva, who addresses Jānaśruti as 'Śūdra' twice, the second time to accede to his request, is speaking matter-of-factly. In India there always have been Śūdra men of importance like Jānaśruti; history even attests to Śūdra rulers and dynasties. So it seems reasonable to conclude from this that, in ancient India, there was flexibility as to the Śūdra's eligibility for instruction in religious knowledge.[311]

3) In the Upaniṣadic period there were *śūdra* rulers and non-Aryan dynasties[312] and therefore, it is likely to have *śūdra* people of importance like Jānaśruti. Having attendants and riches do not categorically prove that a person is *kṣatriya* and not *śūdra* as pointed by Śaṅkara.[313]

---

[311] Lipner, *The Hindus*, 57. Caṭṭampiswāmikal observes, if Jānaśruti was not really a *śūdra*, when Raikva called him a *śūdra*, Jānaśruti would have thought that he was misunderstood and at least tried to point out that he was not a *śūdra*. See Caṭṭampiswāmikal, *Vedādhikāranirūpaṇam*, 37.

[312] Such as Koliyas, Mallas, Vṛijjis, Vṛṣnis, Ābhiras, Malvas, Nanda dynasty, etc. See Thapar, *Early India*, 147–150, 210–212; Lipner, *The Hindus*, 57.

[313] Śaṅkara's *bhāṣya* for this Upaniṣadic passage, Ch U Bh 4.2.3, states "Or, he (Jānaśruti) approached him (Raikva) like a *śūdra* who would try to get knowledge by offering wealth only, but not service" (Ch

4) If the etymologically derived meaning of *śūdra* is to be preferred than the conventional one, this meaning could be retained at least in the same *adhikaraṇam*. The conclusion of the discussion states that 'a *śūdra* is unfit for knowledge through Vedas'. If the word *śūdra* meant not caste by birth, as Śaṅkara's meaning runs, this final conclusion would mean that the 'one who is struck by grief' is not worthy of Vedic knowledge.[314]
5) Śaṅkara's attempt to prove Jānaśruti's *kṣatriyatva* is not very much credible[315] and the two factors on which the argument is based are sufficiently weak: (1) on the *kṣatriyatva* of Citraratha, which is proved using an anonymous scriptural text; (2) on the 'mentioning the names together': the 'mentioning together' of Abhipratārin and Śaunaka and that of Jānaśruti and

U Bh 4.2.3 p. 253–254). This statement indicates, for Śaṅkara, it is possible to have *śūdra* men of wealth and even they tried to acquire knowledge by offering wealth. But here in BS Bh 1.3.34,35 he holds just the opposite.

[314] Caṭṭampiswāmikal observes that there is no Vedic prohibition to instruct Vedic knowledge to the one who comes with desire for knowledge, and therefore, with the consequent sorrow for not having the knowledge. See Caṭṭampiswāmikal, *Vedādhikāranirūpaṇam*, 39.

[315] For Śankara, since Jānaśruti's name is mentioned along with Abhipratārin (who is proved to be a *kṣatriya*) and since the mention is on the occasion of discussing same kind of knowledge, Jānaśruti also must be a *kṣatriya*. Then Śaṅkara goes on proving the *kṣatryatva* of Abhipratārin. Since his name is mentioned with Śaunaka Kāpeya who is a *kṣatirya*, Abhipratārin also must be a *kṣatriya*. Then quoting *Tāṇḍya Brāhmaṇa* 20.12.5, 'The Kāpeyas made Citraratha perform this *Dviratra* sacrifice', he proceeds to prove the *kṣariyatva* of Śaunaka Kāpeya. Since Citraratha and Kāpeyas are mentioned in connection with the sacrifice they muṣt be of same lineage. Next, the proof for *kṣatriyatva* of Citraraha is given and for which he quotes from an anonymous text "from him issued one named Citrarathi who was a *kṣatriya* king."

Abhipratārin is not of same kind. In dealing the *samvarga vidyā*—which is presented as Raikva's advice to Jānaśruti—the Upaniṣad takes a complementary discussion in the context of an incident took place in the life of Abhipratārin and Śaunaka. They are mentioned together as they were together for a meal and the whole incident took place in which both of them were partakers. But this is not the type of connection between Jānaśruti and Abhipratārin.

6) Coming to the case of Raikva, the great teacher, he is unlikely to be a traditional *brāhmaṇa* teacher.[316] Upaniṣadic knowledge, as Romila Thapar observes, "reflected a spectrum of interests, and incorporated what appears to be a folk or subaltern knowledge. This is included, for example, by the inclusion of Raikva as a teacher. He sits under his cart, scratching himself and hardly behaves as would upper caste teachers."[317] This

[316] The attendant of Jānaśruti came back unsuccessful after making a search for Raikva. Then Jānaśruti sends him for a second time with the instruction "go for him where a *brāhmaṇa* should be searched for." Most probably, when he looked for him, for the first time, he must have done it among the traditional teachers. Here Śaṅkara in his *bhāṣya* for the same Upaniṣad explains the word *brāhmaṇa*as 'knowers of *Brahman,*'and gives the example for the places to be looked for as "in solitary places, in the forest, or on the banks of the river" (Ch U Bh 4.1.7 p. 250). Then, for Śaṅkara, the servent found him in a solitary place which is under the cart. Knowers of *Brahman*, whether it be a *brāhmaṇa* or a *kṣatriya* are likely to be found in a solitary place; but not under a cart with itches all over as Raikva is.

[317] Thapar, *Cultural Pasts,* 813–814. Upper caste teachers received the disciples with proper rites. Usually they have residence of their own and they were happy about the gifts offered. Here Raikva is a homeless street dweller, without having expected ritual and non-ritual purity of body, having itches all over, and despises the offer of cows and gold (which the *brāhmaṇas* always liked). See Doniger, *The Hindus*, 183.

could be an indication of Upaniṣadic challenge to the *brāhmaṇic* social order[318] and non-*brāhmaṇa* and subaltern contributions to the Upaniṣadic store of knowledge.[319] To add another point, Raikva is always second named with '*sayugva*' which means 'the one who is with a cart'. Probably he belonged to the caste of *rathakāra*, a chariot maker, and so must be a *śūdra*.[320] Even if with much difficulty Jānaśruti is proved to be a *kṣatriya* with high spiritual achievement, but Raikva's (who is most likely to be a low caste) knowledge is still higher. It trumps Jānaśruti's ace of Vedic generosity.[321]

7) Raikva's dissatisfaction over the offering must have been intended to test the real depth of Jānaśruti's inquisitiveness and the sincerity of his inquiry into higher knowledge for it must not be very common that a *śūdra* king becoming very much desirous of knowledge.[322] When the King was even ready to offer

---

[318] Doniger, *The Hindus*, 21.

[319] Doniger, *The Hindus*, 182. When Doniger makes the opinion that 'nor were *kṣatriyas* the only non-*brāhmiṇas* who contributed new ideas to the Upaniṣads' gives the example, "Raikva the man under the cart." This suggests Raikva was of a low birth, at least neither a *brāhmaṇa* nor a *kṣatriya*.

[320] Uma Chakravarty, "Teacher-Student Concept in the Brāhmaṇas and Upaniṣads," *Annals of Bhandarkar Oriental Institute* 78, no. 1–4 (1997): 220.

[321] Doniger, *The Hindus*, 183.

[322] Caṭṭampiswāmikal makes a significant comment on this. If Raikva wanted to test the authenticity of the desire of Janasruti, 1) he could know it with his intuition as he could realise that this person was coming with sorrow, 2) he could have accepted him, and as per the tradition could keep him as an aspirant and only after knowing his authenticity and maturity for knowledge, he needed to impart

his daughter and village for the sake of knowledge it was a proof for his quest for knowledge.[323] For Jānaśruti—for the Upaniṣads in general—the wisdom of a person was taken into consideration and not his age, caste or social status.[324]

3.2.1.3 Satyakāma Jābāla

BS Bh1.3.37 deals with the case of Satyakāma which is taken from Ch U 4.4–9. Satyakāma, the son of Jabālā, addressed his mother and said: "I wish to become a *brahmacārin* (religious student), mother. Of what family am I?" She said to him: "In my youth when I had to move about much as a servant, I conceived you. I do not know of what family you are. I am Jabālā by name, you are Satyakāma." He went to the great *ācārya* Gautama Haridrumata with his request for knowledge. *Ācārya* asked him "Of what family are you?" He replied: "I do not know teacher" then repeated what his mother told him and added "I am therefore Satyakāma Jābāla." Then the *ācārya* replied him, "Not a non-*brāhmaṇa* would thus speak out. Go and fetch fuel, I shall initiate you. You have not swerved from the truth." He initiated him and imparted with knowledge.

---

knowledge. Therefore, the sending him away was only because he wanted more wealth. See Caṭṭampiswāmikal, *Vedādhikāranirūpaṇam*, 39–40.

[323] Bhat openions, it could be common that some one offering wealth and land for the sake of knowledge; but offering one's own beloved daughter to a philosopher, especially when he did not have even normal good health could be considered as a proof for the thirst and readiness to take up any commitment for the acquisition of knowledge. See Bhat, "Teacher-Pupil Relationship," 175.

[324] Chakravarty, "Teacher-Student Concept in the Brāhmaṇas and Upaniṣads," 220.

3.2.1.3.1 Śaṅkara's Pro-Exclusive Interpretation

Gautama accepted Satyakāma as a pupil with the remark, 'an *a-brāhmaṇa* (non-*brāhmaṇa*) will not speak thus'. Taking cue from Satyakāma narrative of *Chāndogyopaniṣad*, Śaṅkara argues for the ineligibility of *śūdra*s for salvific knowledge as: "When owing to the utterance of truth (by Satyakāma Jābāla), the absence of Śūdrahood had been established, then Gautama proceeded to initiate and instruct (Satyakāma) Jābāla" (BS Bh 1.3.37 p. 233).[325] Śaṅkara's point is that the initiation of Satyakāma cannot be considered as *śruti* vindication of *śūdra*s' eligibility. Non-*śūdratva* of Satyakāma was ascertained before he was accepted. Therefore, *śūdra*s are not qualified for salvific knowledge. [326]

3.2.1.3.2 An Inclusive Response to Satyakāma Narrative

Satyakāma's mother being a service girl and had physical contacts with many irrespective of caste or whose caste she did not know and not knowing who exactly fathered him indicate his low birth or at least doubtful lineage. In spite of a lower and doubtful descendent he was initiated to *brahmacarya* with the traditional rite of initiation and later

---

[325] यत्सत्यवचनेन शूद्रत्वाभावे निर्धारिते जाबालं गौतम उपनेतुमनुशासितुं च .... (BS Bh 1.3.37) Cf. Śaṅkara, *Brahmasūtra with Śāṅkarabhāṣya*, ed., Ministry of Education, India 108.

[326] In his *bhāṣya* for the concerned *sūtra* (Ch U Bh 4.4.2), Śaṅkara interprets the word *pricāriṇī* (servant girl) of the text as *upacāriṇī* with the meaning of services done as a young wife. For Śaṅkara, Jabālā was so immersed in many services in the house of her husband including serving many guests and visitors so that she had no idea even of asking the lineage. It seems to be a farfetched explanation. It is difficult to think, if she had a normally wed husband, that she did not know his lineage and even his name (she had to second name her son with her own).

became an authority on spiritual knowledge and had his disciples initiated in the traditional *brāhmaṇic* rite (Ch U 4.10).[327]

Śaṅkara argues that this Upaniṣadic narrative cannot be taken as a proof for eligibility of *śūdra* for knowledge. But from the perspective of pro-subaltern stance of Upaniṣads certain points could be noted in response to this:

1) This narrative is an indication that caste was not important in getting initiated into Vedic knowledge.[328] It can be argued that Satyakāma was accepted not because the social status of those taught was irrelevant, but because, having spoken the truth, he was recognized as a *brāhmaṇa.*[329] But, his uncertain origin was sufficient to suggest that the question of his being born in an upper caste was not central.[330]
2) The initiation of Satyakāma into Vedic knowledge proves that the caste status was decided very much by character than by birth.[331] The teacher was impressed by the truthfulness of the boy and his utter sincerity in

---

[327] Upakosala Kāmalāyana, who was a *brāhmaṇa,* and whose *brāhmaṇatva* is clear from "he tended his fires for twelve years," became his disciple (Ch U 5.2.3; Bṛ U 4.3.1.12).

[328] Umesh Chandra Sharma, "Satyakāma Jābāla: A Socio-Historical Study," *Annals of Bhandarkar Oriental Institute* 54, no. 1–4 (1973): 198.

[329] S. Ramaswami agrees to this by making mention of Tagore's observation: "Rabindranath Tagore thinks that *Satya-vacana* is the only *Brāhmaṇa-lakṣaṇa* that Gautama looked for and found in Satyakāma." S. Ramaswami, "Satyakāma," *Brahmavidya: The Adyar Library Bulletin* 59 (1995): 120.

[330] Thapar, *Cultural Pasts,* 811; Doniger, *The Hindus,* 184.

[331] Arvind Sharma, *Textual Studies in Hinduism* (New Delhi: Manohar Publications, 1980), 42.

his desire for knowledge.[332] The caste, by way of birth, with its barriers did not come in the way.[333]

3) This narrative could be considered as the Upaniṣadic motive to go beyond sterile orthodoxy.[334] The three important characters in this narrative swim against the *brāhmaṇic* traditional practices. First of all, Satyakāma, who is unlikely to be a traditional *brāhmaṇa,* but possessingthe higher values of truthfulness and desire for knowledge; wanted to learn in a traditional *brāhmaṇic* way. Secondly, Jabālā the mother of Satyakāma. When her son asked about his lineage she was admirably truthful about her nonconforming sexual activity; she can be considered as the real 'truth-lover'. If 'being honest' is the mark of deciding one to be *brāhmaṇa* then such praise should come first to Jabālā. It is most likely that Gautama—and the author of this Upaniṣadic narrative—had the mother in mind when he associated truth-telling with being a *brāhmaṇa*. Thirdly, Gautama the teacher; for him speaking the truth was credential enough to impart Vedic knowledge. He acts in defiance

---

[332] Śaṅkara in his Ch U Bh 4.4.5, interprets "a non-*brāhmaṇa* will not be able to say this clearly in a truthful way, because the *brāhmaṇas* are stairght forward by nature, not others." It would mean that the other upper castes (*kṣatriya* and *vaiśya*) who are considered eligible for Vedic study is liable to be untruthful and it is possible such among them be excluded from Vedic study. *Kṣatriyas* who have played not less role in the formulation of the Upaniṣads (which carries anti-*brāhmaṇic* attitude in general) and an Upaniṣadic narrative which is derogatory of them is a matter not to be accepted without critical reflection.

[333] Bhat, "Teacher-Pupil Relationship," 174; Caṭṭampiswāmikal, *Vedādhikāranirūpaṇam*, 47–48.

[334] Lipner, *The Hindus,* 111.

of custom[335] making it not a serious matter to get ascertained of the genealogical caste status.

4) This narrative indicates the co-existence of unorthodox teachers with traditional, and the Upaniṣadic acceptance of their teachings. After Satyakāma was initiated by Gautama he gave him four hundred lean and weak cows and asked him to tend them (Ch U 4.4.5). After spending a number of years in forest he returned to the teacher's house. The teacher noticed that his student shone like a person who knew *Brahman*. To the questions about from where had he learned about *Brahman*, Satyakāma replied that it was not from humans (Ch.U 4.9.2). The teachers were bull, fire, flamingo, and diver bird (Ch U 4.5–8). These represent non-traditional unorthodox teachers and could symbolize, perhaps, other cultural traditions, observation of natural phenomena, etc.[336] As per the request of the aspirant, Gautama taught him; the same knowledge; nothing was left out (Ch U 4.9.2). The content of the knowledge was same, and the mode of imparting alone differed. This narrative indicates Upaniṣadic acceptance of non-traditional form of education and therefore, it cannot be without its implications of *śūdra* having the salvific knowledge.
5) It is important to note that the narratives such as Satyakāma became part of Upaniṣads, i.e. of *brāhmaṇic* orthodox textual corpus. This could be an indication to the inclusivism and openness of

---

[335] Lipner, *The Hindus,* 111.

[336] Black, *Priests, Kings, and Women in the Early Upaniṣads*, 55.

Upaniṣadic *brāhmaṇism* which undercuts strictness and exclusivism of some of the Dharmasūtras.

3.2.2 The *Mahābhārata* Characters in *Apaśūdrādhikaraṇam*

The epics—the *Mahābhārata* (ca. 300 BCE–300 CE) and the *Rāmāyaṇa* (ca. 200 BCE–200 CE)—are *smṛti* texts, and unlike *śruti* they are human textual tradition which have universal accessibility. These texts include more input from non-*brāhmaṇa* authors and shows better concern for the lower classes. It is possible that they were originally in charge of the care and feeding of these two great Sanskrit poems, which *brāhmaṇas* took over only sometime later.[337] Upaniṣadic renewal of Vedism, rise of Buddhism, *Vaiṣṇavism* and *Śaivism* must have had their influence on these great epics. During this time the sectarian worship of particular deities, personal devotion which included *pūja* (daily as well as occasionally) and pilgrimage began to replace Vedic sacrifice.[338]

Apaśūdrādhikaraṇam mentions two characters from the *Mahābhārata*—Vidura[339] and Dharmavyādha[340]—both of them are taken as a case study to prove the ineligibility of *śūdra* for salvific knowledge.

---

[337] Doniger, *The Hindus*, 218–219.

[338] Doniger, *The Hindus*, 258.

[339] Vidura is a famous character spread throughout the *Mahābhārata*. The birth of Vidura is narrated in *Ādiparva* (the first *parva*) of *Mahābhārata* Chapters 90–101.

[340] The narrative and the great advice of Dharmavyādha is found in *Āraṇyaka parva* (third *parva*), chapters 197–206 of the *Mahābhārata*.

3.2.2.1 Vidura and Dharmavyādha: The *Śūdras* of the Epics

Vidura was a cursed birth given to Dharma, the God of Justice, due to his miscarriage of justice. He did not award sage Maṇḍavya heaven after his death. The sage demanded for the reason. Dharma said, "You stuck blades of grass up the tails of a little butterfly when you were a child, and this is the fruit of that *karma*." Then the sage said, "For a rather small offence you have given me an enormous punishment. Because of that, Dharma, you will be born as a man, in the womb of a *śūdra"* (M Bh 1.101).[341] Therefore Dharma, the God, had to be born on earth as *śūdra* in penalty for wrong dispensation of justice.[342]

---

[341] Once a fisherman caught a fish, found a baby girl in its belly, named her Satyavatī and raised her as his daughter. A sage seduced Satyavatī, and she gave birth to her first son, Vyāsa and abandoned him (M Bh 1.99.1–15). Satyavatī later married king Śāntanu and gave birth to another son, who became king but died childless, leaving two widows, the *kṣatriya* princes Ambika and Ambālika. (M Bh 96.55–59). Satyavatī who did not want the lineage to end, summoned Vyāsa to go to the beds of the two widows in order to father children with his half-brother's widows. Vyāsa was ugly and foul smelling. Since Ambika closed her eyes when she conceived her son, Dṛtarāṣtra, the child was born blind. Ambālika turned pale and conceived Pāndu the pale. When Vyāsa was sent to Ambika a second time, she sent in her place a slave girl (*dāsī*). She gave birth to a healthy son, Vidura, but since his mother was not a *kṣatriya*, he could not become king (M Bh 1.99–100).

[342] Being born as a human is different both from fathering a child (as Dharma fathers Yudhiṣṭira) and from getting incarnated (as Viṣṇu does for Rāma and Kṛṣṇa). When Dharma is born on earth (as Vidura), he ceases to exist in heaven until Vidura dies; that is the nature of curse. Being born as a *śūdra* is a terrible curse, one from which you cannot escape in this life, is an attitude that endorses the extant class system. See Doniger, *The Hindus*, 280.

Dharmavyādha was a *brāhmaṇa* in his previous birth. Mistakenly he happened to shoot an arrow, and caused the death of a sage and in his death pain he cursed him to be born as *śūdra* (M Bh 3.205.21–29). Once a *brāhmaṇa* who heard about the great knowledge of Dharmavyādha reached him for advice and found him to be a butcher, doing his work faithfully.[343] Dharmavyādha welcomed him, took him to his house imparted him with great knowledge of *dharma*. The *brāhmaṇa* was greatly enlightened by Dharmavyādha's advice, which can be summarised as, doing one's own duty pertaining to each one's *varṇa* and *āśrama* is worthy of salvation, and was impressed how honestly and diligently he observed his own *dharma* (M Bh 3.205–216).

3.2.2.2 Vidura and Dharmavyādha: The Pseudo-*Śūdras* of *Apaśūdrādhikaraṇam*

The name Vidura appears twice in *Apaśūdrādhikaraṇam*: BS Bh 1.3.34 and 1.3.38. In 1.3.34 it comes as the part of opponent's arguments for the eligibility of

---

[343] There was a *brāhmaṇa*, named Kauśika who being a *brahmacāri* studied Vedas. One day, he sat under a tree reciting Vedas. A crane defiled his body with its droppings. His angry look killed the bird and it fell down dead (M Bh 3. 197.1–5). Some time later, he went as usual to beg alms and reached in a house. The housewife made him to wait for a long time. She was very much engaged in serving her husband who came tired and hungry. When she came out with alms the *brāhmaṇa* became angry. She said: "Be not angry with me and remember that I kept you waiting only because I was dutifully serving my husband. I am no crane to be killed by a violent thought and your rage can do no harm to the woman who devotes herself to the service of her husband" (M Bh 197.25). From the woman he came to know about Dharmavyādha who could instruct him on *dharma* (M Bh 197).

śūdra for knowledge and shows Vidura, the *śūdra* of the *Mahābhārata* as an example. "And in the *smṛti*s are mentioned Vidura and others as born in the Śūdra caste but endowed with special knowledge. Hence Śūdras have competence for different kinds of knowledge" (BS Bh 1.3.34 p. 230). The second mention of Vidura appears together with that of Darmavyādha in the final portion of the *adhikaraṇam.* Śaṅkara's argument is that the great knowledge of both Vidura and Dharmavyādha is the result of their eligibility and the consequent acquisition of knowledge in their previous birth where they were not *śūdra*s. The argument runs as "but from those to whom knowledge dawns as a result of (good) tendencies acquired in the past lives, as for instance to Vidura, Dharmavyādha, and others, the reaping of the result of the knowledge cannot be withheld, for the result of knowledge is inevitable" (BS Bh 1.3.38 p. 234).

3.2.2.3 Vidura-Dharmavyādha Narratives: Through the Lens of Inclusivism

Both the narratives, from the larger context of the *Mahābhārata,* point to the fact that it is character than biological birth (caste) that matters. For instance, even though being a *brāhmaṇa*, being initiated formally into Vedic study, the *brāhmaṇa* who approached Dharmavyādha did not know what *dharma* is. The epic has portrayed him as inferior to the butcher who observed his duties of the caste, clan and the duties as a householder (M Bh 3.205). Both the narratives show even the high profile *brāhmaṇa* life in the previous birth is fallible and even in the low birth one can live enlightened.

Dharmavyādha's advice makes clear that the traditional Vedic education need not necessarily help one to attain salvific knowledge if one has strayed from *dharma* according to one's *varṇa* and *āśrama*. It is *brāhmaṇa*s' *dharma* to learn Veda; in order to fulfil this *dharma* they have to follow all traditional method pertaining to their *varṇa* and *āśrama*. But for *śūdra*s, Vedic learning is not part of their *dharma*. But this does not curtail *śūdra* from knowledge. He can gain the same knowledge from sources other than Vedas, through the means which are in accordance with his *varṇa* and *āśrama*.[344]

Neither Vidura as God nor Dharmavyādha as *brāhmaṇa* in their previous lives (also in their present birth) were leading a renunciant mode of life (*sannyāsa āśrama*), and still they were eligible for knowledge which bore result in this life. It shows the formal taking up of *sannyāsa āśrama* was not essential to the acquisition of salvific knowledge. If it was considered as necessary, only the three upper class males could attain it for they alone were permitted to enter into *sannyāsa*. If it is not the case, the scope of salvation becomes more open and universal, including the householders (*gṛhasta*).

According to Śaṅkara a realised person is beyond rebirth (BS Bh 4.3.1). But Vidura and Dharmavyādha were liable to be cursed and born again. This would mean that they did not have the self-realizing knowledge in their previous life; but only were disposed to it. If, they became enlightened in this *śūdra*-birth it must be either through Vedas or texts other than

---

[344] In BG Bh 18.44–48 Śaṅkara has argued against the position of Āp Dh S 2.2.2–3 that one should desire rebirth in a higher caste to be saved. He holds the view that being a member of a particular caste does not hinder one's salvation; the self-realising knowledge is possible from any caste. If Vedas are inaccessible to *śūdra*s, and at the same time, if they can have liberation, there must be some other means other than Vedas, which according to Śaṅkara, is *smṛti* texts of Itihāsas and Purāṇas.

Vedas, i.e. *smṛti*. Śaṅkra must be admitting that it must be through the latter. This would suggest the scope of salvation more open.[345]

3.3 *Smṛti* Replacing *Śruti*: Is *Śruti* Necessary for Salvation?

The focus point of *Apaśūdradhikaṇam* is proving the ineligibility of *śūdra* for Vedic study and the impossibility of salvation. But, in the final part of the discussion, *sūtra* 38, Śaṅkara gives a *smṛti* quote[346] and states: 'one should read out to the four castes,' which declares the competence for all the castes for the acquisition of Itihāsas and Purāṇas, but the conclusion stands that a *śūdra* has no right to knowledge through the Vedas (BS Bh 1.3.38). This indicates that *śūdra*s can have *brahmajñāna* by means of Itihāsa-Purāṇas. That is to say, what one can achieve through Vedas, which are *śruti,* is also possible through Itihāsa-Purāṇas which are *smṛti*, i.e. *śruti* can be bypassed with *smṛti*.[347] It is enlightening here to analyse

---

[345] This proves against the position that salvation is possible exclusively through Vedas. If then, prohibition for Vedic study does not impede salvation.

[346] Which is this *smṛti* passage is not conclusive. As Gambirananada points out, most probably it could be from M Bh (See Śaṅkara, *Brahmasūtra Bhāṣya of Śri. Śaṅkarācārya*, trans., Swami Gambhirananda, 234n57). It is likely to be from M Bh 12.328.47–50. If then, this passage is from Śuga's advice to his disciples in which he admonishes them that they were competent to lecture the Vedas unto persons of all orders, keeping *brāhmaṇa* in front. If Śaṅkara is using this passage, it could be that he is trying to bring a synthesis and to limit the inclusivism of the *Mahābhārata*: asserting Vedas are not for *śūdra*s but Itihasas and Purāṇas are for all the *varṇas*.

[347] Kane, *History of Dharmaśāstra*, vol. 5, pt. 2, 921–922; Kane, *History of Dharmaśāstra*, vol. 5, pt. 2, 921n1468; Young, "Śaṅkara on the Salvation of Women and Śūdras," in *Goddesses and Women in the Indic Religious Tradition*, 135–137.

how *Śāṅkaravedānta* conceives the scope of *śruti* and how far it is central as far as *brahmajñāna* is concerned. An enquiry into two factors is significant here: (1) how far the textual and *pramāṇa* nature of *śruti* supports the inclusion, and (2) in the epistemic operation of *śruti* as a *pramāṇa,* is *anubhava* (experience)—which is supportive of inclusion—primary.

3.3.1 *Śruti*: *Pramāṇa* and Text

In the *Advaitic* tradition, the term *śruti* means both *pramāṇa* by which the eternal mysteries are revealed and also those texts in which such truths are embodied. As a *pramāṇa*, *śruti* has epistemic status, and it has to be open to any normal human being who is capable of epistemic operations. As the texts, embodying the eternal truth, Śaṅkara widens the scope of *śruti*—not limiting it with the texts of four Vedas, but—even to include *smṛti* texts. In these respects the quest for *Brahman* through *śruti* becomes all the more open to those who are traditionally considered to be excluded from Vedas. *Śruti* taken in both these senses, make the intention of *Apaśūdrādhikaraṇam* to exclude *śūdra* from salvific knowledge very weak.

3.3.1.1 *Śruti*: The *Pramāṇa*

A *pramāṇa* is "an active and unique cause (*karaṇa*) of the *pramā* or valid knowledge,"[348] and therefore, is the means of valid knowledge. In addition to other *pramāṇa*s—perception, inference, comparison, non-cognition, and postulation—*Śāṅkaravedānta* admits *śabda* or verbal

---

[348] D.M. Datta, *The Six Ways of Knowing: A Critical Study on the Vedanta Theory of Knowledge* (London: George Allen & Unwin, 1932), 27.

testimony as a *pramāṇa*.[349] Generally speaking, *śabda* can be seen as a *pramāṇa* for our knowledge of the empirical world, and of the ultimate reality as well. *Advaita*, however is not primarily concerned with *śabdapramāṇa* as a vehicle of secular knowledge (BS Bh 1.4.14; Bṛ U Bh 3.3.intro.). As a *pramāṇa* of the empirical world, it does not have a sphere which is exclusively its own and which, by nature, it alone is capable of transmitting. The special nature of *śabda* for *Advaita*, therefore, lies in its function as a means of knowledge for ultimate reality.[350] Thus *śabdapramāṇa*, which has its object the ultimate reality, has recourse only to *śruti*, because *śruti* alone, and not any other *pramāṇa*, can reveal the nature of ultimate reality, other *pramāṇas* remain contributing to the attainment of Self realizing knowledge.[351] *Śruti* texts are important because they are the eternally revealed texts and the knowledge of its subject matter i.e. the nature of ultimate reality, cannot be gained by any other means of knowledge (BS Bh 1.1.3). In this capacity *śabdapramāṇa* is synonymous with *śruti*.[352] Thus *śruti* as a *pramāṇa* is the unique means to achieve knowledge about the eternal and ultimate reality through the words that are capable of revealing such reality; it is revelation through words.

Śruti, in its capacity as *pramāṇa* with its all epistemological operations which is capable of providing valid

[349] Datta, *The Six Ways of Knowing*, 19.

[350] Satchidanadendra Sarasvati, *The Method of Vedanta: A Critical Account of the Advaita Tradition*, trans., A.J. Alston (Delhi: Motilal Banarsidas, 1989), 61; De Smet, "Theological Method and Vedānta," in *Understanding Śaṅkara*, 194.

[351] Richard De Smet, "Śaṅkara's Perspective on Meaning and Truth," in *Understanding Śaṅkara*: *Essays by Richard De Smet,* ed. Ivo Coelho (Delhi: Motilal Banarsidas, 2013), 262.

[352] Rambachan, *Accomplishing the Accomplished*, 30.

knowledge, has to be open to any human person who is capable of epistemic activity and should not be excluding anyone on the basis of caste and modes of life.[353]

3.3.1.2 *Śruti*: The Text

Śruti as a *pramāṇa* is the means of acquiring knowledge of eternal realities through the words capable of it. The textual embodiment of these words is also called *śruti*. Considering *śruti* as those texts which are canonical and through which the eternal mysteries are revealed, an enquiry into the scope of *śruti* is significant as far as an enquiry into exclusion from such texts are underway: for *Śāṅkaravedānta*, what are the texts included in serving the purpose of *śruti*.

In his introduction to BS Bh Śaṅkara points out, to acquire the knowledge of the unity of the self, the present study takes up a discussion on "all the Upaniṣads" (BS Bh intro. p. 6).[354] Besides this, the whole text is centred on exposing the *Vedāntic* ideals by proving the unity of Upaniṣadic statements, *Brahman* as their purport. Thus it looks, for Śaṅkara, the scriptures by which *Brahman* can be known are exclusively Upaniṣads. But it is not exactly true.

In BS Bh 1.1.3 Śaṅkara explicitly makes clear that *Brahman* can be known through *śāstra*s.[355] In Śaṅkara's

---

[353] Rambachan, "Rethinking *Advaita*," 9.

[354] अस्यानर्थहेतोः प्रहाणाय आत्मैकत्वविद्याप्रतिपत्तये सर्वे वेदान्ता आरभ्यन्ते । (BS Bh intro.) Cf. Śaṅkara, *Brahmasūtra with Śāṅkarabhāṣya*, ed., Ministry of Education, India, 3.

[355] *Śāstra* is generally interpreted as scriptures. The word *śāstra* is formed out of *śās*, 'to control' with the addition of the suffix *ṣtrun*, 'the means thereof'. Therefore, literally it meant 'the means to control'; derivatively and popularly it means 'knowledge-texts' held as a source of valid knowledge. This word occurs in the first time in ṚV 8.33.16. In

commentary on *śāstrayonitvāt* (BS Bh 1.1.3) the term '*śāstra*' has been explained by him as '*Ṛgveda* and others' (*śāstram ṛgvedādih*). *Bhāṣyakāra* states: "*Brahman* is the *yoni* (the material and efficient cause) of great scriptures (*śāstra*s) like the Ṛg-Veda etc. which are supplemented by other scriptures that are themselves sources (of various kinds) of knowledge, which reveal all things like a lamp, and which are almost omniscient" (BS Bh 1.1.3 p. 18).[356] Here, in the expression 'the *Ṛgveda* and others', 'others' refers, according to his commentator Vācaspati, to the rest of the fourteen *vidyāsthānas*.[357] When Śaṅkara gives an alternative

---

Ch U 7.1.1–5, Nārada seeking spiritual instruction from Sanat Kumāra gives the list of all that he knew. All the disciplines in the list came to be known as *śāstra*. They are eighteen in number and they are: *Śikṣa, Kalpa, Vyākaraṇa, Nirukta, Jyotiṣa, Chandas, Ṛgveda, Yajurveda, Sāmaveda, Atharvaveda, Mīmāṁsā, Nyāya, Dharmaśāstra, Itihasa-Purāṇas* (fifth Veda), *Āyurveda, Dhanurveda, Gāndharvaveda,* and *Arthaśāstra*. The list obviously is inclusive of Vedas and those branches of knowledge that help in their study, as well as those meant for the application of Vedic knowledge to the task of maintaining order in society. See Rao, *Encyclopedia of Hinduism*, s.v. "*Śāstra*." From the Vedic and *brāhmaṇic* point of view *śāstra* includes the texts or scriptures belonging to Vedic tradition.

[356] महत ऋग्वेदादेः शास्त्रस्यानेकविद्यास्थानोपबृंहितस्य प्रदीपवत्सर्वार्थाविद्योतिनः सर्वज्ञकल्पस्य योनिः कारणं ब्रह्म। (BS Bh 1.1.3) Cf. Śaṅkara, *Brahmasūtra with Śāṅkarabhāṣya*, ed., Ministry of Education, India, 7.

[357] Given in: B.N.K. Sharma, *The Brahmasūtras and Their Principal Commentaries: A Critical Exposition*, vol. 1 (Bombay: Bharatiya Vidyabhavan, 1971), 2. See also, Young, "Śaṅkara on the Salvation of Women and Śūdras," in *Goddesses and Women in the Indic Religious Tradition*, 137–138.

Vidyāsthānas are the sources of traditional wisdom. They are fourteen in number. They are: 4 Vedas (*Ṛg, Yajur, Sāma* and *Atharva*), 6 *Vedaṅgas* (*Śikṣa, Vyākaraṇa, Chandas, Nirukta, Jyotiṣa* and *Kalpa*) and 4 *Upavedas* (*Mīmāṁsā, Nyāya, Purāṇa*s and *Dharmaśāstra*s). See Rao, *Encyclopedia of Hinduism*, s.v. "*Vidyāsthāna.*"

explanation to the same *sūtra*, as: "The scriptures, viz the Ṛg-Veda etc., just enumerated are the valid means of knowing [*pramāṇa*] the real nature of this *Brahman*" (BS Bh 1.1.3 p. 19),[358] the same meaning of '*śāstra*' is retained. Vedas—Saṁhitās, Brāhmaṇas, Āraṇyakas and Upaniṣads—alone are not the source of *brahmajñāna* but it also includes other texts of the Vedic tradition.[359]

Śaṅkara's predilection for Upaniṣads as expressed in his *Brahmasūtra Bhāṣya* is not without reasons. BS Bh 1.1.4, "*tattu samanvayāt*" is Śaṅkara's response to the *Pūrvamīmāṁsā* view of excluding Upaniṣads from canonical texts. *Mīmāṁsakas* accepted Saṁhitā and Brāhmaṇa portions of Vedas as canonical. In Ja Mī S 2.1.32–40, when Jaimini enumerates the various parts of Vedas, he mentions only three—*Atharvaveda* is missing—but they are said to consist only of Mantras and Brāhmaṇas. Neither Āraṇyakas nor Upaniṣads, which are generally regarded as the end portions of Vedas, find any mention in these *sūtra*s.[360] BS Bh 1.1.4 places

---

[358] अथवा यथोक्तमृग्वेदादिशास्त्रं योनिः कारणं प्रमाणमस्यब्रह्मणो यथावत्स्वरूपाधिगमे । (BS Bh 1.1.3) Cf. Śaṅkara, *Brahmasūtra with Śāṅkarabhāṣya*, ed., Ministry of Education, India, 7.

[359] This view receives support from Upaniṣads themselves. In Bṛ U 2.4.10, for example, it is said: Just as, when a fire is laid with damp wood, proceeds smoke, spark etc. of various kinds, so behold, is the breathing of this great Being *Ṛgveda*, *Yajurveda*, *Sāmaveda*, the hymns of the *Atharvans* and *Aṅgirāsas*, Itihasas, Purāṇas, the sciences, Upaniṣds, *Ślokas*, *Sūtras*, the explanation of the tenets, the explanation of *mantras*; all these have been breathed forth from him. This means all these sources of knowledge are originated from the same great Being. Śaṅkara being committed to the Upaniṣads is unlikely to abandon this view.

[360] But it is possible to argue in defence of this non-mention of Upaniṣads by saying; it could be the case that they were regarded by Jaimini as parts of Brāhmaṇas themselves. But this cannot be held

this *Mīmāṁsaka* view, expressed in Ja Mī S 1.2.1, in the mouth of the opponent as: "Since the Vedas are meant to enjoin action, those portions of them which have not this purpose in view are useless" (BS Bh 1.1.4 p. 20). This means, for *Pūrvamīmāṁsakas*, Upaniṣads are useless for they do not enjoin actions; cannot be the valid means for liberation, therefore, cannot be titled as *śruti*. Śaṅkara responds to this *Mīmāṁsaka* attitude in BS Bh 1.1.4. It proves *Brahman* can be known from Upaniṣads for It is their import.[361] This is the

---

reasonable because his senior or at least his contemporary Bādarāyaṇa—the other celebrated thinker of those times and the author of *Brahmasūtras*—had chosen to concentrate exclusively on *Upaniṣads*, trying to understand their import in a manner very different from Jaimini's. In this context it is surprising that Jaimini does not make any mention of Upaniṣads. From the point of view of *Mīmāṁsika* ritualism which gave importance for *karmakāṇḍa,* and from the evidences from his *Mīmāṁsāsūtra*s (for example, Ja Mī S 1.2.1), this silence of Jaimini could be understood that *Upaniṣads* were not *śruti* for them. See M.R. Bhavanamma, and Srinivasa Rao, "Were the Vedāntic Texts (*Upaniṣads*) Always Accepted as "*Śruti*" in Classical India?" *Journal of Indian Council of Philosophical Research* 25, no. 3 (July–September 2008): 98.

[361] For the *Pūrvamīmāṁsakas*, Upaniṣads have no independent purpose but are merely an appendage to the main body of injunctive text. Injunctions (*vidhi*) inculcating the performance of acceptable acts and prohibitions (*niṣedha*) on acts opposed to *dharma* alone have direct and independent authority. The utility of the Upaniṣads lies only in praising the prescribed action or in providing some useful information. Injunctions on *dharma* alone is contributive to liberation. But Śaṅkara developed a comprehensive view of the authority of the Vedas in which the special significance of the Upaniṣads could be preserved. See Anantanand Rambachan, "Where Words Can Set Free: The Liberating Potency of Vedic Words in the Hermeneutics of Śaṅkara," in *Texts in Context: Traditional Hermeneutics in South Asia,* ed. Jeffrey R. Timm (Delhi: Sri Satguru Publications, 1997), 33–34. Rambachan argues that Śaṅkara, in his works, establishes that the Upaniṣads are the adequate, logical and fruitful source of knowledge about *Brahman* which will

subject matter of first *adhyāya* and of the entire *Brahmasūtra Bhāṣya*, i.e. the various Upaniṣadic passages can be reconciled through a proper interpretation and can be proved that *Brahman* is their import. Thus in opposition to *Pūrvamīmāṁsā,* as a *Vedāntin,* Śaṅkara's intention—all throughout his *Brahmasūtra Bhāṣya*—is to state that Upaniṣads are capable of revealing *Brahman* and making liberation possible. While *Pūrva* (earlier) *Mīmāṁsā* restricted the application of the term '*śruti*' only to the Mantras and Brāhmaṇas, the *Uttara* (later) *Mīmāṁsā* (*Vedānta*) extends the scope of the term to include Upaniṣads as well.[362] In addition to this, Upaniṣads have expressed that they contain the sublime knowledge which even those who studied Vedas might not achieve (Mu U 1.1.5; Ch U 3.5.4; 5.3–10; 6.1; 7.1; Ta U 2.3) and have vindicated that they are the source of knowledge of *Brahman* (Mu U 2.2.3–4; 1.1.5). Śaṅkara, being a strong holder of *Vedāntic* thinking, must be having a preference for Upaniṣads than other Vedic texts.

This does not mean, for Śaṅkara, the *śāstra*s through which *Brahman* can be known are Upaniṣads alone. In his commentary on BS 3.3.4, '*darśayati ca*', he says "The Vedas

---

provide liberation. See Rambachan, "Where Words Can Set Free," in *Texts in Context*, 33–42.

[362] This becomes obvious from an examination of the way in which the central import of '*śruti*' or Vedas comes to be conceived in the two systems. According to the *Mīmāṁsakas* *śruti*-sentences are to be understood literally and also as either injunctions or as exhortations. From such a point of view it is difficult to regard Upaniṣadic sentences as genuine *śruti*-sentences; for they are not injunctions or exhortations. Besides, Upaniṣads only describe *Brahman* and they also suffer from the additional defect of not describing it literally, i.e. in terms intelligible in ordinary parlance. See Bhavanamma, "Were the Vedāntic Texts (*Upaniṣads*) Always Accepted as "*Śruti*" in Classical India?" 104.

are also show the unity of the knowledge, for in all the Upaniṣads the selfsame entity to be known is taught" (BS Bh 3.3.4 p. 650). In support of this interpretation, Śaṅkara cites two *śruti* texts: (1) that the goal which all the Vedas with one voice proclaim (Ka U 1.2.15); (2) the followers of *Ṛgveda* (i.e. *Hotṛs*) discuss this very one in the context of the great *Ukta* (hymn), the priests of *Yajurveda* (i.e. *Athavāryus*) sacrifice to this one in the fire and *Chaṇdogas* (*Udgātā* priests following *Sāmaveda*) sing to this one in their great vow' (Ai Ār 3.2.3). BS Bh 3.3.4 proves, for Śaṅkara, *Brahman* is the final theme of both Vedas and Upaniṣads and not merely of the latter. Besides this, he makes great use of non-*Upanṣadic* Vedic corpus in his *Brahmasūtra Bhāṣya* to establish his philosophy as it is found in BS Bh 3.3.55–56. Added to this, *Apśūdradhikaraṇam* (BS Bh 1.3.38) testifies the competency of Itihāsas and Purāṇas.[363] But, from the valuational and comparative point of view, his preference for *śruti* (four Vedas, inclusive of Upaniṣads) as primary and efficient than *smṛti*, in matters of *brahmajñāna*, is clear. He states: "Vedas have an independent authority with regard to what they reveal ..., whereas the authority of any human being [*smṛti*] is remote, since it depends on some other source of knowledge and since the memory of the speaker intervenes" (BS Bh 2.1.1 p. 304).[364]

---

[363] Ch U 7.1.4 states that Itihāsa-Purāṇas are the fifth Veda. Śaṅkara, in his *bhāṣya* for this *sūtra*, agrees with the same (Ch U Bh 7.1.4). Kane makes it clear that Ithihāsas and Purāṇas can replace Vedas for the salvation of the *śūdra*s and women are concerned. According to him, Śaṅkarācārya in his BS Bh 1.3.38 asserts the same. See Kane, *History of Dharmaśāstra*, vol. 5, pt. 2, 921–922. See also Kane, *History of Dharmaśāstra*, vol. 5, pt. 2, 921n1468.

[364] वेदस्य हि निरपेक्षं स्वार्थे प्रामाण्यं रवेरिव रूपविषये । पुरुषवचसांतुमूलान्तरापेक्षंवक्तृस्मृतिव्यवाहितंचेतिविप्रकर्षः। (BS Bh 2.1.1) Cf. Śaṅkara,

From the above discussions it is obvious, for Śaṅkara, scriptures (*śāstra*s) belonging to the Vedic tradition, with a preference for Vedas and Upaniṣads, are the means for *brahmajñāna*. When properly interpreted with the help of the principles formulated in the '*samanvayadhyāya*' and elsewhere in the *Brahmasūtra Bhāṣya*, they are competent to give us the correct knowledge of *Brahman*.[365] But, among Vedic corpus he devotes primacy for Upaniṣads as it is clear from the whole of *Brahmasūtra Bhāṣya*. This could be because: (1) As the *Vedāntic* adherent it could be his conviction that among the scriptures through which *Brahman* can be deliberated, the excellent and the most preferred are Upaniṣads; (2) In the background of *Pūrvamīmāṁsaka* rejection, the *bhāṣya* of Śaṅkara must have laid greater emphasis on Upaniṣads for liberation; (3) As the interpreter of *Brahmasūtra*, which itself is Bādarāyaṇa's attempt to systematise the teachings of Upaniṣads, he must have remained doing justice to his duty as interpreter. His predilection for Uapaniṣads does not mean he precludes the other texts in the pursuit of salvation.

3.3.2 The Question of Primacy of *Śruti* or *Anubhava* for *Brahmajñāna*

It is confusing in the study of *Śāṅkaravedānta* whether it is *śruti* or *anubhava*[366] that causes realisation of *Brahman*. If

---

Brahmasūtra with Śāṅkarabhāṣya, ed., Ministry of Education, India, 142.

[365] Sharma, *The Brahmasūtras and Their Principal Commentaries*, vol. 1, 3.

[366] The word *anubhava* literally means 'experience'. From the religious and theological point of view it is the proper goal of religious and meditative/contemplative life; it is direct/immediate experience or

śruti is considered as the only *pramāṇa* through which *Brahman* is known, then what would be the role of *anubhava* in it; or if *anubhava* is the means for knowing *Brahman* what is the role of *śruti*. This debate is very much related to the question whether the salvation is inclusive or exclusive: if *śruti* is the cause for liberation, the access is restricted, and if *anubhava* is the cause, the access is open. Exclusion is from the Vedas (*śruti*) not from *anubhava*. There are different opinions among the scholars on the role of *anubhava*; scholars like Arvind Sharma emphasize on transcendental experience resulting *brahmajñāna*, the liberation; but scholars like Anantanand Rambachan argues, for Śaṅkara, scriptures are the only *pramāṇa* which can reveal the nature of *Brahman* and thus experience cannot be held as another *pramāṇa* over and above the six which *Advaita* tradition has accepted.

3.3.2.1 Can *Anubhava* Be Another *Pramāṇa*?

One of the most revealing passages concerning Śaṅkara's analysis of experience comes in BS Bh 1.1.2. This *sūtra* establishes *Brahman* as the source of the origin and the dissolution of the world. Here Śaṅkara surveys the various means at our disposal for gaining the knowledge of the supreme. While holding *śrutipramāṇa* as the appropriate means, he makes room for inference and reasoning as significant helps in this intellectual process. In this context he states the following:

---

intuition; it is the self-realization which is also termed *avagati*. See Rao, *Encyclopedia of Hinduism*, s.v. "*Anubhava*." See also A.G. Ranade and V.P. Bhatta, eds., *An Ecyclopaedic Dictionary of Sanskrit on Historical Principles*, vol. 6 (Pune: Deccan College Postgraduate and Research Institute, 2003), s.v. "*Anubhava*."

> As far as the delibration on Brahman is concerned, the direct texts, indicatory marks, etc. are not the sole means of the valid knowledge of Brahman, as they are when religious duties are deliberated on. But in this former case, the Vedic texts, personal experience [*anubhava*], etc. are the valid means as far as possible; for the knowledge of Brahman culminates in experience (BS Bh.1.1.2 p. 15–16).[367]

This passage brings clouds on Śaṅkara's position whether *śruti* or *anubhava* is the immediate cause for the knowledge of *Brahman* and the consequent liberation. When he states that the knowledge of *Brahman* culminates in *anubhava*, in which the quest for *Brahman* attains its goal, he seems to oppose those statements where he has asserted that *śruti* is the only means for knowing *Brahman* (BS Bh 1.1.3; 2.1.31).

Those who affirm *anubhava* to be a *pramāṇa*, argue that in BS Bh 1.1.2, Śaṅkara explicitly refers to *anubhava* as a *pramāṇa*; and *anubhava* validates the knowledge received through *śruti* in matters of ultimate reality.[368] *Anubhava* can act

---

367 न धर्मजिज्ञासायामिव श्रुत्यादय एव प्रमाणं ब्रह्मजिज्ञासायाम्। किंतु श्रुत्यादयोऽनुभवादयश्च यथासंभवमिह प्रमाणं, अनुभवावसानत्वाद्भूतवस्तुविषयत्वाच्च ब्रह्मज्ञानस्य । (BS Bh.1.1.2) Cf. Śaṅkara, *Brahmasūtra with Śāṅkarabhāṣya*, ed., Ministry of Education, India, 142.

368 Bina Gupta, *Reason and Experience in Indian Philosophy* (Delhi: Indian Council of Philosophical Research, 2009), 268. This view of the function of *śruti* is shared by S.K. Belvalker, according to him the *Advaitin* found it necessary to appeal to the authority of the *śruti* only because the experience upon which it was founded was beyond the reach of all. Whenever the scriptures are cited, Belvalker claims, it is merely for the purpose of supporting a conclusion "which has been reached independently of the scriptures." Given in: Anantanand Rambachan, "Śaṅkara's Rationale for *Śruti* as the Definitive Source of Brahmajñāna: A Refutation of Some Contemporary Views," *Philosophy East and*

as a *pramāṇa* in the matters pertaining to *Brahman* in a way that it cannot in matters pertaining to *dharma.*[369] And again it is argued, for Śaṅkara, *śruti* is a valid means of knowledge about *Brahman* in the practical (*vyāvahārika*) world, and *anubhava* is a means of valid absolute (*pāramārthika*) knowledge. Because knowledge through *śruti* implies duality of knower and the known, but *anubhava* does not.[370]

Those who affirm *śruti* and deny the *pramāṇa* status for *anubhava* show that, for Śaṅkara, *śruti* is the sole valid source of knowledge for *Brahman*; it is not only the logical source, but also an adequate and fruitful source leading to *mokṣa*.[371] His commentary on BS 1.1.2 must be read along with the commentary on BS 1.1.3, where he clearly states that *śruti* is the only *pramāṇa* for *brahmajñāna*.[372] In BS Bh.1.1.2 he uses *anubhava* in a wide sense "to include any experience which can be analyzed to support and reinforce Vedic revelations of *śruti*."[373] According to Rambachan:

> He [Śaṅkara] is unwavering in his position that *brahman* is knowable, and that *śruti* is the valid means. It is not possible, according to Śaṅkara, even to guess about

---

West: A Quarterly of Asian and Comparative Thought 36, no.1 (January 1986): 25.

369 Arvind Sharma, "Is *Anubhava* a *Pramāṇa* According to Śaṅkara?" *Philosophy East and West: A Quarterly of Asian and Comparative Thought* 42, no. 3 (July 1992): 521.

370 Sharma, "Is *Anubhava* a *Pramāṇa* According to Śaṅkara?" 522.

371 Rambachan, "Śaṅkara's Rationale for *Śruti* as the Definitive Source of Brahmajñāna," 25–40; Rambachan, *Accomplishing the Accomplished*, 123.

372 अथवा यथोक्तमृग्वेदादिशास्त्रं योनिः कारणं प्रमाणमस्य ब्रह्मणो यथावत्स्वरूपाधिगमे । (BS Bh 1.1.3) Cf. Śaṅkara, *Brahmasūtra with Śāṅkarabhāṣya*, ed., Ministry of Education, India, 7.

373 Rambachan, *Accomplishing the Accomplished*, 114.

> *brahman* without the assistance of *śruti*. He leaves no room for any doubt about this conclusion. *Brahma-sūtra* 1.1.2, for instance, reads, "That (is *Brahman*) from which (are derived) the birth, etc., of this (universe)." The following *sūtra* (1.1.3) reads, "...because of being the source of scriptures."[374]

If one considers *anubhava* as another *pramāṇa* it raises various problems in *Śāṅkarite* epistemology. Since any *pramāṇa* is an active and unique cause of *pramā* or the valid knowledge, if *anubhava* is considered another *pramāṇa* validating *śruti*, it undermines the theory of intrinsic validity of knowledge which Śaṅkara holds. For him any knowledge is valid in itself unless it is contradicted by subsequent knowledge.[375] If *anubhava* is placed as the *pramāṇa* which validates *śruti*, then it needs another *pramāṇa* to validate its knowledge and the chain will go to the infinity. It would mean valid knowledge is impossible and it is amount to say that the liberation is not possible.[376] If *anubhava* is the proper *pramāṇa* for the knowledge of *Brahman*, then *śruti* cannot be considered as a *pramāṇa*, for any *pramāṇa* has its own unique area of knowledge which other *pramāṇās* cannot reach, but can only contributively assist.[377] Every *pramāṇa* makes known only what is not an object of another *pramāṇa*.[378] If *anubhava* and

---

[374] Rambachan, "Śaṅkara's Rationale for *Śruti* as the Definitive Source of Brahmajñāna," 29.

[375] N.K. Devaraja, *An Introduction to Śaṅkara's Theory of Knowledge* (Delhi: Motilal Banarsidas, 1962), 119.

[376] Rambachan, *Accomplishing the Accomplished*, 22.

[377] Rambachan, *Accomplishing the Accomplished*, 17.

[378] Devaraja, *An Introduction to Śaṅkara's Theory of Knowledge*, 59.

śruti have the same area and object of knowledge which is *Brahman*, either of them ceases to be *pramāṇa*.

Knowledge through any *pramāṇa*, in its final phase culminates in '*anubhava,*' i.e. there is revelation of their particular objects. *Śruti*, in its role as a *pramāṇa*, while revealing the knowledge, culminates in *anubhava*. Since the object of *śruti* is supreme, the consequent *anubhava* also is supreme. Śaṅkara has expressed this variously: knowledge of *Brahman* 'culminates', literally 'ends', in *anubhava* (BS Bh 1.1.2); The direct object of the desire (which animates *brahmajijñāsā*) is a knowledge culminating in full apprehension (*avagatiparyantam jñānam*) (BS Bh 1.1.1); that knowledge which discriminates *Brahman* and discards nescience, terminates in intuition (*anubhavāvasānam*) (BS Bh 2.1.4). If *pramāṇa*s culminate in *anubhava*, it cannot be the case that *anubhava* itself is another *pramāṇa*.[379] In the case of *śruti*, it leads to *anubhava*—immediate knowledge—of the identity of *Ātman* and *Brahman*; and this *anubhava* itself cannot be another *pramāṇa*. There is no indication that Śaṅkara ever held the view that there is a supreme *pramāṇa* or means of knowing called "*anubhava.*" *Brahmānubhava* or the experience of the *Brahman* is not, according to Śaṅkara, another *pramāṇa* besides the six, which *Advaitins* accept.[380] *Brahman* can be known only through scripture, and through no other *pramāṇa*.[381]

---

[379] K.N. Upadhyaya, "Śaṇkara on Reason, Scriptural Authority and Self-knowledge," *Journal of Indian Philosophy* 19, no. 2 (June 1991): 130.

[380] Gupta, *Reason and Experience in Indian Philosophy*, 278.

[381] Devaraja, *An Introduction to Sankara's Theory of Knowledge*, 68.

Anubhava is the non-dual direct experience of *Brahman*, which is liberation itself.[382] *Brahmānubhava*, the liberating *jñāna*, is not a *pramāṇa* but it is beyond the distinction of *pramāṇa* and *prameya*[383] (*prameya* is 'knowables' i.e. the object of knowledge). *Brahman* of Śaṅkara, while it transcends the *pramāṇa*s, does not transcend the experience itself.[384] Śaṅkara's understanding of *anubhava* of the Self is in keeping with his fundamental position that the Self is pure awareness and self-luminous. He says that the nature of *Brahman* and *Ātman* is experience itself (*anubhavātmaka, anubhavātman*) (BS Bh 4.1.2; Upad 1.18.104; 1.18.205, 206). The Self, as pure awareness is not 'an experience' but 'is experience', for its nature is *anubhava.*[385] That is to say, this *anubhava* is not a *pramāṇa*, an instrumental to produce another realization; rather this *anubhava* is the *jñāna* and is the self-realization. Thus it is not surprising that this immediate knowledge in *Advaita* literature is called '*śabdajanyāparokṣa jñāna*', meaning thereby that 'immediate knowledge which can arise through *śrutipramāṇa*'.[386]

---

[382] Kim Skoog, "Śaṁkara on the Role of *Śruti* and *Anubhava* in Attaining *Brahmajñāna*," *Philosophy East and West: A Quarterly of Asian and Comparative Thought* 39, no. 1 (January 1989): 71.

[383] Upadhyaya, "Śaṇkara on Reason, Scriptural Authority and Self-knowledge,"130; Gupta, *Reason and Experience in Indian Philosophy*, 278.

[384] Devaraja, *An Introduction to Śaṅkara's Theory of Knowledge*, 70.

[385] Comans, *The Method of Early Advaita Vedānta*, 306–309.

[386] Gupta, *Reason and Experience in Indian Philosophy*, 141.

3.3.2.2 Can *Anubhava* be Independent of *Śruti*?

Brahmajijñāsā, which necessarily involves *śravaṇa-manana-nididhyāsana* treatment of *śruti* by the qualified aspirant, culminates in *anubhava*. It is not that scriptures remotely make the stage ready for *anubhava*. For Śaṅkara, the statements of the scriptures which can reveal the nature of *Brahman*, the *Ātman-Brahman* identity, have the potency to directly liberate the hearer, provided the hearer is sufficiently qualified; to be able to sift the meaning of the words and grasp their true import as they are heard (BS Bh 4.1.2).[387] This is so because the reality which is being revealed by the *śruti* is immediate; it is the Self, the Awareness which is self-revealing (BS Bh 1.3.22; 2.3.7; Bṛ U Bh 4.3.6; 4.3.23; Upad 1.18.104).[388] "Since knowledge [of the supreme Self] produces an immediately felt direct result, there can be no fear of non-acquisition of it," (BS Bh 3.3.32 p. 705) i.e. there is no need to doubt the lack of a result. In the case of the results of *karma*, like heaven etc., which are not met within experience, there can be a doubt as to whether that result will occur or not. But the

---

[387] Comans, *The Method of Early Advaita Vedānta*, 302. While discussing on the utility of repeated instruction, Śaṅkara makes provision for those who are able to be enlightened from even a single hearing of the *mahāvākya* '*tattvamasi*'. He says: repetition would be useless to one who is able to experience that the Self is *Brahman* on being told just once: "you are that". But repetition is certainly of use to him who is unable to do so (BS Bh 4.1.2). A little later he says: Those whose minds are cute, for whom the meaning of the words is not obstructed by either ignorance, doubt, or misunderstanding, are able to experience the meaning of the statement "*tattvamasi*" even when it is uttered once (BS Bh 4.1.2).

[388] Comans, *The Method of Early Advaita Vedānta,* 302–303.

result of knowledge is present to experience.[389] Upaniṣads vindicate this when they point out *Brahman* as direct and immediate (Bṛ U 3.4.1), and as they state "you are that (*tattvamasi*)" (Ch U 6.8.7) which teaches that *Brahman* is something already accomplished. This statement cannot be interpreted to mean you will become 'That', after you are dead (BS Bh 3.3.32).[390] BS Bh of Śaṅkara shows that the result of knowledge as "present to experience" (अनुभवारूढः, *anubhavārūḍha*), and as something that is "directly felt" (प्रत्यक्षीकृत, *pratyakṣīkṛta*) (BS Bh 3.3.32; 3.4.15).

Brahmajijñāsā which culminates in *anubhava* is not completely without the aid of reason. Śaṅkara legitimises the use of reason that is in keeping with the tenor of the '*śruti*'—especially in the process of *śravaṇa-manana-nididhyāsana*—and limits the scope of reason when he says that such reasoning can be accepted, as it is "a help to *anubhava*" (*anubhavagatvena*) (BS Bh 2.1.6). At the same time, any kind of reasoning independent of *śruti* will not provide the desired *anubhava* (BS Bh 2.1.11).

It is not the case that *śruti pramāṇa*—in which *śravaṇa-manana-nididhyāsana* is integral and which is not without the aid of reason—only remotely prepare and adequately culture the qualified aspirant, but fruitfully effect the self-realising *anubhava*. But at the same time, the genesis of *brahmānubhva*—the self-realizing intuition—cannot be causally depending on *śruti* and its operations even if it is undertaken by adequately qualified person with its proper

---

389 प्रत्यक्षफलत्वाच्च ज्ञानस्य फलविरहाशंकानुपपत्तिः । .... अनुभवारूढं तु ज्ञानफलम् 'यत्साक्षादपरोक्षाद्ब्रह्म' इति श्रुतेः । (BS Bh 3.3.32) Cf. Śaṅkara, *Brahmasūtra with Śāṅkarabhāṣya*, ed., Ministry of Education, India, 336.

390 Comans, *The Method of Early Advaita Vedānta,* 309.

measures.[391] The *anubhava* which Śaṅkara is speaking is the self-realizing intuition or insight of oneself as pure Awareness. It cannot be something which is 'produced' that did not previously exist, nor can it be an experience involving the objectification of Awareness. It is rather the experience of oneself as Awareness (BS Bh 4.1.2).[392] Through the process of *brahmajijñāsā* one does not 'achieve' the liberating reality, for Reality, being ever present to us, is not to be accomplished; truth cannot be created by research. The sole fruit of the knowledge is the removal of the obstacles opposed to this intuition.[393] The aim of the *pramāṇa*s is to dispel the ignorance, the removal of the appearance of the not-self on the self and vice-versa.[394] Though *brahmajijñāsā* cannot 'produce' that intuition, yet, when it is completely sincere and animated by pure love for its end, it is the most proximate disposition towards it, and the most worthy pursuit to which a person can devote himself.[395] Therefore, the self-realising *anubhava* cannot be considered as causally depending on *śruti* with all its operations, namely, *brahmajijñāsā*; but *śruti*—and it alone—

---

[391] Brahman transcends all direct definitions and explanations and the categories of being and non-being (Ta U Bh 2.9.1; BG Bh 13.12). Therefore, the words of the text do not reveal the intrinsic nature of *Brahman*. See Rambachan, *The Advaita Worldview*, 64.

[392] Comans, *The Method of Early Advaita Vedānta,* 310.

[393] De Smet, "Language and Knowledge of the Absolute According to Śaṅkara," in *Understanding Śaṅkara*, 47, 69; Devaraja, *An Introduction to Śaṅkara's Theory of Knowledge*, 69. "Liberation is discovering and owning oneself to be what one already is: self-existent, limitless awareness." Rambachan, *The Advaita Worldview*, 45.

[394] Devaraja, *An Introduction to Śaṅkara's Theory of Knowledge*, 210.

[395] De Smet, "Theological Method and Vedānta," in *Understanding Śaṅkara*, 103.

is the most adequate, sure and excellent means in disposing the aspirant reaching that experience.[396]

3.3.2.3 Necessity of *Śruti* for *Brahmānubhava*: Viewed Through the Optic of Inclusivism

In the light of the above discussions, Śaṅkara's understanding of *śruti*, its scope and role in *brahmajijñāsā* and the nature of *anubhava* in relation to *śrutipramāṇa,* could be subjected to an inclusive critique. It is obvious that Śaṅkara affirms *jñāna mārga*—through *śravaṇa*, *manana* and *nididhyāsana* of scriptures—for liberation.[397] *Śruti* alone can become adequately potent in making *brahmānubhava* possible for an aspirant who is qualified with prerequisites.

For Śaṅkara, *anubhava* is the culmination of *brahmajijñāsā*. If *śruti pramāna* did not reach the final culmination, one has to repeat it until one achieves. In this sense *anubhava* gets primacy than *śruti pramāna*. This final experience cannot be said to be strictly caused by *śruti*. But, for Śaṅkara, it is his conviction that the *śruti pramāna* will excellently and surely dispose the aspirant, and will not go without fruition, i.e. self-realising experience. For him, after

---

[396] De Smet, "Language and Knowledge of the Absolute According to Śaṅkara," in *Understanding Śaṅkara*, 70.

[397] अत्र 'पिताऽपिता भवति' इत्युपक्रम्य 'वेदा अवेदाः' इति वचनात् इष्यत एवास्माभिः श्रुतेरप्यभावः प्रबोधे । (BS Bh 4.1.3) Cf. Śaṅkara, *Brahmasūtra with Śāṅkarabhāṣya*, ed., Ministry of Education, India, 388.

Bhakti and *karma* finally result in *jñāna*, i.e. the realization of *Brahman-Ātman* identity. BS Bh 4.1.18 says rites like *agnihotra*, performed with or without meditations in this or prior life, are efficacious for *Brahman*-realization if done with liberation as the aim. Activities like rites destroy sins acquired. Rites and actions (*karma*) and devotion are therefore, disposes one for liberation.

the self-realising experience, in the state of enlightenment, the person is beyond *śruti*: "For according to the texts starting with, "In this state the father is no father" and ending with "The Vedas are no Vedas" (Bṛ U IV. iii. p. 22), we do admit the absence of the Vedas themselves in the state of enlightenment" (BS Bh 4.1.3 p. 821).[398] From this point of view—though it is not proper to say *brahmānubhva* has 'means' through which one can 'achieve' it—we can say, compared to *anubhava,* which is the culmination (and thus goal), *śruti* is means. On dealing with this same topic Katherine K Young makes an observation: "After all Śaṅkara's basic position is aphoristically stated to be that liberation cannot be attained without *jñāna*, not that it can't be attained without *śruti*."[399]

The discussion on whether *śruti* is the necessary and the only means for *brahmajñāna,* can be summarised as follows: (1) *Śruti*, in its capacity as *pramāṇa* with its epistemic operations, has to be open to any intelligent person; (2) Experience (*anubhava*) which is the culmination of *śrutipramāṇa* and which is independent of *śruti* keeps the possibility of *brahmajñāna* open, because exclusion, as it is claimed, is from *śruti* not from *anubhava*; (3) *Śruti,* as the embodiment of salvific knowledge, is not demarcated with the four Vedas alone. *Śāstra*, the source of knowledge of *Brahman* has an extended scope than the texts of four Vedas. For Śaṅkara, *śūdra*s may be excluded from Vedas but not from salvific knowledge.

[398] This same idea is also expressed in his BG Bh. Scriptures are "purposeful in the sphere of ignorance" and "not in the case of the enlightened one" (BG Bh 13.2 p. 504, 506).

[399] Young, "Śaṅkara on the Salvation of Women and Śūdras," in *Goddesses and Women in the Indic Religious Tradition*, 156.

3.4 *Sannyāsa* as Sine Qua Non for *Brahmajijñāsā*

Sannyāsa, if considered as a strict prerequisite for *brahmajijñāsā,* excludes householders (*gṛhastāśrami*) and those who are not included in any stages of life (*āśrama*s) such as widower, from the quest for *Brahman.* Since taking up of *sannyāsa* pre-supposes Vedic study, it excludes also *śūdra*s and women from *brahmajijñāsā.*[400] Śaṅkara demands *sannyāsa* as a prerequisite (BS Bh 3.4.17; 3.4.20; Upad 2.1.2; BG Bh 2.69; 3.3).

But in *Apaśūdrādhikaraṇam* 38, Śaṅkara points out, from those to whom knowledge dawns as a result of (good) tendencies acquired in the past lives (*pūrva-kṛta-saṁskāra*), i.e. due to the *saṁskāra*s[401] of what is done (the good works) early (in the previous birth)—as for instance, to Vidura and Dharamavyādha—the reaping of the result of knowledge cannot be withheld, for the result of knowledge is inevitable. Vidura and Dharmavyādha in their previous birth were not those who had accepted the *sannyāsa* mode of life. Being non-*sannyāsin*s they could become eligible for *brahmajñāna* and they have it even in this *śūdra*-birth where they did not and could not take up the *āśrama* of *sannyāsa.* So, BS Bh 3.4.38 underlines the connection between deeds (*karma*s) and knowledge. At this point of controversy it is important to note

---

[400] The one who has completed the initial study of Vedas were only permitted to adopt *sannyāsa* mode of living. To get initiated to the Vedic study the investiture of the sacred thread was a must. For this the aspirant must be a male member from any of the three upper castes—*brāhmaṇa, kṣatriya* and *vaiśya.*

[401] *Saṁskāra* here means impression of the past deeds. According to the *karma* theory one is born with a vast store of *saṁskāras*, i.e. impressions or traces of past deeds or experiences, gathered over past lives. See Rao, *Encyclopedia of Hinduism*, s.v. "*Saṁskāra.*"

how Śaṅkara understood *sannyāsa* when he placed it as a prerequisite for *brahmajijñāsā*.

3.4.1 Formal and Informal Renunciation

According to the *āśrama* theory, those who have completed their Vedic studies (*brahmacarya*) could select an *āśrama*: householder (*gṛhasta*) or forest dweller (*vānaprastha*) or renunciant (*sannyāsa*). Vedic study was not only permitted but obligatory for all twice-born upper caste males i.e., *brāhmaṇa*, *kṣatriya* and *vaiśya*. Renunciation was open to all twice-born men, but not compulsory.[402] Their renunciation is considered legitimate and formal which included the 'rite of renunciation'.[403]

A person has to undergo the rite of initiation and complete Vedic study before renouncing. Now, *śūdra*s are not entitled to be initiated or taught Vedas, and therefore, they were not permitted to take up renunciation. However, it is equally certain that *śūdra*s did renounce.[404] Their renunciation was

[402] Patrick Olivelle, *Ascetics and Brahmins: Studies in Ideologies and Institutions*, Cultural, Historical and Textual Studies of Religions (Delhi: Anthem Press India, 2012), 276.

[403] The one who accepts formal *sannyāsa* had to perform the rite of renunciation. This includes abandonment of fire and rituals and saying '*pariśa*'. *Pariśa* is a technical term for the formula: '*sannyāstam maya*' (I have renounced). It is recited three times, first softly, then in a medium voice, and finally aloud. This is considered as the essential act of the rite whereby one actually becomes a renouncer. See Olivelle, *Ascetics and Brahmins*, 208.

[404] Generally, the *smṛti* texts assert a *śūdra* could not become a *sannyāsin*. But there are clear indications that *śūdra*s did assume even in the times of ancient *smṛtis* the ascetic's garb and mode of life. When the Mahābhārata, in Āśramavāsika Parva 26.33, states that Vidura was buried as an ascetic, the commentator Nilakanda remarks that this

considered to be illegitimate and informal. Ollivelle makes the point clear:

> Both Viṣṇu and Yātnavalkya [Dharmaśāstrās] levy a fine of one hundred *paṇās* [money, currency] on a person who feeds a *śūdra* renouncer at a feast in honour of the Gods or manes. ....there is however a tendency in the Dharamśāstrās to group together *śūdra* and heretical renouncers because their position is similar vis-à-vis the *śāstric* provisions. ....it was thus possible to renounce outside the *śastric* prescriptions, and the evidence points to the fact that many *śūdras* did so.[405]

That is to say, there were *śūdra* renouncers, their renouncing was not formal but informal. Their renunciation was tolerated, although it went against the *śāstra*s.

3.4.2 Physical and Mental Renunciation

The primary meaning of the term *sannyāsa*, the most common word for the renunciation, is the 'abandonment of rites'—the rites one performs during *brahmacarya* and *gṛhastāśrama*, with a motive of 'this worldly' goals such as wealth, son, etc., or the 'other worldly' such as attainment of heaven.[406] In the *brahmāṇical* literature, especially of non-Upaniṣadic, the word '*karma*' (action) primarily stands for these rituals and sacrifices[407] and abandoning of these rites is *karmasannyāsa*. The word *karma* also means everything that is prescribed by the scriptures for those who pursue a socially

---

indicates that even *śūdra*s can follow the mode of ascetic life. Given in: Kane, *History of Dharmaśāstra*, vol. 2, pt. 2, 945.

[405] Olivelle, *Ascetics and Brahmins*, 278.

[406] Olivelle, *Ascetics and Brahmins*, 52.

[407] Olivelle, *Ascetics and Brahmins*, 52.

active life, usually centred on family ties and obligations.[408] Thus *karmasannyāsa* includes abandonment of possessions, cessation of rites and duties prescribed for that person. It is also known as physical renunciation which is applicable, in its complete sense, to the formal renouncer;[409] not to the informal renouncer, for this person has no rites and sacrifice to renounce.

Mental renunciation or inner renunciation means renouncing the rewards of action in which there is total absence of self-interest in any action undertaken.[410] This inner renunciation also includes abandonment of incorrect apprehensions about self, i.e., any knowledge of the self which does not hold the self to be pure non-dual consciousness free from action and its results.[411] This implies the removal of superimposition on self, such as self as body, mind, etc. Mental renunciation grows to the higher level when one achieves the renunciation of the 'doer-ship' (BS Bh intro.). This would mean that one becomes permanently devoid of the sense of being a doer and naturally experiences his/her self as the infinite, action-less and free witness (*sākṣin*) of all mental and bodily activities.[412] This is, for Śaṅkara, the state of *brahmasaṁstha*, 'established in *Brahman* or steadfast in *Brahman*'. Both formal and informal *sannyāsi* can achieve this inner renunciation, i.e. it is possible irrespective of *āśrama*s (BS Bh 3.4.20).

The physical or formal *sannyāsa,* which includes formal Vedic study, entering into *sannyāsa āśrama* with the

---

408 Marcaurelle, *Freedom Through Inner Renunciation*, 30.

409 Marcaurelle, *Freedom Through Inner Renunciation*, 16.

410 Marcaurelle, *Freedom Through Inner Renunciation*, 17.

411 Marcaurelle, *Freedom Through Inner Renunciation*, 18.

412 Olivelle, *Ascetics and Brahmins,* 19.

rite of renunciation, and following the outward signs; carrying a staff and the like, could be adopted only by upper caste men. But the informal and mental renunciation, renouncing the 'doer-ship,' is open to all including women and *śūdra*s.[413]

3.4.3 *Sannyāsa*: Mark and Means of Enlightenment

Śaṅkara states in his BG Bh as follows: "For in all the scriptures without exception, dealing with spirituality, whatever are the characteristics of the man of realization are themselves presented as the disciplines for an aspirant, because these (characteristics) are the result of effort. And those that are the disciplines requiring effort, they become the characteristics (of the man of realization)" (BG Bh 2.54–55 p. 102).[414] This passage taken in the background of *sannyāsa* reveals that *sannyāsa* may be said to be of two classes: (1) to be the 'means' of true knowledge which every seeker aims at, and (2) to be the 'mark' of the person who has already had the vision of Truth and has become the enlightened even while living.[415] Śaṅkara expresses this same idea in Bṛ U Bh 4.5.15

---

[413] Kane, *History of Dharmaśāstra*, vol. 2, pt. 2, 946. Women and *śūdra*s are considered as of the same category of those 'born of sin' or those of evil womb or bad birth (*pāpayonayah*) and are debarred from Vedic study (BG Bh 9.32) See Young, "Śaṅkara on the Salvation of Women and Śūdras," in *Goddesses and Women in the Indic Religious Tradition*, 134, 140–141, 158.

[414] यो हि आदितः एव संन्यस्य कर्माणि ज्ञानयोगनिष्ठायां प्रवृत्तः, यश्च कर्मयोगेन, तयोः 'प्रजहाति' इति आरभ्य आ अध्यायपरिसमाप्तेः स्थितप्रज्ञलक्षणं साधनं च उपदिश्यते। सर्वत्रैव हि अध्यात्मशास्त्रे कृतार्थलक्षणानि यानि तान्येव साधनानि उपदिश्यन्ते, यत्नसाध्यत्वात्।यानियत्नसाध्यानिसाधनानिलक्षणानिचभवन्ति .... (BG Bh 2.54) Cf. Śaṅkara, *The Bhagavad-gītā with the Commentary of Śrī Śaṅkarācārya*, ed., Dinakar Vishnu Gokhale, 2nd Rev. ed. (Poona: Oriental Book Agency, 1950), 36.

[415] Kapil N. Tiwari, *Dimensions of Renunciation in Advaita Vedānta* (Delhi: Motilal Banarsidas, 1977), 26.

and BG Bh 2.55–72. The values that the seeker-after-liberation tries to achieve is means for liberation, in this sense *sannyāsa* is 'means' for the aspirants who try to live a perfect *sannyāsa* and it becomes a spontaneous nature or characteristic 'mark' for them once they attain the enlightenment.[416] Thus the real *sannyāsa* in its perfect form can be a spontaneous outcome of an enlightened (Bṛ U Bh 4.4.22–23; Ai U Bh intro.). If *sannyāsa* is a spontaneous, defining mark or characteristic of the liberated sage, then it has to be cultivated by the seeker-after-liberation.[417]

3.4.4 Mental Renunciation as Necessary for *Brahmajijñāsā*

The very essential dimension of renunciation, for Śaṅkara, is not physical but inner (BS Bh 4.1.2; BG Bh 18.2; Upad 1.17.49; 2.1.32). Even if physical renunciation is successfully adopted but fails in mental renunciation, the aspirant cannot achieve liberation.[418] Physical renunciation in its fullest sense—renouncing of rites and sacrificial fire and sacred thread, etc.—is possible only in the case of formal renunciation. Śaṅkara's preference for mental renunciation than physical is reasonable from his teachings.

---

[416] Rambachan, *The Advaita Worldview*, 20–21.

[417] Reid B. Locklin, "Integral *Samnyasa*? *Adi Shankaracharya and Liberation Hermeneutics*," *Journal of Hindu-Christian Studies* 20 (2007): 47. For the seeker, the renunciation is recommended because it is efficacious for bringing forth self-knowledge. See Young, "Śaṅkara on the Salvation of Women and Śūdras," in *Goddesses and Women in the Indic Religious Tradition*, 152.

[418] Marcaurelle, *Freedom Through Inner Renunciation,* 137.

3.4.4.1 Immediate Self-Knowledge: The Direct Means for Liberation

For Śaṅkara immediate self-knowledge as taught by the Upaniṣads, which is independent of rites (BS Bh 3.4.17, 25) and other human activity (Bṛ U 4.4.6), is the sole cause of liberation. He argues against the views that the direct means of liberation consist in obligatory rites alone, or their combination with Self-knowledge (BS Bh 1.1.4).[419] Once direct Self-knowledge is established, it leads spontaneously to liberation without the need of any other means. Hence, at once the ignorance is destroyed one acquires the state of remaining established in Self-knowledge, which is identical with liberation.[420] Since the liberation is independent of human actions—ritual or social or mental—abandoning them cannot be considered necessary for liberation.

3.4.4.2 Possibility of Self-Knowledge Irrespective of Modes of Living

Physical renunciation implies one entering in *sannyāsa āśrama* with its formal rites. For Śaṅkara, the one who does not belong to any *āśrama* also can attain self-realising knowledge, the liberation (BS Bh 3.4.20). In BS Bh 3.4.35–36, a doubt is raised, whether widowers, and others who do not belong to any *āśrama* were competent for knowledge or not. The opponent argues that they do have no competence, for they

[419] Some *Pūrvamīmāṁsaks* held that obligatory rites alone can lead one to liberation. But some *Vedāntins* of Śaṅkara's time such as Manḍaṇa Miśra, advocated a combination of knowledge and rites (*jñāna karma samucaya*). But Śaṅkara argued against these both. See Marcaurelle, *Freedom Through Inner Renunciation*, 22.

[420] Marcaurelle, *Freedom Through Inner Renunciation,* 26.

do have no duties to perform which makes them conducive for the rise of knowledge. Śaṅkara's answer is that people unqualified for rites may be qualified for self-knowledge. He proceeds giving examples from the scriptures: Raikva (a widower,[421] Ch U 4.1.3), Gārgī (a woman,[422] Bṛ U 3.6; 3.8) and Samvarta (an ascetic who roamed about naked, BS Bh 3.4.37). In BS Bh 3.4.38, he affirms nothing stands in the way of qualification of widowers and others.

In Ta U Bh 1.11.4, the opponent claims that the rise of immediate self-knowledge depends on rites and as a consequence, scriptures allow only *gṛhasta āśrama* for the

---

[421] Vācaspati Miśra in his commentary on *Brahmasūtra* 3.4.36 describes Raikva as a widower. Given in: Marcaurelle, *Freedom Through Inner Renunciation,* 220n13.

[422] Bṛ U 3.6 and 3.8 opens with the queries of Gārgī. She is described as the daughter of Vācaknu and is said to be unmarried. The sage Yājñavalkya imparted to her the knowledge of the supreme Reality. Thus, she earned the title *Brahmavādini* which means "one who discourses on sacred texts or Vedas" or "one who asserts the identity of all things with *Brahman*, the Absolute." She is found in the royal assembly of Janaka engaging in religious and philosophical discussions. Women participating in public deliberations in the most honourable courts of the kings in the second century BCE, is an amazing feature of the culture of that time. See K.R. Rajani, "Three Women in the Brhadaranyaka Upanishad," *Satyanilayam* 16 (2009): 35–42; Rao, *Encyclopedia of Hinduism*, s.v. "*Gārgī*"

The significance of this passage and the examples quoted by Śaṅkara indicates that *brahmajñāna* is possible for: (1) those not included in any *āśrama* (Gārgī was unmarried; this does not mean she belonged to the *āśrama* of *brahmacarya* for it was reserved for the male members of the upper class; her presence in the court-assembly for discourses makes it clear that she was not in the state of student-hood), (2) women, and (3) *śūdra* (the possibility of a women being a *brahmajñāni* implies the same for *śūdra*; for both *śūdra* and women were considered on the same rank (*pāpayonayah*) as far as *brahmajñāna* is concerned.

acquisition of it, precluding *sannyāsa* which has none of these rites. Śaṅkara establishes rites are not unique and necessary pre-requisites for arriving at immediate self-knowledge; people who belong to the *āśrama*s other than *gṛhasta* who do not perform rites also have access to knowledge.[423] The *sūtra* concludes: "people in all the stages of life can aspire for knowledge" (Ta U Bh 1.11.4 p. 300).[424] This mainly aims at establishing that a *sannyāsa āśrami* also has access to it, and also implies the eligibility of a *gṛhasta āśrami* still engaged in rites,[425] indicating that physical renunciation is not a must for liberation, but it is inner renunciation which Śaṅkara emphasizes.

3.4.4.3 Possibility of Liberation While Not Being a Physical Renunciant

The Upaniṣads do not completely reject Vedic *karma*s at the expense of *brahmajñāna* (Mu U 3.2.10; Bṛ U 4.4.22). They can dispose the aspirant for the knowledge of the highest truth.[426] Śaṅkara, being faithful to the spirit of Upaniṣads, must

---

[423] Here Śaṅkara points out that practices such as *agnihotra* ritual are not the only ones conducive to self-knowledge; there are also celibacy, austerity, truthfulness, control of mind, control of senses, non-injury, and similar practices, particularly meditation which are commonly associated with other *āśrama*s are also included.

[424] सर्वेषां चाधिकारो विद्यायां... (Ta U Bh 1.11.4) Cf. Śaṅkara, *Īśādidaśopaniṣadaḥ*, ed., Ministry of Education, India, 354.

Direct quotes from Ta U Bh of Śaṅkara (translation), throughout this dissertation, are given page number followed by 'p.' Page numbers are from: Śaṅkara. *Eight Upaniṣads with the Commentary of Śaṅkarācārya*, vol. 1. Translated by Swami Gambhirananda. 1957. Reprint, Kolkata: Advaita Ashrama, 2013.

[425] Marcaurelle, *Freedom Through Inner Renunciation,* 31.

[426] Kane, *History of Dharmaśāstra*, vol. 5, pt. 2, 918.

be accepting the value of Vedic ritualism, but putting it in its proper place in the pursuit of the highest knowledge. He admits that one can attain salvific knowledge even without physical renunciation. In Bṛ U 4.4.23, at the end of the dialogue between Yājñavalkya and king Janaka, Śaṅkara confirms that the latter—who was a king and not a *sannyāsa āśrami*—has now "become *Brahman,*"(एवं ब्रह्मभूतो जनको ...) i.e. attained liberation-in-life.

Commenting on BG 3.20, which states that "by action only, did Janaka and others attain perfection," Śaṅkara proposes two possible interpretations: (1) if Janaka and others continued performing actions even after achieving liberation, then their actions had no other purpose than guiding people (*lokasṁgraha*); (2) if, on the other hand, they had not yet attained liberation, then ritual actions helped them in reaching that state through their purifying effect.[427] Śaṅkara states in his Bṛ U Bh; "But in the case of those who perform the regular rites disinterestedly, just for the purification of the mind, they help towards realisation. … Because these rites indirectly help those people, they are aids to realisation as well" (Bṛ U Bh 3.3.intro. p. 318). This would mean *karma*s, including rituals, if performed with right motivation with the unselfish mind can create perfection of the qualities suitable for devotion to knowledge.[428] In his commentary to BG 4.20 and 23, Śaṅkara accepts that the enlightened persons may continue to perform the activities associated with their stage of life. The enlightened persons may abandon rites together with their

---

[427] Marcaurelle, *Freedom Through Inner Renunciation,* 40; Comans, *The Method of Early Advaita Vedānta*, 325.

[428] Young, "Śaṅkara on the Salvation of Women and Śūdras," in *Goddesses and Women in the Indic Religious Tradition*, 140.

accessories as they do not see any purpose in rites and actions. But, if for some reason anyone among them is unable to abandon them can continue to be engaged in action. They do it without attachment to actions or to their results and it is for the welfare of the world. The actions done by them are certainly inactions, since they are endowed with the realization of the actionless self (BG Bh 4.20).

This indicates that there can be a *brahmajijñāsu* who is a householder. Actions can prepare the way for the knowledge of *Brahman*, contributing to the construction of an environment in which knowledge can occur—an environment which is comprised essentially of the prepared, competent aspirant.[429] A householder may continue their ritual practices but change their motivation: instead of performing them for the usual ritual goals,[430] they perform them now "for the sake of knowledge."[431]

3.4.5 The Role of Physical Renunciation

For Śaṅkara, it is mental renunciation, not physical which is indispensable for liberation. At the same time, he endorses physical renunciation—renunciation of ritual and social actions—before and after the enlightenment. For him, physical renunciation, though not necessary, have a significant role in making the *brahmajñāna* possible.

---

[429] Clooney, *Theology After Vedānta,* 123.

[430] The ritual goals are happiness here in this world through wealth, progeny, etc. and the enjoyment of heaven hereafter.

[431] De Smet, "From Catholic Theology to Śāṅkara Vedānta and Return with Fr F.X. Clooney," in *Understanding Śaṅkara*, 408.

3.4.5.1 Śaṅkara's Understanding of 'Action'

Action or *karma* primarily means ritual actions and then social actions which pertain to one's *varṇa* and *āśrama*. For Śaṅkara, an action is that which is done with a motive of reward, with the wrong notion of the self as the doer (BS Bh 18.2). Action arises from the innate conviction "I am an agent; this is mine" (Upad 1.1.13 p. 104).[432] This conviction results from false superimposition of non-*Ātman*—such as body, senses, and inner organ—upon the action-less *Ātman* (BS Bh intro.).[433] Agency and desire, as components are what count as 'action'. Bodily and mental activity performed independently of the notion, "I am an agent," does not qualify an action.[434] So, one may take up rites and other social actions, both before and after the enlightenment, with the spirit of inner renunciation which becomes a means or *sādhana* before enlightenment and characteristics or mark after the enlightenment.

3.4.5.2 Śaṅkara's Insistence on Physical Renunciation

Śāṅkaravedānta approves inner renunciation, not the physical, as the necessary requirement for liberation. Even if one has achieved the latter, but not qualified with the former, that aspirant cannot become a successful *brahmajijñāsu*. For Śaṅkara, all rituals and their requisites such as sacred thread

---

[432] Direct quotes from Upad of Śaṅkara (translation), throughout this dissertation, are given page number followed by 'p.' Page numbers are from: Śaṅkara. *A Thousand Teachings: The Upadeśasāhasrī of Śaṅkara*. Translated and edited by Sengaku Mayeda. Tokyo: University of Tokyo Press, 1979.

[433] Mayeda, introduction to *A Thousand Teachings*, 84.

[434] John J. Thatamanil, *The Immanent Divine: God, Creation, and the Human Predicament* (Minneapolis: Fortress Press, 2006), 46.

are considered necessary by those who hold that *Ātman* is different from *Brahman* (Upad 2.1.32). But, at the same time, he insists on physical renunciation as it is clear from the texts such as BS Bh 3.4.20; Upad 2.1.2; BG Bh 3.3 and from the physical *sannyāsa* he took up for himself. Some reasons for this could be the following:

1) His disciples were mostly from the *Pūrvamīmaṁsā* background and who had a staunch belief that rites alone will save. To them Śaṅkara was strong to suggest actions do have no use at all.[435] There are some passages where he seems to emphasise *sannyāsa* for the *brāhmaṇa* caste (BS Bh 3.4.20; Mu U 1.2.12; Bṛ U 3.5.1; 4.5.15). This does not mean only a *brāhmaṇa* can take up *sannyāsa*. Here Śaṅkara is arguing against the *Pūrvamīmāṁsāka* belief that a *brāhmaṇa* should not renounce *karma* and shall not take up *sannyāsa*, and he establishes *brāhmaṇas* are eligible for renunciation and a real *brāhmaṇa* is the one who knows the Absolute, i.e. *Brahman*.[436]

---

[435] Mayeda, introduction to *A Thousand Teachings*, 91.

[436] Young, "Śaṅkara on the Salvation of Women and Śūdras," in *Goddesses and Women in the Indic Religious Tradition*, 149. After having made an analysis on the three passages from Śaṅkara's *Upaniṣadbhāṣya*—Mu U 1.2.12; Bṛ U 3.5.1; 4.5.15—which are emphatic on the point that only a *brāhmaṇa* can renounce, Young makes the following observation: "Śaṅkara's main concern in his commentary here is to overcome *brāhmaṇical* objections to the idea of renunciation because of other Vedic statements that *brāhmaṇas* must wear the sacred thread, perform rituals, and study the Vedas throughout their lives. The entire discussion is to resolve such argument for the exclusivity." Young, "Śaṅkara on the Salvation of Women and Śūdras," in *Goddesses and Women in the Indic Religious Tradition*, 149.

Reid B Locklin gives another understanding while dealing with the eligibility of a seeker, in reference to Mu U Bh 1.2.12–13 and Upad

2) For the seeker-after-liberation, who aims at steadfastness or total absorption in *Brahman*, the value of physical renunciation and monasticism lies in allowing full-time dedication to the most direct means of self-knowledge (BS Bh 3.4.20). Since the monastic mode of living does not entail the obligation of performing ritual actions as in the other modes, it allows full absorption in the discipline of knowledge (BS Bh 3.4.20), and is in this sense it is more conducive to the goal of liberation than other modes of life.[437]

3.4.6 Physical Renunciation as Mandatory: The Post-Śaṅkara Development

Śaṅkara placed emphasis on renunciation of doer-ship. He did not consider physical renunciation of rites and actions indispensable both before and after enlightenment. But post-Śaṅkara *Advaitins*, often understood him as advocating the

---

2.1.2: "Sankara himself seems to have insisted that only Brahmins, along with upper-caste males, are specially qualified for spiritual instruction; but it is also possible to argue that only those who are qualified for spiritual instruction can really be counted as Brahmins. That is, "Brahmin" becomes a kind of shorthand for any person, of any gender or social class." Reid B. Locklin, *Spiritual But not Religious? An Oar Stroke Closer to the Farther Shore* (Minnesota: Liturgical Press, 2005), 20.

In addition to this, it is significant to note whenever Śaṅkara mentions on the qualified teacher he uses the phrase "knower of *Brahman*" without any reference to *varṇa*. (Upad 2.1.6; 2.2.45). Śaṅkara shows that the teacher has to instruct the aspirant that the *varṇa* distinctions are superimpositions and the real aspirant has to come out of such divisions (Upad 2. 1. 10–16).

[437] Marcaurelle, *Freedom Through Inner Renunciation,* 146.

necessity of physical renunciation for the one who aspires for self-knowledge and liberation.[438]

One of the reasons for such disorientation could be how the term *uparati* or *uparama* (quietness) which is one of the six 'qualities' within the fourfold requirement for *brahmajijñāsā* received a different interpretation.[439] While describing the third requirement, Śaṅkara, in his BS Bh. 1.1.1, mentions only the first two 'qualities' (*śama*, *dama*, etc.) and does not comment on them. According to *Vedāntasāra, Vedāntaparibhāṣa*[440] and to the *Advaita* tradition as a whole, the remaining qualities of the third requirement which are left unsaid by Śaṅkara are; quietness (*uparati*), endurance (*titikṣa*), collectedness (*samādhāna*) and faith (*śraddhā*).[441] This list originates from Bṛ U 4.4.23, which makes clear the characteristics of the one who has knowledge of *Brahman*as: one's mind is controlled, one's senses are controlled, one is quiet (*uparata*), enduring, concentrated, and sees the self in the [individual self itself]. Here Śaṅkara glosses 'quiet' (*uparata*) by a renouncer (*sannyāsin*) who is completely free from all desires (Bṛ U Bh 4.4.23). These verses describe an already enlightened person: Yājñavalkya, the speaker of the verse, declares to his disciple, Janaka, that he has attained complete realization of *Brahman*.

---

[438] Marcaurelle, *Freedom Through Inner Renunciation,* 11.

[439] In BS Bh 1.1.1, Śaṅkara simply writes that the fourfold requirement is: (1) *Viveka* (discrimination between the eternal and non-eternal); (2) *Vairāgya* (non-attachment of the results of one's actions here or hereafter); (3) *Śamadamādhisādhanasampat* (accomplishment of qualities, such as *śama*, *dhama*, etc. referred to as the wealth of six disciplines; and (4) *Mumukṣutvam* (the burning desire for *mokṣa).*

[440] These are works of two well-known *Advaita* teachers. *Vedāntasāra* is by Sadānanda, and *Vedāntaparibhāṣa* by Dharmarāja.

[441] As given in: Marcaurelle, *Freedom Through Inner Renunciation*, 5.

Janaka who was a king was not obviously a physical renouncer; but still Yājñavalkya certifies him to be *uparata*. For Śaṅkara, *uparata* (quiet) must be, one who has direct knowledge of *Brahman* and due to which is inwardly free from all desires.[442] When *uparama* is suggested for a *brahmajijñāsāu* it would mean that the aspirant should make it a disciplineand means to attain *mokṣa* by which internal freedom from all desires is achieved. But some *Advaitins* believed *uparati* consists in physical renunciation of Vedic rites as a part of the initiation into monastic life.[443] The reasons for misrepresenting Śaṅkara in this regard could be:

1) Physical and formal *sannyāsa* of Śaṅkara and of the *Advaita* tradition at large—before and after Śaṅkara—must have led to an emphasis on leaving *gṛhastāśrama* and abandoning *karma*.
2) The post-Śaṅkara *Advaitins* could not explain the creation of the world from *Brahman* without violating the non-dual nature of It. They interpreted Śaṅkara's concept of ignorance as the cosmic power and material stuff out of which the world is created, and therefore, world was wrongly considered illusion; attributed inferior value,[444] and any positive engagement with it was looked down upon.[445] Consequently, world-

---

[442] Marcaurelle, *Freedom Through Inner Renunciation*, 158.

[443] Marcaurelle, *Freedom Through Inner Renunciation*, 5.

[444] Richard De Smet, "*Māyā* or *Ajñāna*? A Textual Analysis," in *Understanding Śaṅkara: Essays by Richard De Smet,* ed. Ivo Coelho (Delhi: Motilal Banarsidas, 2013), 122; Rao, "Two Myths in Advaita," 265. This article argues against the two 'post-Śaṅkara myths' which are those ideas in fact Śaṅkara did not intent: one is the conception of world as illusion and the other is the concept that once realization is achieved this world ceases to exist.

[445] Rambachan, *The Advaita Worldview*, 69–80, 109.

negation was appreciated as a religious value, and it contributed extra emphasis on renunciation of all actions.

The above discussions on *sannyāsa* can be concluded as: for Śaṅkara, it is not physical or formal, but mental and informal *sannyāsa* is what is necessary for the quest for *Brahman*. Referring to Śaṅkara and his *bhāṣya* on BS 1.3.34, Kane makes the same opinion and adds that the latter can be "resorted to by women, *śūdra*s and mixed castes."[446] If so, the possibility of salvation is more universal and open even to *śūdra*s.[447]

Conclusion

A critical enquiry into *Apaśūdrādhikaraṇam* shows *Śāṅkaravedānta* cannot and do not exclude *śūdra* from the quest for *Brahman*. The result of the study could be summarised as follows:

1) *Śāṅkaravedānta* is even criticised by the succeeding *Vedāntin*, Rāmānuja for it is relaxed and cannot but be so, in the matter of *śūdra*-exclusion.

---

[446] Kane, *History of Dharmaśāstra*, vol. 2, pt. 2, 946.

[447] Analyzing Śaṅkara's *bhāṣya* on BG 18.44–66, which discusses mainly on how *karma* is related to salvation, Young makes the following observation: "To conclude, scrutiny of these passages has failed to turn up any specific statement that women and *śūdras* are barred from taking *sannyāsa* after attaining eligibility for *jñāna-niṣtha*. Indeed, the whole discussion begins with the context of the four castes. Nowhere are *brāhmaṇas* then singled out for special consideration regarding eligibility for *sannyāsa*. Similarly, nowhere it is said that only twice-born men (*dvijas*) are eligible." See Young, "Śaṅkara on the Salvation of Women and Śūdras," in *Goddesses and Women in the Indic Religious Tradition*, 143.

2) Śaṅkara's attempts to show the *śūdra*s from Upaniṣads (Jānaśruti and Satyakāma) and from the *Mahābhārata* (Vidura and Dharmavyādha) who had great knowledge, as pseudo-*śūdra*s (*apa-śūdra*s) remains drained of sound logic. These narratives in their original contexts are loud for their pro-*śūdra* stance and give a larger space to conceive them as the scriptural vindication for the possibility of *śūdra*s having salvific knowledge.
3) *Śruti* considered in its capacity and operation as a *pramāṇa,* cannot be made inaccessible to someone on the basis of *varṇa* and *āśrama*; it must be open to any intelligent person. Primacy of *anubhava* than *śruti,* in the sense of the former as independent and the culmination of the latter, makes the possibility of self-realising *anubhava* more open. For Śaṅkara, *brahmajñāna* is possible from the scriptures (*śāstra*s) which do not strictly demarcate the four Vedas alone but consist of other texts belonging to Vedic tradition including the *smṛti* texts of Itihāsas and Purāṇas. Therefore, *Apaśūdrādhikaraṇam*'s final instruction on barring *śūdra*s from Vedas does not preclude them from their quest for *Brahman* for it is possible through the texts other than Vedas.
4) *Sannyāsa* is considered indispensable for *brahmajijñāsā* and, if so, *śūdra*, women, *gṛhastāśrami* and those who have not adopted any *āśrama* like a widower are excluded. But, for Śaṅkara, it is not the formal taking up of *sannyāsa* but the internal *sannyāsa*, detachment to the fruits of works done, is what necessary for a *brahmajijñāsu*. In this sense, *sannyāsa*

(and also *brahmajijñāsā*) is possible for aspirants of every walk of life, irrespective of *varṇa* and *āśrama*. This is evident in the case of the *Mahābhārata* characters mentioned in *Apaśūdrādhikaraṇam*, Vidura and Dhrmavyādha. Despite being *śūdra*s they were endowed with salvific knowledge. For Śaṅkara they had their knowledge from their previous life in which they were not *śūdra*s. But neither in their previous life nor in this life had they undertaken formal *sannyāsa*. This indicates, for Śaṅkara, *brahmajñānā* is open also to a non-*sannyāsa āśrami*.

Taking account of all the discussions made in this chapter, two general conclusions can be deduced: (1) For Śaṅkara, being a *sannyāsa āśrami*, non-*śūdra* and knower of Vedas, which are part of external criteria for *brahmajijñāsā*, are not the necessary prerequisites for the quest for *Brahman*; they can be interpreted, and (2) due to this, he cannot do away with the possibility of a *śūdra brahmajijñāsu*.

These two concluding remarks point to the inclusivism and universal character of *Śāṅkaravedāntic* soteriology. But, at the same time, the external criteria for *brahmajijñāsā* which Śaṅkara repeatedly demand from aspirants—which makes his soteriology less universal—are not without any relevance. For him, they provide an ambience for the promotion of a culture and environment for nurturing *brahmānubhava.* His hermeneutical disposition and his convictions as a *sannyāsi* must have played a great role in emphasising the need for external criteria in the pursuit for the quest for *Brahman*. Therefore, Śaṅkara appears to be in a dilemma between exclusivism and inclusivism. Before making a polemic conclusion by placing Śaṅkara on the point of an 'either … or' question to choose between inclusivism and exclusivism, one has to analyse the reasons for such dilemma. The following chapter is entitled for this purpose.

CHAPTER 4

TEXT VERSUS TRUTH: INCLUSION-EXCLUSION DILEMMA IN ŚAṄKARA

Introduction

According to Śaṅkara, *brahmānubhava* is possible only through *jñānamārga,* in which *śravaṇa-manana-nididhyāsana* of Vedic scriptures are integral. To take up this programme of *brahmajijñāsā* the aspirant must be eligible; both internally and externally. Internally one has to get qualified with *sādhanacatuṣṭaya*, the fourfold discipline which includes: *viveka, vairāgya, śamadamādisādhanasampatti* and *mumukṣutvam.* These internal moral virtues can excellently flourish, if the aspirant gets qualified with external criteria of eligibility—being a *sannyāsi*, an upper caste, etc. It is these demands of external criteria exclude many such as *śūdra*s, women, householders, etc. from the program of liberation, whereas, the internal qualities remain open to all, and make *brahmajijñāsā* universal and inclusive.

Later *Vedāntin*s and those who have critiqued *Śāṅkaravedānta* were not unanimous on Śaṅkara's position on *śūdra*-exclusion. He is criticised by his immediate succeeding *Vedāntin*s of being inclusive, for he showed leniency towards the salvation of *śūdra*s, but later on, he is accused on the charge of being an exclusivist for he has not opened Vedas for *śūdra*s. So, it is significant to identify what is Śaṅkara's position in this regard. Previous chapter has given an indication: for him, *śūdra* is excluded only from the study of Vedas, and not from the quest for *Brahman* and the possibility of salvation, and therefore, a *śūdra brahmajijñāsu* is possible. It seems, Śaṅkara is in an in-between position, in a dilemma between inclusion and exclusion. It is significant to make an enquiry into the nature of this dilemma, and then to explore the reasons for it. This chapter is focused on bringing out the salient features of this dilemma, especially by identifying it as a tension between Vedic 'truth' which is open for all and Vedic 'text' which is accessible to few and then to look into the reasons for such dilemma.

The social and religious context and the hermeneutical disposition of Śaṅkara reveal that his position on *śūdra*-exclusion was deliberate with ample reasons. It must be taken as his creative response to the challenges that were raised against the *Vedāntic* ideals which he held uncompromisingly, and to the Vedic tradition at large. Hence, it is worth making a study on the rationale behind his inclusion-exclusion dilemma. This can be fruitfully done by considering Śaṅkara as an exegete of his time and by analysing his hermeneutical prejudices and agenda.

The discussions of the preceding chapter have narrowed down the scope of the problem of exclusion to the exclusion of *śūdra* from Vedas alone, and not from the liberation at large. Study of the Vedas and the prerequisites—both internal and external—are the two important factors which determine the inclusive or exclusive nature of *brahmajijñāsā*. This chapter, in its first part, takes up these two factors: (1) a critical study on the reduced scope of exclusion—exclusion from Vedas—and (2) a revisit to the prerequisites for *brahmajijñāsā*, especially the internal. This is done with an eye of exploring the inclusive impetus implied in them. This will give a clear focusing and will deepen the study on the exclusion of *śūdra* from *brahmajijñāsā* and will shed better light into the major theme of this chapter, the dilemma and its reasons.

4.1 Reducing the Problem of Exclusion: *Brahmajijñāsā* for All and Vedas for a Few

Brahmasūtra Bhāṣya, especially *Apaśūdrādhikaraṇam,* shows Śaṅkara does not exclude *śūdra*s from the quest for *Brahman*, but from the Vedic study alone.[448] Further reflections on this will raise the question, if Śaṅkara were to admit and instruct a *brahmajijñāsu*, would he take the chance of scriptures other than Vedas? That is to say, whether the texts other than Vedas, preferably Itihāsas and Purāṇas, be the first choice as the excellent means for *brahmānubhava*? Although, for Śaṅkara, Vedas are not the exclusive and *sine qua non* for *brahmānubhava*, the answer to these questions, with all possibility, would tend to be negative. For him *śruti*, especially the Upaniṣads are the excellent and sure means through which *Brahman* can be quested. Therefore, one may reduce the problem of exclusion from 'the exclusion of *śūdra*s from *brahmajijñāsā*' to 'the exclusion of them from Vedas', but this will not annihilate the *Śāṅkarite* problem of 'exclusion from *brahmajijñāsā*'. The specificities of Śaṅkara's programme of *brahmajijñāsā* include the study of Vedas. He shows little attention to the means other than Vedas, except in admitting their competence. They are only a byway for those who are ineligible for the highway, the Vedas. Thus, exclusion of *śūdra*s from Vedas is not without consequences, and implications to the exclusion of them from *brahmajijñāsā*. Though Veda is not the exclusive means for *brahmajijñāsā*, and the exclusion from them will not directly affect *brahmajijñāsā*, Śaṅkara is not free from the charge of exclusion: he excludes a group consist of *śūdra*s from the

---

448 Rambachan, *The Advaita Worldview*, 29.

excellent means for *brahmajijñāsā* (*śruti*) on the basis of their birth into particular social class.

4.2 Requisites of *Sādhanacatuṣṭaya* and Study of Vedas: Revisiting Exclusion from the Quest for *Brahman*

There are two important factors which are pivotal in the inclusion-exclusion discussions which contribute to narrow down or widen the scope of exclusion, i.e. to determine *brahmajijñāsā* to be inclusive or exclusive. They are (1) the internal and external criteria for *brahmajijñāsā*, and (2) the demand of getting qualified with Vedic knowledge. If these two are held strict, *brahmajijñāsā* will become exclusive, if they are open for interpretation it will be inclusive and universal. A critical study of *Apaśūdrādhikaraṇam* reveals that the external criteria and the study of Vedas are not a *sine qua non* for salvation. Considering the program of *brahmajijñāsā* from the point of predilection and specificity of Śaṅkara, wherein he denies the 'excellent' means (*śruti*) to a group of people (*śūdra*s) on the basis of their birth, a re-reading of these two factors is relevant. Therefore, firstly, having accepted the inclusive scope of external criteria, now the attention is turned to the question how far the internal criteria (*sādhanacatuṣṭaya*) are inclusive. Secondly, by agreeing the narrowed position of exclusion, i.e. *śūdra* is excluded only from Vedas, now the focus is on the question, how far the arguments for the exclusion of them from Vedas are well-founded. This will make the study on the *Śāṅkarite* reasons for the exclusion from *brahmajijñāsā* more focused and solid.

4.2.1 Inclusivism of *Sādhanacatuṣṭaya*

For Śaṅkara, the external qualities, such as being a *sannyāsi* and non-*śūdra*, which promote and demand exclusion are not 'necessary' for salvation. But he does not make any compromise with internal moral virtues, the *sādhanacatuṣṭaya*.[449] Salvific knowledge is impossible for the one who has all the external eligibilities but does not have the internal moral virtues.

Sādhanacatuṣṭaya do not contain any stipulations about caste. Rambachan observes: "These requirements share a great deal with the demands of the religious path in many traditions and their disconnection from the caste order and patriarchy would enhance the rationality and human claims of the Vedānta."[450] For Clooney, "There is nothing specific to Advaita, nor to Vedic orthodoxy, about these interior prerequisites, nor do they bear any necessary textual component."[451] Most probably Śaṅkara must have chosen these four virtues as important for *brahmajijñāsā* from his experience as a *sannyāsi* after the ideals of Upaniṣads.[452] Nowhere has Śaṅkara mentioned that *śūdra* cannot attain those

---

[449] De Smet opinions, for Śaṅkara, it is these internal *sādhanas*—not the external status related with *varṇa* and *āśrama*—that are the necessary and sufficient condition for *brahmajijñāsā*. See De Smet, "Theological Method and Vedānta," in *Understanding Śaṅkara*, 109; See also Caṭṭampiswāmikal, *Vedādhikāranirūpaṇam*, 49.

[450] Rambachan, *The Advaita worldview*, 29.

[451] Clooney, *Theology After Vedānta,* 130. When Śaṅkara gave this *sādhanacatuṣṭaya* in his BS Bh 1.1.1, he has not given any scriptural reference. Later *Śāṅkarite*s have connected it with quotes from Upaniṣads. See the third chapter of this dissertation 3.4.6.

[452] De Smet, "From Catholic Theology to Śāṅkara Vedānta and Return with Fr F.X. Clooney," in *Understanding Śaṅkara*, 407.

four-fold requirements,[453] and thus disqualified from *brahmajijñāsā*.

Not all the aspirants are readily qualified with the internal prerequisites. The unqualified aspirants need to get training to attain these virtues, and thus they become qualified in order to receive the teachings of *Vedānta*. Śaṅkara, in his life, has attempted to motivate those who have not attained the four-fold qualifications by illustrating the ways and means for it. He considered it as the duty of those who have received enlightenment. In *Apaśūdrādhikaraṇam* Śaṅkara seems to introduce one group of human beings namely, the disqualified—consist of *śūdra*s—apart from the qualified and unqualified. But they are prohibited not from getting qualified with *sādhanacatuṣṭaya* and acquiring knowledge of *Brahman* but only from studying the Vedic texts.[454]

Therefore, from the point of view of internal criteria for *brahmajijñāsā*, the quest for *Brahman* is successful only to those who are qualified with *sādhanacatuṣṭaya* which is universal in its scope. People might be unqualified for it but cannot be disqualified from it. When *sādhanacatuṣṭaya* and the study of Vedas are placed as the options for the question, which is *sine qua non* for *brahmajijñāsā,* the answer will be the former, not the latter. In this sense, *brahmajijñāsā*, is universal, open to all, because, *sādhanacatuṣṭaya,* without which there is

---

[453] Rao, "Inconsistencies in the *Brahmasūtra* and *Śāṅkarabhāṣya*," 139–145.

[454] *Apaśūdrādhikaraṇam* (BS Bh 1.3.38) offers *smṛti* texts of Itihāsas and Purāṇas for *śūdras'* salvation. It is noteworthy that among the three sources of *Vedānta* (*prasthānatraya*) except Upaniṣads, other two—*Bhagavadgītā*, and *Brahmasūtra*—are *smṛti* texts, and *śūdra*s have access to it. The knowledge received through them cannot possibly be considered insufficient for salvation.

no quest for *Brahman*, is beyond any caste barriers and is accessible to all.

4.2.2 Exclusion from Vedas: Pitfalls of *Apaśūdrādhikaraṇam*

Śaṅkara concludes *Apaśūdrādhikaraṇam* (BS Bh 1.3.38) by admitting that the exclusion of *śūdra*s is not from *brahmajñāna* but from the study of Vedas. Even if the arguments of the *adhikaraṇam* are intended to prove that the exclusion is only from Vedas, they remain inconsistent. Hence those reasons cannot be accepted without subjecting them to a critical study. The crux of Śaṅkara's argument in *Apaśūdrādhikaraṇam* is that those born *śūdra*s are prohibited to study Veda. They may aspire for liberation and also can have ability but they are debarred by the scriptures to have access to Vedas. But the arguments against *śūdra*s' competence for Vedas become weaker when they are viewed through the background of some of the strongly held *Śāṅkarite* convictions: (1) caste as something which is superimposed on self and (2) it is *śruti*, not *smṛti*, which takes precedence in self-realising knowledge. Before entering into these explorations it is important to identify what exactly is the group that *Brahmasūtra Bhāṣya* of Śaṅkara, especially *Apaśūdrādhikaraṇam,* excludes.

4.2.2.1 Identifying the Excluded: *Śūdra*s in Śaṅkara's *Brahmasūtra Bhāṣya*

Apart from *Apaśūdrādhikaraṇam* (BS Bh 1.3.32–38), *Brahmasūtra Bhāṣya* of Śaṅkara takes up little discussions on *śūdra.*[455] Though the word 'Veda' occurs very many times apart from *Apaśūdrādhikaraṇam,*[456] the word '*śūdra'* occurs only here in the discussions on excluding them from the Vedic study. In this *adhikaraṇam* the word *śūdra* stands for the one who is born in the fourth *varṇa*. Śaṅkara uses the term *jātiśūdra* (BS Bh 1.3.34; 1.3.35)[457] which means 'born *śūdra'* or '*śūdra* by birth'; and to such ones the study of the Vedas are denied. Though he gives a different interpretation for the word *śūdra* to mean 'the one who is struck with grief', that is only from the point of view of refuting the claim of eligibility for *śūdra* by explaining away the *śūdra*-utterance of Raikva while accepting Jānaśruti as his disciple. The reason for *śūdra*-exclusion is that they are named in the scriptures as those who cannot have the *adhikāra* (eligibility) for Vedic study; Vedas themselves have set the limit. It is nothing concerned about lack of capacity such as, intelligence, desire, moral purity etc. but only because they are named as those who are to be barred.[458] Therefore, for *Brahmasūtra Bhāṣya* of Śaṅkara, the term *śūdra* stands for a born *śūdra* belonging to the fourth *varṇa*, representing the one who is mentioned by the scriptures to be ineligible for the study of Vedas.

4.2.2.2 Caste as Superimposition

Śaṅkara maintains in his introduction to *Brahmasūtra Bhāṣya*, that *varṇa* and *āśrama* are mere superimpositions,

---

[455] T.M.P. Mahadevan, ed., *Word Index to The Brahma-sūtra-bhāṣya of Śaṅ*kara, pt. 2 (Madras: University of Madras, 1973), 921.

[456] Mahadevan, ed., *Word Index to The Brahma-sūtra-bhāṣya of Śaṅ*kara, pt. 2, 879.

[457] जातिशूद्रस्यानधिकारात्। (BS Bh 1.3.34) Cf. Śaṅkara, *Brahmasūtra with Śāṅkarabhāṣya*, ed., Ministry of Education, India,107.

[458] Clooney, "Finding One's Place in the Text," 12–13.

which an aspirant has to—and the enlightened has already—overcome (See also Upad2.1.12, 13). For him, the knowledge of the absolute reality is free from differentiation as *brāhmaṇa*, *kṣatriya*, etc. He states, "Such scriptural injunction as "A *Brāhmaṇa* shall perform a sacrifice" can become effective only by taking for granted various kinds of superimposition of caste, stage of life, age, condition, etc." (BS Bh intro. p. 5).[459] This implies just as the scriptural injunction 'A *brāhmaṇa* shall perform a sacrifice' is based on *varṇāśrama* which is only superimposition, the scriptural prohibition such as, '*śūdra* is unfit for performing a sacrifice' are ineffective because they also are based on the superimpositions of *varṇāśrama.* In Bṛ U Bh, Śaṅkara states, "The different castes such as the Brāhmaṇa or the Kṣatriya, the various orders of life, and so on, up on which rites depend, and which consists of actions, and their factors and results, are objects of notions superimposed on the Self by ignorance—i.e. based on false notions like that of a snake in a rope" (Bṛ U Bh 2.4.5 p. 247).[460] To conceive of oneself as a *brāhmaṇa* who must perform the fire sacrifice or as a warrior obliged to fight in a righteous battle is to superimpose onto oneself these contingent identities.[461] For Śaṅkara, the aspirant of *Vedānta* has to overcome these

---

[459] तथाहि ब्राह्मणो यजेत इत्यादीनि शास्त्राप्यात्मनि वर्णाश्रमवयोवस्थादिविशेषाध्यासमाश्रित्य प्रवर्तन्ते । (BS Bh intro.) Cf. Śaṅkara, *Brahmasūtra with Śāṅkarabhāṣya*, ed., Ministry of Education, India, 2.

[460] यद्ब्रह्मक्षत्रादिकर्मनिमितं वर्णाश्रमादिलक्षणं आत्मन्यविद्याध्यारोपितप्रत्ययैषयं क्रियाकारकफलात्मकं अविद्याप्रत्ययविषयं रज्ज्वामिव सर्पप्रत्ययः... (Bṛ U Bh 2.4.5) Cf. Śaṅkara, *Īśādidaśopaniṣadaḥ,* ed., Ministry of Education, India, 142.

[461] Thatamanil, *The Immanent Divine*, 32.

superimpositions[462] and an enlightened is beyond such distinctions (Upad 1.17.43–46).

4.2.2.3 Caste by Birth or Character: Primacy of the Opinion of *Śruti* than *Smṛti*

Reflection on excluding *śūdra*s from *brahmajijñāsā*, has to be appended with the question, can a *brāhmaṇa*, who lacks proper intelligence, who has not qualified with fourfold moral requirements be admitted for *brahmajijñāsā* only on the merit of being born as *brāhmaṇa*? Śaṅkara would answer negatively to this (Ka U Bh 2.2.8): caste which is based on the birth cannot be an 'exclusive' and 'necessary' factor for *brahmajijñāsā*.

There can be two versions of the criterion of caste; namely, (1) caste should be determined by birth and (2) caste is determined by one's own qualities. The *smṛti* texts give different opinions on this matter.[463] In the event of *smṛti* opposing another *smṛti*, Śaṅkara himself suggests a method that, its authority is decided by the criterion of its being in harmony with the *śruti* from which alone it derives its own validity (BS Bh 2.1.1).

The *śruti* texts have never made any emphatic statements on the prohibition of *śūdra*s from Vedic

---

[462] Therefore, this has to become part of his *sādhana*, the spiritual discipline.

[463] For example, "a kind-hearted man is called a *brāhmaṇa* irrespective of whether he does anything else or not" (MS 2.87) and "the *śūdra* belongs to the fourth caste and has but a single birth" (MS 10.4). For further examples see MS 3.15; Ga Dh S 9.1 and MS 2.87; Bh Pu 1.4.25.

knowledge,[464] at the same time gives ample indications on the other way.[465] In *Apaśūdrādhikaraṇam* Śaṅkara has not quoted any *śruti* passage in support for *śūdra*-exclusion; he has only made attempts to explain away those passages which supports *śūdra*'s admission to knowledge.[466] This itself shows *śūdra*-exclusion was not very much scriptural but traditional.[467] The

---

464 Murty, *Vedic Hermeneutics*, 15; Caṭṭampiswāmikal, *Vedādhikāranirūpaṇam*, 27.

465 In *śruti* itself there is examples of *śūdra*s like Kavaṣa having knowledge and taking part in the Vedic sacrifice (Ai Br 2.3; Ka Br 12.3).

466 Among the seventeen scriptural texts that Śaṅkara has quoted in *Apaśūdrādhikaraṇam*, nine are from *śruti* texts, seven are from *smṛti* and one is anonymous.

Among the nine *śruti* quotes: four of them are intended to explain away the pro-*śūdra* stance implied in them (Ta Sa 7.1.1.6; Ch U 4.1.3; 4.4.5; 5.11.7); three of them are to show the rite of initiation was preceded for Vedic study (Ch U 7.1.1.1; Pr U 1.1; Śa Br 11.5.3.13); the other two (Ch U 4.3.5; *Tāṇḍya Brāhmaṇa* 20.12.5) are used to prove *kṣatriyatva* of Jānaśruti.

Among the seven *smṛti* quotes: six are to support prohibition of *śūdras* for Vedic learning (MS 10.4; 10.126; 4.80; Ga Dh S 12.4; 9.1; Va Dh S 18.11–14); the remaining one is possibly M Bh 327.49 (There is confusion on exactly which is this quote. For explanation, see chapter three of this dissertation, 3.3 and the foot note no. 328) is used in support of *śūdra*'s access to Itihāsas and Purāṇas.

The anonymous text comes in the attempt to prove the *kṣatriyatva* of Jānaśruti.

467 The *śruti* indications which treated *śūdra*s comparatively inferior were interpreted in such a way as to exclude them from the study of the Vedas. The later *smṛti* texts like Dharmaśāstras, especially Manu, were very strict on the exclusion of *śūdra*s which had also social and political reasons besides religious. For explanation, see the second chapter of this dissertation.

During the *Vedāntic* period *śūdra*-exclusion became very much formal than factual; it almost become a hallmark for the *brāhmaṇa* tradition to profess the exclusion of *śūdra*s from the Vedas, if not, it would indicate the author or the preacher to be on the camp other than *brāhmaṇic.* See second chapter of this dissertstion, 2.8.2.

characters from *śruti*, such as, Jānaśruti, Raikva (Ch U 4.1–3), Satyakāmajābāla (Ch U 4.4–9), Maitreyī (Bṛ U 2.4; 4.5) and Gārgī Vācaknavī (Bṛ U 3.6; 3.8) give strong evidence for character than birth that accounts for knowledge. Caste is determined by heart and mind than birth is in harmony with *śruti*.[468]

Among the Upaniṣadic characters mentioned above, Gārgī Vācaknavī and Maitreyī needs special attention. Śaṅkara in BS Bh 3.4.37 has mentioned Gārgī Vācaknavī as an example for Upaniṣadic characters who do not belong to any particular *āśrama* but are having *brahmajñāna*.[469] But the example proves more than what is intended in this particular *sūtra*. This woman character was as competent a Vedic scholar as anybody else. It is unlikely that she had her knowledge through Itihāsas and Purāṇas.[470] Śaṅkara accounts Maitreyī as the one who had

---

[468] Paul Deussen, *The System of the Vedanta*, trans. Charles Johnston (Chicago: Open Court, 1912), 64. See also Rao, "Inconsistencies in the *Brahmasūtra* and *Śāṅkarabhāṣya*," 143; Caṭṭampiswāmikal, *Vedādhikāranirūpaṇam*, 69–71.

[469] Gārgī is described as the daughter of Vācaknu. No reference is made about her marriage and is said to be unmarried. When Yājñavalkya was in the court of Janaka, Gārgī came to him to participate in the great conference of Vedic deliberation. The sage imparted to her the knowledge of the supreme Reality. Thus, she earned the title *Brahmavādinī* which means "one who discourses on sacred texts or Vedas" or "one who asserts the identity of all things with *Brahman*, the Absolute." See Rajani, "Three Women in the Brhadaranyaka Upanishad," 35–42.

[470] The *smṛti* texts of Itihāsas and Purāṇas have later origin than Upaniṣads. The discussions which Gārgī undertakes show she is proficient in Vedic texts. She put herself forward as an opponent as the sage Yājñavalkya, and by virtue of her erudition and wisdom, dared challenge his assertion of pre-eminence in the great philosophical congress which assembled at the court of King Janaka (Bṛ U 3.6; 3.8). Gārgī was thus as much a student of the Veda as anybody else. See

great knowledge. He in his *bhāṣya* for Bṛ U, while introducing Yājñavalkya's dialogue with Maitreyī (Bṛ U Bh 2.4.intro.) makes it clear that the dialogue was not merely for giving an explanation of why he was leaving his wives and seeking his own salvation, but rather, it was an occasion to enlighten her.[471] Here too the instruction is unlikely to be through *smṛti* texts. In the course of the same discussion Śaṅkara adds that caste, various orders of life, and so on up on which rites depend, and which consist in actions, are superimposed on the self by ignorance (Bṛ U Bh 2.4.5). If so, and if women and *śūdra*s are equal in status, in privileges and disabilities,[472] it may be reasonably inferred that the study of Veda (not merely the acquisition of knowledge through texts other than Vedas) must be open to *śūdra*s too.[473]

Radha Kumud Mookerji, *Ancient Indian Education* (1947; repr., Delhi: Motilal Banarsidas, 1974), 270–275.

[471] Śaṅkara agrees that she is ineligible for rituals. But for him this does not hinder her from salvific knowledge. "Moreover, the knowledge of Brahman as a means to immortality has been imparted to Maitreyī, who was without the means to perform rites. … Therefore, this story is introduced with a view to enjoining renunciation of the world as part of the knowledge of the Self" (Bṛ U Bh 2.4.intro. p. 243).

[472] Women and *śūdra*s are considered belonging to same category of those 'born of sin' or 'those of evil womb' or 'bad birth' (*pāpayonayah*) and are debarred from Vedic study (BG Bh 9.32). See Young, "Śaṅkara on the Salvation of Women and Śūdras," in *Goddesses and Women in the Indic Religious Tradition*, 134, 140–141, 158.

[473] Mookerji, *Ancient Indian Education,* 270–275. Nowhere throughout these discussions does Śaṅkara hint that Maitreyī is ineligible for salvation or that she must wait for another life. Through the instance of Maitryī's acquisition of knowledge, Śaṅkara has made the point clear that caste and orders of life are superimpositions and are real only in the realm of the ignorance. It implies just as Maitreyī, *śūdra* also are eligible for *Jñāna-niṣṭha*. See Young, "Śaṅkara on the Salvation of Women and Śūdras," in *Goddesses and Women in the Indic Religious Tradition*, 151.

In excluding *śūdra*s from Vedic study, Śaṅkara seems to rely heavily upon *smṛti* than *śruti.* He should have discarded *smṛti* when a *smṛti* rule conflicts with *śruti* which is the practice of Vedic tradition of interpretation (Ja Mī S 1.3.1–4).[474] Here, in *Apaśūdrādhikaraṇam*, a *smṛti* instruction is brought in another *smṛti* text which is *Brahmasūtra* and it is affirmed again in another *smṛti* text *Brahmasūtra Bhāṣya.* So the weight put on the debarring of a born *śūdra* is lighter.

In addition to this, in his *Brahmasūtra Bhāṣya,* Śaṅkara quotes *Manusmṛti* 2.87 "a kind-hearted man is called a *brāhmaṇa* irrespective of whether he does anything else or not" (BS Bh 3.4.38 p. 794)[475] which indicates it is the quality of a person than caste matters. Therefore, the above discussions indicate the attempts of *Apaśūdrādhikaraṇam* to argue for the exclusion of *śūdra*s from Vedic study is inconsistent because:

1) It flouts some of the very strong convictions of Śaṅkara such as; (a) distinctions based on *varṇa* are superimpositions (which the aspirant has to overcome and the enlightened have gone beyond) and (b) *śruti* is primary and important than *smṛti.*
2) Śaṅkara himself, in his *Brahmasūtra Bhāṣya*, shows that it is not birth, but character matters.

---

[474] Kane, *History of Dharmaśāstra*, vol. 3, 832. According to Caṭṭampiswāmikal there is no Vedic injunction to consider *śūdra*s as ineligible for Vedas. But then, if at all, anyone finds any indications of this, Vedas themselves exhibit the instances of *śūdra*s having knowledge, and because of this, the eligibility of *śūdra*s for the Vedic knowledge has to be accepted. See Caṭṭampiswāmikal, *Vedādhikāranirūpaṇam*, 53, 55.

[475] कुर्यादन्यन्न वा कुर्यान्मंत्रो ब्राह्मण उच्यते" इत्यसंभवदाश्रमकर्मणोऽपि जाप्येऽधिकारं दर्शयति । Cf. Śaṅkara, *Brahmasūtra with Śāṅkarabhāṣya*, ed., Ministry of Education, India, 374–375.

4.3 Truth in-and-through the Text: Salient Features of Inclusion-Exclusion Dilemma

Brahmajijñāsā, the creative and dynamic enquiry for *Brahman*, the self-realization, is the supreme end (*mokṣa*) of every human being. It involves not an intellectual enquiry alone, but the conversion and transformation of the whole person.[476] In this sense, and from the theoretical framework of *Śāṅkaravedānta* at large, a *śūdra brahmajijñāsu* is possible because here there is no scope of any restriction based on *varṇa* and *āśrama*. The inclusivism of Śaṅkara can be deduced from the following:

1) *Brahmajñāna*, the final self-realization is immediate and is independent of any means, requirements and dispositions[477] and *brahmānubhava* cannot be considered as a mere product of an esoteric body of texts.[478]
2) From the point of view of *Advaita*, *Brahman* is the one without a second; the root cause and source of everyone and everything; the ultimate goal of every human being; which one has to realize rather than achieve.[479] Therefore, Śaṅkara has little scope to divide

---

[476] Richard De Smet, "Language and Knowledge of the Absolute According to Śaṅkara," in *Understanding Śaṅkara*, 68. See also the first chapter of this dissertation 1.1.1.

[477] De Smet, "Language and Knowledge of the Absolute According to Śaṅkara," in *Understanding Śaṅkara*, 47; De Smet, "The Fundamental Antinomy of Sri Śaṅkarācārya's Methodology," in *Understanding Śaṅkara*, 80. See also the third chapter of this dissertation, 3.3.2.2 and 3.3.2.3.

[478] Clooney, *Theology After Vedānta,* 137.

[479] See the third chapter of this dissertation, 3.3.2.1 and 3.3.2.2.

people on the basis of caste, and to deny the very possibility of self-realization on the basis of birth.[480]

3) From the epistemological point of view of *Śāṅkarite*s, knowledge cannot be denied to someone on the basis of birth into a particular caste. Ignorance which is the fundamental human problem is not the problem of a few but of the entire humanity. The solution that Śaṅkara offers for the removal of ignorance cannot be for a few, but for anyone who can conduct a sound epistemic operation.[481]
4) For Śaṅkara, *varṇa* distinctions are superimpositions on the real nature of self and the enlightened goes beyond all these. This 'going beyond' of these distinctions should become a means or *sādhana* for the aspirant and a mark for the enlightened.[482]
5) A study on the prerequisites for the *brahmajijñāsā* reveals it is the internal requirements (*sādhanacatuṣṭaya*) that are *sine qua non* for the quest for *Brahman*, and these are universally accessible irrespective of one's *varṇa* and *āśrama*.[483] The external requirements—such as the aspirant must be a non-*śūdra, sannyāsi,* etc.—which come under *varṇa* and *āśrama* restrictions are not 'necessary' for

---

[480] *Śūdra*s also have self, the soul which is *Brahman.* They are also infected by ignorance, the human problem. Therefore, in fact, they also are in need of self-realising knowledge. There is no reason why they should not have it. See Rambachan, *The Advaita Worldview,* 28; Deussen, *The System of the Vedanta,* 60.

[481] See the third chapter of this dissertation, 3.3.1.1

[482] See this chapter 4.1.3.1

[483] See this chapter 4.2.1.

brahmajijñāsā, not unalterable, and are liable to be interpreted.[484]

6) In *Brahmasūtra Bhāṣya* while establishing that those who are not included in any *āśrama* also can attain knowledge and the consequent ṣalvation, Śaṅkara asserts, "it is possible for knowledge to be helped by such virtuous acts as repetition of *mantra*s (*japa*), fasting, worship of Gods, etc. which can be resorted to men in general, and which do not clash with the fact of one's standing outside any stage of life" (BS Bh 3.4.38 p. 794). These devotional and austere practices have nothing to do with *varṇa* and *āśrama* duties.[485]

But at the same time, *Śāṅkaravedāntic* exclusivism is explicit. First of all, Śaṅkara holds, *brahmajijñāsā* can be fruitfully carried out only through *jñānamārga* (way of knowledge)—through *śravaṇa-manana-nididhyāsana* of *śruti* (BS Bh 1.1.1; 1.1.2; 1.1.4). Secondly, Śaṅkara emphasises the traditional mode of initiation to Vedic study and *sannyāsa* as the most conducive disposition for the quest for *Brahman* (BS Bh 3.4.17; 3.4.20; Upad 2.1.1–2). These two cases would mean knowledge of *Brahman* is reserved only for elite upper caste male renouncer and it excludes many: householders, *śūdra*s, outcastes, women, and those who have not included in any of the four *āśrama*s, such as widower.[486]

---

[484] The third chapter of this dissertation discusses this matter and concludes that it is not the external requirements that are necessary for *brahmajijñāsā*, but internal, i.e. *sādhanacatuṣṭaya*, which has universal accessibility, and therefore, for Śaṅkara, salvation of *śūdra* is possible (although it is through the means other than Vedas).

[485] Mookerji, *Ancient Indian Education,* 270–275.

[486] See the first chapter of this dissertation 1.3.4.

Although Śaṅkara's arguments for exclusion go unsound and inconsistent he does not agree to an unconditional inclusive stand on the quest for *Brahman* and does not make direct statements on the possibility of a *śūdra brahmajijñāsu.* He is explicit in holding or building the fort of exclusion, but then, gives ample implications for the inclusion, i.e. makes some openings or side-doors for the possibility of *śūdra*s' salvation[487] by suggesting caste as superimposition, Itihāsa-Purāṇas can replace *śruti*, mental renunciation than physical is necessary, etc.[488] Though there is robust inclusivism implied in Śaṅkara, it is most unlikely, that he would guide an aspirant who is questing for *Brahman,* through the texts other than Vedas, such as Itihāsas and Purāṇas, which are universally accessible irrespective of gender, *varṇa* and *āśrama.* Therefore, Śaṅkara's inclusivism remains not as the first and best choice in his programme for the quest for *Brahman,* but it is only an alternative that could be adopted for those who are ineligible for the excellent.

---

[487] This is clearly evident in his Upad 2.1.2, 12, 13. In Upad 2.1.2, Śaṅkara gives qualifications for the aspirants who are desirous for *mokṣa* and to whom this knowledge to be imparted. The aspirants have to abandon the desire for sons, wealth and worlds, and have to reach the state of *sannyāsa* and must be *brāhmaṇa* who is pure, and must be examined in respect of their cast, profession, conduct, learning and parentage. But, in Upad 2.1.12 and 2.1.13 we find explaining the caste title *brāhmaṇa* as superimposition, if that is not removed there can have no liberation.

It could be the case that primarily he closes the door of salvation to *śūdra*s and then leaves lot of openings for their inclusion. Sometimes the back-door becomes the main just as informal becomes more than formal for all the practical matter of facts; but for all the theory the formal remains as main. See Lipner, *The Hindus*, 57.

[488] See the third chapter of this dissertation 3.3. and 3.4.

Śaṅkara cannot but be inclusive, but at the same, is adamantly exclusive, at least, in the case of accessibility of the Vedas. In fact, it indicates a kind of tension inherent in *Śāṅkaravedānta*—a tension between inclusivism and exclusivism. This exclusion-inclusion dilemma which is implied in Śaṅkara can be made clear as follows:

1) On the one hand, there is a basic, original desire to know (*jijñāsa*) and the realization is immediate,[489] on the other, the task and path to be undertaken for this realization is narrow where the aspirant has to be the kind of person intellectually, socially, religiously and scripturally fit and thus can become the proper knower of *Brahman.*[490] The entire project of *brahmajijñāsā*, takes into consideration the innate aptitude of the aspirant, caste, educational capabilities, etc. In fact, *Śāṅkaravedānta* looks for persons who are ripe for the knowledge from the social, cultural and religious context of the time.
2) The inherent tension in *Śāṅkaravedānta* could be the tension between 'truth' and the 'text'. For Śaṅkara, the 'truth' of the text is simple and universal; but this truth is available in-and-through the 'text', which belongs to a particular tradition.[491] It is a tension between the simple event of insight and the complex requirements of listening and studying. The truth is universally available, but it is available only under certain

[489] See the third chapter of this dissertation 3.3.2.1 and 3.3.2.2.

[490] Francis X. Clooney, "From Anxiety to Bliss: Argument, Care, and Responsibility in the Vedanta Reading of *Taittirīya* 2.1–6a," in *Authority, Anxiety, and Canon: Essays in Vedic Interpretation*, ed. Laurie L. Patton (Delhi: Sri Satguru Publications, 1995), 161.

[491] Clooney, *Theology After Vedānta,* 129.

pedagogically prescribed circumstances, after the text is listened and mastered, for which, all the regulations and practices of the tradition are to be maintained.[492]

3) If the truth, the 'goal', is simple and universal, can the text, the 'means' to achieve the goal be not made free from the *varṇa* and *āśrama* barriers? But Śaṅkara does not do it, but places himself in between exclusivism and inclusivism. This tension is the crux of the problem with *Apaśūdrādhikaraṇam* and it runs throughout Śaṅkara: a tension between 'text' and its 'truth'. On the one hand there is the insistence on the centrality of the *śruti* (text) and its appropriate and formal reception in accordance with the tradition, and on the other hand, *Śāṅkaravedānta* equally insists on the simplicity and un-restrictedness of its truth. According to the latter, *śūdra*s, women, non-*sannyāsāśrami* are ought to be included; according to the former, they cannot be.[493]

4.4 Rationale for the Inclusion-Exclusion Dilemma

Exclusion of *śūdra*s, whether it is from Vedas or from the liberation at large, Śaṅkara argues, from the narrowest textual and logical grounds. It is curious to note, in spite of being weak and inconsistent in his arguments, he remains on the side of exclusion, particularly, strict with excluding *śūdra*s from Vedas. It remains a matter of concern that the greatest historical exponent of *Advaita* remained almost untroubled with his exclusive stance, even when there were social awareness and protests against such exclusion, inequality and discrimination by Buddhist and other heterodox traditions and

---

[492] Clooney, *Theology After Vedānta,* 119.
[493] Clooney, *Theology After Vedānta,* 141.

even by the orthodox movements such as *Vaiṣṇavism* and *Śaivism*. There were various attempts, in later period, to justify Śaṅkara's stance on exclusion, and also on the dilemma related to it. Although all those reasons are not equally strong and convincing, a study of them will throw better light into Śaṅkara's position on exclusion and into his philosophy at large. An enquiry from the perspective of his hermeneutical context and agenda will make the result more solid and convincing.

4.4.1 Justifying Śaṅkara's Insistence on Exclusion of *Śūdra*s

Śaṅkara's position on exclusion is explained variously. Not all of them are well-founded and convincing. Some of the possible justifications are given below:

1) Śaṅkara had to hold on the exclusion of *śūdra*s, as Comans observes, due to the circumstances of his own times.

> In a similar way to Śaṅkara, Rāmānuja too interprets the statements of the Brahmasūtras as prohibiting Śūdras from the Vedic study. These ācāryas reflect the circumstances of their own times, and they ought not to be condemned as discriminatory from the vantage point of our times when the principle of political equality, stemming from the European Enlightenment, is now widely accepted as a moral right.[494]

[494] Comans, *The Method of Early Advaita Vedānta*, 317. Rambachan also shares the same view. See Rambachan, *The Advaita Worldview*, 28.

Kane also makes the same opinion. Referring to Śaṅkara's explanation on the term '*śūdra*' by which Jānaśruti was addressed by Raikva and the authors' attempt to establish that this Upaniṣadic narrative does not indicate *śūdra*'s education, Kane comments: "But this farfetched explanation had to be given because of the practice current in the times of the Vedāntasūtras that the śūdra is not entitled to study the Veda."[495] The very 'circumstances of the time' points out, due to various social, religious and cultural reasons.

2) Śaṅkara's program of liberation is the way of knowledge and it aims at those who have already studied the Veda and have developed desire for *mokṣa*. *Śūdra*s were exempted primarily not because they are born from particular parents belonging to a particular caste, but in the context of the then society, they represented the illiterate group, especially in the matters of Vedic Study.
3) Śaṅkara was only interpreting *Brahmasūtra*, authored by Bādarāyaṇa and suffered all the limitations of an interpreter. The exclusion of the *śūdra*s was the idea of Bādarāyaṇa and Śaṅkara could not leave it altogether. Therefore, Śaṅkara is irresponsible for the idea of exclusion.
4) According to the theory of *karma,* being born as *śūdra* is not mere chance of birth in a particular family. It is the consequence of that person's past *karma*s. Therefore, for Śaṅkara, the exclusion is not merely because one is born of particular parents.

---

[495] Kane, *History of Dharmaśāstra*, vol. 2, pt. 1, 155.

Taking Śaṅkara as an intellectual genius and spiritual reformer these reasons seem to be inadequate. Few responses could be made on the reasons mentioned above:

1) It is true that Śaṅkara was influenced by his social, religious and cultural context but he was not a prisoner of those. He, as an exegete and original thinker, has tried to come out of the ideas and practices, and to go beyond what he understood as having a little or no value. He had his own hermeneutical prejudices and agendas as well, to repute him as an original thinker.
2) *Śūdra*-exclusion cannot be interpreted as the exclusion of the illiterate. In *Apaśūdrādhikaraṇam*, he has made it clear that the exclusion is of '*jātiśūdra*' i.e. *śūdra* by birth. Besides this, *śūdra*s were not totally illiterate; at least since from the time of Upaniṣads, there were people from the low rank, like Jānaśruti, who were literate and had proved their ability in the knowledge of various disciplines. Śaṅkara might not be unaware of this. Therefore, his intention cannot be considered as the exclusion of illiterate, but clearly of *śūdra* by birth.
3) Śaṅkara's position on *śūdra*-exclusion cannot be brushed aside as the helplessness of an interpreter. He cannot be considered merely as an interpreter whose task was only to be faithful to the author, Bādarāyaṇa. He has used all his hermeneutical skill to interpret the text, *Brahmasūtra* to the *Vedāntic* ideals of his time and by finding foundations to base them on Upaniṣads.[496] "If Śaṅkara had wished to argue the

---

[496] Francis X Clooney states that Śaṅkara for the most part attended directly to the Upaniṣdas through BS as a neutral lens helping to

opposite, radical view, that Śūdras ought to be entitled to Vedic study, it would not have been impossible for someone of his ability to mount a substantial argument in favor of that position."[497] He could find out some scripture passage in support of it from the vast resources of *śruti* and *smṛti*.[498] In *Apaśūdrādhikaraṇam*, he has used all his ability to explain away those scriptural quotes supportive of *śūdra*-inclusion and uses all the possibilities, although scripturally and logically narrow, to support *śūdra*-exclusion. If he wanted, he could argue the other way, i.e. could find out the scriptural basis for the inclusion of *śūdra*s. Therefore, Śaṅkara as an interpreter, in his *Brahmasūtra Bhāṣya*, must not be repeating the idea of Bādarāyaṇa, and *śūdra*-exclusion cannot be the mind only of Bādarāyaṇa and the social practice of his time.

---

structure the reading of the Upaniṣads. He sometimes even deferred to Bādarāyaṇa's viewpoint. See Francis X. Clooney, "Binding the Text: Vedanta as Philosophy and Commentary," in *Texts in Context: Traditional Hermeneutics in South Asia*, ed. Jeffrey R. Timm (Delhi: Sri Satguru Publications, 1997), 60.

[497] Comans, *The Method of Early Advaita Vedānta*, 317.

[498] For example: In *Apaśūdrādhikaraṇam* he brings an unfamiliar or anonymous text to support for *śūdra*-exclusion. In the same *adhikaraṇam* he uses a text probably from M Bh. In its original context the text is more prone to *śūdra's* eligibility even for Vedas. But Śaṅkara limits its scope in such a way to restrict *śūdra*s from Vedas and to support their accessibility only to Itihāsas and Purāṇas. See third chapter of this dissertation 3.3, foot note no. 328.

In BS Bh when Śaṅkara argues that *sannyāsa* could be adopted from any stage of life, he does it on the basis of a single text (Jābāla Upaniṣad 4), restricts the scope of other texts that could be used to support the opposite view (BS Bh 3.4.17).

4) For Śaṅkara liberation implies liberation from the cycles of rebirth. The effects of past life are destroyed after the rise of self-realizing knowledge (BS Bh 4.1.13; 3.3.30), whether it is through Vedas or Itihāsa-Purāṇas.[499] "There is no journey after death for one who knows the non-difference of the self and *brahman.*"[500] The very fact that Śaṅkara admits the salvation of *śūdra*s (even if it is through the texts other than Vedas) shows, for him, a *śūdra* need not have to be born again as an upper caste in order to attain salvation. Past *karma*s do not make one totally ineligible for salvific knowledge.

It is most unlikely that Śaṅkara was unaware of the social and religious problems concerning exclusion; or he took it for granted as the established practice of the time; or he considered it very negligible. From the time of Upaniṣads onward and even during the time of Śaṅkara there were movements, mainly by Buddhism, Jainism, *Śaivism* and *Vaiṣṇavism,* against exclusion and inequality based on caste. Hence, Śaṅkara must be reasonably deliberate in his position on exclusion, placing himself in an inclusion-exclusion dilemma, and must be aware of its impacts.

4.4.2 Inclusive-Exclusive Tension: Through the Optic of Hermeneutical Context of Śaṅkara

Śaṅkara, as a philosophical genius, developed his ideas principally through a series of commentaries reinterpreting and reformulating ancient Vedic texts and traditions. In his literary

---

[499] Kane, *History of Dharmaśāstra*, vol. 5, pt. 2, 921–922.
[500] Rambachan, *The Advaita Worldview*, 3.

as well as philosophical and theological career, to a great extent, he was the making of his own times or at least was influenced by that.[501] His writings exhibit a precise acquaintance with the whole land scape of philosophical and religious thinking as developed up to his time. This does not mean that he remained merely as a bearer of his own time without making a forward step. Śaṅkara, from the foundations of his Upaniṣadic convictions, religious and social context, allegiance to the *Vedānta* tradition of *Advaita*, and from the *sannyāsa* mode of life that he adopted, has creatively responded to the religious, cultural, philosophical and theological context of his time through his writings. As an exegete he has maintained certain agenda which is very significant in recognising him as an original thinker. A study on these will contribute to shed light on why he could not accept or reject either exclusion or inclusion and had to take an in-between position.

4.4.2.1 Social and Religious Context of Śaṅkara

A fair critique of Śaṅkara, especially of his idea of *śūdra*-exclusion, will be limping if the study on his ideas is done independent of historical and cultural context of their development. Hence an exposition of his context will be a fitting starting point to understand how they contributed to frame his hermeneutical prejudices which will also throw light on the reason for his inclusion-exclusion dilemma.

---

[501] Rambachan, *The Advaita Worldview*, 3.

4.4.2.1.1 Date and the Historical Facts of Śaṅkara

The dates of Śaṅkara's life are uncertain; but at the same time, setting the time of his life and activity is important to study him from the context of his time so that he may be understood with better clarity.[502] After exploring the whole question scholars now agree to place him in the eighth century CE and more probably in the second half of that century.[503]

---

[502] Mayeda, introduction to *A Thousand Teachings*, 3.

[503] Śaṅkara's life time is generally taken to be 788–820 CE. See Thapar, *Early India*, 349; Doniger, *The Hindus*, 503; De Smet, "Language and Knowledge of the Absolute According to Śaṅkara," in *Understanding Śaṅkara*, 32; Sastri, *A History of South India, 386;* Avari, *India*, 215; A. Sreedhara Menon, *A Survey of Kerala History* (Kottayam: DC Books, 2007), 129. For Govind Chandra Pande, Śaṅkara has to be placed between 650 and 700 CE. See Govinda Chandra Pande, *Life and Thought of Śaṅkarācārya* (Delhi: Motilal Banarsidas, 1994), 41–52. Some of the scholars are of the opinion that he must be placed in the first half of the eighth century. See Comans, *The Method of Early Advaita Vedānta*, 163; Mayeda, introduction to *A Thousand Teachings*, 6.

K. Kunjunni Raja has made an elaborate study on this matter and has concluded *Śaṅkara*'s date to be the second half, probably the close of the eighth century. He concludes his studies as: "Śaṃkara is later than Bhartṛhari, Diṅnāga, Gauḍapāda, Dharmakīrti and Kumārila, and cannot be earlier than A.D. 650. Since Vācaspati wrote one of his works in A.D. 841, and since he is later than Śaṃkara by one or two generations, Śaṃkara has to be placed before A.D. 800. The absence of any reference to the philosophical system of Śaṃkara in the works of Śāntarakṣita and Kamalaśīla, even when they discuss an Advaitavāda under the heading of Upaniṣadvāda, and also in the works of Haribhadrasūri shows that Śaṃkara's theories had not spread by the second half of the eighth century. Hence the works of Samkara must have been composed towards the close of the eighth century A.D." K. Kunjunni Raja, "On the Date of Śaṃkarācārya and Allied Problems," *Brahmavidya: The Adyar Library Bulletin* 24, pts. 3–4 (December 1960): 146–147.

Śaṅkara is believed to be born to *nambūtiri brāhmaṇa*[504] parents at Kālaḍi in Kerala, deep in the south west corner of India. But, what we know about the life of Śaṅkara is almost entirely based on undated oral traditions and later biographies.[505] According to A.J. Altson what could most likely to be true of Śaṅkara is: "The idea that Śaṃkara was a

[504] M.Sudhakar Rao and V. Raghavendra Reddy, *Encyclopaedia of South India*, vol. 3 (New Delhi: Mittal Publications, 2009), 184. *Nambūtiri brāhmaṇas* are those orthodox *brāhmaṇas* of Kerala, who occupy the highest position in Kerala caste system. Orthodox in the extreme, its members regarded themselves as the true repositories of the ancient Vedic religion and of the traditional Hindu code. They follow the ritualistic *śrauta* traditions, mainly of *Pūrvamīmaṁsā*. See Rao, *Encyclopaedia of South India*, 184.

[505] The account of the life of Śaṅkara is almost constructed on oral traditions and later biographies. One of the accounts is Śaṅkara Digvijaya of Mādhava which cannot be early as it quotes a seventeenth century author. According to this work and other legends the important events of Śaṅkara's life can be sketched as follows:

Leaving home while yet young, Śaṅkara travelled north to the banks of the Narmada and met his teacher Govinda, studied the *Vedānta* texts with him. From there he journeyed to Banāres, where he assembled a band of pupils and expounded *Brahmasūtras* to them. Then he moved to Ganges, into the Himalayan region.

Later he travelled the length and breadth of India, holding debates with *Mīmāṁsākas*, Buddhists, etc. Tradition mentions Padmapāda, Sureśvara, Toṭaka and Hastāmalaka as his prominent disciples. The four monasteries said to have been found by him are: Śringeri in the south, Puri in the east, Dwāraka in the west, and Badarīnāth in the north. According to a dearly-cherished tradition, he performed the funeral rites of his mother, amid the opposition from *Mīmāṁsākas*, for technically he was not competent to do so as a wandering monk. Eventually he returned to the Himālayas and disappeared from amidst his pupils after revealing to them that he was an incarnation of the deity Śiva. See A.J. Altson, *Śaṃkara on the Absolute,* vol. 1 of *A Śaṃkara Source-Book* (London: Shanti Sadan, 1980), 42–44; Rajan Gurukkal, "Sankara: Buddhist in Disguise," *The Week,* December 27, 2015, 38–40; Menon, *A Survey of Kerala History,* 129–130; Sastri, *A History of South India*, 386–387.

Brahmin from the south who taught and wrote mainly in the north, who gathered many pupils about him, who won fame travelling about and engaging in debates and who was devotee of Viṣṇu[506] can be supported from the surviving writings of Śaṃkara himself and his early followers."[507] For De Smet: "A

---

[506] Weather Śaṅkara was a devotee of *Viṣṇu* or *Śiva* is a matter unsettled, but scholars, with most probability, take him to be a *Vaiṣṇava*. See Bradley J. Malkovsky, "Śaṃkara on Divine Grace," in *New Perspectives on Advaita Vedānta: Essays in Commemoration of Professor Richard De Smet, S.J*, ed. Bradley J. Malkovsky (Leiden: Brill, 2000), 82–83.

It is true that Śaṅkara often explains away references to the personal aspect of the Lord Kṛṣṇa or Viṣṇu in his commentary to Bhagavadgītā. He interprets them as references to the impersonal (supra personal), Absolute (*Brahman*) of Upaniṣads. Yet, there is undoubtedly a devotional component in his spiritual personality and in his works as well. When Gītā speaks of the "lamp of wisdom" (BG 10.11), Śaṅkara elaborates the metaphor and speaks of the lamp as 'filled with the clear oil of devotion'. Here as elsewhere in Śaṅkara's writings, knowledge and devotion are fused. See Altson, *Śaṃkara on the Absolute,* 12.

Altson proves from the texts of Śaṅkara and from the works of his early disciples that he had a predilection for devotion to Viṣṇu. He concludes: "Probably we should assume that the belief that Śaṃkara was an incarnation of Śiva first arose at a much later date when Śaṃkara was an established classic but already a distant legendary figure, and that it arose originally among circles devoted to Śiva and spread from them to the people at large." Altson, *Śaṃkara on the Absolute,* 45–46. Mayeda also proposes him to be a *Vaiṣṇava*: "It is said that Śiva, one of the principal Gods in Hinduism, was Śaṅkara's family deity and also that he was by birth, a *Śākta*, or worshiper of Śakti, the consort of Śiva and female personification of personal deity. Later he came to be regarded as a worshipper of Śiva and even as an incarnation of Śiva himself. But his doctrine is very far removed from *Śaivism* and *Śāktism*. It can be ascertained from his works that he had some faith in, or was favourable to, *Vaiṣṇavism*." Mayeda, introduction to *A Thousand Teachings*, 4.

[507] Altson, *Śaṃkara on the Absolute,* 44. Altson, from the texts of Śaṅkara and from the works of his first disciples proves the above-mentioned statement. See Altson, *Śaṃkara on the Absolute,* 44–47.

Brahmin, he was probably born at Kāladi (Malabar) and spent many years in the monastery which he founded in Śṛṅgeri (Mysore). He is generally reported to have died relatively young either in Kedarnāth (Himālaya) or perhaps in Kāñci. The other traditional details of his life are legendary."[508] Rajan Gurukkal, one of the historians of our time, considers that the "Traditional beliefs likely to be historical are Śaṅkara's tutelage under Govindapada, higher learning at Kanchi, travel to Varanasi, debates with scholars, journey to the source of Ganga, return to Varanasi, composing of main texts, continuation of debates, attainment of Digvijaya and founding of a monastic order."[509] He confirms that "Śaṅkara was of the acarya-brahmacari tradition of Upanishadic learning that was confined to be relatively small number of nambuthiri households in Kerala. His acarya, Govindapada, was a brahmacari of Gaudapada."[510]

More than three hundred works—commentaries, expositions and poetry—are attributed to Śaṅkara. Most of them are not accepted as authentic. The works accepted as authentic by most of the scholars are: *Brahmasūtra Bhāṣya,* the commentaries on *Bṛhadāraṇyaka*, *Chāndogya*, *Aitareya*, *Taittirīya*, *Kena*, *Īśa*, *Kaṭha*, *Muṇḍaka*, *Praśna*, and *Māṇḍūkya Upaniṣads*, and one non-commentarial work, *Upadeśasāhasrī*.[511]

---

[508] Richard De Smet, "Śaṅkara's Non-Dualism," in *Understanding Śaṅkara: Essays by Richard De Smet,* ed. Ivo Coelho (Delhi: Motilal Banarsidas, 2013), 305.

[509] Gurukkal, "Sankara," 38.

[510] Gurukkal, "Sankara," 40.

[511] Mayeda, introduction to *A Thousand Teachings*, 6. De Smet also accepts this but excludes the commentary on *Māṇḍūkya Upaniṣad*; for him, its authorship continues to be disputed. See De Smet, "Śaṅkara's Non-Dualism," in *Understanding Śaṅkara*, 307–308.

4.4.2.1.2 Salient Social Features of the Time

Gupta period, which historians consider to be the 'Golden Age' in the history of ancient India, got eclipsed during the sixth century CE and Huns emerged as the political power. The first half of the sixth century is remarkable with the reign of King Harṣa. He, as the powerful administrator, brought peace in north India.[512] After him it was a time of chaos: lacking strong political power and administration; rising of small kingdoms without steady rule; increased influence of many invading powers such as Arabs, Turks, Chinese, etc.[513] Kingdoms rising in Deccan played the role of a bridge between north and south in transmitting goods as well as ideas.[514]

By the sixth century, in South India, the polity of chiefships and small kingdoms from earlier times gave way to larger kingdoms.[515] Besides the larger political units such as *Chālukyas*, *Pallavas*, *Pāṇḍyas*, *Raṣtrakūḍas*, etc. the country was divided into certain well marked territorial divisions, such as, *Kuntala*, *Andhra*, *Tonḍainad*, *Choḷa*, and *Chera*. The people of each section had separate traditions and habits of their own.[516] In the succeeding period, by the seventh century, in the southern tip of peninsula *Choḷa, Chera* and *Pāṇḍya* kingdoms became strong: the west coast of the southern tip of India was ruled by *Cheras*.[517]

---

[512] Thapar, *Early India,* 280–290.

[513] Thapar, *Early India,* 405–418.

[514] Thapar, *Early India,* 408.

[515] Thapar, *Early India,* 326.

[516] Sastri, *A History of South India,* 284.

[517] This is the part including central Kerala, which is considered to be the birth place of Śaṅkara. He is said to be a younger contemporary of Kulaśekhara Alwar and an elder contemporary of Rājaśekhara

During the seventh century, in India, people generally enjoyed social security. *Brāhmaṇism* retained its supremacy with its political ties. The performance of Vedic rituals and sacrifices gave high status to the authority of the King.[518] The presence of new social groups—by way of trade, invasion, migration, etc.—was increasing. The earlier process of Sanskrit becoming the hegemonic language with some adaptations was continued. However its hegemony was not absolute, because in the south, the languages derived from Draviḍian roots retained authority and were more widely used.[519] Debates and discussions among scholars were common practice. Gradually the debates focused on well-defined philosophical systems. It was also an age of commentaries and exegesis on what was regarded as established tradition, which was now being re-interpreted among new social groups.[520]

The bulk of the population was Hindus, organised in castes. The lower caste often came up with various occupations than what was assigned to them in spite of the protest from the conservative *Brāhmaṇism*.[521] The status of the *śūdra*s improved and they enjoyed more rights. They entered into farming, in capacities other than labourers, and turned into sharecroppers and peasants, some became craftsmen, and some even could join army.[522] Śaṅkara himself gives a glimpse of his

---

Varman (Cheramān Perumān Nāyanār), the Chera rulers. See Menon, *A Survey of Kerala History,* 129.

[518] Thapar, *Early India,* 348.

[519] Thapar, *Early India,* 348.

[520] Thapar, *Early India,* 308–310.

[521] Sastri, *A History of South India,* 285.

[522] Avari, *India,* 167; Pande, *Life and Thought of Śaṅkarācārya,* 64.

age where *varṇa* and *āśrama* rules were unstable (BS Bh 1.3.33). This could be because of the growing influence of various religious groups, such as Jainism, Buddhism, *Vaiṣṇavism*, *Śaivism*, Islam, Christianity, etc., and other social groups—mercantile, migrating, etc., for example, Turks and Arabs—who thoroughly disregarded caste rules and the consequent discriminations.[523]

Brāhmaṇas still continued with the distinction between *dvijas* and *śūdra*s. Some concessions were made in allowing *śūdra*s for some rites of worship by using the *mantra*s only from *smṛti* but never from Vedas. It could be to deter and bring back those *śūdra*s who were attracted to the heterodox religions.[524] Formal education was available in *brāhmaṇa* hermitages, which later located in temples, and in Buddhist and Jain centres. In the former it would have been restricted to the upper caste. But there were educated *śūdra*s.[525] They were taught scriptures—most likely, other than Vedas—and could receive vocational training. The term *śūdra*, in the *brāhmaṇic* circles, began to be used more of an offensive term than representing genealogical social group. This term was used generally to anyone who did not follow the *brāhmaṇic* caste

---

[523] Sharma, *Śūdras in Ancient India*, 325.

[524] Kane, *History of Dharmaśāstra*, vol. 5, pt. 2, 922; Sharma, *Śūdras in Ancient India*, 300.

[525] Avari, *India*, 167; Thapar, *Early India*, 462–466.

and ritual rules. In this sense even the Buddhists, Jains, *Ājīvakas*,[526] etc. are at times labelled as *śūdra*s.[527]

In fact, when the challenge from religious and other social groups, from those who did not have any regard on caste-rules, especially from Buddhism, was acute the *brāhmaṇic* thinkers loosened the caste rules and barriers. But later, when the challenges, especially from Buddhism, became minimal they have stiffened the attitude. Kane makes an observation as follows:

> In the times of the Dharmasūtras the only mantras employed [in religious rites] were mostly Vedic and therefore in the case of śūdras Gautama provided that the śūdras were allowed the alternative of saying 'namaḥ' in place of a Vedic mantra. In the centuries preceding Christ, the *śūdra*s would naturally have been attracted to Buddha's teaching as it was addressed to all including *Śūdra*s. …. Therefore, the learned brāhmaṇas who wanted to wean sections of the masses (including śūdras) away from Buddhist teachings composed new Paurāṇika mantras by the thousand and employed in all religious rites like śrāddhas…. It was, therefore, that earlier *nibandha* writers like Śrīdatta were prepared to allow *śūdra*s to recite Paurāṇika mantras. But when centuries had elapsed, after Buddhism had disappeared from India, orthodox brāhmaṇa writers like Kamalākara (who wrote

[526] *Ājīvakas* were the sect outside the pale of Hinduism, founded by Makkahali Gośāla. They believed in an inexorable *niyati* (destiny) which human was unable to counteract. They practised severe asceticism. See Sastri, *A History of South India,* 395–396; Rao, *Encyclopedia of Hinduism*, s.v. "*Ājīvaka*."

[527] Sharma, *Śūdras in Ancient India*, 324. See the second chapter of this dissertation 2.8.2. Even the labouring mass who did not pay taxes was also placed in the category of *śūdra*s. See Sharma, *Śūdras in Ancient India*, 315.

> his N.S. [Nirṇayasindhu] in 1612 A.D) showed a stiffer attitude by confining śūdras merely to the listening to Purāṇas read by a brāhamaṇa and by not allowing them even to recite a Paurāṇika mantara.[528]

But, the groups consisted of untouchables and outcastes suffered all the disabilities which *śūdra*s once suffered, even more pitiably than that.[529] Their labour was sought for, but their physical and social presence was detested.

4.4.2.1.3 Religious Scenario

By the sixth century CE Buddhism and Jainism became popular religions.[530] Their ideals of renunciation, emphasis on the practise of moral virtues, acceptance of people irrespective of caste, the organization of monks and nuns of all castes with the mission of spreading their faith, and their use of vernaculars in religious teaching instead of Sanskrit contributed to the spread of these religions with great appeal among the common people. These religions, especially Buddhism, challenged the rationale of Vedic sacrifice and its caste context. But, by the end of the eighth century they began to lose their importance, except in some isolated pockets.[531] Such decline was partly because of the Hindu revival—effected by the Purāṇic religions, mainly *Vaiṣṇavism* and *Śaivism*, and by the *brāhmaṇic* religions of *Pūrva* and *Uttara Mīmāṁsakas*—and

---

[528] Kane, *History of Dharmaśāstra*, vol. 5, pt. 2, 925–926.

[529] Sastri, *A History of South India,* 290; Thapar, *Early India,* 303.

[530] Jainism was particularly prominent in Karnataka and Deccan, and Buddhism, from the time of Aśoka, had been firmly established among the Choḷas and Pāṇḍyas. See Doniger, *The Hindus,* 362.

[531] Mridula Tripathi, *Renaissance of Hinduism and the Decline and Eclipse of Buddhism* (New Delhi: Abhijeet Publications, 2015), 263.

partly because of the internal disintegrations and ideological differences within those heterodox systems.[532]

Responding mainly to the Buddhist and Jaina challenge, there arose a renaissance within Hinduism which gathered momentum by the eighth century. Consolidation of Vedic *Brāhmaṇism* and Purāṇic Hinduism was the cause and consequence of this revival. Purāṇic Hinduism took the revival in the form of *Bhakti* Movements especially that of *Śaivism* and *Vaiṣṇavism*, which was very much facilitated by the emergence of Purāṇic texts to which they claimed greater authority. They emerged on the one hand, as a response to the heterodox systems, on the other, to the *brāhmaṇic* ritualism. It gained momentum by reacting to the formalistic Sanskrit culture and religious practice introduced in the elite circles, and a

[532] Thapar, *Cultural Pasts*, 885–890. Comans makes the observation that by the time of Śaṅkara, Buddhism had already declined in importance. He saw *Pūrvamīmāṁsakas* as his principal opponents. See Comans, *The Method of Early Advaita Vedānta,* 164. Mayeda points, the eighth century, the time of Śaṅkara, found "a weakening, esoteric-oriented Buddhism which was the target of strong criticisms of Kumārila and others." Sengaku Mayeda, "Śaṅkara and Buddhism," in *New Perspectives on Advaita Vedānta: Essays in Commemoration of Professor Richard De Smet, S. J*, ed. Bradley J. Malkovsky (Leiden: Brill, 2000), 27. Avari observes, by 645 CE in many parts of India, Buddhism was in great decline. The Challenge to Buddhism and Jainism came, not so much from Vedic *Brāhmaṇism* as from the two great schools of *Śaivism* and *Vaiṣṇavism*. See Avari, *India*, 194.

For Krishnasamy Aiyar, Buddhism in its later period became corrupt in many ways. Gross idolatry in practice, formal atheism in doctrine, decayed monasticism, were only a few of its bad features. Its enemies, *brāhmaṇas*, at length felt that the time had come for them to use the logic and rhetoric of Buddhists against themselves, and they began to do it effectively. See C.N. Krishnasamy Aiyar and Sitanath Tattvabhushan, *Sri Sankaracarya* (Madras: G.A. Natesan, n.d.), 7.

reluctance to subordinate to this culture.[533] Deity oriented worship, temple centred religion, simple form of offerings made to deity in the form of *pūja* instead of elaborate rituals of Vedas, disregard for caste restrictions were some of the important features of these devotional sects.[534] Although it was usually *brāhmaṇas* who enjoyed the royal patronage, in the later centuries, it was extended to these religions, because, by then, these were popular among the common people and had a substantial following, that is to say, apart from the religious conviction, the royal acceptance had political reasons too.[535] These movements, to an extent, stemmed the flow of low caste to the non-Hindu religions.[536] Besides these major religions, people practised *Tantrism*[537] and there were other minor sects

---

[533] Sastri, *A History of South India,* 4–5; Thapar, *Early India*, 355.

[534] Aiyar, *Sri Sankaracarya*, 8. Devotional poets of these sects belonged not only from *brāhmaṇic* fold but also from lower castes; including women. See Thapar, *Early India,* 354–355; Doniger, *The Hindus,* 359.

[535] Thapar, *Early India,* 356.

[536] Doniger, *The Hindus,* 363.

[537] *Tantra* is the processes and methods of a particular form of ritualised study. This system originally represented an attempt of the early religious thinkers of India in making available to the common people the wisdom of Vedas. Its mode of worship was devised for those who could not perform the Vedic sacrifice to obtain their wishes. But later it tended to become an easy road to immorality, vice and crime. See K.V. Krishna Ayyar, *A History of Kerala* (Palghat: Malabar Printers, 1965), 120–121; Rao, *Encyclopedia of Hinduism*, s.v. "*Tantra*."

such as *Kāpālikas*[538] with their own ritualism.[539] But, as they grew, there developed many negative elements which distanced them from the true spirit of religion.[540]

Within the *brāhmaṇic* world there were two groups which responded, on the one hand, to the heterodox religions, and on the other, to the growth of the *Bhakti* Movements.[541]

---

538 *Kāpālikas* are one of the heretical sects of *Śaivism* known for its ascetic and crude religious practices. They are so called from their use of the *kapāla*, the skull, as a drinking and eating bowl. They performed worship with the dead body in the cremation ground at midnight, believing that their deity would descent upon their corpse, and through it speak and grant their wishes. See Ayyar, *A History of Kerala*, 120–121; Rao, *Encyclopedia of Hinduism*, s.v. "*Kāpālikas*."

539 Ayyar, *A History of Kerala*, 120–121.

540 During this period, *Śaiva* and *Vaiṣṇava* cults were the order of the day. Devotion to God was supposed to be the path of salvation. Truth seemed being veiled in mists of sentiments. Interested priests were spreading their tentacles everywhere through festivals and temples. Apart from these there were other sects such as *Bhairavas*, *Śāktas*, *Gaṇpatyas*, etc. with many sub-divisions. They had all based their faiths, however on the texts of Vedic tradition, sometimes with peculiar interpretations. Several of them had begun to claim greater authority for Purāṇas on which they had based their belief. The practices of some of these religious sects were abominable or terrible. For example, *Kāpālikas* were offering human victims to their God *Bhairava*. As a reaction to all this *mīmāṁsikas* were advocating a go-back campaign towards the Vedic sacrifices. Every sect grew intolerant of every other. In fact, true religion was fast disappearing under narrow sectarianism and some immoral practices during the time of Śaṅkara. There arose a general sense of weariness which seemed to have come over people, and an earnest hankering after some kind of harmonizing principles, and general religious peace. See Satchidananda Murty, *Hinduism and its Development*, rev. ed. (New Delhi: D.K. Printworld, 2007), 94; Aiyar, *Sri Sankaracarya*, 8; Ayyar, *A History of Kerala*, 120–121.

541 The *Pūrvamīmāṁsā* doctrine gained ascendency in the seventh and eighth centuries "as a protest against the Puranic religion of the people and was opposed both to the Buddhist and Upanishadic thoughts"

One among them was *Pūrvamīmāṁsakas*, generally known as *Mīmāṁsakas*, religiously powerful upper caste minority, at whose hands the ritual use of the Vedas remained alive.[542] They generally hardened the caste rules and ritual purity laws against the popular *Bhakti* Movements and heterodox systems to which many people, especially the lower caste, took a large flow. They thrived during this period with the leading personalities such as, Kumārila Bhaṭṭa and Prabhākara.[543] Another *brāhmaṇic* group was *Uttaramīmāṁsakas*, who came to be known as *Vedāntin*s, whose influence and numbers increased from the early centuries of CE. They gave importance to knowledge, contemplation, *sannyāsa* and moral virtues. For them, Vedic ritual was not to be abandoned, but it was to be practiced in the light of *Vedānta*, that is, as a stepping-stone to the more insight-oriented religious ideals of Upaniṣads. They wanted to found the theological ideals and the religious practices on *śruti*, especially Upaniṣads, and many were involved with the exegesis of Upaniṣadic texts.[544] Śaṅkara belonged to this tradition of Upaniṣadic learning.[545] In

---

Tripathi, *Renaissance of Hinduism and the Decline and Eclipse of Buddhism*, 267.

[542] Lipner, *The Hindus*, 58.

[543] *Mīmāṁsakas* believed that salvation is through *karmamārga*, i.e. faithful performance of *karma*s or the daily and the other periodical ceremonial rite enjoined by Vedas and *smṛtis*. It is from south India arose two schools of Vedic exegesis—*Mīmāṁsā*—that go by the names of Kumārila Bhaṭṭa and Prabhākara. They met the challenges from other religions, especially Buddhism, and argued in favour of Vedic religion. See Sastri, *A History of South India,* 381; Aiyar, *Sri Sankaracarya*, 7.

[544] Lipner, *The Hindus*, 58.

[545] Gurukkal, "Sankara," 40. Śaṅkara was from the tradition of Upaniṣadic learning that was confined to be relatively small number of *nambūtiri* households in Kerala. At the time of Śaṅkara, in Kerala, there was Vedic religion of *Brāhmaṇism* with its strict observance of caste

any case, for both camps—*Mīmāṁsā* and *Vedānta*—the Vedas were still the active, normative source of saving knowledge. But *Mīmāṁsakas* had started gaining precedence over the Upaniṣadic *Vedāntin*s, during the time of Śaṅkara.[546]

There was another religious orientation among the Vedic *brāhmaṇas*. They accepted religious aspects of *Vaiṣṇavism* or *Śaivism* especially in the day to day matters of worship. Therefore, there were *śaiva* or *vaiṣṇava brāhmaṇas.* This was not the feature only of *brāhmaṇas* but also of other castes; there were *Śaivites* from any caste and *Vaiṣṇavas* of any caste.[547] Many *Śaiva* and *Vaiṣṇava* temples were built during this time and they became centres of worship and education.[548]

---

rules as a group of *brāhmaṇas* called *nambūtiris* as its champions. The caste system became established in Kerala, with *nambūtiris* at the top of the hierarchy, *śūdra*s remained just below, and then many outcastes at the bottom as *izhvas* and *pariahs* as the lowest of all. There were no proper *kṣatriyas* and *vaiśyas*. See Gurukkal, "Sankara," 40.

[546] Gurukkal, "Sankara," 40; Tripathi, *Renaissance of Hinduism and the Decline and Eclipse of Buddhism*, 267.

[547] Sastri, *A History of South India,* 382; Thapar, *Early India,* 350; Altson, *Śaṃkara on the Absolute,* 9.

[548] Thapar, *Early India,* 357–359.

Apart from these indigenous religions, there were foreign religions such as Islam[549] and Christianity[550] to which people were attracted mainly because they preached the possibility of worship for all, irrespective of caste-rules.[551]

4.4.2.1.4 Śaṅkara's Theoretical Audience

The works of Śaṅkara, due to its solidity of the content, style of dialogue and debate, and the use of Sanskrit which was not the vernacular of the common people, shows his immediate listeners were elite of the society.[552] Śaṅkara's theoretical audience consists of the three higher castes, *brāhmaṇas*, *kṣatriyas* and *vaiśyas*, all of whom are entitled to study Veda, whose life is especially defined by the duties of the four stages

---

[549] The contact of south India with Islam is much older (in the first half of seventh century) than that of the North. Muslim traders settled in numerous parts of Malabar Coast, married the women of the country, and the issue of such unions became the Māppiḷḷas (Moplahs). Such Muslim traders were encouraged by the Hindu *rajas* who used them to produce horses for their cavalry and to operate their fleets. A doubtful legend relates the conversion to Islam of the last of the Perumal rulers of Kerala, Cheraman Perumal. He is said to have made the pilgrimage to Mecca and to have sent directions from there to the rulers of his home land to receive Muslims hospitably and to build mosques for them. See Sastri, *A History of South India,* 396.

[550] A persistent but doubtful tradition ascribes the introduction of Christianity in South India to St. Thomas, in the first century CE. The strength of the community was increased by a number of immigrations of Christians from western countries, from Bagdad, Nineveh, Jerusalem, and other places. See Sastri, *A History of South India,* 397.

[551] Clooney, "Finding One's Place in the Text," 3.

[552] Gurukkal points out, Śaṅkara had in mind that Vedas offer the normative for the commons, because Vedic rituals aimed at earthly rewards, while Upaniṣads provide the universal truth to the wise. Therefore, as an adherent to Upaniṣads he must have preached his *Vedānta* to those who are above the worldly desires with certain high moral and intellectual standards. See Gurukkal, "Sankara," 40.

of life.[553] His discourses and his pedagogy that appears in his works generally show that it was not directly intended to the common folk for a general reading but to a selected audience, most probably, *sannyāsins* who had renounced the world and hailed mainly from a *Mīmāṁsaka* background.[554] It is probable that he concentrated on the intellectuals in the villages rather than the city dwellers and he gradually won the respect of *brāhmaṇas* and feudal Lords.[555]

4.4.2.2 Hermeneutical Task and Agenda of Śaṅkara

The issue of caste and the exclusion of *śūdras* from the study of Vedas are located within the Vedic corpus which is by and large the liturgical, theological and philosophical discourses of *brāhmaṇa* authors. Exclusion from *brahmajijñāsā*, which amounts to the denial of the possibility for self-realisation on the basis of birth, might take a different intensity from the background of present emphasis on the human person, and the value of equality. So, the problem of *śūdra*-exclusion cannot be studied from the bare point of view of sociology or from the sole framework of subaltern empowerment which depends on social analysis through the collected data on the existing social factors. Hence, a fair attempt to understand Śaṅkara demands that the enquirer has

---

[553] Comans, *The Method of Early Advaita Vedānta,* 316.

[554] Mayeda, introduction to *A Thousand Teachings*, 5, 91.

[555] Mayeda, introduction to *A Thousand Teachings*, 5. Mayeda opinions, in the cities the power of the Buddhism was still strong (though already declining), and Jainism prevailed among the merchants and manufactures. *Śaivism* and *Vaiṣṇavism* occupied the minds of the ordinary people. There were also hedonists in the cities. It was difficult for Śaṅkara to preach his philosophy to these people. See Mayeda, introduction to *A Thousand Teachings*, 5.

to get into the context and the ideologies of his time. Therefore, in understanding Śaṅkara's position on *śūdra*-exclusion, it is important to consider his hermeneutical context and to make an attempt to grasp his prejudices and intentions in his task as an exegete. While analysing the hermeneutical disposition of Śaṅkara it is important to note the following:

1) While theorizing, Śaṅkara, being an *ācārya* or *guru* with Vedic philosophy and theology, held certain priorities which are strongly based on scripture and the Vedic tradition to which he belonged. It is important to get into the question, what must be those convictions which he considered *apriori* and never questioned and on which, most probably, he placed his stance on *śūdra*-exclusion.
2) It is unlikely that Śaṅkara, as an interpreter, was solely focusing on the exact meaning of the text and the intention of the author. He has very creatively responded to his time through his interpretative task. An enquiry into the question, did Śaṅkara completely turn a deaf ear to the social and religious changes of his time, especially those focused on equality and dignity of human person, is very significant. This would give some light into why he could not openly admit *śūdra* for the Vedic study and had to maintain a dilemma in this regard.

4.4.2.2.1 Hermeneutical Prejudices of Śaṅkara

As a thinker from the Vedic tradition of *Brāhmaṇism* and as a *sannyāsin*, Śaṅkara held certain convictions and beliefs uncompromisingly. Here the point is not to enquire why Śaṅkara accepted these without questioning them, but to recognize the fact that he accepted them, and how he, remaining within the framework of these, made all possible attempts to come in terms with changing social realities.

4.4.2.2.1.1 Faith in the Scriptures

Śaṅkara had great faith and devotion to the Vedic scriptures. From the Vedic tradition—both from *Mīmāṁsā* and *Vedānta*—he inheritedthe faith in the eternal, authorless and infallible character of *śruti* (Ta U Bh 2.3; BS Bh1.3.28; 1.3.29; 1.1.2; 1.1.4). As a result of this, and of his study of other systems of religious philosophies, his erudition in Upaniṣads, and above all, from his own experience, he believed that *śruti*, especially Upaniṣads, are the source of valid knowledge regarding *Brahman* (BS Bh 2.1.31). For him, they are capable of providing a *brahmajijñāsu* with excellent and sure results.[556] Prior to *nididhyāsana* that leads to the self-realising experience, the aspirant must get ascertain the truth of the teaching through a thorough rational questioning (*manana*) lest one would interiorize untruth (Ke U Bh 2.1; Upad 18. 123–126). This ascertaining of the truth would be the chief aim of his commentaries. Therefore, in his exegetical task he was guided by the primacy of *śruti*, and wanted to establish the inner connectedness by explaining away the apparent contradictions in them (BS Bh 3.2.21).[557]

---

[556] De Smet, "Śaṅkara's Non-Dualism," in *Understanding Śaṅkara*, 310.

[557] Richard De Smet, "Śaṅkara's Perspective on Truth and Meaning," in *Understanding Śaṅkara,* 261.

4.4.2.2.1.2 Appreciation for and Allegiance with True Tradition

Śaṅkara in his search for truth came across *ācāryas* of true wisdom. He had his *ācārya* as Govindapāda who was the disciple of Gauḍapāda. He had great regard for the lineage of teachers (*parambara*).Through them alone, he believed, the true wisdom can be effectively and fruitfully mediated.[558]

Śaṅkara's works show a persistent emphasis on the importance of receiving traditional instruction. This is evident from his frequent compounding of the two words "scripture" (*śāstra*) and "teacher" (*ācārya*) such as, *śāstrācāryopadeśa* (instruction by way of the scripture and the teacher) and *vedāntācāryopadeśa* (instruction by way of the Upaniṣads and the teacher) (BS Bh 3.4.51; Bṛ U Bh 1.4.2; BG Bh 8.8; 13.30; 13.34; 18.16; 18.17; 18.50). Thus knowledge of *Brahman* is not just a matter of a serious, solitary engagement with the text, accompanied with reasoning and austerities (Ke U Bh 1.4). It is a matter of committed seeker seriously engaging the scripture by listening it under the guidance of a competent teacher with a deep devotion to him.[559] "Knowledge imparted by those who have full enlightenment becomes effective, not any other" (BG Bh 4.34).[560]

The whole endeavour of Śaṅkara consists in imparting to his disciples the meaning of the scriptures which he

---

[558] Comans, *The Method of Early Advaita Vedānta*, 183.

[559] Comans, *The Method of Early Advaita Vedānta*, 183.

[560] ये सम्यग्दर्शिनः तैः उपदिष्टं ज्ञानं कार्यक्षमं भवति, न इतरत् इति भगवतः मतम् ॥ (BG Bh 4.34) Cf. Śaṅkara, *The Bhagavad-gītā with the Commentary of Śrī Śaṅkarācārya*, ed., Dinakar Vishnu Gokhale, 81.

considered as true.[561] His works take the character of pedagogy, and it is dialogical, and the author is the pedagogue or *guru*. His teaching indicates that he himself has thoroughly grasped the entire doctrine which he exposes. It even seems to imply that he has mystically realized the truth of the doctrine, although he never refers explicitly to such an experience of as his own, but only as the experience of the enlightened men as testified by the *śruti* (BS Bh 4.1.15; 2.1.14; 4.1.19; Bṛ U Bh 1.4.7). As such it is not an enquiry performed by the *guru* for his own account, but it is pedagogical enquiry performed by the *guru* for the sake of disciples.[562]

4.4.2.2.1.3 Acceptance of *Varṇa* Division of Society

Śaṅkara, from his firm faith in Vedas and the respect for true tradition, accepted the Vedic social system of *varṇa*. Not only for Śaṅkara, but for the *brāhmaṇic* tradition at large, the *varṇa* system is good and the best in itself. It is not merely an ordering of society but rather it includes Vedic cosmogony and Vedic ritualism.[563] Brian K. Smith makes an observation:

> The varṇa scheme, like the Vedas themselves, is traced back in the Vedic texts to the dawn of time: canon and

---

[561] De Smet, "The Fundamental Antinomy of Sri Śaṅkarācārya's Methodology," in *Understanding Śaṅkara*, 75.

[562] De Smet, "The Fundamental Antinomy of Sri Śaṅkarācārya's Methodology," in *Understanding Śaṅkara*, 75–76.

[563] Brian K. Smith gives an account of how Vedas and *varṇa* are related. The interconnectedness between Vedic origin of cosmos and Vedas and meters and social class are expounded. See Brian K. Smith, "The Veda and the Authority of Class: Reduplicating Structures of Veda and *Varṇa* in Ancient Indian Texts," in *Authority, Anxiety, and Canon: Essays in Vedic Interpretation*, ed. Laurie L. Patton (Delhi: Sri Satguru Publications, 1995), 67–85.

> social classification are both part of creation itself according to Vedic cosmogonies. Canon and class are not only primordial; both are also represented in the Veda as structurally reduplicative of a generalized cosmic pattern and are therefore both supposedly part of the "natural order of things."[564]

Hence, Vedic concept of *varṇa* cannot be ignored or bypassed (BS Bh 1.1.3; 1.3.30; 1.3.29). The access to Vedic hymns, primarily being the speech-acts for the religious rituals, is very much related to the notions of sacred, and cannot be treated as any other texts which also might give knowledge. In this sense, the person's eligibility and exclusion had a great role to play. For an outsider, the one who does not belong to and have no faith in the Vedic tradition, from the point of sociology or other axiological sciences it may be evil. But Śaṅkara worked out within the framework of *varṇa* rules and the hierarchical notion of the society; but denied as far as possible the evils implied in it when it is put into practice. His *a-dvaitic* notion that every person has same source and cause, the *Brahman*, indicates how his theorizing has enough scope for speaking against evil practices in the name of *varṇa*.

4.4.2.2.1.4 Looking at Society through Vedas

The whole *brāhmaṇic* theologising and philosophising, with their faith in Vedas, looked at society through Vedas; and not vice versa. That is to say, Vedas were not thought to be a revelation added later to an already created and ordered natural world. But they, as authorless and eternal, contain the structure of the world and social order from its

---

[564] Smith, "The Veda and the Authority of Class," in *Authority, Anxiety, and Canon*, 68.

beginning;[565] Vedas precede society, and indeed was a key factor in the construction of it (BS Bh 1.3.28). It is not the case that the social facts existed first and then, after observing them, Vedic injunctions are modelled. Śaṅkara, being true to his tradition, worked within a realm of intelligibility defined by the Vedas. "The Veda is not only a normative guide to how one should act; as constitutive of the world itself, it also insures that such right action will be occurring within a setting properly conformed to the values and patterns of right action. If humans act according to the Veda, their lives will go well."[566] From this point of view, according to Śaṅkara, *varṇa* classification and *śūdra*-exclusion is not a fact first found in the society and later included in the Vedas but rather Vedas have ordered the society in this fashion and thus those are to be accepted.

4.4.2.2.1.5 Śaṅkara the Valuationist: Focus on the Excellent

Śaṅkara, the *guru* who taught wisdom, was keen on ascertaining the values, evaluating them and choosing the best among them in view of leading one to eternity. Therefore, discernment (*viveka*) has become primary virtue for him. The first of four qualifications laid down by Śaṅkara for the study of *Vedānta* is *viveka,* which is, 'the capacity to discriminate between eternal and impermanent realities' (BS Bh intro.). The wise people discriminate the excellent from the merely

---

[565] Clooney, "Finding One's Place in the Text," 8. Śaṅkara states: "it goes without saying that, that great Being has absolute omniscience and omnipotence, since from Him emerge the Ṛg-veda, etc.—divided into many branches and constituting the source of classification into gods, animals, men, castes, stages of life, etc., and the source of all kinds of knowledge" (BS Bh 1.1.3 p. 19). He argues for the beginninglessness of the Vedas in BS Bh 1.3.29.

[566] Clooney, "Finding One's Place in the Text," 20.

pleasant (Ka U Bh 2.2.12–13). Human life is presented with various values and disvalues. However, Śaṅkara is "not interested in a hierarchy of values but only in the top ones which he feels, are alone worthy of our whole-hearted pursuit."[567] "What he sought was exclusively the Excellent; he shunned the rest."[568]

For Śaṅkara the most excellent which a human being can desire is self-realization i.e. *mokṣa*, than *artha*, *kāma* and *dharma*. *Mokṣa* is knowledge of the true nature of *Brahman* as identical to *Ātman*. To achieve this aim the most effective and excellent means is *śruti*, thus he emphasizes the primacy of *śruti*. From among *śruti*, *jñānakāṇḍa*—the domain of knowledge which consists of Upaniṣads—has to be preferred than *karmakāṇḍa* which is centred on sacrificial ritual. Even in Upaniṣads those propositions which directly refer to *Brahman* possess primacy and independent authority.[569]

Among all other *pramāṇas*, *śabda* or *śruti* is supreme, for it alone can provide us with knowledge which results in liberation. All other means for knowledge subservient to and

---

[567] De Smet, "Śaṅkara's Perspective on Meaning and Truth," in *Understanding Śaṅkara*, 256.

[568] De Smet, "Śaṅkara's Non-Dualism," in *Understanding Śaṅkara*, 308.

[569] Even from among those indicative injunctions, those concerning the material world and physical realities need not be given importance. Because, physical realities can be known through other means for knowledge such as perception and inference; they are subservient to the purpose of teaching *Brahman* (Bṛ U Bh intro.; BS Bh 1.4.14). The validity of *śruti* holds good only with regard to matters concerning ends and means which are not known through other *pramāṇas*. A hundred *śrutis* may declare that fire is cold or dark; still they possess no authority in that matter (BG Bh 18.66).

may contribute to the *śruti*-knowledge in its function of revealing and realizing the ultimate.[570]

To achieve this knowledge through *śruti* the most apt disposition is monastic renunciation. Among the castes, the chief one is the *brāhmaṇa* and also other upper castes that are formally entitled for the study of Vedas.[571] Therefore, in the quest for *Brahman*, which is the supreme goal of human life, Śaṅkara must be adamant on choosing the excellent and getting qualified with the prerequisites.

4.4.2.2.2 Hermeneutical Intentions and Inclusion-Exclusion Dilemma of Śaṅkara

Śaṅkara's program of liberation and the implied inclusion-exclusion dilemma in it are to be observed within the frame of his firm convictions that have substantially affected his theorizing. To delve further into how he reached in the dilemma, we have to reflect, how far he has responded to the social realities of his time as an exegete, within the confines of constraints which he did not substantially question. These carry the attention to the hermeneutical agenda and task of Śaṅkara which would shed light into the reasons for his position on exclusion;in between inclusion and exclusion.

4.4.2.2.2.1 Exclusion: Not Factual, But Textual

According to Śaṅkara, as it is made clear in *Apaśūdrādhikaraṇam*, the reason why *śūdra*s are excluded

---

[570] See the third chapter of this dissertation, 3.3.1.1.

[571] These, according to Śaṅkara, taking his context into account, are the best dispositions or environment which will make *brahmajijñāsā* unfailingly fruitful. This does not mean their exclusivity to lead one to self-realisation.

from the Vedic study is that they are prohibited by the scriptures. There is nothing about the *śūdra*s that disqualifies them, except that they are those corresponding to the word '*śūdra*' in Veda. He never argues that *śūdra* is disqualified for lack of intelligence or desire or moral qualities or other basic human qualities that make learning impossible.[572] Sociologically and anthropologically, they might be qualified in all these. For Śaṅkara, the only reason for exclusion is that *śūdra* is named in scripture as ineligible for the study of the Vedas.[573] The knowledge received through the texts other than Vedas, possibly through Itihāsas and Purāṇas and the consequent experience of realisation by no way are of a second category, but are of the same as that the upper caste could get through Vedas.[574] Therefore, *śūdra*-exclusion is based not on human nature but on text.

Added to this, it is important to observe, that Śaṅkara was primarily concerned with *varṇa*, and not with *jāti*. He must

[572] Clooney, "Finding One's Place in the Text," 9–10.

[573] In *Apaśūdrādhikaraṇam*, when the opponent argues that Vedas prohibit *śūdra*s only from the performance of sacrifice (Ta.S 7.1.1.6) and not from the acquisition of knowledge, Śaṅkara replies, since it is based on a logic having common application, it suggests that they have no right to knowledge as well, for the logic applies both ways (BS Bh 1.3.34). That is to say, the reason why *śūdra*s are excluded from the sacrifice is the same for the exclusion of them from knowledge. They are excluded only because their name is spelled out in the Vedas as prohibited. The rite of initiation is a necessary prerequisite for the Vedic learning. This requisite is equally applicable whether the learning is for the sake of sacrifice or for the sake of knowledge, for both requires learning. Once *śūdra*s are debarred from learning it applies to both the cases. Hence *śūdra*s who are excluded from initiation, must also be excluded from the acquiring the knowledge, regardless of what they are capable of in theory. See Clooney, "Finding One's Place in the Text," 12–13.

[574] Kane, *History of Dharmaśāstra*, vol.5, pt. 2, 921–922.

not be unaware of the social fact that the people were grouped under more complicated system of *jāti*, than the four *varṇas*. There existed various *jātis* and its sub divisions, mixed castes and so on, among which some were considered on the same or lower status than *śūdra*s. Although *jāti* divisions were a social reality, for him, it was *varṇa* that played a significant role behind the exclusion for it was authorised by Vedas.[575] He considered *varṇa* not as a social structuring done by humans from their practical knowledge for the better functioning of the society. But, for him, *varṇa* was as eternal in its origin as the Vedas were. He points out that it is from the great being who has absolute omnipotence and omniscience emerged *Ṛgveda*, etc. with its classifications of *varṇa* and *āśrama* (BS Bh 1.1.3).

The above discussions underline, for Śaṅkara, the exclusion was not factual, i.e. he did not consider the social reality of *jāti* and the social fact of relegated status of *śūdra*s. It was not based on anthropological or psychological or of any norms of human worth that they are excluded from (the study of Vedas) what they might be capable of (from the point of view of other human sciences). The reason for the exclusion is purely scriptural. Śaṅkara, who looked at society through the Vedas, could not just do away with *varṇa* division and *śūdra*-exclusion.

4.4.2.2.2.2 Accommodating the Value of Equality into the Vedic Norm of *Śūdra*-Exclusion

Śaṅkara, as an exegete, with the available possibilities, has tried to respond to the social situations of his time without

[575] Clooney, "Finding One's Place in the Text," 7–8.

compromising his commitment to the Vedic tradition and Upaniṣadic ideals.

Society, especially the upper caste, considered *śūdra*s to be intellectually and culturally inferior and lacking enough moral and religious purity. Hence there were practices of discriminations which violated the value of equality and worth of the human person. At the same time, society witnessed a growing awareness against this, which took the form of various religious movements such as Buddhism. These movements did their theorizing and based their arguments primarily on the social practice of treating *śūdra*s with low status, and the resulting vices of discrimination such as denial of social and religious rights. For them, *śūdra*s meant those who are inferior especially in moral, social, economic, intellectual and cultural spheres and who are deprived of many rights. Whereas, *brāhmaṇas* meant persons excelling in intelligence, and the moral qualities of truth-telling, etc.[576] From this understanding they worked out for finding the reasons for the existing social practices of discrimination, exclusion and violation of human rights. They found Vedas as giving sanction for these and challenged the Vedic norm of *śūdra*-exclusion.

For Śaṅkara, a *śūdra* is not inferior and a *brāhmaṇa* is not superior inherently. A *brāhmaṇa* or a *śūdra* is identified and recognized so only because of that person's birth in a particular family or from particular parents. This has nothing to do with one's intrinsic value. The distinction is not based on abilities or disabilities such as intellectual, moral, psychological, physical, etc.[577] There is nothing inherently making a *brāhmaṇa* superior and a *śūdra* inferior; no *śūdra* is

---

[576] Clooney, "Finding One's Place in the Text," 11.
[577] Clooney, "Finding One's Place in the Text," 11.

de-humanized and no *brāhmaṇa* is super-humanised. Śaṅkara's reason for exclusion is precisely that *śūdra*s are named in Vedas as those who are ineligible for the study of it. In the Vedic world, it is not *śūdra*s alone but upper caste also suffered some kind of prohibition. Śaṅkara shows in his *Brahmasūtra Bhāṣya*, that *brāhmaṇas* also suffered some kind of ineligibilities, for example, their incompetence for *Rājasūya* sacrifice. For him, if Vedas suggest exclusion of some groups from some privileges, those are to be followed (BS Bh 1.3.33).

He was not looking at the social fact and then interpreting the text, rather for him Vedic text from eternity has defined the society and therefore, he was re-appropriating the society into the textual frame.[578] This being the basic attitude, he had no difficulty in agreeing with the salvation of *śūdra*s. The nature and character of the salvific knowledge, self-realising experience and the liberated life (*jīvanmukta*) are same for *śūdra* and for the upper caste irrespective of whether they acquired it from Vedas or Itihāsa-purāṇas.[579] Here Śaṅkara's effort to deal with "the tension between hierarchical notions of society and the sacred on the one hand and non-hierarchical perceptions of human person and the "core" of religion on the other"[580] is significant. He was aware of the value of the human person and the evils of social discrimination. He took also into account the growing social

---

[578] There is something peculiar in this kind of interpretation. Here, the text is denying what a person (*śūdra*) is really able to (e.g. to learn). The non-*brāhmaṇic* movements, from the received empirical social data tried to denounce the text. But for Śaṅkara, Vedic words are eternal; the society runs or has to run as it is described in the Vedas. See Clooney, "Finding One's Place in the Text," 9–13.

[579] Kane, *History of Dharmaśāstra*, vol. 5, pt. 2, 921–922.

[580] Clooney, "Finding One's Place in the Text," 2.

awareness against the existed evils in the practices of caste rules. He made use of his hermeneutical skill and opened all possible avenues to respond to these but without compromising his basic convictions. Therefore, salvation is open to all including *śūdra*s through the means other than Vedas. Exclusion and inclusion have nothing to do with any inherent virtues or vices; but it is only because Vedas have put the restriction. Thus, neither exclusion from nor inclusion in *brahmajijñāsā*, can be considered unconditional and absolute. Here it is important to note, how Śaṅkara's commitment to Vedas enabled him to define and defend the Vedic position of exclusion, although it is from the narrowest textual ground[581] despite running the risk of being inconsistent in the arguments adduced for it. New ideas and the changes in society are accommodated without letting it touch the core of religious belief.

4.4.2.2.2.3 Revival of Religion in the Spirit of Synthesis and Harmony

Śaṅkara, in his hermeneutical task, had in his mind the intention of reviving and restoring the Vedic religion in the fashion of Upaniṣadic ideals.[582]

The guiding principle in this attempt was the spirit of synthesis and harmony which Śaṅkara nurtured all throughout his task as an exegete and thinker. As the one who was committed to Upaniṣads and of the religion based on it, his task included: first, to expose and oppose the elements in the

---

[581] Clooney, "Finding One's Place in the Text," 21.

[582] De Smet, "Śaṅkara's Non-Dualism," in *Understanding Śaṅkara*, 305. See also Sastri, *A History of South India,* 386; Ayyar, *A History of Kerala*, 111–129.

heterodox and other rival systems, which were against the spirit of *śruti*; secondly, to weld together into a coherent and powerful system the teachings of *śruti*.[583] His spirit of finding harmony extends to (1) establishing the inner harmony of the apparently contradicting Upaniṣadic passages, (2) proving the inner connectedness between *karmakāṇḍa* and *jñānakāṇḍa* of Vedas (3) showing the relatedness between *śruti* and *smṛti*, (4) exposing how other systems of thought are related (or unrelated) to the principles of *śruti,* and (5) finding and bringing the various religions of his time to a synthesis and harmony.[584]

The attempt for revival or renaissance had to address diverse issues existed in the then religious scenario. Śaṅkara had to respond to, on the one hand, the universal soteriology, disregard for cast-rules and simple form of worship preached and practised by non-*Mīmāṁsaka* religions and the large acceptance and following of the common people to these religions, and on the other, *Mīmāṁsakas'* commitment to safeguard the Vedic tradition which they treasured greatly.

Keeping his basic convictions rooted in Upaniṣads intact, Śaṅkara criticised *Mīmāṁsakas* for their extreme ritualism which aimed primarily at happiness and benefits here on earth and in heaven. He wanted to show that there is something noble than these which human heart can and should aspire for, which is the self-realization, and to that end religion should serve. At the same time, he joined with them in sharing their dedication to the Vedic tradition including social ordering

---

583 Devaraja, *An Introduction to Śaṅkara's Theory of Knowledge*, 4.

584 Comans, *The Method of Early Advaita Vedānta*, 169; See the third chapter of this dissertation 3.3.1.2.

of the society through the original spirit of *varṇāśrama* system. Śaṅkara, in tune with Purāṇic religions, did not denounce popular practices of devotion, but rather put them in their proper place; they should dispose the aspirants in their quest for self-realisation, the supreme goal. This realisation is beyond emotion, and is the matter of *jñāna* leading to *brahmānubhava*, which requires the transformation of entire life of the person.[585] He did not regard the devotional practices taught in the *smṛtis*—such as temple worship or repetition of the name of God—as forming the part of the discipline of the *sannyāsi* who has embarked on the Upaniṣadic path to liberation. But he held them, though not mandatory, to be efficacious for the preliminary purification of the mind.[586] He was also influenced by Islam and Christianity and his missionary zeal could be ignited by inspirations received from them.[587]

Śaṅkara's attempt for harmonising the various religions and reviving the Upaniṣadic tradition was done primarily by offering the *Advaitic* metaphysics and theology as the foundation for all diverse religions. In his *Advaitic* spirit he established a basic unity among the existing religions by offering non-dual *Brahman* —which is the absolute reality and the source and cause of everything—as the foundation for them. Basing on this foundation, he could also admit the

---

[585] Rambachan, *The Advaita Worldview*, 20.

[586] Altson, *Śaṃkara on the Absolute,* 10.

[587] According to Murty, Śaṅkara was the first Hindu who travelled debating, convincing and converting people to his *jñānamārga* all over India. His insistence on the non-dual *Brahman* as the only one supreme reality and his missionary zeal must have been very much influenced by Islam and Christianity. See Murty, *Hinduism and its Development,* 95–96.

diversities; the various devotional practices, provided they were not against *śruti* and the Vedic tradition and were observed as the means to serve the ultimate aim, the self-realisation.[588] "Union and friendliness were possible only when a common basis could be so fashioned as to be comprehensive and able to allow for large differences of secondary importance, philosophically as well as practically."[589] This kind of unification is attempted by Śaṅkara through his *Vedānta*, which can make the basis of every religious sect that India has known.[590]

Apart from its philosophical and religious turn, from the political and social point of view, renaissance also included coming in some conciliation with other popular religions; because, even the rulers had started to become active collaborators of popular religions.[591]

In his attempt to renew the *brāhmaṇic* religion from the point of Upaniṣadic tradition and philosophy, Śaṅkara had to be very careful not to get derailed from his Vedic identity and from the true tradition of his teachers. By this time, Vedas had become very much a symbol of authentication. An idea or a thinker, if proved to be rooted in Vedas then it would be established as sanctioned by eternal and divine wisdom.[592] Besides this, it was the mark of heterodox religions to publically challenge the *varṇa* rules and *śūdra*-exclusion. Therefore, unconditional and open proposal to make *śūdra*s eligible for Vedic study would stamp Śaṅkara as a heterodox

---

[588] Murty, *Hinduism and its Development,* 94; Menon, *A Survey of Kerala History,* 130.

[589] Aiyar, *Sri Sankaracarya*, 7–8.

[590] Aiyar, *Sri Sankaracarya*, 8.

[591] Thapar, *Early India*, 325.

[592] Thapar, *Early India*, 309; Lipner, *The Hindus,* 62.

and lose his Vedic credibility. At the same time, Śaṅkara was not unaffected by the universal soteriology of these heterodox, Purāṇic and foreign religions which offered salvation to every one irrespective of caste and which made them popular. He also must be intending to reach the Upaniṣadic ideals and the religion based on it out to the people.[593] Therefore, Śaṅkara, (1) in his spirit of harmony and synthesis, (2) from the intention of renewing the Upaniṣadic view of religion, and (3) from the need of coming to conciliation with the popular religions, became inclusive to the most by keeping *sādhanacatuṣṭaya* and the salvific knowledge open to all irrespective of *varṇa*. But at the same time, as a faithful observer of the Vedic tradition, he could not but hold the exclusion of *śūdra*s from Vedas.

The above discussions draw the conclusion that the inclusion-exclusion dilemma of Śaṅkara, from its historical, social and religious point of view, was mainly the result of: (1) his attempt to revive the Vedic and Purāṇic Hinduism based on Upaniṣadic ideals, in which, the spirit of harmony and synthesis remained as undercurrent; (2) his holding on to "a new brahmanical universalism to compete with the heterodox religions and to come to terms with social change;"[594] (3) at the same time, it was also "a reinforcement of brahmanical exclusivity to stem the tide of change and regroup under the banner of the duties of caste and stages of life (*varṇa-āśrama-*

---

[593] It is important to note that this revival within the Vedic tradition after the ideals of Upaniṣads had remarkable impact on the elite, and less among the common people. Solidity of the ideas and the use of Sanskrit could be some of the reasons. See Sastri, *A History of South India,* 386; Menon, *A Survey of Kerala History,* 130.

[594] Young, "Śaṅkara on the Salvation of Women and Śūdras," in *Goddesses and Women in the Indic Religious Tradition*, 132.

dharma)."[595] Śaṅkara's hermeneutical skill is evident in his reconciliation of these seemingly contradictory goals which must be also the part of his hermeneutical agenda.

4.4.2.2.2.4 Liberation through the Text and the Need for Culture of Liberation

According to Śaṅkara, the final realization is through *jñānamārga*, through *śravaṇa-manana-nididhyāsana*. The 'truth' at the point of its realization is located after the 'text' i.e. after the text is studied. This is amount to say, the simple event of revelation of truth, the *brahmānubhava* is possible after the engagement with text, through the linguistic understanding of its meaning. Communication through language, especially in the case of grasping the truth from the texts of Vedas, will effectively take place when it is done in a proper environment, under certain pedagogically prescribed circumstances.[596] Hence, a fitting circumstance or environment which makes the aspirant socially, religiously and morally ripe for the reception of truth is highly suggested through both internal and external prerequisites. The internal requisite consists in growth of moral virtues through the fourfold *sādhanas* and the external criteria is being qualified with the social and traditional factors, such as non-*śūdratva*, *sannyāsa*, etc. which makes cultivation of moral virtues and liberation possible. This environment which makes the aspirant

[595] Young, "Śaṅkara on the Salvation of Women and Śūdras," in *Goddesses and Women in the Indic Religious Tradition*, 132.

[596] Clooney, *Theology After Vedānta,* 119.

most disposed for the liberation through text can be termed as 'culture of liberation', which has to be fostered carefully.[597]

The question is, to what extent the various elements of this 'environment' are necessary for the experience of liberation. If it is taken to be absolutely necessary, then the universal aspect of *Advaita* program of liberation will be subjected to, and limited by a particular culture, and it becomes exclusive. If the culture of liberation is considered interpretable and is relativized in significant ways then it is not absolutely necessary, and then, it becomes inclusive by opening a great space in *Advaita* for trans-cultural, universal approach to salvation.[598] But at the same time, if it is open to interpretation without any restrictions, then the very essential of the liberation program, the *brahmānubhava* could be lost. Thus it needs a balancing.

According to Śaṅkara, an aspirant, however qualified the person be, if not with internal prerequisites of *sādhanacatuṣṭaya* cannot achieve the goal of this quest. That is, the internal aspect of the culture of liberation, the moral environment for the liberation is held uncompromised. But the external aspect is relativized, subject to interpretation as per the need arises.[599] That is why, though Śaṅkara is advocating that a *brahmajijñāsu* must be a non-*śūdra*, *sannyāsi* etc., he makes proper interpretations for those rules in view of giving priority for the direct means of liberation and the internal moral virtues

[597] Thomas A. Forthoeffel, *Knowing Beyond Knowledge: Epistemologies of Religious Experience in Classical and Modern Advaita* (Delhi: Motilal Banarsidas, 2002), 58.

[598] Forthoeffel, *Knowing Beyond Knowledge*, 57.

[599] Forthoeffel, *Knowing Beyond Knowledge*, 57.

which makes the liberation possible. Therefore, Śaṅkara can be placed on the side of inclusivism.

But then, taking the reflection further, another question has to be on the dais: although the internal requisites are necessary, are they adequate? If they are not fostered and assisted by certain externally cultured environments, the growth in the moral virtues and the salvific knowledge would become extremely difficult; the aspirant even might miss the target. Thus, those external requirements for *brahmajijñāsā* are—though not unalterably *sine qua non* for liberation, at least in its interpreted and altered form, tailored to the context with the purpose of better result—are not without relevance.

The aspirants who take up *Vedāntic* study can be of two types: *mumukṣu* (the one who has an intense desire for liberation) and *jijñāsu* (the one who has desire to know, one who might commit the study of scriptures out of intellectual curiosity or of any other reasons).[600] Swami Tapovanam states: "Vedanta is not for mere intellectual recreation, or for a mere expansion of one's intellectual fancy. One has to dedicate one's life to it and thus strive to realise this Supreme Truth."[601] From the *Śāṅkaravedāntic* point of view, it is significant to note: (1) Śaṅkara's program of liberation addresses and is designed for a '*mumukṣu*', and (2) *Advaita* tradition does not distinguish between *mumukṣu* and *jijñāsu* i.e. every *jijñāsu*

[600] Rambachan, "Rethinking *Advaita*," 10.

[601] Swami Tapovanam, "The Glory of Brahma-vidyā," trans. Swami Chinmayananda, in *Advaitāmṛtam*, ed. Sandhya Sundar and Dilip Kumar Rana (Ernakulam: Chinmaya International Foundation, 2015), 15. Swami Tapovanam (1889–1957) of Uttarkashi, was an *Advaitic sannyāsi* and scholar.

must be a *mumukṣu.*[602] Because, the knowledge of *Brahman* is such that the knower acquires transformation, and lives his/her life as the enlightened (Mu U Bh 3.2.9).

The specificity of Śaṅkara's programme of *brahmajijñāsā* indicates, for him, Upaniṣads are the excellent source and *sannyāsa* is the best disposition in the quest for *Brahman.* He preferred always the best, and paid little attention to the rest. This is because, (1) the quest for *Brahman* is the supreme, ultimate goal of a human person, and (2) it demands the wholehearted pursuit of the aspirant.

From the discussion above, the need for external requirements—although they might exclude many from *brahmajijñāsā*—is evident. Two sets of reasons can be identified for the same. The first set of reasons are based on "the truth is realizable after the text is grasped" and the other set is on "the knowledge of *Brahman* is transformative." The reasons could be summarised as follows:

1) The truth is realizable after the text is grasped.

   The need for external reqirements, and therefore, the consequent exclusion is in place because: (a) For Śaṅkara, the truth is posterior to the text. Only through a prepared reading, i.e. the skillful engagement with the text by the committed reader, the realization can take place. The discovery of truth from the text has to be done carefully and patiently without breaking its threads of interconnectedness.[603] Thus, competence is restricted to conscious, intelligent persons, who are

---

[602] The one who takes up the study of Vedic texts are expected to do it with the faith in it and with the purpose of *mokṣa*. See Rambachan, *Accomplishing the Accomplished*, xi.

[603] Clooney, *Theology After Vedānta,* 126.

equipped with physical, mental and moral capacities.[604] (b) The knowledge of *Brahman* is gradual; not because *Brahman* is a temporal reality, but because knowledge's venue is textual. It requires an eligible listener gradually making a transition from the necessary words which speak of *Brahman* to the simple knowledge of *Brahman.*[605]

2) The knowledge of *Brahman* is transformative.

   The exclusion occurs because: (a) Knowing *Brahman* from/through the text is not a mere rational grasping and not mere intellectual information; it is the realization of the identity between *Ātman* and *Brahman* which amounts to the transformation of the aspirant.[606] The entire *Vedānta* program of liberation, seeks to produce persons who are ripe for knowledge of *Brahman*, precisely because they have been affected by what they study.[607] Therefore, the quest for *Brahman* demands, unless the aspirant's life-style and value systems are in harmony with the demands of the truth they cannot hope for real enlightenment. (b) Śaṅkara's program of liberation is addressed to the *mumukṣu*, who has a desire for liberation and who has a faith in *śruti* tradition as the adequate means for liberation. It is not designed for those who wish to be passive consumers, or merely grateful assimilators of neatly labeled conclusions, or for those who engage in

---

[604] Clooney, *Theology After Vedānta,* 136.

[605] Clooney, *Theology After Vedānta,* 126.

[606] Rambachan, *The Advaita Worldview*, 20.

[607] Clooney, "From Anxiety to Bliss," in *Authority, Anxiety, and Canon*, 161.

> learning the text for the sake of intellectual curiosity.[608] This will do a great to avoid misreading, wrong interpretation and thus leading people away from the truth of the text.[609]

Śaṅkara, who looks for the excellent which are worthy of wholehearted pursuit, demands the prerequisites for *brahmajiñāsā* lest the quest go unsuccessful. The restrictions are attempts to ensure that the 'transformation' occurs in the engagement with text.[610] Therefore, Śaṅkara, on one hand, is on the side of inclusivism for he holds that it is not the external but internal requirements that are uncompromisingly necessary, but on the other, he is exclusivist because, with ample reasons, he stresses the need for an environment, external criteria for the fruitful quest for *Brahman*.

4.4.2.2.2.5 *Dharmajijñāsā* and *Brahmajijñāsā*: Bridging *Pūrva* and *Uttara Mīmāṁsā*

Pūrvamīmāṁsā (*Mīmāṁsā*) and *Uttaramīmāṁsā* (*Vedānta*) are closely connected. They represent two streams belonging to Vedic tradition and share the common aim of systematising the meaning of the Vedas. Both these traditions accept *śruti* as: (1) the single means to know about those things which are beyond the scope of sense perception, (2) eternal and authorless. Hence they accept that the Vedic knowledge can have no possibility of any defect[611] (Br U Bh 1.1.intro; 1.3.1; BS Bh 2.1.1; 2.1.27; 2.3.1).

---

[608] Clooney, *Theology After Vedānta,* 34.
[609] Clooney, *Theology After Vedānta,* 151.
[610] Clooney, *Theology After Vedānta,*32.
[611] Comans, *The Method of Early Advaita Vedānta*, 168.

But they differ in certain important matters. For *Vedāntins*, *mokṣa* means self-realization, and it is the knowledge of *Brahman*; whereas for *Mīmāṁsā* it is in the attainment of heaven through rituals.[612] *Vedānta* took Upaniṣads as primary for it is the *jñānakāṇḍa* which give emphasis on knowledge of *Brahman*; but for *Mīmāṁsā, Saṁhitā* and *Brāhmaṇa* portions of the Vedas are important for it is *karmakāṇḍa*, dealing with the sacrificial rituals. Therefore, for *Vedāntins*, quest for *Brahman* (*brahmajijñāsā*) is the most desirable aim of a human person but for *Mīmāṁsakas* quest for *dharma* or *karma* (*dharmajijñāsā*) replaces it.[613]

For *Mīmāṁsā*, injunctions or *vidhi* (enjoining the performance of acceptable actions) and prohibitions or *niṣedha* (forbidding actions that are opposed to *dharma*) are authoritative. All other parts of Vedas are secondary and they, for their significance and meaning, dependon a connection with the injunctions. The final section of Vedas, the Upaniṣads, are viewed by them as an appendage to the injunctive texts which either praise these texts or provide information that is useful for the performance of Vedic rituals. The Upaniṣads, they claimed, do not have any independent subject matter.[614] Therefore, for them, the *karmakāṇḍa* portion of the Vedas are concerned with providing ritual methods for the attainment of

---

[612] *Mīmāṁsakas* aimed at mundane riches and pleasures and well-being as the aim of life. These they tried to achieve through sacrifices and other rituals. Even in life after death they sought heaven where all these joys are met with. But for *Vedāntins* renouncing all these pleasures and enjoyment were considered the best means for *mokṣa* which they considered as being freed form the cycle of re-birth. See Kane, *History of Dharmaśāstra*, vol. 5, pt. 2, 1649; Lipner, *The Hindus*, 39.

[613] Lipner, *The Hindus*, 45.

[614] Rambachan, "Where Words Can Set Free," in *Texts in Context*, 33–34.

wealth, power, fame and pleasure, here and in the hereafter, which are considered the final goal of human life. It specifies the proper ethical and ritual action, which is meant by the word *dharma*, for the accomplishment of these ends.[615] But for *Vedāntin*s, Upaniṣadic statements are authoritative by themselves. They can lead one to self-realisation, the final aim of every human person (BS Bh 1.1.7). Vedic injunctions of *karmakāṇḍa* are of secondary importance.[616] Comans observes:

> According to Mīmāṁsakas, the entire Veda is ultimately about *dharma*, and *dharma* is characterised by an injunction to do something or to refrain from doing it. Śaṅkara argues repeatedly against this position. He does agree that the majority of the Veda is concerned with *dharma* and concerns injunctions to do or to refrain from doing certain types of specified activity, but against the Mīmāṁsakas he strenuously upholds that the Upaniṣad portion of the Veda is distinct from the rest of the Veda in so far as the Upaniṣads aim to teach Self-knowledge, and through this they alone can fulfil the ultimate human-goal, liberation from the sorrows of transmigratory existence (*saṁsāra*).[617]

About the difference between *Mīmāṁsā* and *Vedānta* Rambachan remarks: "If the qualified student for the ritual section is the one who is desirous of pleasure in this or other worlds, the qualified student for the knowledge section is the one who has discovered the limits of pleasure by reflecting

[615] Rambachan, *The Advaita Worldview,* 50.

[616] Rambachan, "Where Words Can Set Free," in *Texts in Context*, 33–34, 42.

[617] Comans, *The Method of Early Advaita Vedānta*, 170.

deeply on the nature of her experiences in the world and has developed an attitude of detachment in relation to these."[618]

For *Mīmāṁsakas*, *dharma,* the goal of life, can be attained through the life lived by following the rituals and social obligations directed by the *karmakāṇḍa* of Vedas. It requires, getting married and having some property. Therefore, the mode of life they considered ideal was *gṛhastāśrama.* For a *Vedāntin,* on the other hand, the goal is quest for *Brahman*, which is considered transcending ritual and social life, hence, *sannyāsa* is considered to be the most preferred *āśrama.*

Though there are differences, this does not mean Śaṅkara took a complete deviation from *Mīmāṁsā* tradition. Śaṅkara explored all possible relations between *Pūrva* and *Uttara Mīmāṁsā* and geared them to the renewal of *Brāhmaṇism. Śāṅkaravedānta* does not deny the study of the earlier portions of Veda and the performance of rituals enjoined by it. In keeping with the spirit of Upaniṣads, for Śaṅkara, these are preparatory as cleansing the mind of its lower passions, and as making a person worthy of receiving the knowledge of the highest truth about the one supreme spirit. If the *karma*s are done in a detached spirit they can very much dispose the aspirant for self-realization. For him, the study of the Veda does not merely consist in learning the *mantra*s by heart, but knowing the reality behind it[619] (BS Bh 1.3.30). In this sense he does not totally deny rituals and *gṛhastāśrama*; but, unlike *sannyāsa*, *gṛhasta* is not a must for attaining realisation, it could even be bypassed.

---

[618] Rambachan, *The Advaita Worldview,* 50.

[619] Kane, *History of Dharmaśāstra*, vol. 5, pt. 2, 918; Kane, *History of Dharmaśāstra*, vol. 2, pt. 1, 356.

Śaṅkara's response to *Mīmāṁsā*, can be summarised as follows:

1) He attempted, as far as possible, to come into conciliation with them. To this end (a) he assigned a proper place for ritualism, (b) *gṛhastāśrama* was taken into consideration and agreed that the salvation is attainable while being a *gṛhastāśrami*, and (c) he did not violate the norm of *śūdra*'s exclusion from the study of Vedas.
2) At the same time, he maintained stand-off with them by being unwilling to make a compromise with his basic *Vedāntic* positions. Therefore, against *Mīmāṁsakas*, he held Upaniṣads as constituting independent means of knowledge; that they teach the liberating knowledge of the non-dual self; and that the knowledge they generate is entirely independent of the performance of the rites.[620]

In consistency with his *Vedāntic* spirit which consists in *jñāna*-oriented and Upaniṣadic-based philosophy and religion, Śaṅkara, admitted the possibility of self-realisation for all; being faithful to Vedic and *Mīmāṁsaka* tradition, restricted its quest through Vedas to the upper caste alone.

Conclusion

The scope of Śaṅkara's problem of *śūdra*-exclusion can be reduced to or can be focused on the exclusion of them only from Vedas and not from salvation. They are not excluded from the possibility of self-realization, the liberation; they can have the liberation through the texts other than Vedas. But this

---

[620] Comans, *The Method of Early Advaita Vedānta*, 164.

reduction does not make the problem of exclusion unrelated to *brahmajijñāsā*. Śaṅkara's program of *brahmajijñāsā*, taken from his specificity, cannot be carried out without having exposure to *śruti*, especially to Upaniṣads. For him, they are the excellent source for salvific knowledge than any other; only in the case of an aspirant who cannot have access to them need to think about another option such as Itihāsa-Purāṇas. But the problem takes another turn, when reflected on the question, how far, the exclusion of human persons from the 'excellent' (i.e. Vedas for salvation) based only on their birth, can be justified. Even the reduced version of exclusion—exclusion is only from the Vedas and not from salvation—is argued in the *Apaśūdrādhikaraṇam* less convincingly and not without pitfalls.

Śaṅkara, neither openly rejects *śūdra*-exclusion nor wholeheartedly accepts inclusivism. He has taken an in-between position: he is an exclusivist, for he strictly holds *śūdra*s are ineligible for the study of Vedas, but he is also on the inclusive side for he agrees *śūdra* can have salvation through the means other than Vedas and the nature of salvific experience and the character of the one who is saved (*jīvanmukta*) are same for the upper caste and for *śūdars*. The *Śāṅkarite* dilemma between inclusion and exclusion is, in fact, a tension between the truth and the text: the truth of the Vedic text is universal, therefore inclusive, but the possessing of the truth is 'in-and-through' the text, in which all the *Mīmāṁsā* rules on getting access to the text and on deriving the meaning of it are to be observed, which makes it on the charge of exclusion.

It is most unlikely that Śaṅkara, being an original thinker and as the one who lived in a time when various religious and philosophical movements were challenging the exclusion, was unaware of the gravity of the issue or did not take it serious enough. Hence his position on exclusion must be intentional and must be with adequate reasons. The reasons for the dilemma are better convincing when they are enquired from the point of his hermeneutical prejudices and agendas. Some of his basic convictions must have become humus for his position on *śūdra*-exclusion. They are: his faith in the scriptures, allegiance with true tradition, acceptance of *varṇa* division of society, attitude of looking at society through Vedas (not vice versa) and his focus on the excellent. Being founded on these he has very creatively responded to the social changes, especially those which are pertaining to *śūdra*-exclusion. Therefore, as an exegete, Śaṅkara must not be only translating the original author, but has creatively brought out his own originality by intentionally incorporating his ideas.

Śaṅkara's dilemma must be understood from the fact that he looked at society through Vedas and not the Vedas through Society. Hence, for him, the problem is primarily textual than factual or social. But at the same time, he has not left out the social reality of caste and the vices related with it. His dilemma can be understood from his attempt to accommodate the value of equality into the Vedic norm of *śūdra*-exclusion making use of all the possible ways but without compromising his basic convictions. In his interpreting task he has maintained the intention of reviving the Vedic religion and coming to some conciliation with *Mīmāṁsā* without diverting from his Upaniṣadic ideals. To achieve this purpose he has accommodated different ideas and this contributed very much to his position on exclusion. Since the liberation is through engaging with the 'text', it consists in the linguistic understanding. This necessitates that the aspirant be qualified with the prerequisites which will foster the culture of liberation and make the aspirant well-disposed for the salvific knowledge. Among the prerequisites external requirements can be subjected to interpretation but not the internal; they are the *sine qua non* for *brahmajijñāsā*. This too indicates why Śaṅkara took an in-between position on exclusion.

The dilemma of Śaṅkara on the problem of inclusion and exclusion, taken in his social, cultural, religious and philosophical context, is reasonable. As an interpreter, from his available textual possibility—though narrow—he has addressed the issue of *śūdra*-exclusion and has responded creatively to the changing notions of society. This will serve as an orientation for the future. The present *Śāṅkaravedāntin*s have to proceed further with it, especially by giving an *Advaitic* response to the problems related with exclusion. Such responses are significant and are challenging as well. It is significant because, it is such creative responses that keep the *Advaitic* tradition dynamic; it is challenging because, the nature of the problems and the dialogue partners for today's *Advaitin* are not the same that of Śaṅkara. A fair attempt in this regard demands a critique of Śaṅkara's reasons for inclusion-exclusion dilemma, instead of accepting it uncritically. This will also throw better light for addressing some of the issues related to exclusion. The next chapter is an attempt towards this aim.

CHAPTER 5

RE-READING *ŚŪDRA*-EXCLUSION: AN INCLUSIVE LISTENING TO THE VOICES FOR *ADVAITA*

Introduction

Brahmajijñāsā, the quest for *Brahman*, consists in the 'desire' and all the 'endeavours' undertaken for *Ātman*/*Brahman*-realisation. As a desire, *brahmajijñāsā* may come at any time; but as a project it is through the *śruti* texts, which needs skilful reading or listening activities.[621] It is not mere intellectual activity but culminates in self-realising experience which calls for integral transformation of the person.[622] Francis X. Clooney expresses it in this way: "Not only are texts invested with internal and external meanings; when understood, they transform their hearers or readers, changing their context. If one dared, one might proffer a slogan: no information without transformation."[623] Therefore, great importance is invested in identifying an authentic seeker, who has a set of intellectual and social expectations that deliberately exclude most potential aspirants.

The eligibility criteria raise the question, who can take up *brahmajijñāsā*. This resonates extensively onto the question, who can speak for *Advaita*. 'Speaking for' is different from 'speaking about' because, the former implies the question

---

[621] Clooney, *Theology After Vedānta,* 133.

[622] Tapovanam, "The Glory of Brahma-vidyā," in *Advaitāmṛtam*, 15.

[623] Clooney, "From Anxiety to Bliss," in *Authority, Anxiety, and Canon*, 160.

of *adhikāra* (authority).[624] There can be two possible solutions. The first opinion could be that those who are from within the tradition, who have faith in Vedas and have *brahmānubhava* through them, alone can speak for *Advaita*. From the post-colonial perspective, which gave importance for restoring power to indigenous voices that have been either silenced or misinterpreted by mainstream cultures and hegemonic authorities of the past, the appreciation for the voice from the 'insider' has become significant. The second opinion is, only those who are outside the tradition can objectively speak for it. Here the voice of the 'insider' is undervalued charging it to be a subjective opinion. For Śaṅkara, the one who has achieved enlightenment alone can lead others to the same experience. In this sense, those excluded can neither take up *brahmajijñāsā,* and therefore, nor can become voices 'speaking for *Advaita*'. Therefore, exclusion from *brahmajijñāsā* directly affects the question of *adhikāra*; whether the voice is 'for' or 'about' *Advaita*.

A fair response to this issue depends very much, on the one hand, whether the *Śāṅkaravedāntic* inclusivism has enough scope to transcend the barriers of caste, gender, culture, tradition, religious practices, etc. and on the other, how essential and original is the purpose of the restrictions and therefore, how the exclusion has to be understood.

---

[624] Literally, the term *adhikāra* carries a range of possible meanings related to one's rightful "place" or field of action, from diligent effort in one's line of work to the sovereign prerogative of a king. For Śaṅkara, it refers more specifically to one's fitness, qualification, authority, eligibility and competence, especially in relation to the quest for *Brahman*. See Locklin, *Spiritual But not Religious?* 18; Rao, *Encyclopedia of Hinduism*, s.v. "*Adhikāra*."

The first part of this chapter responds to Śaṅkara's reasons for exclusion so as to discover inclusive possibilities implied in them. This is done in view of exploring its scope to become guidelines for the present-day *Advaitin*. It would shed light in his/her engagement with issues related to inclusion-exclusion whose context, implications and articulations are not the same as that of the time of Śaṅkara. In the light of this, the second part of this chapter, tries to address some of the issues which are related to religion and exclusion. Through the lens of inclusivism it views the question, who can be an insider or outsider for *Advaita*, and focuses on listening to the voices of people from different walks of life, speaking for/about *Advaita*.

5.1 Śaṅkara's Inclusivism: Śaṅkara Through the Prism of an Inclusivist Critique

Śaṅkara's position on exclusion—placing himself in between inclusion and exclusion—was not arbitrary. He might be reasonable from his cultural and philosophical context and from the point of his hermeneutical agenda. Those are to be critically assessed by the present-day *Advaitin* in his/her engagement with today's world, which has got not the same context that of Śaṅkara. A close observation will reveal that those reasons have enough scope to provide light for the forward steps so as to make *Śāṅkaravedānta* meaningful and dynamic for the world today, without violating the philosophical or theological foundations of Śaṅkara. Recognizing the essentials of *Śāṅkaravedāntic brahmajijñāsā* as 1) truth-oriented and 2) *sādhanacatuṣṭaya*-based, the following part attempts to assess and explore the possibilities of transcending the exclusive norms implied in the *Śāṅkaravedāntic* reasons for exclusion.

5.1.1 *Śāṅkaravedāntic Brahmajijñāsā*: Truth-Oriented Theorizing and *Sādhanacatuṣṭaya*-Based Axiology

Śaṅkara's reasons for exclusion can be summarised into two: hermeneutical (or scriptural) and axiological. According to the former, *śūdra*s are excluded solely because they are mentioned in the Vedas by name as those to be excluded; *śruti* itself has made the restriction. *Śruti* which is eternal and canonical has defined the society, and everyone is obliged to follow it, and therefore, society has to be viewed through Vedas not vice versa.[625] The axiological reasons restrict the aspirant by demanding eligibility with psychological and moral values. Here the role of internal and external prerequisites becomes significant.

The scriptural reasons for exclusion have to be reflected in the light of Śaṅkara's priority for truth. He gave importance for *mokṣa* than *dharma*; truth than text; knowledge than ritual.[626] Liberation through knowledge is the central axiom of his soteriology. Everything else is subservient to this truth.[627] Śaṅkara, in his interpretive task has taken all the care to identify the meaning, and to establish the inter connectedness between various Vedic ideals—a candid attempt to bring out the truth, in relation to which text is

---

[625] See the fourth chapter of this dissertation, 4.4.2.2

[626] Lipner, *The Hindus*, 33–39. Caṭṭampiswāmikal illustrates this point, i.e. it is truth which is important than text. He asks, which is important; jewels and gems or the box in which these are kept safely. For him, the truth of Vedas is available to the *śūdra*s through *smṛti*,and then, talking about their ineligibility for Vedic texts in which these truths are embodied is not reasonable. He proceeds with showing how Vedas themselves agree the importance of truth than text. See Caṭṭampiswāmikal, *Vedādhikāranirūpaṇam*, 65–67.

[627] Malkovsky, "Śaṃkara on Divine Grace," in *New Perspectives on Advaita Vedānta*, 77.

inferior. The text indicates the truth, the real, which is extra-textual.[628] He held truth as independent and immediate. *Brahmānubhava* cannot be considered as something 'achieved' through the mastery of the text.[629] "The knowledge is not the guaranteed result of those activities, even if they are well performed. By its nature knowledge eludes reduction to the predictable availability of either repeatable statements or imitable actions."[630] Therefore, Śaṅkara's theorizing is truth-oriented, in which, the role of the text is always subservient to the truth.

The axiological reasons for *śūdra*-exclusion are based on prerequisites for *brahmajijñāsā*: the aspirant has to be qualified with internal and external eligibilities.[631] The purpose of the prerequisites—both internal and external—is to make sure that the aspirant might not miss the target which is *brahmānubhava*. Extreme care has to be taken in this regard because the quest consists not merely in information, but transformation;[632] it is the ultimate goal of one's life which requires the wholehearted pursuit and to which one commits his/her entire life.[633] *Brahmajijñāsu* should not take chances in this regard but should go for excellent and sure means with fitting preparations. Therefore, he/she has to be a person ripe for knowledge lest his/her attempts go fruitless.

---

[628] Language cannot adequately express but can only indicate the essence of *Brahman* (Ta Up Bh 2.6.1).

[629] See the third chapter of this dissertation, 3.3.2.2; 3.3.2.3 and the fourth chapter, 4.3.

[630] Clooney, *Theology After Vedānta,* 123.

[631] See the first chapter of this dissertation, 1.1.2.1 and 1.1.2.2.

[632] If the information is capable of transformation the wrong information may cause wrong transformation too.

[633] Tapovanam, "The Glory of Brahma-vidyā,"in *Advaitāmṛtam*, 15. See also the fourth chapter of this dissertation, 4.4.2.2.2.4.

According to *Śāṅkaravedānta*, among the prerequisites, the internal criteria of moral eligibility, the *sādhanacatuṣṭaya*, are the necessary condition for *brahmajijñāsā*.[634] They are inclusive and universal in their scope.[635] These virtues are perfect in the state of enlightenment and are to be *sādhana* for an aspirant before enlightenment. Other requisites are interpretable keeping in mind the spirit behind the demand for requisites. That is to say, an aspirant may be restricted to take up *brahmajijñāsā*, not because of his/her caste or gender, but only on the point of ensuring *brahmānubhava*, so that his/her life-long commitment might not go ineffective. *Śāṅkaravedāntic* soteriology consists in *sādhanacatuṣṭaya*-based axiology which always provides scope for conceiving inclusive programme for liberation.

Śāṅkaravedāntic programme for *brahmajijñāsā* and the reasons for exclusion have to be evaluated keeping in mind these two important and uncompromising aspects: truth-oriented theorizing and *sādhanacatuṣṭaya*-based axiology. Among these two, the former, truth than text—that is related to the scriptural and hermeneutical reasons for exclusion—calls for further study and is taken up in the following part.

---

[634] De Smet, "Theological Method and Vedānta," in *Understanding Śaṅkara*, 109. When Swami Tapovanam, one of the 20th century *Advaitin* (1889–1957), speaks about a fitting *Vedānta*-disciple he focuses on virtues of *sādhanacatuṣṭaya* without any reference to *varaṇa* or *āśrama*.SeeTapovanam, "The Glory of Brahma-vidyā,"in *Advaitāmṛtam*, 15.

[635] "Considered as external status, *varṇa* and *āśrama* do not therefore condition *Brahmajñāna* in the same necessary way as the four internal *sādhanas*." De Smet, "Theological Method and Vedānta," in *Understanding Śaṅkara*, 109. See also the fourth chapter of this dissertation, 4.2.1.

5.1.2 The Sacred in-and-through the Secular: Deciphering Truth from the Text

The discussions on exclusion from Vedas consist of conciliation of secular and sacred. From the secular point of view, Vedas as the texts have their historical, literary and ritual formation, and have to be subjected to the epistemic operations of linguistic derivations of meaning just like any other texts. From the point of view of sacred, the texts are scriptures divine and they are eternal and infallible; since these are the theological aspects of the text,a theological understanding of those are called for.

The text indicates or announces the truth, the *Brahman,* which is an extra-textual reality. But text is the location in-and-through which this reality can be known.[636] The formation of texts, in which the embodiment of truth has taken place, is subjected to historical and epistemological influences. The text is the locus where both divine and humane aspects get involved: sacred is within the structures of secular. But truth-realisation transcends these secular aspects.[637] Though the interplay between truth and text are granted, the canonicity can be appropriated to truth than texts.

From the epistemological point of view, Vedas as texts provide knowledge. The epistemological operation in this process is same as that of any other texts. The language, which has the power to indicate *Brahman*, also possesses the power

---

[636] Rambachan, "Where Words Can Set Free," in *Texts in Context*, 48; Clooney, "Binding the Text," in *Texts in Context*, 63.

[637] *Brahman* transcends all direct definitions and explanations; the categories of being and non-being and existence and non-existence. Such terms are only properly applicable to objects in time and space (BG Bh 13.12; Ta U Bh 2.9.1). See Rambachan, *The Advaita Worldview*, 64.

to signify It through analogy to reach it to its supreme meaning.[638] But, is it necessarily because of its eternal, infallible and revelatory nature that these *śruti* texts are conferred this power of 'faithfully signifying the true nature of the absolute', is a question relevant taking *śruti* in its operations as *pramāṇa*.[639] But it is the conviction of *Śāṅkaravedāntin* that *śruti* as a *pramāṇa* is significant in the matters of trans-natural reality, and is the source of valid knowledge concerning the Absolute. In deciphering truth from the text, attention has to be paid to the interplay between sacred and secular.

5.1.2.1 Embodying the Truth: Historical, Ritual, and Literary Formation of the Text

The embodiment of the truth in the text has its historical, ritual and literary dimensions. From the historical point of view, Vedic corpus cannot be the work of one single author. It must have evolved through the religio-literary activity of many generations of the authors (ca. 1700–500 BCE).[640]

Tracing back to the origin of Vedic hymns reveals that they were speech-acts—which also could be wisdom-

---

[638] De Smet, "Language and Knowledge of the Absolute According to Śaṅkara," in *Understanding Śaṅkara*, 51–52.

[639] De Smet, "Language and Knowledge of the Absolute According to Śaṅkara," in *Understanding Śaṅkara*, 69.

[640] Dandekar, "Vedic Literature," 5. Evolution of the Vedas taking centuries is also evident from the facts that (1) the variations, improvement, difference and development in the language used ranging from Mantras to Upaniṣads and (2) the existence of various Vedic branches (*śākhas*) and traditions with their own recensions. See Dandekar, "Vedic Literature," 4, 19.

sayings—primarily of the nomadic group called Aryans,[641] in the form of hymns relating to their religion and mythology. These were used in the rituals which were simple in their form. The later period witnessed two-way developments: on the one hand, the simple form of rituals gave way to more complex sacrificial rituals, on the other, the Vedic words began to be conferred with mysterious power.[642] The appropriate use of them—i.e. the correct form and the proper recitation by the properly disposed reciter in a ritually and socially correct context—would yield the desired benefits.[643]

This made a great impact. Vedic words, which were the communicable, knowledge-filled speech-acts, were changed into "partially unintelligible fixed chunks of sounds"[644] which are mysterious and powerful to bring the benefits while using them in the complicated rituals. They were decontextualized—their origin and development were disconnected from their history—and were impersonalized, and super-human authorship was sought.[645] Oral transmission was preferred even

---

[641] Scholars also suggest the possibility of influence of various cultures in the formation of Vedic corpus. See Doniger, *The Hindus*, 99–101. See also the second chapter of this dissertation 2.3.1.

[642] Deshpande, "Changing Conceptions of the Veda," 12.

[643] David Carpenter, "The Mastery of Speech: Canonicity and Control in the Vedas," in *Authority, Anxiety, and Canon: Essays in Vedic Interpretation*, ed. Laurie L. Patton (Delhi: Sri Satguru Publications, 1995), 20–25.

[644] Deshpande, "Changing Conceptions of the Veda," 29.

[645] This attitude tried to transcend all notions of human seers being authors of the Vedic hymns. For example, *Śatapathabrāhmaṇa* says that *Ṛgveda* was born from *agni*, *Yajurveda* from *vāyu*, and *Sāmaveda* from sun (Śa Br 1.1.58). See Deshpande, "Changing Conceptions of the Veda," 20–22.

after its written form was introduced.[646] Gradually the meaning of the text became insignificant.[647] In the later period, Upaniṣads made the quest for meaning than the ritual use of Vedic hymns.[648]

5.1.2.2 Eternity of Vedas: A Theological Doctrine

As the Vedas were believed to be sacred and conferred with mysterious power, Vedic theologians were very much concerned about the non-contradiction, coherence and infallibility of Vedic corpus. To serve this purpose they sought for transcendental single origin of the Vedas. The historical elements of origin of Vedas were "gradually replaced by theological conception of single authorless Veda."[649] The theories related to Vedas—*apauruṣeyatva* (no human being is responsible for the creation of Vedas), *vedanityatva* (the eternity of Veda) and *vedaprāmāṇya* (the ultimate and absolute epistemological authority of Veda)—which are the features that emphatically bring out the character of Veda as scripture, are to be understood as theological ones. These are to be

---

[646] It has been suggested that the reason for the oral transmission was the absence of written script at the time when the Vedas were composed. Even long after writing was introduced there was a clear preference for the oral transmission of scripture, and the religious learning through the written word was looked down upon. Vedic words had to be handed down exactly as they had been heard, and correct sounds and pronunciation became all important. See Rambachan, "Where Words Can Set Free," in *Texts in Context*, 44n1.

[647] Barbara A. Holdrege, "Veda in the Brāhmaṇas: Cosmogonic Paradigms and the Delimitation of Canon," in *Authority, Anxiety, and Canon: Essays in Vedic Interpretation*, ed. Laurie L. Patton (Delhi: Sri Satguru Publications, 1995), 39.

[648] Deshpande, "Changing Conceptions of the Veda," 26.

[649] Deshpande, "Changing Conceptions of the Veda," 30.

accepted critically placing them at the considerations of historical and cultural development of the texts.

In the earlier Vedic periods, these characteristics—*apauruṣeyatva*, *vedanityatva* and *vedaprāmāṇya*—of Vedic hymns were not considered emphatic and specific. Dandekar observes: "However, the references to the *apauruṣeyatva* of the Veda in the Vedic texts themselves are but few and not particularly explicit or compelling. It is mostly in the later ancillary literature that the *apauruṣeyatva* has been made the starting point of Vedic exegesis."[650] The interpretation of the Vedas began within the Vedic corpus itself, starting from Saṁhitā and Brāhmaṇa traditions which were the attempts to interpret the Vedic hymns for the use of rituals. It is these texts that began to show the tendency to establish the authority of Vedas.[651] There were also various textual attempts to prove the authority and infallibility of the Vedas such as connecting its origin with creation of the universe, demonstrating its identity with primary deity, linking it with part of genealogy, etc.[652] The subsequent texts of Vedic tradition show greater emphasis on articulating *apauruṣeyatva* and related features of Vedas. This must be to defend the Vedic authority (1) in the context of tension between the established *brāhmaṇical* norms and the alien 'barbaric' cultures of non-Aryan origin, (2) when *brāhmaṇism* faced the challenges from heterodox systems, such as Buddhism and Jainism, and (3) as an attempt of later traditions to get authenticated, i.e. the texts of these traditions

[650] Dandekar, "Vedic Literature," 2.

[651] Smith, "The Veda and the Authority of Class," in *Authority, Anxiety, and Canon*, 68.

[652] Frederick M. Smith, "Purāṇaveda," in *Authority, Anxiety, and Canon: Essays in Vedic Interpretation*, ed. Laurie L. Patton (Delhi: Sri Satguru Publications, 1995), 100–102.

pay great respect for Vedas by praising them as eternal and infallible to assert that they were also belonged to the great Vedic tradition.[653]

Apauruṣeyatva and related doctrines are not primarily concerned with secular knowledge but of the knowledge of ultimate reality which cannot be gained through any other ordinary means of knowledge (BS Bh 1.1.3; 1.4.14; Bṛ U Bh 3.3.intro.). Śaṅkara states:

> The Validity of the Vedas holds good only with regard to matters concerning the relation between ends and means of Agnihotra etc., which are not known through such valid means of knowledge as direct perception; but not with regard to objects of direct perception etc., because the validity of the Vedas lies in revealing what is beyond direct perception. … Surely, even a hundred Vedic texts cannot become valid if they assert that fire is cold or non-luminous! … Vedas become logically meaningful in respect of knowledge of Brahman" (BG Bh 18.66 p. 757–758).[654]

It might be true that the authors of the Vedas are unknown but the Vedic corpus cannot be considered altogether as without human authors.[655] *Apauruṣeyatva* of the Vedic texts cannot be

---

[653] Dandekar, "Vedic Literature," 10; Smith, "Purāṇaveda," in *Authority, Anxiety, and Canon*, 105.

[654] प्रत्यक्षादिप्रमाणानुपलब्धे हि विषये अग्निहोत्रादिसाध्यसाधनसम्बन्धे श्रुतेः प्रामाण्यं, न प्रत्यक्षादिविषये, … न हि श्रुति शतमपि 'शीतः अग्निः, अप्रकाशो वा' इति, ब्रूवत् प्रामाण्यं उपैति। यदि ब्रूयात् 'शीतः अग्निः, अप्रकाशो वा' इति, यथाऽपि अर्थान्तरं श्रुतेः विवक्षितं कल्प्यम्, प्रामाण्यान्यथाऽनुपपत्तेः, न तु प्रमाणान्तरविरुद्धं स्ववचनविरुद्धं व कल्प्यम ॥ (BG Bh 18.66) Cf. Śaṅkara, *The Bhagavad-gītā with the Commentary of Śrī Śaṅkarācārya*, ed. Dinakar Vishnu Gokhale, 278.

[655] Malati J Shendge, while dealing about the poems of *Ṛgveda* writes: "The maṇḍalas II to VIII are called family books, because they are composed by poets belonging to particular families. These poets are Gṛtsamada, Viśvāmitra, Vāmadeva, Atri, Bhāradvaja, and Vasiṣṭha or

understood as factual and historical truth about Vedic texts but as a theological doctrine taking account of the context of its development. Vedic *apauruṣeyatva* would mean that the Vedic truths on supernatural reality are not merely the outcome of human reasoning, but rather they are trans-empirical and trans-rational. "They are the outcome of the seeing (*darśana*) of the eternal ultimate reality and of the hearing (*śruti*) of the rhythm of the infinite by inspired seers through their superhuman (*apauruṣeya*) intuitive and insightful faculty."[656] Clooney makes an observation on *apauruṣeyatva* doctrine as follows:

> The doctrine of *apauruṣeyatva*—the Veda has expositors, but no authors (*puruṣa*)—reflected the Mīmāṁsā School's desire to show that the Vedic complex of sacrifice and text was not dependent on any transitory and self-motivated agents and things;

---

their descendants. Each poem has a ṛṣi (a seer composer), devatā (a deity to whom it is addressed) and chandas (metre)." See Malati J. Shendge, "The Authors of the Ṛgveda," *Annals of the Bhandarkar Oriental Research Institute* 81 (2000): 169. Cattampiswamikal gives various references from within Vedic corpus to show human agency in their authorship. See Chatampiswamikal, *Vedādhikāranirūpaṇam,* 23–25. Upaniṣads makes some mention of its authors. Radhakrishnan states: "some of the chief doctrines of the Upaniṣads are associated with the names of renowned sages as Āruṇi, Yājñavalkya, Bālāki, Śvetaketu, Śāṇḍilya. They were, perhaps, the early exponents of the doctrines attributed to them." See Radhakrishnan, *The Principal Upaniṣads*, 51. Bādarāyaṇa makes mention of considerations of intentions of various authors. See Clooney, "Binding the Text," in *Texts in Context*, 56.

In understanding *apauruṣeyatva*, historical and humane dimension in the formation of the Vedas cannot be side-stepped. Radhakrishnan points out: "The Vedas were composed by the seers when they were in a state of inspiration. … Inspiration is a joint activity, of which man's contemplation and God's revelation are two sides." See Radhakrishnan, *The Principal Upaniṣads*, 23.

[656] Dandekar, "Vedic Literature," 3.

> external reference to impermanent realities threatened ultimately to undercut the posited eternity and permanence of the sacred text itself. The system had to be nonreferential, meaningful in itself, and expressive of that meaning, in order to be protected from a changing and unpredictable world. Vedānta follows the Mīmāṁsā lead and develops ways of explaining texts without appealing to an author's intention.[657]

Being *apauruṣeya*, Vedic truth is not contaminated by the frailties and inadequacies of the human sense organs and intellect. It is not accessible to, and is beyond the normal means of knowledge.[658] *Vedaprāmāṇya* was always formal and epistemologically motivated.[659] These texts from their very origin were subjected to editing, synthesizing and interpretation because they contained various doctrines sometimes even contradicting and unconnected which makes it impossible to believe that those were derived from a single coherent doctrine. Even those systems which have accepted *vedaprāmāṇya* has interpreted it differently deriving their own specific doctrines. It is possible that "*vedaprāmāṇya* was not the result of the *apauruṣeyatva* of the Veda but that *apauruṣeyatva* was imposed on the Veda in order to bestow on it ultimate *prāmāṇya*."[660]

These theological doctrines convey that the Vedic truths which deal with the supernatural reality originated not

---

[657] Clooney, "Binding the Text,"in *Texts in Context*, 56.

[658] Rambachan, "Where Words Can Set Free," in *Texts in Context*, 35–37.

[659] For Śaṅkara, Vedas are direct revelations. It meant "they do not depend on any other means of knowledge for their validity" (BS Bh 1.3.28 p. 210).

[660] Dandekar, "Vedic Literature," 4.

through the normal human sense knowledge and are in unfailing potency to lead one to have supernatural experience of *brahmānubhva*. These doctrines also suggest that there is an extra textual reality that serves as a reference point by which one can detect a wrong interpretation and understanding of the texts and make sure his/her engagement with the texts to be genuine and can attain liberation.[661]

It is true that *varṇa*, at first as three and later as four, have entered into Veda and has been conferred with great approval by affirming its eternal origin, and by placing it side by side with the origin of Vedas and cosmos. But a proper understanding of this cannot leave the social context of Vedas, and also of the formation of the fourth class (the *śūdra*), unnoticed. Vedic conformation of *varṇa* has to be reflected on the one hand, together with the social, ritual, and literary influence in the formation of the text in its role of embodying truth, and on the other, with the theological nature and the development of its canonicity.

5.1.3 Ineligibility for Rituals and Knowledge: Applying the Same Logic to Both

In *Apaśūdrādhikaraṇam*, the opponent argues by quoting Ta Sa 7.1.1.6 that *śruti* prohibits *śūdra*s for performing sacrifice alone, not for knowledge. Śaṅkara's reply indicates 'being unfit for sacrifice' implies 'unfit for learning'. That is to say, the reason why *śūdra*s are excluded from the sacrifice is the same underlying reason for the exclusion of *śūdra*s from knowledge. These reasons are textual or scriptural. But the tenability of *Śāṅkaravedāntic* claims to apply the same reasons

---

[661] Clooney, "Binding the Text," in *Texts in Context*, 63.

equally to both the case of ritual and knowledge cannot be accepted uncritically.

Dharmajijñāsā of *Mīmāṁsaka* and *brahmajijñāsā* of *Vedāntin* differ in their goal and method. For *dharmajijñāsā* the goal is *dharma* which includes happiness here in the world and in heaven hereafter. But for *Vedānta* it is self-realising knowledge. The method of *dharmajijñāsā* is sacrifices and other rituals but that of *Vedānta* is acquisition of knowledge. For the former, Vedic learning is solely for the rituals; knowing 'how' of the rituals[662] therefore, the Vedic texts are understood from the point of ritualistic meanings. If one is ineligible for rituals due to some reasons it implies he/she cannot learn Vedas. Śaṅkara's intention on working for a *bhāṣya* for Brahmasūtra, he states, is to provide a different understanding on it than that of the *karma*-oriented *Mīmāṁsā* understanding. "Hence it is proved that the unembodiedness, called liberation, is eternal and different from the results of works that have to be performed. … (Since liberation is different from the result of work, it being unrelated to virtue and vice), therefore liberation is the same as Brahman about which this deliberation is started" (BS Bh 1.1.4 p. 27–28).

Śaṅkara makes a thorough breakaway from the ritual-oriented *Mīmāṁsaka* thinking and constructs his entire philosophy and theology on truth or knowledge-oriented theorizing. He advocates a soteriology, wherein the ultimate goal of human quest is self-realising knowledge, which is based on truth and virtue, and which has little role for ritualism.[663] Being ineligible for sacrifice cannot in anyway

---

[662] Lipner, *The Hindus*, 33, 34–39.

[663] One does not need to perform sacrifices in order to be able to know *Brahman*.

hinder the desire and endeavours taken for the acquisition of knowledge. But such clear-cut discontinuance from *Mīmāṁsā* is very much compromised when it comes to the case of eligibility for taking up the quest for *Brahman.* In both *Mīmāṁsā* and *Vedānta* the quest is satisfied through the engagement with texts. All the *Mīmāṁsaka* rules for the accessibility of text are accepted also by *Vedānta.*[664] Śaṅkara, while giving specific norms for the eligibility for reading Vedas, directly applies those criterions for *dharmajijñāsā* to the *brahmajijñāsā* which has a different aim and method.[665] The distinction from *Mīmāṁsā* which is very central to *Vedānta* has to be consistently carried out in designing the programme of *brahmajijñāsā*, especially in the case of engaging with the text for knowledge.

5.1.4 *Śūdra*-Exclusion: Formal than Factual

A study on exclusion, taken from the social point of view, has to address the following issues: what purpose did the *śūdra*-exclusion serve and who benefitted out of it in the specific historical period of *Śāṅkaravedānta.*

During this period the economic and social status of *śūdras* was not that derogatory as it was before. The word *śūdra* denoted not only those born of *śūdra* parents but also those who belonged to different social and religious culture.[666] Outside the fold of Aryan *varṇa* there existed, sometimes with an inferior status than *śūdra*s, groups of people such as outcastes, mixed castes, various *jātis* and those belonged to the

---

[664] Clooney, *Theology After Vedānta,* 131–132.

[665] Rao, "Inconsistencies in the *Brahmasūtra* and *Śāṅkarabhāṣya,*" 148.

[666] See the second chapter of this dissertation, 2.3; 2.8.

foreign religion and culture. But the dictum remained that *śūdra*s—for Śaṅkara specifically *jāti śūdra*s—are ineligible for Vedas. For Śaṅkara, the reason why *śūdra* is to be excluded is simply because their name is mentioned in the Vedas as those to be excluded. The historical reasons how a group called *śūdra*s were formed, and why their name appeared in the Vedic texts as those to be excluded cannot go unattended. Thus, from the social and secular point of view, *śūdra*-exclusion very much means keeping a 'group' as excluded; not necessarily '*śūdra*s'. In the succeeding *Vedāntic* period the outcastes and other groups whom the mainstream society considered lower, replaced *śūdra*s with the social disabilities and exploitations once *śūdra*s suffered.[667]

Vedas had become very much a symbol of authentication by the time of *Vedāntin*s. In the textual world citing from the Vedas in support of any particular theories very much meant establishing that theory or position as part of eternal divine wisdom enshrined in the Vedas. Invoking the Vedas did not require that the text conforms to Vedic knowledge, for it could be a way of seeking legitimation.[668] Allegiance to Veda served a high profile and became a symbol of religious authority also. One of the reasons why certain social movements, which simultaneously developed as religious traditions such as *Bhakti* Movements, were brought under Vedic fold was to get it authenticated.[669] Conducting Vedic sacrifice became a matter of social and political

---

[667] See the fourth chapter of this dissertation, 4.4.2.1.2 and second chapter, 2.8.2.

[668] Thapar, *Early India*, 309.

[669] Lipner, *The Hindus*, 62.

legitimacy.[670] Having allegiance to Vedas became a matter of identity with a high profile culture.[671]

In the light of what is being said, one important question is: during the time of Śaṅkara, what did the excluded group miss due to their inaccessibility for Vedas? It was not education, not the possibility of self-realisation, not the economic security but it was mainly the admission to a high profile status.[672] The feeling of being excluded involved also the desire for admittance into it and then to become a part of it.

What did those upper castes who exclude them gain? It was no more the availability of permanent manual labour. By the time of *Vedānta, śūdra*s did not strictly constitute the servile group; there were people from other low caste who took up this role. Exclusion did not serve the purpose of protecting the Vedic truth by keeping it secret and to save it from misinterpretations because Vedic truth was available to *śūdra*s in various ways.[673] Excluding a group as the 'other' might

---

670 For example, performing Vedic sacrifices, especially the *aśvamedha* (horse-sacrifice) by the rulers. This is an elaborate ritual by which its patron affirmed territorial sovereignty. The royal performance of these sacrifices would have been a public event, designed to display to maximum effect the king's adherence to the *dharma* of Vedas. This would have reinforced, in the public eye, the symbolic value of the authority of the Vedas as final. See Lipner, *The Hindus*, 63.

671 What being canonized is Vedic actions; primarily ritual and the Vedic culture at large. As a result, canonical interpretation implies the linking of this system of actions within the sacrifice to the system of actions surrounding and supporting it—in other words, the joining of sacrificial structure and social structure. See Carpenter, "The Mastery of Speech," in *Authority, Anxiety, and Canon*, 27–31.

672 In the eyes of upper caste *śūdra*s lost the possibility of rituals and the consequent benefits of happiness of this world and the heaven hereafter.

673 Caṭṭampiswāmikal, *Vedādhikāranirūpaṇam*, 65–67. According to Caṭṭampiswāmikal, truth is important than texts, the truth is already

become something constitutive of the self-identity—collectively and individually—and of the social status of those who exclude. This does not mean exclusion did not exist as a social fact, but rather the purpose of exclusion was no more the same when it was practised during the early Vedic period. Therefore, *śūdra*-exclusion does not evoke and stick on to the questions such as which are the texts to be strictly demarcated as inaccessible; who all are to be included in the group of *śūdra*s; can all non-*śūdra*s, such as outcastes and those whom upper caste consider to be lower than *śūdra*s, have access to those texts.[674]

5.1.5 Highlights of the Critique

In the light of the above discussions on Śaṅkara's reasons for exclusion, certain significant observations can be made. Among the arguments supporting exclusion, those based on scriptures are important. For him *śūdra*s are excluded not because of any physical or psychological or moral incapacity, but only because the scriptures mention their name as those to be excluded. Since scriptures are eternal and infallible its restriction cannot be bypassed. But this reason is not without setbacks, and triggers some relevant remarks. First of all, it implies anyone who is a non-*śūdra*—even those belonging to the lower status than *śūdra*, such as outcastes—can have access to Vedas, provided their names are not mentioned in Vedas as

considered universal and is accessible to all through *smṛti*. There is nothing against making the Vedas universally accessible. For him, by imparting the Vedas to anyone who really desires for it, and thus by making Vedas more inclusive and universal they do not lose their greatness rather it increases. See Caṭṭampiswāmikal, *Vedādhikāranirūpaṇam*, 74–75.

[674] See the second chapter of this dissertation, 2.8.2.

those to be excluded. If so, it really questions the very reasonableness of exclusion, and the restriction seems to be purposeless. Secondly, Vedas do not make any injunctive statement on the exclusion of *śūdra* from the Vedic knowledge. This fact flouts the very basis on which Śaṅkara has placed his reasons for exclusion. While arguing for the exclusion he has not brought out any Vedic injunction which admonishes exclusion of *śūdra*s from Vedas. He has only explained away those Vedic passages and narratives which would support inclusion. But the explanations given to them are far-fetched, inconsistent and difficult to agree with. He also has conveniently forgotten Vedic character Kavaṣa who is a *śūdra* with Vedic knowledge (Ai Br 2.3; Ka Br 12.3). If he wanted to argue for a strict inclusive position he had the entire scriptural avenue open enough; he could do it as he has done with some of his convictions by bringing out very narrow scriptural support. But he is deliberate in not doing it, and the reason relies very much on his devotion to *brāhmaṇic* tradition. In the matter of exclusion, Śaṅkara seems spporting the Vedic tradition and thereby deviating from his conviction on priority for Vedic Truth.

If the *śūdra*-exclusion is taken to be Vedic, then a third point of observation could be made on the basis of his conviction on validity of *śruti*. For Śaṅkara, *śruti* is valid in the matters of transcendental realities not of mundane and empirical realities. Even among the statements on the ultimate reality the statements that define the nature of *Brahman*/*Ātman* are primary. The Vedic statements that might suggest exclusion cannot be taken to be non-empirical and to be about the transcendental reality. Why the social group called *śūdra* was formed, why they were incorporated into Aryan fold, why they were denied the Vedic learning, and why their name has appeared in the *brāhmaṇic* texts as those to be excluded have social reasons. These reasons also bear the negative tone of vested interests, exploitation and oppression. Fourthly, Śaṅkara affirms Vedic truths are to be followed because they are infallible and eternal. Infallibility and eternity of the Vedas are theological doctrines. Understanding them to be theological, precludes accepting them matter-of-factly, i.e. denying any kind of human interventions in the formulation of the Vedic scriptures. Therefore, the social reasons for the development and insistence of these doctrines must be noticed. It includes the intention of safeguarding the authority of Vedas in the midst of dissenting and divergent voices which were growing against Vedic religion. The sacredness was highlighted by distancing the 'unworthy'. It also helped the Vedic proponents to stem its use by those critiques and to get subjected to thorough criticism. It also worked reversely, i.e. ascribing eternity and sacredness of the Vedas also contributed to the intention of excluding *śūdra*s and keeping them to be low and exploited. The upper caste society had to maintain a group of dependent and amenable people to be at their beck and call mainly for the manual service. Therefore, *brāhmaṇism* considered them and took all the possible measures to make them believe that they are ineligible for Vedas, and therefore, not to be educated and shall not enter into the Vedic culture which they considered high profile or mainstream culture.

Śaṅkara's reasons for inclusivism, within his inclusive-exclusive dilemma, are not solid. He treats this dilemma in such a way that the norm of exclusion is primary, giving only a secondary provision for inclusivism where he finds some space to accommodate the value of equality of human persons and also the social reformations and responses based on it. His intention of inclusivism in relation to the revival of religion also included nurturing the *brāhmaṇic* tradition even at the cost of sabotaging the growth of other religions by curbing the flow of people from lower caste to those religions. Even his disagreement with the sacrificial ritualism was not a total isolation from the tradition but was a part of the revival of the same. The primary interest here seems to be a religiously motivated compromise and adjustment than defending the values of equality and freedom of human person.

5.1.6 *Śūdra*-Exclusion: Forward Steps in *Śāṅkaravedānta*

The discussions that are held so far point out Śaṅkara's position on *śūdra*-exclusion as precarious. Here the significant question is: has the present or future *Śāṅkaravedāntin* any scope of becoming an inclusivist, and thus the light for the world which is overshadowed by exclusivism. This question could be addressed from the point of view of, how weak/strong is Śaṅkara in his arguments for or against inclusivism.

It is obvious Śaṅkara's arguments for exclusion are very weak but at the same time, his arguments for inclusivism also are not strong. But, when the discussions on exclusion are taken to the platform of the very essentials of his thinking—especially of his soteriology—which he held uncompromisingly, we can have very strong inclusive orientations and inspirations. In articulating those basic convictions he must have been very much affected by his context and must be limited. Thinking from the present context, which is not the same as that of Śaṅkara, the present-day *Śāṅkaravedāntin*s can disregard Śaṅkara's reasons for exclusivism for they are unsound. They, by ignoring the pitfalls in articulating the inclusivism, can focus on, and can explore the inclusivism implied in the very essential teachings of Śaṅkara. *Śāṅkaravedāntin*s, with their genuine desire for becoming creative and meaningful for the world today, and readiness to subject themselves to radical self-criticism, can find solid guidelines in Śaṅkara for their engagement with the exclusive-inclusive discourses.

It is true that Śaṅkara was not immune to the social, cultural and axiological changes of his time, no matter how successful he was in his response to them. He had taken all the care to respond to the context with the available textual grounds carefully safeguarding fundamentals of its truth. This invites the present-day *Śāṅkaravedāntin*s to respond constructively and dynamically to the present context with their *Advaitic* realisation.

Śaṅkara's theorizing was truth-oriented than text or tradition. He uncompromisingly held *sādhanacatuṣṭaya* as the principal ethical norm. Both these have the potential to transcend the norms of exclusion based on *varṇa*, *āśrama*, gender, culture, nationality, etc. The prerequisites other than *sādhanacatuṣṭaya* which Śaṅkara suggests might imply exclusion, but are not *sine qua non* for self-realisation. The intention of prerequisites is that the truth which is eternal and infallible—having their origin in trans-natural means of knowing, and which is unfailingly potent to bring self-realizing knowledge—cannot be approached as any other text but with preparations fitting to the nature of its truth. In addition to this, very serious attention has to be given for 'preparing a fitting aspirant' lest his/her effort—the wholehearted life-long commitment—might go ineffective. The prerequisites other than *sādhanacatuṣṭaya* are interpretable according to the context without losing the spirit behind suggesting prerequisites for *brahmajijñāsā*.

The word '*śūdra*' itself need not represent a genealogical group but rather anyone who is ineligible for the Vedic truth.[675] Anyone, irrespective of being born to particular parents, if he/she has the necessary qualifications, can become a fruitful *brahmajijñāsu*.[676] Therefore, *śūdra*-exclusion, from the formal and theological point of view can mean those ineligible for the truth will run the risk of unfruitful effort.[677] But the ineligibility for truth has to be understood as natural, such as inadequate intelligence and imperfections in possessing *sādhanacatuṣtaya.* Therefore, the very essentials of *Śāṅkaravedānta*, which obviously is inclusive, give basic insight and orientation for the present-day *Advaitin*. It is his/her task to carry forward with the original and essential insights of

---

[675] *Śūdra* represents and can be considered as a blanket term for the excluded and the marginalised. From the social and religious point of view it is always possible there emerge '*śūdra*s' in the society whom the mainstream groups exclude for various reasons and with various criteria.

[676] Swami Chinmayanada—as it is pointed out by Swami Advayananda—while explaining BG *sūtra*s such as BG 4.13 and 18.41 afirms character as the basis of caste not birth. He takes an inclusive stand on the possibility of enlightenment. See Swami Advayananda, "The Holy Geeta – In a Class All by Itself," in *Advaitāmṛtam*, ed. Sandhya Sundar and Dilip Kumar Rana (Ernakulam: Chinmaya International Foundation, 2015), 43–47.

[677] In dealing with Śaṅkara's mentions on *brāhmaṇa* as the specially qualified, in reference to MU U Bh 1.2.12–13, Reid B Locklin gives a possible understanding of it "only those who are qualified for spiritual instruction can really be counted as Brahmins. That is, "Brahmin" becomes a kind of short hand for any person, of any gender or social class." Locklin, *Spiritual But not Religious?* 20. If the term *brāhmaṇa* can be understood in this way, the term *śūdra* could be understood as the one 'who is ineligible for the knowledge' regardless of caste, class, gender, culture, nation, etc.

the system by enriching it with critical explorations and by creatively applying it to the present context.

5.2 *Brahmajijñāsā* for Some or for All: The *Adhikāra* of Various Voices Speaking for *Advaita*

According to *Śāṅkaravedānta*, the one who has *Advaitic* enlightenment can lead the other to this experience; he/she has the *adhikāra* and can speak for *Advaita*. But then, if it excludes some group of human beings from the possibility of enlightenment, their voices on *Advaita* becomes feeble or of little value. Therefore, *Śāṅkaravedāntic* discourse on exclusion from *brahmajijñāsā* is interfaced with insights on the issues such as, 'exclusion-inclusion', 'outsider-insider', 'speaking for or about' and '*adhikāra*'.

The present-day context really calls for an in-depth insight on *adhikāra* for *Vedāntic* truths. The society today witnesses that the values such as human freedom, respect for life, dignity of human person, indigenism, nationalism, etc. are at times downplayed or interpreted narrowly and sometimes hijacked with negative values such as extremism. Besides this, there is a growing tendency that some groups, sometimes with political influences, have taken it to be their duty to speak for *Vedānta* and the related traditions. In such context, if *Advaita*, which is a living tradition that continues to be studied, discussed and practised in daily life, does not creatively respond, especially to the axiological changes, it ceases to be dynamic and meaningful to the present world.

In the light of inclusive understanding of *brahmajijñāsā,* present-day *Advaita Vedāntin* has to listen to the voices from various spheres speaking for *Advaita*: voices of academicians who are not Vedic believers, of those seeking self-realization without the aid of religion, of those *Advaitin*s who are engaged in social activities without being strictly contemplatives or academicians, and of those from a different nation and culture other than Indian and Hindu. The *Advaitin* today cannot refrain from dialoguing with the movements of subaltern empowerment and cross boarder ideologies and cultures.

5.2.1 Academic and Religious *Advaitin*: 'Speaking For' or 'Speaking About'

The question, who can speak for *Advaita,* can be readily answered with 'an *āpta* (reliable or trustworthy)[678] alone is eligible'. But the matter is, who can be an *āpta*? Śaṅkara's opinion on this regard is clear from the passages such as BG Bh 4.34; Ch U Bh 6.14.2; MU̥ U Bh 1.2.12; Upad 2.1.6; 2.2.45. For Śaṅkara, an *āpta* must be (1) *brahmaniṣṭhaḥ,* the one who is absorbed in *Brahman*, (2) knower of the scriptures and, (3) the one who is mature in moral virtues.

According to Śaṅkara, "knowledge imparted by those who have full enlightenment become effective, not any other" (BG Bh 4.34 p. 223).[679] In Ch U Bh, while mentioning about who can help another for attaining liberation, Śaṅkara states,

---

[678] An *āpta* is a person who is trustworthy. Vatsyāyana, while commenting on *Nyāyasūtras*, defines *āpta* as the one who 1) possesses direct and valid knowledge, 2) intends to communicate his knowledge correctly, and 3) has the ability to communicate his knowledge adequately. A person who is devoid of any of the above characteristics cannot be regarded as *āpta*. See Rao, *Encyclopedia of Hinduism*, s.v. "*Āptatva.*"

[679] ये सम्यग्दर्शिनः तैः उपदिष्टं ज्ञानं कार्यक्षमं भवति, न इतरत् इति भगवतः मतम् ॥ (BG Bh 4.34) Cf. Śaṅkara, *The Bhagavad-gītā with the Commentary of Śrī Śaṅkarācārya*, ed., Dinakar Vishnu Gokhale, 81.

"The knower of Existence which is *Brahman*, who is free from bondage" (Ch U Bh 6.14.2 p. 487–488) is capable of it. According to *Upadeśasāhasrī* a seeker after final release has to approach a knower of *Brahman*, who is established in *Brahman* (Upad 2.2.45). Therefore, a *brahmaniṣṭhaḥ*—the one who "remains absorbed in the non-dual *Brahman*" (MU U Bh 1.2.12 p. 104),[680] i.e., the one who has *Advaitic* enlightenment—alone is the *āpta* to speak for *Advaita*.

The enlightened one is supposed to know scriptures. MU U Bh 1.2.12 characterises the teacher as; "*śrotriyam brahmaniṣṭham*, (a teacher) who is versed in the meaning of the Vedas that he recites and hears, and who is absorbed in *Brahman*" (MU U Bh 1.2.12 p. 104).[681] The enlightenment has to be complimented with intellectual acumen. While stating the need for virtues and purity of mind for a *brahmaniṣṭah*, in Ch U Bh, Śaṅkara adds, the capacity for well-reasoning. "(In understanding anything) other auxiliaries (such as reasoning) also function in keeping with the make of a person's mind" (Ch U Bh 8.9.2 p. 636). The real teacher has to be the one who "is able to consider the pros and cons [of an argument], is endowed with understanding" (Upad 2.1.6 p. 212). "The one who has enlightenment but not well-versed in scriptures may not be familiar with the methodology necessary to help the student understand the self as *Brahman*. She may not have the words

---

[680] All the direct quotes from the Mu U Bh of Śaṅkara (translation) is given page number followed by 'p.' throughout this dissertation. The page numbers are from: Śaṅkara. *Eight Upaniṣads with the Commentary of Śaṅkarācārya*, vol. 2. Translated by Swami Gambhirananda. 1957. Reprint, Kolkata: Advaita Ashrama, 2013.

[681] समिप्याणिः समिद्धारगृहीतहस्तः श्रोत्रीयं अध्ययनश्रुतार्थसंपन्नं ब्रह्मनिष्ठं हित्व सर्वकर्माणि केवलेऽद्वये ब्रह्मणि निष्ठा यस्य सोऽयं ब्रह्मनिष्ठो, जपनिष्ठस्तपोनिष्ठ इति यद्दत्। (MU U Bh 1.2.12) Cf. Śaṅkara, *Īśādidaśopaniṣadaḥ,* ed., Ministry of Education, India, 509.

or skill to use words properly to impart knowledge."[682] But, at the same time, academic and intellectual knowledge without enlightenment will not constitute *āptatva* (reliability or trustworthiness). "A teacher who is well versed in the scripture, but who has not grasped the immediacy of *Brahman* as her own self and who does not therefore, see herself or others from this understanding, will, at best, impart mere words. Knowledge imparted by such a teacher will be indirect and the self may appear to be a remote entity, difficult to attain."[683]

It is the conviction of Śaṅkara that the pure intellectual sharpness alone will not bring about *brahmajñāna*. *Āptatva* is determined very much by the growth in the necessary virtues and the consequent purity of mind. "It is well-known that although the word heard may be the same, still its understanding occurs according to the purity or impurity of the hearer's mind" (Ch U Bh 8.9.2 p. 636). The virtues suggested in the passages such as MU U Bh 1.2.12; Upad 2.1.6; Ch U Bh 6.14.2, shows the significance of compassion. All the virtues exposed here in these passages can be included in *sādhanacatuṣṭaya* (which are comprised of *mumukṣutvam* and *śraddhā*). The scholarship on Vedic scriptures which is purely of academic interest without believing in the Vedic efficacy for salvation, and without practising the necessary virtues might not bring about *brahmānubhava*, without which one cannot be an *āpta* for *Advaita*. The study of the scriptures by a *brahmajijñāsu* includes transformation of the person. The

---

[682] Rambachan, *The Advaita Worldview*, 63. The enlightened is the authority for *Advaita*. In his/her mission to lead others to this enlightenment his/her ability to impart the knowledge is significant.

[683] Rambachan, *The Advaita Worldview*, 63.

scholarship that ignores the possibility of the transformation of the one who engages with it, is incomplete yielding no fruit.[684]

Among all these, primacy is given for enlightenment. All other virtues follow from it as the spontaneous expression of enlightenment. An enlightened person integrates moral virtues and his/her scholarship. In dealing with the question of an ideal teacher, after analysing *Upadeśasāhasrī* 2.1.6 and 2.2.45, Locklin writes: "His descriptions begin with an assumption that the ideal teacher truly knows *Brahman*, the divine Self at the root of all creation, and thus fully embodies the source and end of spiritual life; other characteristics from the facility with scripture to a personal demeanor of comfort and compassion, follow from this interior knowledge itself."[685]

It is generally understood that only the one who is born into the tradition can rightly speak for *Advaita*; not the one who is outside the tradition. The insider is usually taken to be the person who is born to that tradition, takes up the religious practises of the tradition and believes in the Vedic efficacy for salvation. But the outsider can claim that his/her voice on *Advaita* would be more authentic for he/she can be objective. It is true that those outside the tradition have the advantage of making an objective critique of the tradition than an insider; at the same time, the insider's understanding is rich. An insider can penetrate deeper into the tradition with his/her experience and engagement with the tradition and by nurturing an appreciation for it. In fact, the voice of both the insider and the outsider are complementary for they make *Advaita* more enriched and insightful. Neither of them needsto be considered

---

[684] Clooney, "From Anxiety to Bliss," in *Authority, Anxiety, and Canon*, 140.

[685] Locklin, *Spiritual But not Religious?* 52.

superior or inferior to each other. Clooney suggests that the benefits of objectivity have to be valued but at the same time the subjective element is not inferior.[686] In understanding a tradition it is possible that the subjective elements appear. Instead of making attempts for eradicating such influences, one has to take it positively and notice how the subjectivity affects one's understanding or study.[687] Arvind Sharma argues that neither the outsider's claim for objectivity nor the insider's claim for subjectivity is absolute from the point of view of *Advaitic* epistemology.[688] For John J.Thatamanil and Douglas

---

686 Clooney, *Theology After Vedānta*, 149–152, 201–207. For Clooney when an outsider gets into the text, he/she might be breaking the strict rules of exclusion of the tradition, but he/she reveres the pure *Advaita* insight. Because, "advaita sees knowledge as pure consciousness not bound by words." See Clooney, *Theology After Vedānta*, 149, 151.

687 John J. Thatamanil, "Managing Multiple Religious Scholarly Identities: An Argument for a Theological Study of Hinduism," *Journal of American Academy of Religion* 68, no. 4 (December 2000): 797n10.

688 In *Advaitic* epistemology the knowing subject itself becomes object. The usual subject-object division in epistemology is replaced with *dṛk* and *dṛśya;* the former means the self or what reveals and the latter what is revealed. According to *Advaita* the knowing subjects are not pure subjects, in as much as one is capable of objectifying oneself in his/her minds. It occurs in the knowledge situation like 'I know myself', where 'myself' refers to some thought or feeling or some particular perception, etc. Here one objectifies oneself. In the same way insider can also distance his/her own tradition and can know it from its objectivity as the outsider would claim. In the process of perceptual knowledge 'mind stuff' goes out through the senses, assumes the form of the object. Here takes place a communion between the knower and the known. In the same way an outsider while looking at another tradition can lose his/her objectivity and can bring into the interiority of the insider. The earlier polarization of authenticity of insider or that of outsider is reduced by the epistemological consideration; both the insider and outsider can speak for *Advaita*. See Arvind Sharma, "Who Speaks for Hinduism? A Perspective from *Advaita* Vedānta," *Journal of American*

R. Brooks the objectivity of the scholar and the subjectivity of the religious person are not exclusive.[689]

But, general understanding of insider/outsider has to be revisited with the *Śāṅkaravedāntic* primacy for truth and *sādhanacatuṣṭaya.* The criteria of caste, gender, territory, culture, nationality, etc. do not come on the way in determining who can be the insider/outsider to *Advaita*. *Śāṅkaravedāntic* soteriology has the potency to go beyond all these.[690] As *mumukṣutvam*, and *śraddhā* are those included among the cardinal virtues, i.e, *sādhanacatuṣṭaya*, a *mumukṣu* with firm faith in the salvific efficacy of *śruti,* irrespective of genealogy

---

Academy of Religion 68, no.4 (December 2000): 756-757. "The great advantage of the outsider is that the outsider can be objective. However, to the extent that an insider from a tradition can objectify his or her own tradition, the insider can also perceptually distance him- or herself from his or her tradition, and, *to that extend*, the outsider's claim to perceptual objectivity no longer remains unique. Similarly, if the outsider's mind can reach out and assume the forms of the tradition he or she is studying, *to that extend*, similarly, the insider's special claim to perceptual interiority in relation to the tradition no longer remains unique." Sharma, "Who Speaks for Hinduism?" 758.

[689] Thatamanil, "Managing Multiple Religious Scholarly Identities," 796; Douglas R. Brooks, "Taking Sides and Opening Doors: Authority and Integrity in the Academy's Hinduism," *Journal of American Academy of Religion* 68, no. 4 (December 2000): 825–826.

Douglas R. Brooks comments, what is more important is, who one is, when he/she speaks on a tradition. One might be penetrating into it from outside, but more than it, how 'one is being penetrated by what one have learnt' is important. "Legitimacy and authenticity are not resolved by being either "outside" or "inside". Instead what is established is a relationship with our subject that everyone in the conversation understands. Standing "outside" the subject or claiming knowledge by entering into it more personally—these are not exclusive categories of understanding." Brooks, "Taking Sides and Opening Doors," 818–819.

[690] The argument that only those from within the religious or cultural tradition and only the natives of the tradition can become an *āpta* is too much polemic and an *Advaitin* can, and has to go beyond it.

or nationality or culture, can take up *brahmajijñāsā* and can be considered as an insider.

The voices of those academic *Advaitin*s who might prefer to be an 'outsider' are not without significance. The authentic desire for *Advaitic* knowledge and the sincere attempts for it cannot be overlooked. They can bring challenges and can critique *Advaita* from the point of their own tradition and area of expertise, such as history, philology, etc. which will keep the *Advaita* tradition always in the process of being constructively dynamic.[691] Their voice might not rank as 'speaking for' but their knowledge and objectivity with which they speak is significantly 'speaking about' *Advaita*. At the same time, "the first responsibility of those scholars from outside the tradition who participate in the tradition shall not credibly dictate how that tradition should function. One has to respect the tradition as one finds it, not as one wish, one could re-create it."[692] Such respect does not take away the scholars' responsibility to critically comment on the inhuman or exploitive structures of the tradition, if there is.[693]

5.2.2 Being Spiritual than Religious: Listening to the Seeker after Spirituality

Śaṅkara is very keen on determining who shall be an authentic seeker. Upad 2.1.2 and Mu U Bh 1.2.12–13 give a significant conformation on this. Except *brāhmaṇatva* and *sannyāsa*, all other characteristics given here of an authentic

---

[691] Rambachan, "Rethinking *Advaita*," 10.

[692] William Harman, "Speaking About Hinduism and Speaking Against It?" *Journal of American Academy of Religion* 68, no. 4 (2000): 739.

[693] Harman, "Speaking About Hinduism and Speaking Against It?" 739.

seeker i.e., the values demanded of an aspirant, can be reduced to *sādhanacatuṣṭaya.*[694] But *Śāṅkaravedānta* has enough scope to go beyond caste and stages of life—and therefore, *brāhmaṇatva* and *sannyāsa*—in recognising a true seeker.[695] The restrictions based on caste, gender, social status, nationality, etc., are not absolute when it comes to seeking self-knowledge.[696] An authentic seeker on his/her way of quest for *Brahman* makes him/herself disposed to, and strives for *sādhanacatuṣṭaya* without which the quest will never bear fruit.

An original seeker emerges from the dissatisfaction that he/she experience on the worldly life. That is, the real quest begins after the realisation that the highest purpose of life is not something that can be achieved through ordinary human effort.[697] He/She like Nārada (Ch U 7. 1. 1–3), Yājñavalkya and Maitreyī (Bṛ U 2.4. 1–5) realises the limits of mundane

---

[694] "If he is a Brahmin who is [internally and externally] pure; if he approaches his teacher in the prescribed manner; if his caste, profession, behaviour, knowledge [of the Veda], and family have been examined" (Upad 2.1.2 p. 211).

[695] The preceding chapters, especially the third chapter of this dissertation, 3.4.4 and 3.4.5, have already discussed on the inclusive features of *Śāṅkaravedāntic brahmajijñāsā*, its potency to go beyond *varṇa, āśrama*, and gender-based restrictions which *sannyāsa* and *brāhmaṇatva* might invoke. In Upad 2.1.2, after suggesting *sannyāsa* and *brāhmaṇatva* for an authentic seeker, Śaṅkara goes on explaining how a teacher has to instruct the aspirant that the caste, stages of life, etc. are superimpositions which the aspirant has to overcome to become a real seeker (Upad 2.1.10–16). In the same portion of the text, while describing on the qualified teacher, Śaṅkara states he must be a 'knower of Brahman' without having any reference to *varṇa* or *āśrama* (Upad 2.1.6; 2.2.45).

[696] Locklin, *Spiritual But not Religious?* 19.

[697] Locklin, *Spiritual But not Religious?* 17.

knowledge, wealth and pleasure and seeks for fulfilment beyond these.[698]

The authentic seeker, *brahmajijñāsu*, can be characterised as a spiritual person.[699] Śaṅkara exhorts that *brahmajijñāsā* is not a solitary engagement with scriptures accompanied with reasoning and austerities (Ke U Bh 1.4). It consists of engaging seriously with the scriptures by the committed seeker who with a deep devotion accepts the guidance of a competent teacher.[700] It invokes always a context, includes certain practices, disciplines, etc. In this *Advaitc* process of search he/she cultivates a set of values, a pattern of behaviour, mode of life, etc. which he/she find most suitable for the successful fruition of his/her search. These would become more profound and spontaneous mark of his/her life after the enlightenment. This context and environment with all its praxis, before or after enlightenment constitutes the religious aspect. In the process of search for enlightenment, living the life of an enlightened, and sharing of it in view of leading the other to it through words and deeds, there always forms a religious context in which the mutuality between expression of the experienced and the experience of the expressed take place. When the aspirants and also the enlightened ones, who are with the same path and mode of search, share in the same pattern of external context which they

---

[698] Rambachan, *The Advaita Worldview*, 9–15.

[699] The concept of spirituality applies to any person who has a belief in the divine or transcendental and fashions a life-style according to it. It is not restricted to any particular religion. It is a vision of life with a system of values and goals that orient and guide one's life. See C. Camillus, "Spirituality in Value Based Integrated Daily Living," *Vaihari* 9, no. 3 (September 2004): 7.

[700] Comans, *The Method of Early Advaita Vedānta*, 183.

find conducive for their self-realisation, it gets the form of a religious tradition, which obviously the members in it finds helpful for them.[701] In this sense to be spiritual is to be religious; though not necessarily becoming a part of its organised and institutionalised form. The voice of the authentic seeker is to be valued irrespective of their membership in established religions.

5.2.3 Listening to the Socially Engaged *Advaitin*

It is possible that the non-dual system of *Śāṅkaravedānta* be understood as illusionism, admitting little value to the world. The reasons for such explanation could be the difficulty of the *Advaita* tradition to explain the origin of the world from the non-dual *Brahman,*[702] and the emphasis on

---

[701] *Śāṅkaravedāntic* metaphysics and theology is suited to serve as a substratum for the diverse religious practises. See the fourth chapter of this dissertation, 4.4.2.2.3.

[702] *Brahman* is eternal, non-dual, the one without a second, absolutely simple and changeless (BS Bh 1.1.1; 1.1.4-5; 1.15.4; 1.1.20; Ch U Bh 6.2.1). How creation, which involves duality, can be explained to be caused by *Brahman* without violating *Brahman*'s non-duality and absoluteness? Therefore, in view of finding a solution, the reality of the world is degraded by relating its creation with *māyā* and lower *Brahman*. Srinivasa Rao, who considers this as a misunderstanding or a 'myth' points out: "Post-Śāṅkarite Advaitic writers attribute only indirect causality to *brahman*. Since *brahman* is the only reality in Advaita, it must perforce be involved in any causal process. Therefore, the post-Śāṅkarites hold that *brahman* serves as the ground for *māyā* which is the actual cause of this empirical world. *Māyā* is the material cause of this world and *brahman* merely serves as a support (*adhiṣṭhāna*) for this *māyā*. This *māyā*, which causes the insentient (*jaḍa*) world, is itself insentient (*jaḍa*) in nature, a nature that is totally opposed to the sentient (*cetana*) nature of *brahman*." Rao, "Two Myths in Advaita," 265. For De Smet it is Śaṅkara's "later disciples diffused his teaching as an authentic form of *māyāvāda*." See De Smet, "*Māyā* or *Ajñāna*?" in *Understanding Śaṅkara*, 122.

sannyāsa which contributed to the attitude of world-negation and ascribing inferior status to the world.[703] Within this framework, *Advaita* tradition becomes indifferent to the engagement with the world and there is practically little space for a social activist, and if at all there is, his/her voice on *Advaita* can have only limited authority.

Taking the case of *sannyāsa*, Śaṅkara valued mental detachment, than physical or formal *sannyāsa*. It is direct self-knowledge and the accompanying interior renunciation of doer-ship that stand at the centre of his concept of *sannyāsa* which is necessary for *brahmānubhava*. This makes liberation accessible to anyone regardless of caste, gender or state of life.[704] He supported a *gṛhastāśrami* becoming *brahmajñāni*. Continuing ritual actions and related social obligations by a *gṛhastāśrami* either before or after enlightenment, in no way impede liberation.[705]

Śaṅkara's teachings reveal that he did not consider the world as *māyā* or illusion.[706] *Brahman* is both the efficient and

---

[703] Rambachan, *The Advaita Worldview,* 109.

[704] Locklin, "Integral *Samnyasa*? 44. See also the third chapter of this dissertation, 3.4.4.

[705] See the third chapter of this dissertation 3.4.4.3.

[706] Śaṅkara has opposed *vijñānavādins* of their subjective idealism who deny the existence of world outside the perceiving mind. He challenges the claim that what appears to be outside of the mind is an illusion and argues for the objective nature of the world (BS Bh 2.2.28).

De Smet proves, Śaṅkara favored the term *ajñāna* or *avidyā* than *māyā*. "In this fundamental text [*Brahmasūtra Bhāṣya*], the ratio of frequency of the terms *ajñāna* (or *avidyā*) and *māyā* is 10 against 2. Besides *ajñāna* is constantly used as a precise technical term of the system (being clearly defined as *adhyāsa*, superimposition), while *māyā* is still an ordinary term with various significations, none of which has yet been privileged." See De Smet, "*Māyā* or *Ajñāna*?" in *Understanding Śaṅkara*, 122. De Smet gives three various meanings and material cause of the universe (Mu U Bh 1.1.7; 2.1.1; Ta U Bh 2.1.1Ch U Bh 6.2.3; Ai U Bh 1.1; BS Bh 1.1.5; 1.1.11; 2.1.1; 1.1.5; 1.1.9; 1.1.2). *Brahman* is the ultimate cause and essence of the world. Causing does not limit or implies change in *Brahman*.[707] This does not mean the world is totally identical with *Brahman* (BS Bh 2.1.9), at the same time, it is not something essentially different from *Brahman* (BS Bh 1.1.25; 2.1.9).[708] *Brahman*-world relation is that of *ananyatva* (not-

---

occasions in which the word *māyā* is used within *Brahmasūtra Bhāṣya* as an ordinary non-technical term. See De Smet, "*Māyā* or *Ajñāna*?" in *Understanding Śaṅkara*, 122–128.

707 Richard De Smet, "A Note About Śaṅkara's Doctrine of Creation," in *Understanding Śaṅkara*: *Essays by Richard De Smet,* ed. Ivo Coelho (Delhi: Motilal Banarsidas, 2013), 464. The rope-snake example that Śaṅkara uses is to show that, *Brahman* causes the world without having any change.

708 If *Brahman* is the material and efficient cause of the world, and if the basic nature of the world in essence is non-different from its cause how the causality of unconscious world can be explained on the basis of *Brahman* who is consciousness. In order to harness this issue some have interpreted *Advaitic* world as *māyā* and have given extra emphasis on the division of *Brahman* into *saguṇa* and *nirguṇa* and the former is associated with creation. But this is unwarranted. For Śaṅkara, according to Srinivasa Rao, "There is only the *cetana brahma* and nothing else. If it is so, this *cetana brahma* itself must be manifesting as the *acetana* world. In that case, "*acetana*" cannot be construed as something that *fundamentally* lacks sentiency; it can only be construed as something that does not manifestly reveal its sentiency. … Since what is regarded as *jaḍa* and what is regarded as *cetana* are not two really separate kinds of things, Śaṅkara has no difficulty or hesitation in declaring that what are regarded as *jaḍa* entities, like cow dung, produce *cetana* entities like scorpions and likewise, what are regarded as *cetana* entities, like human body, produce insentient nails and hair (BS Bh 2.1.6)." See Rao, "Two Myths in Advaita," 268. Aurobindo in his *Advaitic* philosophy agrees with this fact. For him, the higher reality (*sat-cit-ānanda*) makes an involution to the lower level reaching to matter and the lower makes an evolution to the higher. The evolution is possible because the higher is already implicit in the lower. See Chandradhar Sharma, *A Critical*

being-another-ness) or *tādātmya* (being-that-ness) (BS Bh 2.1.9; 3.2.32).[709] This implies, world, as an effect, depends on *Brahman* for its existence, but *Brahman* is independent (BS Bh 2.1.14).[710] It is not the existence of the world that Śaṅkara denies but only its existence independently of *Brahman* (BS Bh 2.1.4; 3.2.13; 2.1.14). The world is celebrative expression of *Brahman*'s fullness (BS Bh 2.1.32–33)[711] which is

---

Survey of Indian Philosophy (1960; repr., Delhi: Motilal Banarsidass, 1994), 381-385.

[709] Rao, "Two Myths in Advaita," 266. De Smet explains *tādātmya* relation as having six characteristics. (1) Unreciprocality: *Brahman* is the *ātman* of its effects; the effects are not the *ātman* of *Brahman*, their cause (Ta U Bh 2.6.1; BS Bh 2.1.9). (2) Dependence: World, the effect, completely depends upon its cause, the *Brahman*, for its existence (BS Bh 2.1.14; Bṛ U Bh 1.5.14). (3) Non-separateness: effect is non-separate from its cause (BS Bh 2.3.6; Bṛ U Bh 1.6.1). (4) Non-otherness: the effect is not totally foreign or 'other' but ontologically related to, and dependent on the cause; it excludes not non-distinction but division (Ta U Bh 2.6.1; Bṛ U Bh 2.3.6. (5). Distinction: the effect is not absolutely equal with cause; in the cause there is an excellence (BS Bh 2.1.6). (6) Extrinsic denominativity: Effects are not intrinsic qualifiers (*viśeṣaṇa*) but extrinsic denominators (*upādhi*) of *Brahman.* The great saying '*neti, neti*', designates *Brahman* unaffected by *upādhis* (Bṛ U Bh 3.8.12). See Richard De Smet, "Spiritual Values of Advaita Vedānta and Social Life," in *Understanding Śaṅkara*: *Essays by Richard De Smet,* ed. Ivo Coelho (Delhi: Motilal Banarsidas, 2013), 165–167; De Smet, "Śaṅkara's Non-Dualism," in *Understanding Śaṅkara*, 315–316.

[710] Comans, *The Method of Early Advaita Vedānta*, 194. As a finite expression world does not fully express *Brahman* and cannot, therefore, enjoy the same value as *Brahman*. *Brahman* is always greater than the sum total of its created effects and enjoys ultimate value. See Rambachan, *The Advaita Worldview,* 80. The relation of *Brahman* to the world in no way defines the ontological nature of the Absolute. Therefore, according to Śaṅkara, Names and forms in all their states have their *ātman* in *Brahman* alone, but *Brahman* has not it's *ātman* in them (Ta U Bh 2.6.1; BS Bh 2.1.9).

[711] *Brahman* is the efficient cause of the world. This implies causality of an intelligent and free agent. Since *Brahman* is transcendent

indefinable for the human intellect.[712] The richness of the value of the world derives from the very fact that (1) *Brahman* is its ultimate cause and essence; (2) it, therefore, is ontologically non-different from *Brahman,*[713] and (3) is the celebrative expression of *Brahman*'s fullness. *Śaṅkara* upholds the transcendence of *Brahman*, which is his primary concern, without denying the value and status of the world.[714]

According to Śaṅkara, the world exists both for the one who knows *Brahman* and the one who does not know *Brahman*. In the state of realization "a false view of the universe, and not the universe itself, is destroyed."[715] The enlightened one, based on his/her realization that *Brahman*

---

and perfect its causality is through infinite intelligence and infinite freedom and it is of a kind of sportfulness (*līlārūpaḥ*) (BS Bh 2.1.33). This would mean the act of creation does not involve any exercise of effort and not out of any inner necessity from the part of *Brahman*. It also implies that the world cannot be orderless, illogical and absurd for its creator is infinite intelligence. *Brahman*'s freedom must include the freedom to create or not to create. The effortlessness with which *Brahman* creates should not be misread to mean that creation is not desired by *Brahman* or that it is not a deliberate action. See De Smet, "A Note About Śaṅkara's Doctrine of Creation," in *Understanding Śaṅkara*, 467–468; Rambachan, *The Advaita Worldview,* 92–93.

[712] Rambachan, *The Advaita Worldview,* 79.

[713] World is not merely illusion; not without any ontological status; it is related to Brahman with *tādātmya* relation where in the excellence of *Brahman* is guaranteed.

[714] All realities other than *Brahman*, although they possess a specific existence (BS Bh 2.1.22) do not constitute another absolute and self-existent reality but they are one with *Brahman*. *Śāṅkaravedāntic* explanation on creation does away with monism or theopanism; it is *a-dvaita* or non-dualism. The created existence is not a modification, or an emanation, or a self-evolution, or a part of *Brahman* (BS Bh 2.1.14; 2.1.26). See De Smet, "A Note About Śaṅkara's Doctrine of Creation," in *Understanding Śaṅkara*, 464, 483.

[715] Rao, "Two Myths in Advaita," 270–276.

alone is the one without a second beyond all finite relations, understands the world which appears manifoldas essentially non-different from *Brahman* and as that which depends on *Brahman* for its existence and reality (Bṛ U Bh 3.5.1).

The behaviour and actions of the liberated is spontaneous to the nature of his/her realization. In BG Bh 6.32 Śaṅkara discusses the nature of the enlightened as the one who looks upon happiness and sorrow as pleasant and unpleasant to all beings, by the same standard as he/she would apply to him/herself. He/she does not act against anyone, is non-injurious and is steadfast in full illumination. This implies compassion or mercy as the characteristic virtue of the enlightened. The same is reflected in Ch U Bh 6.14.2. But compassion, as it is conceived by Śaṅkara, is a private, individual virtue articulated in its passive form such as refraining from harming others, hatred, etc. For him, teaching seems to be the only, positive activity born out of compassion.[716] The teacher is the enlightened person who teaches because of his/her compassion for the suffering of the student (Ch U Bh 6.14.2). This virtue of compassion does not discriminate human beings for it has become very much the spontaneous nature of the one who has realised the non-dual enlightenment and is the *sādhana* for an aspirant.[717] Caṭṭampiswāmikal concludes his critique of *Vedādhikāram* (*Vedādhikāranirūpaṇam*) by statingthat the imparting of

[716] Śaṅkara's reason on the teaching role of the *jīvanmukta* ought to be seen in the light of the *Advaita* emphasis on self-ignorance as the root of suffering and on the assumption that *jīvanmuktas* are few in number. See Rambachan, *The Advaita Worldview,* 108.

[717] Compassion has become his/her nature. It is like the flower which has its sweet smell. Wherever the flower may be, and to whom ever be the person come near to it, it cannot but spread its smell.

salvific knowledge of Vedas to anyonewho sincerely desires for it—irrespective of caste, class, gender, etc. —is the supreme form of compassion and is the supreme *dharma*. He compares the denial of Vedic knowledge with the merciless act of denying food for the hungry.[718]

Compassion cannot be construed as passive virtue and cannot be limited to the teaching ministry. "If the *jīvanmukta* [the liberated one while living] is motivated to teach because of compassion for the suffering student and a desire to set her free, there is no good reason why other kinds of actions, similarly motivated by the compassion for the suffering of others, are not possible."[719] The realized person is to lead others also to the same experience motivated by the compassion, and has to work for the integral well-being of the world (*lokasṃgraha*). Liberation does not alienate, isolate, or separate one from the community of other beings but awakens one to the truth of life's unity and interrelatedness. This calls for his/her positive engagement with the world, human relationships, social structures, ecological integrity, etc. liberating them from their ignorance-ridden engagements.[720]

The above discussion provides a strong impetus for the possibility of an *Advaitin* who is socially engaged, and his/her *āptatva* will enrich the critique of *Śāṅkaravedānta* by making it more dynamic and meaningful for the world today.

---

[718] Caṭṭampiswāmikal, *Vedādhikāranirūpaṇam*, 75.

[719] Rambachan, *The Advaita Worldview,* 108.

[720] Rambachan, *The Advaita Worldview,* 110–111. For an enlightened these characteristics are perfect and spontaneous but these also could become part of the *sādhana* or discipline for the aspirant. See Locklin, "Integral *Samnyasa*? 48.

5.2.4 The *Advaitic* Voices from Other Cultures and Traditions

Crossing the boundaries of society, culture, religion, etc., are found very common in the world today: Buddhist-Jews, Buddhist-Christians, Hindu-Christians—crossing the boundaries are endless and enriching. Religious practices and ideas have their give-and-take and float across religious boundaries and take root in new soil. For example, Christians do Zen, Buddhist engage in social activism, and anyone does yoga. At this point, it is important to reflect: can a person from another tradition and culture who is ready to accept *Advaitic* faith take up *brahajijñāsā*; can his/her voice on *Advaita* be legitimate; how far the attempts of other traditions for self-realization in their own ways can be appreciated by the *Advaitin*.

The teachings of Śaṅkara were not totally new as he was part of the great living tradition, the *Advaita*. As a great interpreter and reformer of the tradition, he was not unaffected by, and independent of the culture, religious practices and the social situations of his time. His life as a renouncer has influenced his teachings, because renunciation traditionally implied a specific attitude to the world, community and family.[721]

In developing and explaining his teachings, Śaṅkara has greatly made use of other systems, both orthodox and heterodox. He always took the critique of these systems seriously and was willing to incorporate elements of rival world views. He expounds his theories in disputation with orthodox schools such as *Pūrvamīmāṁsa*, *Sāṁkhya*, *Yoga*, and

---

[721] Rambachan, "Rethinking Advaita," 8.

Nyāya and heterodox traditions like Buddhism and Jainism. He demonstrates a remarkable effort to present and engage these perspectives. In the process of engaging these traditions and attempting, when necessary, to refute some of their claims, Śaṅkara incorporated many of their insights and the *Advaita* tradition was enriched.[722] On the question of accepting doctrines from *Yogadarśana*, Śaṅkara remarks that if the doctrine of another tradition or scholar is not inconsistent with our own, it becomes an accompaniment of our own (BS Bh 2.4.12).[723] He does not become stingy in accepting *smṛti* texts—which unlike *śruti*, were not infallible—in so far as *smṛti* is consistent with *śruti*. For instance, he writes a commentary on *Bhagavadgītā* which he interpreted in the *a-dvaita* (non-dualistic) mode.[724]

In addition to this, the enlightened one who is beyond caste, tradition, etc. who is compassionate, looks for the happiness or well-being of all beings. He/She has the vision of sameness (*samatva*); the knowledge of the identity of the self and *Brahman* everywhere even in the clump of grass (BG Bh 6.29, 32).[725] "The response to seeing oneself in another is love. It makes it possible for us to identify with others beyond the boundaries of our nationality, ethnicity, tribe, religion, and

---

[722] Rambachan, "Rethinking Advaita," 11.

[723] एवंतर्हि "परमतमप्रतिषिद्धमनुमतं भवति" इति न्यायादिहापि योगशास्त्रप्रसिद्धा मनसः पंचवृत्तयः परिगृह्यन्ते "प्रमाणविपर्ययाविकल्पनिद्रास्मृतयः" नाम । Cf. Śaṅkara, *Brahmasūtra with Śāṅkarabhāṣya*, ed., Ministry of Education, India, 257.

[724] De Smet, "Śaṅkara's Perspective on Meaning and Truth," in *Understanding Śaṅkara*, 266.

[725] सर्वभूतस्थं सर्वेषु भूतेषु स्थितं स्वं आत्मानं सर्वभूतानि च आत्मनि ब्रह्मादीनि स्तम्बपर्यन्तानि च सर्वभूतानि आत्मनि एकतां गतानि ईक्षते पश्यति योगयुक्तात्मा समाहितान्तः करणः सन् सर्वत्र समदर्शनः सर्वेषु ब्रह्मादिस्थावरान्तेषु विषमेषु सर्वभूतेषु समं निर्विशेषं ब्रह्मात्मैकत्वविषयं दर्शनं ज्ञानं यस्य सः सर्वत्र समदर्शनः॥ (BG Bh 6.29) Cf. Śaṅkara, *The Bhagavad-gītā with the Commentary of Śrī Śaṅkarācārya*, ed., Dinakar Vishnu Gokhale, 111.

culture, to share their suffering and rejoice in their well-being."[726] This experience motivates the *Advaitin* to be open to the one who is really in search for self-realization leaving aside his/her all other identities.

At the same time, we find Śaṅkara advising his disciples to denounce the rival doctrines (Upad 1.16. 64–67). The aim here is the student, after understanding all those,[727] has to reach an unperturbed state with the conviction that the *Advaitic* truth is really worthy of wholehearted pursuit, which he/she can adhere with faith and devotion. He/She shall not get divided in mind or become half-hearted in the quest for truth. Śaṅkara's assimilation of other philosophies and traditions was not uncritical. In accepting other traditions he was very careful not to compromise with his basic insights and convictions, and the essentials of his philosophy and theology.

The *Advaitic* enlightenment of non-duality recognises the underlying ontological unity of everything but does not deny the differences and uniqueness. The other traditions need not be brought into one single tradition, perhaps *Advaita*, creating a hybrid unity. Various religious traditions in their uniqueness can enrich the spiritual pursuit of each other. They can share a communion that is neither entirely foreign nor entirely recognizable as one's own.[728]

Therefore, *Śāṅkaravedāntin*s, taking cue from Śaṅkara's openness to the richness of other traditions, his commitment to truth than ritual and to *sādhanacatuṣṭaya* than other requisites, can gladly recognize the attempts of other

---

[726] Rambachan, *The Advaita Worldview,* 110–111.

[727] Śaṅkara himself in his writings exhibits an in-depth knowledge of all these.

[728] Locklin, *Spiritual But not Religious?* 134.

religious traditions and cultures for achieving self-realization. At the same time, they can hold on to their own conviction that *Advaitic* programme for self-realization as excellent and sure. In this vein of thought *Śāṅkaravedānta* has the potency to rise above caste, gender, tradition, and to extend a warm welcome to anyone from any tradition who can commit him/herself to the virtues of *sādhanacatuṣṭaya*, for taking up the quest for *Brahman*. Their enlightenment and scholarship can be taken to the point of 'speaking for' *Advaita*.

Conclusion

The fundamentals of *Śāṅkaravedāntic brahmajijñāsā* is based on knowledge than rituals and *sādhanacatuṣṭaya* than external criteria such as *sannyāsa* and *brāhmaṇatva.* The goal of all the prerequisites is to lead the aspirant unfailingly to achieve the aim, *brahmānubhva*, the self-realisation. The care given to the process of *brahmajijñāsā* is significant, because the failure in this regard will be grave for it is one's wholehearted pursuit needing a life-long commitment. The essentials of *brahmajijñāsā*—knowledge and *sādhanacatuṣṭaya*—are inclusive having the potency to go beyond the restrictions of caste, gender, social status, culture, nationality, etc.

The main reason for *śūdra*-exclusion, as it is presented by *Apaśūdrādhikaraṇam,* is that the name '*śūdra*' is mentioned in the scripture as those to be excluded. Since Vedas being eternal and canonical this mandate remains obligatory. But the formation of the Vedas, the emergence of the social group called *śūdra*s and the inclusion of the name *śūdra* into the Vedic texts as the one to be excluded have historical reasons too. *Apauruṣeyatva* of the Vedas has to be understood theologically and therefore, it means, that the Vedic truths on ultimate reality is derived not from ordinary human perceptual mechanisms; those truths have unfailing potency to lead one to the fruitful realisation of his/her ultimate goal, *brahmānubhva*. Taking all these into account *śūdra*-exclusion need not be taken in the literal sense; *śūdra* stands for anyone who is ineligible for *brahmajijñāsā*; eligibility criterion need not be based on one's birth, social status, culture, nationality, etc. but on being qualified with moral virtues of *sādhnacatuṣṭaya*. Śaṅkara's reasons for exclusion are weak and inclusivism implied in his essentials of *brahmajijñāsā*—primacy for truth and *sādhanacatuṣṭaya*—are strong. The *Advaitavedāntin* of the present-day has all the scope to explore the inclusivism implied in Śaṅkara.

The answer to the question, who can speak for *Advaita*, depends very much on an inclusive or exclusive understanding of *Advaita*. If the one who has achieved enlightenment is the *āpta* in speaking for *Advaita*, and if some are disqualified from taking up *brahmajijñāsā*, then the *āptatva* is exclusive. *Śāṅkaravedāntic* soteriology has given the orientation to go beyond caste, gender, etc. and have the potency to become inclusive. *Advaita* being a living tradition, the present *Advaitin*s have to explore these orientations and bring them to the present day religious and social circumstances of exclusive ideologies and practices. An inclusive revisiting of the questions concerning listening to the voices from various *Advaitic* spheres is significant. The voice of anyone, irrespective of caste, gender, culture, nationality, etc., who has qualified with *sādhancatuṣṭaya* and has *brahmānubhva* can be considered as an *āpta* speaking for *Advaita*. Any authentic seeker who has the faith in the Vedas and is devoted to its truth for the self-realisation can be considered as an insider. The enlightened scholar, whether from within *brāhmaṇic* tradition or not, whether contemplative or social activist, is an *āpta* and can speak for *Advaita*. Academic knowledge about *Advaita* is not without significance, but without enlightenment, it 'speaks about' *Advaita*; not 'for' it.

CONCLUSION

Delimiting, Furthering and Forwarding this Study

This study on exploring the inclusive potentials of *Śāṅkaravedānta* by analysing *Apaśūdrādhikaraṇam* from *Brahmasūtra Śāṅkara Bhāṣya* is not exhaustive. It has attempted to explore only from the theoretical point of view the inclusivism and pro-subaltern possibilities of *Śāṅkaradarśana* by analysing the particular text, *Apaśūdrādhikaraṇam.* Being an attempt for a theroretical exploration and a textual study, it has given less attention to its practical applications in the particular cases of exclusion, and also has not focused on social and practical renaissant-thinkers who has contributed to the abolition of exclusive practices. This study has limited itself by taking up texts only of *brāhmaṇic* tradition and has given scant attention to non-*brāhmaṇic* texts and traditions. Buddhist and Jaina texts, indegenous floklore sources and vernacular literature from the women fold, low caste or out-caste of the then society would have contributed very much to this study. The scriptures and practices of *bhakti* traditions such as *Vaiṣṇavism* and *Śaivism* which have originated partly as the reaction to the caste system of the *brāhmaṇic* religion, would speak aloud the story of exclusion. These are studied only in nutshell; not analysed in detail. An analysis of inclusivism in the *advaitins* immediately after Śaṅkara, and also the later non-academic religious *advatins,* such as Ramaṇamaharṣi, is still another posibility to strengthen this study. An exposition on practical applications of the advaitic inclusivism, a detailed analysis on the texts and traditions other than *brāhmaṇic* and exclusive/inclusive interpratation and practices of *Advaita* in the non-academic religious texts and institutions are beyond the scope and focus of this study. An in-depth knowledge of

Sanskrit language would take this study which is textual and hermeneutical to a further depth.

This study has further avenues and posibilities. It could be carried forward with the questions such as: if Śaṅkara had to develop a social philosophy from his *a-dvaitic* metaphysics, how it could be? How *Śāṅkaradarśana* would dialogue with post-colonial subaltern studies? Do a solidarity-ethics need a substatial non-dual metaphysics? This study could serve as the foundation for developing an *advaitic* eco-philosophy; a world-view which is very much inclusive, accepting every diffrences and uniquness which looks, not for homogenity and unity, but for harmony and integrity. Inclusivism and the non-dual metaphysics of *Advaita* can contribute very much to the philosophy of self and its other. It can also strengthen the feminist theorising, i.e. philosophial response to the marginilaised and the exploited; it could be 'women' in a male-dominated society or 'body' which is forgotten in the world of philosophy where mind and soul is celebrated. This study can further join hands with practical or pragmatic *advaitism* by responding to the particular issues of exclusion and exploitation in the cases such as LGBT persons, Dalit, etc.

Final Comments in Concluding this Study

Advaitavedānta of Śaṅkara, or any philosophical or theological system for that matter, bears the mission of becoming the light for the world, and therefore, has become an inspiration and aid for people to achieve integrity in their lives. If it has to continue to be so, the original insights and the fundamental orientation given to it by Śaṅkara, are to be nurtured by the subsequent following. For which, first of all, the system shall be taken not as a finished and closed piece of theology or philosophy, but rather, must be considered as a process: a process of theorising, opening up the possibilities for revision and renewal which will invite it to be self-critical. Secondly, it should be prudent and audacious to identify and to confront the 'darkness' of the present-day society. Thirdly, it has to be creative and constructive in responding to the changing issues and concerns of the present world which Śaṅkara might not have addressed, for it might not be a concern for his historical period. If these are not attended well, the mission of *Advaita* becomes hardly successful and it ceases to be meaningful for the people and can eventually get extinct.

The present world, which is negatively affected by the exclusive policies and practices, is in need of light. Exclusion can be considered as an attitude which begets many negative practices in various areas. The reasons why a particular group of people are excluded could be political, social, cultural, educational, occupational, economic, gender, religious, ideological and so on. Whatever be the criteria and the form of exclusion, it involves discrimination, exploitation, disrespect for the dignity of the person, and it negatively affects the integrity of the human person, society and the cosmos at large. Sometimes exclusive interests are systematically theorised, interpreted, justified and are at times normalised, so that applying them would cleverly effect exclusion and consequent exploitations whereby justice, right and dignity of the weak and the minority are robbed away. Exclusion, therefore, is the cause and consequence of the marginalisation of the weak, and therefore, the formation of subalterns. Inclusive thinking and practices give a ray of hope against this. Inclusivism has to become the underlying nature of theorizing in which the discriminative and exploitive structures, policies and strategies are challenged. *Advaita vedānta*, therefore, in its mission of becoming light for the world has to be inclusive.

Being inclusive does not mean, bringing everything into one single fold, into a kind of hybrid unity. *Śāṅkaravedānta* does not deny the existence of the world either before or after enlightenment and does not do away with the differences and uniqueness that exist. In fact, it is the enlightenment on basic ontological non-duality that can recognize and appreciate the differences of the phenomenal world; of each and every person, gender, culture, religion and so on, and of every creature at large. It remedies the evils such as discrimination, exploitation, disrespect for human personhood, etc. Without this basic insight it is possible that the differences and uniqueness are either considered totally alien to each other which would perpetuate hostile attitude between them, or the differences are tailored or reduced to form a kind of sameness.

Śāṅkaravedāntic tradition, from its early beginnings, was attentive to the problem of exclusion. The specific issue of *śūdra*-exclusion has received Śaṅkara's attention as it is obvious from the *Apaśūdrādhikaraṇam* of his *Brahmasūtra Bhāṣya.* A cursory reading and a general understanding of the *adhikaraṇam* and his *bhāṣya* for *Brahmasūtra* at large, gives an inclination to understand Śaṅkara as an exclusivist. This is mainly because, the text supports *varṇāśrama* system, emphasises the importance of Vedas for *mokṣa* and argues for the exclusion of *śūdra*s from the Vedic learning. In addition to this, *Brahmasūtra Bhāṣya*, and Śaṅkara's other works also, insists on *sannyāsa* as the requirement for *brahmānubhava*. If Vedas and *sannyāsa* are held to be the *sine qua non* for salvation, then, according to the Vedic religious tradition, *śūdra*s, women of all *varṇa*, non-*sannyāsa āśramis* such as householders, and those who do not belong to any *āśrama* such as widower, are excluded from salvation, and therefore, the possibility of salvation is limited only to the male members of the upper caste. This characterises *Śāṅkaravedānta* as pro-exclusive and categorises it to be elite monasticism. A careful listening to Śaṅkara's treatment on the problem of exclusion points to an important observation. He takes an in-between position: on the one hand, he does not explicitly admit the eligibility of *śūdra*s for Vedas, and therefore, he remains as an exclusivist, but on the other hand, his texts give lot of indications, by way of exceptions, provisions, and implications which suggest the possibility of salvation for *śūdra*s and even their eligibility for Vedas, and this keeps him on the side of inclusivism. Śaṅkara seems to be first closing the door of salvation to *śūdra*s, but then, opening a lot of side doors for them to attain it. Śaṅkara's arguments for such a position, especially for his exclusive inclinations, could be justified from his hermeneutical context, but from the present context of growing exclusivism, they are inadequate. His arguments are inconsistent and unsound, especially when they are viewed from the platform of his non-dualistic philosophy and of his basic convictions. Therefore, his treatment and position on this issue has to be revisited in the spirit of a true critique. The possible and general understanding on Śaṅkara as pro-exclusive and therefore, anti-subaltern is to be re-visioned through the lens of an inclusivist critique.

A critique on Śaṅkara's position on exclusion can be done in two ways: first of all, by bringing out the inconsistencies and unsoundness of his arguments for exclusion, and secondly, by exploring the inclusivism of his fundamental teachings. Taking the former, one significant observation is, his arguments for exclusion depend very much on placing Vedas and *sannyāsa* as prerequisites for *brahmajijñāsā*. If these are taken to be absolutely necessary for salvation, then it is true that *Śāṅkaravedāntic* soteriology is clearly exclusive. But, in fact, this is not the case. *Apaśūdrādhikaraṇam* gives evidences that Vedas are not *sine qua non* for salvation; *smṛti* texts also are competent for it. He argues, *śūdra*s are excluded from Vedas because Vedas themselves have named them as those to be excluded. But, in fact, Vedas have not made any injunctive statement on *śūdra*-exclusion, and Śaṅkara has not brought out any of such in favour of his arguments. Even if those are there, Śaṅkara's basic convictions on the validity of *śruti* do not agree accepting the exclusive norms. According to Śaṅkara, *śruti* is valid, not of empirical matters but of transcendental reality, and the validity of *śruti* lies in their being eternal and infallible. Considering the former case, a historical survey on the formation of *śūdra*s, the practice of exclusion, and its appearance in the texts show that the *śūdra*-exclusion was very much motivated by social reasons and has little to do with the nature and realisation of the truth, the transcendental reality. Taking the latter case, the conception of Vedas as eternal is a theological doctrine and it cannot be taken as literal and factual. Why such doctrine entered into the Vedic tradition has social and contextual reasons. It was to affirm the authority of Vedas in the context of growing challenges and criticisms to the Vedic religion. The doctrine is to affirm the authority of Vedas in the matters of transcendental reality and it declares the unfailing potency of Vedas to lead one to the self-realising experience. Another factor that makes Śaṅkara exclusive is his insistence on *sannyāsa*. But an analysis of his concept of *sannyāsa* shows, for him, it was not physical *sannyāsa* as a formal *āśrama* but the internal *sannyāsa* of detachment that was necessary for *brahmānubhava*. This breaks the boundaries of exclusivism. Vedas and *sannyāsa* as the requisites for *brahmajijñāsā* leave the scope of inclusive and universal understanding of *Śāṅkaravedānta*.

The fundamental among the teachings of *Śāṅkaravedānta* is: *Brahman*, the Absolute, is one without a second and is the ontological cause and essence of everything else. Śaṅkara emphasized the transcendence of non-dual reality. *Mokṣa* is the self-realizing experience of this non-duality. In dealing with the possibility of this experience, he emphasized knowledge than ritual, and the virtues of *sādhanacatuṣṭaya* than any other prerequisites. These remain essential to his soteriology. Every other requirement is supportive of this, and is interpretable according to the context without losing the spirit of deploying the requirements. The intention behind the restrictions by way of prerequisites is that the aspirant who quests for *Brahman* should not miss his/her goal. This quest requires one's wholehearted pursuit, and therefore, one shall not take chances but should go for excellent means with adequate preparations. Therefore, in designing the program for liberation, i.e., *brahmajijñāsā,* the uncompromisingly important factors are knowledge and *sādhanacatuṣṭaya*. Both these have the potency to go beyond the discriminations based on *varṇa*, *āśrama*, gender, culture, nationality, etc. Therefore, from the fact that (1) Śaṅkara's arguments for exclusion are inconsistent and unsound, and (2) the essentials of his soteriology are universal and inclusive,

Śāṅkaravedāntic brahmajijñāsā can be characterised as inclusive and Śaṅkara as non-exclusivist.

Though Śaṅkara, due to various reasons, is not explicit on inclusivism, he has left all the possibilities for the present-day *Śāṅkaravedāntin* to explore it and fight against the exclusive ideologies, policies and practices. He/she can get into this task in two ways. First of all by theorising Śaṅkara for the present context. It could be done by taking account of his primary convictions on which he remained uncompromising, i.e. his emphasis on non-dual enlightenment and *sādhanacatuṣṭaya* ethics. Secondly, he/she has to enrich and carry forward thc basic inspiration and orientation which the thinker has initiated. Such orientation includes Śaṅkara's shift from ritualism to the enlightenment of the truth, and his creative responses to the social and axiological changes. Śaṅkara was not immune to the social reformations based on equality of human person. From the available and possible textual and contextual grounds he has opened himself up. He becomes comparatively less exclusive when he held that the exclusion is only from Vedas and not from liberation. The final *brahmānubhava*, whether it is through *śruti* or *smṛti*, is same for all, the upper or lower *varṇa*. These are to be the direction and inspiration for the present *Advaitin* to go ahead with this spirit, and to be creative and dynamic in responding to the contexts of the society.

The inclusion-exclusion discourse on *Advaitic brahmajijñāsā* points also to the question, who can speak for *Advaita*. If, one who has *brahmānubhava* alone is authorised for *Advaita*, and if some groups of people are excluded from the possibility of having it, then the answer to this question become very much exclusive. *Sādhanacatuṣṭaya*, the primary requisite for *brahmajijñāsā*, reveal that those who have grown in the required moral virtues, who have the desire for *mokṣa*, and have the faith in Vedic scriptures can become a real *Advaitic* seeker and can fruitfully reach the goal, *brahmānubhava*. If then, caste, class, gender, culture, nationality and so on do not hinder one to become an authentic spiritual seeker, a *brahmajijñāsu*. He/She can have *brahmānubhava*, and can become the voice for *Advaita*. Those who approach the Vedic scriptures with a pure academic interest may speak about it, and their contribution to it from the context of their academic erudition and cultural difference are significant in keeping the tradition creative and dynamic. The understanding that only a contemplative *guru* can speak for *Advaita* has to be reviewed. The enlightened, with his/her compassion for the creatures and desire for the well-being of the world, can get into the social activities other than teaching. Therefore, the voice from a socially engaged *Advaitin* shall not go unattended.

The critique on *śūdra*-exclusion can be considered as a response to any exclusive, exploitive and oppressing system. '*Śūdra*s', the oppressed and 'upper-caste', the oppressors get changed from time to time. It is even possible that the oppressed of today become tomorrow's oppressor. The mode of exploitation and from what the exclusion is, also change according to the context. Revisiting *śūdra*-exclusion in *Śāṅkaravedānta*, based on a critical and inclusive reading of his *Apaśūdrādhikaraṇam* invites one to become inclusive in his/her thinking, attitude and engagement with society and environment. It challenges, especially the *Advaitins*, to become the light, dispelling the darkness caused by exclusive ideologies and structures. It speaks loudly to the exclusivists, especially to those who might take Śaṅkara to be on their side, that *Śāṅkaravedānta* is not anti-inclusive and anti-subaltern. Those oppressors—whether it be from the social, political, cultural, religious or domestic spheres—have to review their attitude and policies. This study does not intend to say that the excluded or the oppressed should strive by all means to get all what they are denied. It does not advocate a blind yearning for what the so called high culture has. Each culture or tradition may have their own ways and means for the attainment of self-realisation which are so beneficial, special and dear to them. Those are not to be abandoned for the sake of another, which some other groups, who claim to be the mainstream ones in the society, consider to be the excellent. The groups of people, whom others might consider to be inferior from their point of view, shall not lose appreciation for their culture, religion, and unique means for self-realisation; but, has to be vigilant not to become prey to exploitation. Exclusion of *śūdra*s from the Vedas and from the related tradition is critiqued not to mean that the excluded have to somehow get into it. But, it speaks to the exclusivists that the critical study of *Śāṅkaravedānta* shows that they have to renew and revise their understanding of Śaṅkara and has to become inclusive.

According to *Śāṅkaravedānta,* to be an enlightened necessarily implies to be inclusive. This invites him/her to creatively respond to the exclusivism and the related evils, such as intolerance, religious fundamentalism, discrimination, oppression and exploitation. This will lead the enlightened to be concerned also about the ecology. Exploitation of the nature by the strong and the powerful makes the weak, the powerless and the poor—human and non-human creatures and the cosmos at large—being excluded from their right for natural resources, the very basics for the sustenance of their life on earth. An enlightened *Advaitin* is inclusive, compassionate and strives for the well-being, the integrity of the people and the entire cosmos. Being so, he/she enters into the culture of respect: respecting the other human beings, other cultures, other creatures, etc. The differences are neither tailored into one single unity nor alienated or denied, but, are respected and celebrated, because the enlightened one realises the underlying ontological non-duality. Therefore, the *Advaitic* enlightenment makes the person an inclusivist who respectfully engages with the world with pro-subaltern and ecological concerns. Those aspirants who strive for enlightenment make this as a discipline, *sādhana*, which would become spontaneous to his/her nature after enlightenment.

The discussions held through out this dissertation states, though Śaṅkara did not adequately develop and explicitly open up, *Śāṅkaradarśana* is inclusive. A re-reading of *Apaśūdrādhikaraṇam* from *Brahmasūtra Śāṅkara Bhāṣya* in the spirit of a true critique reveals that it is non-exclusive. The inclusive potentials and insights of *Śāṅkaravedānta* can be further enriched and carried forward as the light for the present context of exploitive structures either caused by or the consequence of exclusivism. A true *Śāṅkaravedāntin* with his/her non-dual insight, the realisation of the Real, has to be inclusive in his/her thinking, attitude and activities, and therefore, is a pro-subaltern.

GLOSSARY

adhikāra Authority, eligibility or competence, especially in relation to the quest for *Brahman*.

Adhikaraṇam A set of aphorisms dealing with a particular topic.

advaita Non-duality, one without a second. It also means the theory or system which is based on non-duality.

Anubhava Experience; from the religious and theological point of view, it is direct/immediate experience or intuition.

apaśūdrādhikaraṇam The set of five aphorisms (*sūtra*s) which deals with the eligibility of *śūdra* for Vedic study. This consists of *sūtra*s 34–38, from the third section constituting ninth topic of the first chapter of *Brahmasūtra,* i.e. BS 1.3.34–38.

apauruṣeyatva A doctrine on Vedic scriptures which states that no human being is responsible for the creation of Vedas.

āpta	A reliable or trustworthy person whose words can be considered authoritative or valid.
āśrama	The stages of life; there are four stages or *āśrama*s. They are: *brahmacarya* (student-hood) *gṛhasta* (house holder), *vānaprastha* (forest-dweller or hermit) and *sannyāsa* (renunciant).
brahmajijñāsā	Quest for *Brahman*
brahmajijñāsu	The one who has taken up the quest for *Brahman*
brahmajñāna	Knowledge of *Brahman*
brāhmaṇism	Vedic religious tradition which consists in ritualism where *brāhmaṇas* are the officiating priests.
brahmaniṣṭhaḥ	The one who is absorbed in *Brahman*
brahmānubhava	Experience of *Brahman*, the experience of self-realisation.
brahmasaṁstha	Established in *Brahman* or steadfast in *Brahman*
Brahmasūtra Bhāṣya	Interpretation given to *Brahmasūtra* which is the work of Bādarāyaṇa.

dāsa	A group of people mentioned in *Ṛgveda* with whom Vedic Aryans were in conflict with.
dharmajijñāsā	The quest for *dharma*. For *dharmajijñāsā* the goal is *dharma* and the method is sacrifices and other rituals. But, for *brahmajijñāsā* the goal is self-realisation through the acquisition of knowledge.
gṛhastāśrama	The second one among the four stages of life. This is the stage of being a householder.
jīvanmukta	The liberated one while living
jñānamārga	The way of knowledge for liberation
manana	Reflection (reasoning) on the scriptures
Mīmāṁsāsūtra	The textual work of Jaimini who belongs to the *Pūrvamīmaṁsā* Vedic tradition
mokṣa	Liberation
mumukṣutvam	Desire for *mokṣa*

nididhyāsana	Meditation on the scriptures
pramāṇa	Means for valid knowledge.
Pūrvamīmaṁsā	Known generally as *mīmaṁsā*; it is the philosophical and religious system belongs to Vedic tradition. It gives emphasis on ritual aspect of the Vedas and gives priority for *saṁhitā* and *brāhmaṇa* portions of Vedas.
pūrvapakṣa	The earlier view or the opponent's view.
sādhana	Spiritual practice or discipline.
sādhanacatuṣṭaya	The fourfold virtues necessary for the quest for *Brahman*: *viveka, vairāgya, śamadamādisādhanasampatti,* and *mumukṣutvam.*
Śaivism	Religious system with the devotion to Śiva who is considered as the supreme deity.
Śamadamādi-sādhanasampatti	Qualities such as *śama, dama*, etc. referred to as the wealth of six disciplines. The six spiritual virtues referred to are: *śama, dama, uparati, titikṣa, samādhāna,* and *śraddhā.*

Śāṅkaravedānta	The *Vedānta* system of philosophy expounded by Śaṅkara.
***Śāṅkarite*s**	Those who follow the philosophical system of Śaṅkara.
sannyāsa	Renunciation or the renunciant mode of life-stage (*sannyāsa-āśrama*).
śāstra	Scriptures, treatise or disciplines
smṛti	The texts other than Vedas which have comparatively later origin. Unlike *śruti* they are considered as authored; e.g. *Bhagavadgītā*, *Manusmṛti*, etc.
śraddhā	Faith
śravaṇa	Listening to the scriptures
śruti	The body of directly received knowledge enshrined in Vedic texts which are considered authorless and eternal. *Śruti* also means the source of valid knowledge for it provides the knowledge from the scriptures.
śūdra	A member of fourth class in the Vedic system of *varṇa* classification of

	society. They are considered to the servile/labourer class.
sūtra	Aphorisms
upanayana	The rite of initiation by which one is introduced to the stage of studenthood.
Uttaramīmāṁsā	A philosophical system of Vedic tradition. It is generally known as *Vedānta*. It takes knowledge portion of the Vedas, mainly Upaniṣads as primary. It considers knowledge of the Vedic truth, and not the rituals, leads one to liberation.
vairāgya	Non-attachment
Vaiṣṇavism	The religious system with devotion to Viṣṇu which considers Viṣṇu as the supreme deity.
varṇa	An order dividing society into four groups arranged in a hierarchy—the *brāhmaṇa* (priestly class), *kṣatriya* (*rājanya* i.e. ruling/warrior class), *vaiśya* (cultivator and the trader) and *śūdra* (servile/labourer class).

vedanityatva	Doctrine on Vedic scriptures which states the eternity of Veda
Vedānta	The word literally means the end (*anta*) portion of Vedas and indicates Upaniṣads. But it popularly understood as those philosophical systems that have developed basing on Upaniṣads, *Bhagavadgītā* and *Brahmasūtra* of Bādarāyaṇa.
vedaprāmāṇya	A doctrine on Vedas which states the ultimate and absolute epistemological authority of Veda.
viveka	Discrimination between the eternal (*nitya*) and non-eternal (*anitya*).

BIBLIOGRAPHY

BOOKS

Adams, George C. *The Structure and Meaning of Bādarāyaṇa's Brahma Sūtras: A Translation and Analysis of Adyāya I.* Delhi: Motilal Banarsidas, 1993.

Aiyar, C.N. Krishnasamy and Sitanath Tattvabhushan. *Sri Sankaracarya.* Madras: G.A. Natesan, n.d.

Altekar, A.S. *Education in Ancient India.* Varanasi: Nand Kishore, 1965.

Altson, A.J. *Śaṃkara on the Absolute.* Vol.1 of *A Śaṃkara Source-Book.* London: Shanti Sadan, 1980.

Arya, Ravi Prakash and K.L. Joshi, trans. and eds. *Ṛgveda Saṁhitā: Sanskrit Text, English Translation, Notes and Index of Verses.* 4 vols. Delhi: Parimal Publications, 2001.

Avari, Burjor. *India: The Ancient Past; A History of the Indian Sub-Continent from c.7000 BC to AD 1200.* London: Routledge, 2007.

Ayyar, K.V. Krishna. *A History of Kerala.* Palghat: Malabar Printers, 1965.

Beteille, Andre. *The Idea of Natural Inequality and Other Essays.* Delhi: Oxford University Press, 1983.

Bhandarkar Oriental Institute. *The Mahābhārata: Text as Constituted in its Critical Edition.* 4 vols. Poona: Bhandarkar Oriental Institute, 1971–75.

Bhandyopadhyaya, Jayantanuja. *Class and Religion in Ancient India*. New Delhi: Anthem Press, 2007.

Bhatt G.H, ed. *The Vālmīki-Rāmāyaṇa*. 7 vols. Baroda: Oriental Institute, 1960–75.

Black, Brian. *Priests, Kings, and Women in the Early Upaniṣads: The Character of Self in Ancient India*. Delhi: Motilal Banarsidas, 2014.

Buhler, Georg, trans. *The Sacred Laws of the Āryas As Taught in the Schools of Āpastamba, Gautama, Vāsishtha and Baudhāyana: Part 1; Āpastamba and Gautama*. Vol. 2 of *The Sacred Books of the East*, edited by F. Max Muller. Rev. ed. Oxford: Clarendon Press, 1897.

———, trans. *The Sacred Laws of the Āryas As Taught in the Schools of Āpastamba, Gautama, Vāsishtha and Baudhāyana: Part 2; Vāsishtha and Baudhāyana*. Vol. 14 of *The Sacred Books of the East*, edited by F. Max Muller. 1882. Reprint, Delhi: Motilal Banarsidas, 1965.

Caṭṭampiswāmikal, Srī. *Vedādhikāranirūpaṇam* (in Malayalam). http://hinduebooks.blogspot.com, 2010. https://archive.org/details/VedadhikaraNirupanam-

ChattampiSwamikal-Malayalam (accessed February 20, 2017).

Clooney, Francis X. *Theology After Vedānta: An Experiment in Comparative Theology*. New York: State University of New York Press, 1993.

Comans, Michael. *The Method of Early Advaita Vedānta: A Study of Gauḍapāda, Śaṅkara, Sureśvara and Padmapāda*. Delhi: Motilal Banarsidas, 2000.

Das, Abhinas Chandra. *Ṛgvedic India.* Rev. ed. Delhi: Motilal Banarsidass, 1971.

Dasgupta, Surendranath. *A History of Indian Philosophy*. Vol. 1. Cambridge: Cambridge University Press, 1922.

Datta, D.M. *The Six Ways of Knowing: A Critical Study on the Vedanta Theory of Knowledge.* London: George Allen & Unwin, 1932.

Deussen, Paul. *The Philosophy of the Upaniṣads.* Translated by A.S. Geden. Edinburgh: T & T Clark, 1908.

———. *The System of the Vedanta.* Translated by Charles Johnston. Chicago: Open Court, 1912.

———, trans. *Sixty Upaniṣads of the Veda*. 2 vols. Translated into English by V.M. Bedekar and G.B. Palsule. Delhi: Motilal Banarsidas, 1980.

Devaraja, N.K. *An Introduction to Śaṅkara's Theory of Knowledge.* Delhi: Motilal Banarsidas, 1962.

Doniger, Wendy. *The Hindus: An Alternative History.* Oxford: Oxford University Press, 2009.

Eggeling, Julius, trans. *The Śatapatha-Brāhmaṇa.* Edited by Maitreyee Deshpande. 4 vols. Delhi: New Bharatiya Book Corporation, 2008.

Forthoeffel, Thomas A. *Knowing Beyond Knowledge: Epistemologies of Religious Experience in Classical and Modern Advaita.* Delhi: Motilal Banarsidas, 2002.

Griffith, R.T.H, trans. *Yajurveda Saṁhitā.* Edited by Ravi Prakash Arya. Rev. ed. Delhi: Primal Publications, 2012.

Gupta, Bina. *Reason and Experience in Indian Philosophy.* Delhi: Indian Council of Philosophical Research, 2009.

Hiriyanna. M. *Outlines of Indian Philosophy*. London: George Allen & Unwin, 1958.

Jaimini. *Mīmāṁsā Sūtras of Jaimini.* 2 vols. Translated by Mohanlal Sandal. 1923–25. Reprint, Delhi: Motilal Banarsidas, 1980.

Johnson, W.J. *Dictionary of Hinduism.* Oxford: Oxford University Press, 2010.

Joshi, K.L, ed. *Atharva-veda Saṁhitā: Sanskrit Text, English Translation, Notes and Index of Verses*. 3 vols. Delhi: Primal Publications: Motilal Banarsidas, 2009.

Kane, Pandurang Vaman. *History of Dharmaśāstra: Ancient and Medieval Religious and Civil Law in India.* 5 vols. Poona: Bandarkar Oriental Institute, 1930–62.

Keith, A.B, trans. *Rigveda Brahmanas: The Aitareya and Kauṣītaki Brahmanas of the Rigveda.* Harvard Oriental Series 25. Cambridge: Harvard University Press, 1920.

———, trans. *The Veda of the Black and Yajus School entitled Taittiriya Sanhita*, 2 pts. Hardvard Oriental Series 18 and 19. Delhi: Motilal Banarsidas, 1967.

———, trans. *The Aitareya Āraṇyaka.* Oxford: Clarendon Press, 1969.

Krishnacharya T.R. and T.R. Vyasacharya, eds. *Sriman Mahābhāratam: A New Edition Mainly Based on the South Indian Texts, with Foot Notes and Readings.* 9 vols. 1906–14. Reprint, Delhi: Divine Books, 2011.

Lipner, Julius. *The Hindus: Their Religious Beliefs and Practices*. London: Routledge, 1994.

Locklin, Reid B. *Spiritual But not Religious? An Oar Stroke Closer to the Farther Shore.* Minnesota: Liturgical Press, 2005.

Madhva. *The Vedanta-sūtras with the Commentary by Sri Madhwacharya*. Translated by S. Subba Rau. Madras: Thompson, 1904.

———. *The Brahmasūtras: With English Translation of Madhva Bhāṣya*. Translated by S. G Mudgal. Mumbai: Archish Publications, 2005.

Mahadevan, T.M.P, ed. *Word Index to The Brahma-sūtra-bhāṣya of Śaṅkara.* 2 pts. Madras: University of Madras, 1973.

———. Foreword to *Brahmasūtra Bhāṣya of Śri Śaṅkarācārya*. Translated by Swami Gambhirananda, v–xii. 1965. Reprint, Kolakata: Advaita Ashrama, 2013.

Mani, Vettam. *Purāṇic Encyclopaedia: A Comprehensive Dictionary with Special Reference to the Epic and Purāṇic Literature*. 1964. Reprint, Delhi: Motilal Banarsidass, 1975.

Marcaurelle, Roger. *Freedom Through Inner Renunciation: Śaṅkara's Philosophy in a New Light*. New York: State University of New York Press. 2000.

Mayeda, Sengaku. Introduction to *A Thousand Teachings: The Upadeśasāhasrī of Śaṅkara*, 3–97. Tokyo: University of Tokyo Press, 1979.

Menon, A. Sreedhara. *A Survey of Kerala History*. Kottayam: DC Books, 2007.

Moniner-Williams, Moniner. *A Sanskrit-English Dictionary: Etymologically and Philologically Arranged.* 1899. Reprint, Delhi: Motilal Banarsidass, 2005.

Mookerji, Radha Kumud. *Ancient Indian Education*. 1947. Reprint, Delhi: Motilal Banarsidas, 1974.

Murty, Satchidananda. *Vedic Hermeneutics*. New Delhi: Shri Lal Bahadur Shastri Rashtriya Sanskrit Vidyapeetha, 1993.

———. *Hinduism and its Development*. Rev. ed. New Delhi: D.K. Printworld, 2007.

Olivelle, Patrick, trans. and ed. *Manu's Code of Law: A Critical Edition and Translation of the Mānava-Dharmaśāstra*. New Delhi: Oxford University Press, 2006.

———. *Ascetics and Brahmins: Studies in Ideologies and Institutions*. Cultural, Historical and Textual Studies of Religions. Delhi: Anthem Press India, 2012.

Pande, Govinda Chandra. *Life and Thought of Śaṅkarācārya*. Delhi: Motilal Banarsidas, 1994.

Pandey, Umesh Chandra, ed. *Yājñavalkyasmṛti of Yogīśwara Yājñavalkya*. The Kashi Sanskrit Series 178. 2nd ed. Varanasi: Chaukhambha Sanskrit Sanstan, 1977.

Radhakrishnan, S, trans. *The Principal Upaniṣads*. London: George Allen & Unwin, 1953.

———. *The Brahma Sūtra: The Philosophy of Spiritual Life*. London: George Allen & Unwin, 1960.

Raja, Kunhan, ed. *Chādogyopanishad of Daśopaniṣad-s*. Vol. 2, pt. 1. The Adyar Library Series 15. Rev. ed. Madras: The Adyar Library and Research Centre, 1996.

Rāmānuja. *The Vedānta-sūtras with the Śri-Bhāshya of Rāmānujāchārya*. Translated by M. Rangacharya and M.B. Varadaraja Aiyangar. Madras: The Educational Publishing, 1964.

———. *The Vedanta-Sūtras with the Commentary by Ramanuja.* Translated by George Thibaut. Vol. 48 of *The Sacred Books of the East*. 1904. Reprint, Delhi: Motilal Banarsidas, 1971.

Rambachan, Anantanand. *Accomplishing the Accomplished: The Vedas as a Source of Valid Knowledge in Śaṅkara*. Honolulu: University of Hawaii Press, 1991.

———. *The Advaita Worldview: God, World, and Humanity*. Albany: State University of New York Press, 2006.

Ranade, H.G, trans. *Kātyāyana Śrauta Sūtra*. Poona: H.G. Ranade and R.H. Ranade, 1978.

Ranade, A.G. and V.P. Bhatta, eds. *An Ecyclopaedic Dictionary of Sanskrit on Historical Principles*. Vol. 6. Pune: Deccan College Postgraduate and Research Institute, 2003.

Rao M. Sudhakar and V. Raghavendra Reddy. *Encyclopaedia of South India*. Vol. 3. New Delhi: Mittal Publications, 2009.

Rao, K.L. Seshagiri and Kapil Kapoor, eds. *Encyclopedia of Hinduism*. 11 vols. New Delhi: India Heritage Research Foundation and Rupa, 2010.

Rengarajan T. *Dictionary of Vedas*. Delhi: Eastern Book Linkers, 2004.

Roer E, ed. *The Twelve Principal Upaniṣads*. 3 vols. 1906. Reprint, New Delhi: D.K. Print World, 2000.

Roy, Pratap Chandra, trans. *The Mahabharata of Krishna-Dwaipayana-Vyasa*, 11 vols. Culcutta: Datta Bose. n.d.

Salam, Jeebanlata. *Social Exclusion and Education*. New Delhi: Indian Social Institute, 2004.

Śaṅkara. *The Vedānta-Sūtras with the Commentary by Śaṅkarācārya*. Translated by George Thibaut. Vols. 34

and 38 of *The Sacred Books of the East*. Oxford: The Clarendon Press, 1890–96.

———. *The Bhagavad-gītā with the Commentary of Śrī Śaṅkarācārya*. Edited by Dinakar Vishnu Gokhale. 2nd Rev. ed. Poona: Oriental Book Agency, 1950.

———. *Īśādidaśopaniṣadaḥ: Ten Principal Upanishads with Śāṅkarabhāṣya*. Edited by Ministry of Education, India. Delhi: Motilal Banarsidas, 1964.

———. *Brahmasūtra with Śāṅkarabhāṣya*. Edited by Ministry of Education, India. Delhi: Motilal Banarsidas, 1964.

———. *A Thousand Teachings: The Upadeśasāhasrī of Śaṅkara*. Translated and edited by Sengaku Mayeda. Tokyo: University of Tokyo Press, 1979.

———. *Eight Upaniṣads with the Commentary of Śaṅkarācārya*, 2 vols. Translated by Swami Gambhirananda. 1957. Reprint, Kolkata: Advaita Ashrama, 2013.

———. *Brahmasūtra Bhāṣya of Śri. Śaṅkarācārya*. Translated by Swami Gambhirananda. 1965. Reprint, Kolakata: Advaita Ashrama, 2013.

———. *Bhagavad Gītā with the Commentary of Śaṅkarācārya*. Translated by Swami Gambhirananda. 1984. Reprint, Kolkata: Advaita Ashrama, 2014.

———. *Chāndogya Upaniṣad with the Commentary of Śaṅkarācārya*. Translated by Swami Gambirananda. 1983. Reprint, Kolkata: Advaita Ashrama, 2015.

Sarasvati, Satchidanadendra. *The Method of Vedanta: A Critical Account of the Advaita Tradition*. Translated by A.J. Alston. Delhi: Motilal Banarsidas, 1989.

Sarma, R.R, ed. *Drāhyāyaṇa Śrauta Sūtram*. Ganganatha Jha Sanskrit Vidyapeeth Text Series 6. Allahabad: Ganganatha Jha Kendriya Sanskrit Vidyapeeth, 1982.

Sarma, Subramanian et al., ed. *Yajurveda: Krishna Yajurveda Works of the Taittiriya Shaka.*http://www.sanskritweb.net/yajurveda/#TB (accessed February 24, 2016).

Sastri, K.A. Nilakanta. *A History of South India: From Prehistoric Times to the Fall of Vijayanagar*. 4th ed. New Delhi: Oxford University Press, 2015.

Selvanayagam, Israel. *Vedic Sacrifice: Challenge and Response.* Delhi: Manohar Publishers, 1996.

Sharma, Arvind. *Textual Studies in Hinduism*. New Delhi: Manohar Publications, 1980.

Sharma, B.N.K. *The Brahmasūtras and Their Principal Commentaries: A Critical Exposition*. 3 vols. Bombay: Bharatiya Vidyabhavan, 1971.

Sharma, Chandradhar. *A Critical Survey of Indian Philosophy.* 1960. Reprint, Delhi: Motilal Banarsidass, 1994.

Sharma, Ram Sharan. *Śūdras in Ancient India: A Social History of the Lower Order down to Circa A.D. 600.* Delhi: Motilal Banarsidas, 1980.

Smith, Vincent A. *History of India.* Oxford: Oxford University Press, 1958.

Stein, Burton. *A History of India.* New Delhi: Oxford University Press. 1998.

Tagore, Ganesh Vasudevo, trans. *The Bhāgavata Purāṇa.* 3 pts. Ancient Indian Tradition and Mythology 7–9. Delhi: Motilal Banarsidas, 1976.

Thapar, Romila. *Cultural Pasts: Essays in Early Indian History.* New Delhi: Oxford University Press, 2000.

———. *Early India: From the Origins to AD 1300.* California: University of California Press, 2002.

Thatamanil, John J. *The Immanent Divine: God, Creation, and the Human Predicament.* Minneapolis: Fortress Press, 2006.

Thibaut, George. Introduction to *The Vedānta-Sūtras with the Commentary by Śaṅkarācārya*, Vol. 34 of *The Sacred Books of the East*, ix–cxxviii. Oxford: The Clarendon Press, 1890.

Thite, G.U, trans. *Āpastamba-Śrauta-Sūtra: Text with English Translation and Notes*. 2 vols. Delhi: New Bharatiya Book Corporation, 2004.

Thorat, Sukhadeo and Narender Kumar, eds. *B. R. Ambedkar: Perspectives on Social Exclusion and Inclusive Policies*. New Delhi: Oxford University Press, 2009.

Tiwari, Kapil N. *Dimensions of Renunciation in Advaita Vedānta*. Delhi: Motilal Banarsidas, 1977.

Tripathi, Mridula. *Renaissance of Hinduism and the Decline and Eclipse of Buddhism*. New Delhi: Abhijeet Publications, 2015.

Vidyasagar, Jibananda. *Śabda-Sāgara: Sanskrit-English Dictionary*. Varanasi: Chowkhamba Sanskrit Series office, 2002.

Vireswarananda, Swami, trans. *Brahma-sūtras*. Calcutta: Advaita Ashram, 1962.

Wolpert, Stanley, ed. *Encyclopedia of India*. 4 vols. Farmington: Thomson Gale, 2006.

Zaehner, R.C, trans. *The Bhagavadgītā*. Oxford: Oxford University Press, 1969.

ARTICLES

Advaitananda, Swami. "The Journey of a Seeker." In *Advaitāmṛtam*, edited by Sandhya Sundar and Dilip Kumar Rana. Ernakulam: Chinmaya International Foundation, 2015: 213–217.

Advayananda, Swami. "The Holy Geeta – In a Class All by Itself." In *Advaitāmṛtam*, edited by Sandhya Sundar and Dilip Kumar Rana. Ernakulam: Chinmaya International Foundation, 2015: 30–48.

Bhal, Vinay. "Relevance (or Irrelevance) of Subaltern Studies." *Economic and Political Weekly* 32, no. 23 (June 1997): 1333–1344.

Bhat, G.K. "Teacher-Pupil Relationship (In the Context of Upanishadic Literature)." *Annals of Bhandarkar Oriental Institute* 54, no.1/4 (1973): 173–178.

Bhavanamma, M.R. and Srinivasa Rao. "Were the Vedāntic Texts (*Upaniṣads*) Always Accepted as "*Śruti*" in Classical India?" *Journal of Indian Council of Philosophical Research* 25, no. 3 (July–September 2008): 97–106.

Brooks, Douglas R. "Taking Sides and Opening Doors: Authority and Integrity in the Academy's Hinduism." *Journal of American Academy of Religion* 68, no. 4 (December 2000): 817–829.

Camillus, C. "Spirituality in Value Based Integrated Daily Living." *Vaihari* 9, no. 3 (September 2004): 4–12.

Carpenter, David. "The Mastery of Speech: Canonicity and Control in the Vedas." In *Authority, Anxiety, and Canon: Essays in Vedic Interpretation*, edited by Laurie L. Patton. Delhi: Sri Satguru Publications, 1995: 19–34.

Chakravarty, Uma. "Teacher-Student Concept in the Brāhmaṇas and Upaniṣads." *Annals of Bhandarkar Oriental Institute* 78, no. 1–4 (1997): 215–222.

Clooney, Francis X. "Finding One's Place in the Text: A Look at the Theological Treatment of the Caste in Traditional India." *Journal of Religious Ethics* 17, no. 1 (Spring 1989): 1–29.

———. "From Anxiety to Bliss: Argument, Care, and Responsibility in the Vedanta Reading of *Taittirīya* 2.1–6a." In *Authority, Anxiety, and Canon: Essays in Vedic Interpretation*, edited by Laurie L. Patton. Delhi: Sri Satguru Publications, 1995: 139–169.

———. "Binding the Text: Vedanta as Philosophy and Commentary." In *Texts in Context: Traditional Hermeneutics in South Asia*, edited by Jeffrey R. Timm. Delhi: Sri Satguru Publications, 1997: 46–68.

Dandekar, R. N. "Vedic Literature: A Quick Overview." *Annals of the Bhandarkar Oriental Institute* 81 (2000): 1–13.

De Smet, Richard. "The Theological Method of Śaṃkara." PhD diss., Pontificiae Universitatis Gregorianae, Rome, 1955. Type-written, unpublished.

———. "Language and Knowledge of the Absolute According to Śaṅkara." In *Understanding Śaṅkara: Essays by Richard De Smet,* edited by Ivo Coelho. Delhi: Motilal Banarsidas, 2013: 30–74.

———. "The Fundamental Antinomy of Sri Śaṅkarācārya's Methodology." In *Understanding Śaṅkara: Essays by Richard De Smet,* edited by Ivo Coelho. Delhi: Motilal Banarsidas, 2013: 75–82.

———. "Theological Method and Vedānta." In *Understanding Śaṅkara: Essays by Richard De Smet,* edited by Ivo Coelho. Delhi: Motilal Banarsidas, 2013: 99–110.

———. "*Māyā* or *Ajñāna*? A Textual Analysis." In *Understanding Śaṅkara: Essays by Richard De Smet,* edited by Ivo Coelho. Delhi: Motilal Banarsidas, 2013: 122–128.

———. "Spiritual Values of Advaita Vedānta and Social Life." In *Understanding Śaṅkara: Essays by Richard*

De Smet, edited by Ivo Coelho. Delhi: Motilal Banarsidas, 2013: 158–172.

———. "Śaṅkara's Perspective on Meaning and Truth." In *Understanding Śaṅkara*: *Essays by Richard De Smet,* edited by Ivo Coelho. Delhi: Motilal Banarsidas, 2013: 255–270.

———. "The Dynamics of Contemplation According to Śaṅkarācārya." In *Understanding Śaṅkara: Essays by Richard De Smet,* edited by Ivo Coelho. Delhi: Motilal Banarsidas, 2013: 285–294.

———. "Śaṅkara's Non-Dualism." In *Understanding Śaṅkara: Essays by Richard De Smet,* edited by Ivo Coelho. Delhi: Motilal Banarsidas, 2013: 305–323.

———. "Śāṅkara Vedānta and Christian Theology." In *Understanding Śaṅkara: Essays by Richard De Smet,* edited by Ivo Coelho. Delhi: Motilal Banarsidas, 2013: 383–397.

———. "From Catholic Theology to Śāṅkara Vedānta and Return with Fr F.X. Clooney." In *Understanding Śaṅkara: Essays by Richard De Smet,* edited by Ivo Coelho. Delhi: Motilal Banarsidas, 2013: 398–412.

———. "A Note About Śaṅkara's Doctrine of Creation." In *Understanding Śaṅkara*: *Essays by Richard De Smet,* edited by Ivo Coelho. Delhi: Motilal Banarsidas, 2013: 463–484.

Deshpande, Madhav M. "Changing Conceptions of the Veda: From Speech-Acts to Magical Sounds." *Brahmavidya: The Adyar Library Bulletin* 54 (1990): 1–41.

Fox, Richard G. "Varna Schemes and Ideological Integration in Indian Society." *Comparative Studies in Society and History* 11, no. 1 (January 1969): 27–45.

Guha, Abhijit. "'Social Exclusion': A Sceptical View." *Journal of the Indian Anthropological Society* 42, no. 3 (November 2007): 287–292.

Gurukkal, Rajan. "Sankara: Buddhist in Disguise." *The Week*, December 27, 2015.

Harman, William. "Speaking About Hinduism and Speaking Against It?" *Journal of American Academy of Religion* 68, no. 4 (2000): 733–740.

Holdrege, Barbara A. "Veda in the Brāhmaṇas: Cosmogonic Paradigms and the Delimitation of Canon." In *Authority, Anxiety, and Canon: Essays in Vedic Interpretation*, edited by Laurie L. Patton. Delhi: Sri Satguru Publications, 1995: 35–66.

Jacobi, H. "The Dates of the Philosophical Sutras of the Brahmins." In vol. 2 of *Studies in the History of Philosophy: An Anthology of Articles by Scholars Eastern and Western*, edited by Debiprasad Chattopadhya. Culcutta: K.P. Bagchi, 1978: 54–87.

K.R. Rajani. "Three Women in the Brhadaranyaka Upanishad." *Satyanilayam* 16 (2009): 35–42.

Kazanas, N. "Indigenism and the Collapse of Aryan-Invasion-Theory." *Brahmavidya: The Adyar Library Bulletin* 78–79 (2014–2015): 365–425.

Kumar, Vivek. "Towards an Epistemology of Social Exclusion: A Critical Perspective." In *Marginality, Exclusion and Social Justice*, edited by Ashish Saxena. Jaipur: Rawat Publications, 2013: 64–83.

Locklin, Reid B. "Integral *Samnyasa*? Adi Shankaracharya and Liberation Hermeneutics." *Journal of Hindu-Christian Studies* 20 (2007): 43–51.

Louis, Prakash. "Social Exclusion." *Social Action* 58, no. 4 (October–December 2008): 343–352.

Malkovsky, Bradley J. "Śaṃkara on Divine Grace." In *New Perspectives on Advaita Vedānta: Essays in Commemoration of Professor Richard De Smet, S.J*, edited by Bradley J. Malkovsky. Leiden: Brill, 2000: 70–83.

Mayeda, Sengaku. "Śaṅkara and Buddhism." In *New Perspectives on Advaita Vedānta: Essays in Commemoration of Professor Richard De Smet, S.J.* edited by Bradley J. Malkovsky. Leiden: Brill, 2000: 18–29.

Raja, K. Kunjunni. "On the Date of Śaṃkarācārya and Allied Problems." *Brahmavidya: The Adyar Library Bulletin* 24, pts. 3–4 (December 1960): 125–148.

Rajani, K.R. "Three Women in the Brhadaranyaka Upanishad." *Satyanilayam* 16 (2009): 35–42.

Ram, Nandu. "Marginalized Groups and the State of Human Rights in India." In *Marginality, Exclusion and Social Justice*, edited by Ashish Saxena. Jaipur: Rawat Publications, 2013: 40–52.

Ramaswami, S. "Satyakāma." *Brahmavidya: The Adyar Library Bulletin* 59 (1995): 116–120.

Rambachan, Anantanand. "Śaṅkara's Rationale for *Śruti* as the Definitive Source of Brahmajñāna: A Refutation of Some Contemporary Views." *Philosophy East and West: A Quarterly of Asian and Comparative Thought* 36, no.1 (January 1986): 25–40.

———. "Where Words Can Set Free: The Liberating Potency of Vedic Words in the Hermeneutics of Śaṅkara." In *Texts in Context: Traditional Hermeneutics in South Asia,* edited by Jeffrey R. Timm. Delhi: Sri Satguru Publications, 1997: 33–46.

———. "Rethinking *Advaita*: Who is Eligible to Read *Advaita* Texts?" *Journal of Hindu-Christian Studies* 22 (2009): 8–13.

Rao, M. Prabhakara. "Inconsistencies in the *Brahmasūtra* and *Śāṅkarabhāṣya*: With Special Reference to the Competence of *Śūdra*." *Journal of Indian Council of Philosophical Research* 19, no. 2 (April–June 2002): 139–155.

Rao, Srinivasa. "Two Myths in Advaita." *Journal of Indian Philosophy* 24, no. 3 (June 1996): 265–279.

Sankaranarayanan, S. "Bādarāyaṇa and Vyāsa as Authors of the Brahmasūtra—A Historical Analysis." *Brahmavidya: The Adyar Library Bulletin* 67 (2003): 91–146.

Sharma, Arvind. "Is *Anubhava* a *Pramāṇa* According to Śaṅkara?" *Philosophy East and West: A Quarterly of Asian and Comparative Thought* 42, no. 3 (July 1992): 517–526.

———. "Who Speaks for Hinduism? A Perspective from *Advaita* Vedānta." *Journal of American Academy of Religion* 68, no. 4 (December 2000): 751–759.

———. "Dr. B.R. Ambedkar on the Aryan Invasion and the Emergence of the Caste System in India." *Journal of the American Academy of Religion* 73, no. 3 (September 2005): 843–870.

Sharma, Umesh Chandra. "Satyakāma Jābāla: A Socio-Historical Study." *Annals of Bhandarkar Oriental Institute* 54, no. 1–4 (1973): 193–198.

Shendge, Malati J. "The Authors of the Ṛgveda." *Annals of the Bhandarkar Oriental Research Institute* 81 (2000): 169–178.

Skoog, Kim. "Śaṁkara on the Role of *Śruti* and *Anubhava* in Attaining *Brahmajñāna*." *Philosophy East and West: A Quarterly of Asian and Comparative Thought* 39, no. 1 (January 1989): 67–74.

Smith, Brian K. "The Veda and the Authority of Class: Reduplicating Structures of Veda and *Varṇa* in Ancient Indian Texts." In *Authority, Anxiety, and Canon: Essays in Vedic Interpretation*, edited by Laurie L. Patton. Delhi: Sri Satguru Publications, 1995: 67–93.

Smith, Frederick M. "Purāṇaveda." In *Authority, Anxiety, and Canon: Essays in Vedic Interpretation*, edited by Laurie L. Patton. Delhi: Sri Satguru Publications, 1995: 97–138.

Tapovanam, Swami. "The Glory of Brahma-vidyā." Translated by Swami Chinmayananda. In *Advaitāmṛtam*, edited by Sandhya Sundar and Dilip Kumar Rana. Ernakulam: Chinmaya International Foundation, 2015: 11–20.

Thatamanil, John J. "Managing Multiple Religious Scholarly Identities: An Argument for a Theological Study of Hinduism." *Journal of American Academy of Religion* 68, no. 4 (December 2000): 791–803.

Upadhyaya, K.N. "Śaṇkara on Reason, Scriptural Authority and Self-knowledge." *Journal of Indian Philosophy* 19, no. 2 (June 1991): 121–132.

Young, Katherine K. "Śaṅkara on the Salvation of Women and Śūdras." In *Goddesses and Women in the Indic Religious Tradition,* edited by Arvind Sharma. Leiden: Brill, 2005: 131–166.

INDEX